Race, Nation, & Empire
in American History

Race, Nation, & Empire in American History

EDITED BY

James T. Campbell, Matthew Pratt Guterl, & Robert G. Lee

THE UNIVERSITY OF NORTH CAROLINA PRESS—CHAPEL HILL

Designed by Heidi Perov
Set in Minion and Scala Sans
by Keystone Typesetting, Inc.

The paper in this book meets the guidelines for permanence and durability of the
Committee on Production Guidelines for Book Longevity of the Council on Library
Resources.

Parts of this book have been reprinted with permission from the following works:
Matthew Frye Jacobson, *Barbarian Virtues: The United States Encounters Foreign Peoples
at Home and Abroad, 1876–1917* (New York: Hill and Wang, 2001); James T. Campbell,
"The Americanization of South Africa," in *Here, There, and Everywhere: The Foreign
Politics of American Culture* (Hanover: University Press of New England, 2000); Louise
Michele Newman, *White Women's Rights: The Racial Origins of Feminism in the United
States* (New York: Oxford University Press, 1999), © 1999 Louise Michele Newman, used
by permission of Oxford University Press, Inc.; and Ruth Feldstein, "I Don't Trust You
Anymore: Nina Simone, Culture, and Black Activism in the 1960s," *Journal of American
History* (March 2005), © 1999 Organization of American Historians, reprinted with
permission.

Library of Congress Cataloging-in-Publication Data

Race, nation, and empire in American history / edited by James T. Campbell, Matthew
Pratt Guterl, and Robert G. Lee.
p. cm.
"The genesis of this book traces to a conference, 'Race, Globalization, and the New
Ethnic Studies,' held at Brown University's Center for the Study of Race and Ethnicity in
2003"—Acknowledgments.
Includes bibliographical references and index.
ISBN 978-0-8078-3127-4 (cloth: alk. paper)
ISBN 978-0-8078-5828-8 (pbk.: alk. paper)
1. United States—Foreign relations—Congresses. 2. United States—Territorial
expansion—Congresses. 3. Imperialism—History—Congresses. 4. Racism—United
States—History—Congresses. 5. Nationalism—United States—History—Congresses.
6. Globalization—Political aspects—United States—Congresses. 7. United States—Race
relations—Congresses. I. Campbell, James T. II. Guterl, Matthew Pratt, 1970–   III. Lee,
Robert G., 1947–
E179.5.R33 2007
305.800973—dc22 2007012186

cloth   11 10 09 08 07   5 4 3 2 1
paper   11 10 09 08 07   5 4 3 2 1

Contents

Acknowledgments

The genesis of this book traces to a conference, "Race, Globalization, and the New Ethnic Studies," held at Brown University's Center for the Study of Race and Ethnicity in 2003. We would like to thank the center's director, Evelyn Hu-DeHart, for her steadfast support and comradeship. To acknowledge everyone who helped to make the conference a success would require more pages than we have, but we would be remiss if we did not offer thanks to Karen Ball, Jennifer Edwards, Jennifer Roth-Gordon, José Itzigsohn, and Paget Henry. We are also pleased to acknowledge President Ruth Simmons, Provost Robert Zimmer, and Dean Mary Fennell, whose offices helped to underwrite the conference, and the Watson Institute for International Studies, which provided a venue.

Our editor at the University of North Carolina Press, Sian Hunter, saw this book from conception to completion, offering wise counsel and only occasional cajoling. Production of the book was overseen by the estimable Paula Wald. Special thanks to Cynthia Gwynne Yaudes of Indiana University, without whose timely intervention this manuscript might never have escaped the editors' desks.

If we have one regret, it is that our friend and teacher Winthrop Jordan did not live to see the book finished. No historian has done more to unearth the roots of our nation's painful racial predicament, and we were pleased and proud when he agreed to participate in our original conference. We were even more touched when he came back to Brown for the weekend workshop at which the volume's authors collectively transformed their conference papers into a coherent book. On both occasions, he exhibited the qualities that had long distinguished his career as a scholar and a teacher: intellectual generosity, a wide-ranging mind, and a scrupulous respect for evidence, all enriched by rare personal graciousness and wry sense of humor. We dedicate the book to his memory.

Introduction

JAMES T. CAMPBELL, MATTHEW PRATT GUTERL, & ROBERT G. LEE

There are many ways to introduce a book, especially one that ranges across as much terrain as this one, but let us begin with a gravestone. The stone, which stands in a cemetery in northwest Connecticut, bears the legend, "In memory of Henry OBOOKIAH, a native of OWHYHEE." The inscription, dated 1818, credits the young Hawaiian with inspiring the creation of the Foreign Mission School at Cornwall, Connecticut. Few today visit the site. Fewer still realize that there is no body buried beneath the stone. But the story of Opukaha'ia—a tale of unlikely connections and ironic reversals, with echoes reverberating into our own time—has much to teach us about the history of the modern world, and about American history in particular.

Opukaha'ia's journey commenced in 1808, just thirty years after Captain Cook's ill-fated visit to Hawaii. He was sixteen years old and an orphan, having lost his family in Kamehameha's wars of unification. Spying a ship anchored in Kealakekua Bay, he swam out to it. The ship was the *Triumph*, an American merchantman out of New York, under the command of Caleb Brintnall. Brintnall signed the lad on as a cabin boy, conferring the name by which he would become known to history: Henry Obookiah.[1]

Opukaha'ia spent the next year at sea, sailing first to the seal hunting grounds of the Pacific Northwest and thence to Macao and Canton, where the *Triumph* exchanged its cargo of furs for tea, spices, and silk. The ship then continued west across the Indian Ocean, restocking at Cape Town in South Africa before braving the Atlantic. It finally arrived in New York in late 1809. Most of the crew was paid off there, but Opukaha'ia accompanied Brintnall to his home in New Haven, Connecticut.

Opukaha'ia was clearly of a pious turn of mind—in Hawaii, he had studied to be a kahuna—and he began to attend Christian services in his new home. But with a limited command of English he had little understanding of what he saw and heard. He was sitting "on the college steps at Yale crying because he had no means of getting an education" when he was befriended by a student, Edwin Dwight, son of Yale's president, Timothy Dwight. Dwight, who later penned a best-selling memoir of Opukaha'ia's life, invited the young Hawaiian to live in the Dwight family's home, where he received religious instruction and learned to read and write. After a year in New Haven, Opukaha'ia moved to nearby Torringford to live with Samuel Mills, a leader of what New Englanders at the time called "the Benevolent Empire," a phalanx of religious and reform organizations dedicated to expanding Christ's kingdom on earth. Though only a few years older than his guest, Mills had already played a central role in the creation of the American Board of Commissioners of Foreign Missions, the nation's first overseas mission society, and the American Bible Society, a group dedicated to placing a Bible in every American home. Under the tutelage of Mills and other local ministers, Opukaha'ia blossomed into a pious Christian and a formidable scholar, conversant not only in English but in Latin and Hebrew. By the time of his death, he had produced the first grammar of the Hawaiian language, as well as a translation of the book of Genesis.[2]

Opukaha'ia's transformation shaped the character of the emerging American mission movement. While the first European missions relied on white ministers to carry the gospel to foreign lands, the American Board initially embraced the principle of native agency, of training indigenous people to serve as missionaries among their own communities. The Foreign Mission School at Cornwall reflected this approach. Established in 1817, the school was dedicated to preparing the children of "heathen" nations—not only Hawaiians and Native Americans but also students from as far afield as India and China—for missionary service. Opukaha'ia helped to raise money to build the school, and he was the first student to enroll. But his dream of redeeming his homeland never came to pass. Stricken with typhus, he died on February 17, 1818, at the age of twenty-six. Such was his stature that Lyman Beecher, the nation's preeminent divine (and father of novelist Harriet Beecher Stowe), conducted the funeral. His body was interred in the cemetery at Cornwall, beneath a stone marker celebrating his passage from "Pagan priest" and "Idolater" to servant of the Lord.[3]

Though Opukaha'ia did not live to see it, Christianity did come to Hawaii. Inspired by the young Hawaiian's life and death, the American Board dispatched the first Christian missionaries to the islands. The company, about twenty people in all, was composed chiefly of white ministers and their wives, though it also included three native Hawaiians, Opukaha'ia's classmates at Cornwall. (In 1822 the American Board dispatched its first African American missionary to Hawaii, a schoolteacher and former slave named Betsy Stockton.) The missionaries anticipated opposition, but on arriving in Hawaii they learned that Kamehameha had died and that the *kapu* system, the elaborate system of religious law that undergirded the traditional order, had been abolished, clearing the way for the rapid spread of Christianity on the islands. For the mission's sponsors, the passing of the old order was a proof of God's favor, the final element in a providential plan that began when a young orphan swam out to an American ship in Kealakekua Bay.[4]

To contemporaries, the life of Henry Obookiah offered a reassuring parable of enlightenment and progress beneath a Christian cross and the American flag. Yet for the historian, it is a story laced with ironies and unexpected connections. Samuel Mills, for example, was not only Opukaha'ia's benefactor but also a founder of the American Colonization Society, an institution dedicated to removing free Africans and African Americans from the nation's shores. Whatever his beliefs in the young Hawaiian's potential, Mills refused to believe that black people could ever be absorbed as citizens in an American republic. In 1817 he sailed to West Africa to locate a site for an African American colony, what would later become Liberia. Stricken with a fever, presumably malaria, he died on the return voyage, just a month after Opukaha'ia.[5]

The Foreign Mission School at Cornwall also met an early demise, a victim of a different kind of fever: racism. The controversy that scuttled the school centered on a pair of Cherokee students from Georgia, Elias Boudinot and John Ridge. The two were cousins and members of a prominent "civilized" family among the Cherokee, a family that had embraced Christianity, individual land tenure, and commercial agriculture. (The family's loyalties were registered in their adopted names: Major Ridge, John's father and the family patriarch, acquired his forename serving alongside Andrew Jackson in the Seminole War, while Boudinot, born Buck Watie, bore the name of the president of the American Bible Society.) The young men were precisely the kind of students for whom the Foreign Mission School had been founded, but they committed a cardinal sin: they fell in love with white women. In 1824 Ridge married Sarah Northrup, the daughter of the school's steward, scandalizing the local community. In marrying Ridge, the local newspaper opined, Northrup had "made herself a *squaw*, and connected her race to a race of Indians." Two years later, Boudinot also married a white woman, Harriet Gold, daughter of a local physician, provoking another outcry, highlighted by a mob's burning an effigy of the bride. The scandal was too much for the leaders of the American Board of Missionaries, who closed the school.[6]

The episode had a grim sequel. Undeterred by their encounter with American racism, Boudinot and Ridge remained leading advocates of Cherokee acculturation and Western-style progress. Boudinot drafted a republican constitution for the Cherokee nation and worked on the first Cherokee translation of the New Testament. In 1826 he founded the *Cherokee Phoenix*, the first Native American newspaper in U.S. history. With pressure on Cherokee lands mounting after the 1830 Indian Removal Act, Boudinot initially took a defiant stand, insisting on the Cherokees' right to "live on land which God gave them . . . surrounded by guarantees which this Republic has voluntarily made for their protection." But as removal became inevitable, he changed tack, advocating negotiation and compromise. In 1835 Boudinot, John Ridge, and Major Ridge signed the Treaty of Echota, ceding Cherokee lands to the United States in exchange for land west of the Mississippi. Though the three had no authority to negotiate on behalf of the tribe (most of whose leaders and members staunchly opposed removal), the treaty was quickly ratified by the U.S. Senate, and the Cherokee were compelled to leave their homes. Thus began the Trail of Tears, on which a third of the Cherokee nation perished.[7]

Boudinot and the Ridges survived the westward journey, settling in Oklahoma. But in signing the treaty they had antagonized most Cherokee people. They had also violated tribal law, which prohibited the sale or transfer of land to non-Cherokees under penalty of death. In 1839 Boudinot was assassinated by a band of Cherokee men; fittingly, the murder occurred as he was walking to the local mission church. John and Major Ridge were killed the same day.

The American mission in Hawaii took the most ironical turn of all. Shielded from the upheavals on the mainland, the mission survived and even prospered, as indigenous Hawaiians, loosed from the *kapu* system and reeling from waves of newly introduced diseases, sought the solace of the new religion. But the years also brought a distinct hardening of racial lines within the mission. By the coming of the Civil War, the spirit of Christian universalism and democratic optimism in which the enterprise had been launched had all but evaporated, taking the commitment to native agency with it. Authority in the mission rested in the hands of whites, with native Hawaiians cast in the role of perpetual minors.

The changes in the mission were associated with Richard Armstrong, a missionary who arrived in Hawaii in 1831 and served as minister of public instruction on the islands from 1840 until his death in 1860. For Armstrong, "Polynesian" people stood far behind whites in the ranks of civilization. While sweet and tractable, they were also improvident, indolent, and emotional, requiring generations of white tutelage before they could safely be entrusted with the responsibilities of self-government. This assessment was reflected in the curriculum that Armstrong installed on the islands, a system that contemporaries called "industrial education." First developed as a pedagogy for the British working class, industrial education eschewed subjects like Greek, Latin, and Hebrew—subjects in which Opukaha'ia had excelled—in favor of courses in brick making, carpentry, agriculture, and other practical pursuits. Such instruction, the argument ran, served not only to equip students with useful skills but also to reform their characters, instilling those "habits of industry"—self-discipline, regularity, a mind to work—that "savage" races were presumed to lack.[8]

Armstrong's legacy was carried forward by his son, Samuel Chapman Armstrong. Born on a Maui mission in 1839, the younger Armstrong left Hawaii in 1860, the year of his father's death, to enroll at Williams College. After service in the Civil War, he served as agent of the Freedmen's Bureau in Hampton, Virginia. Not surprisingly, Armstrong saw his charges through the prism of his upbringing in Hawaii. Though emerging from slavery rather than savagery, African Americans were also a backward race, without experience of self-government or self-directed labor; like Hawaiians, they would require white tutelage as they confronted the challenges of modern civilization. Significantly, Armstrong's first act on arriving at Hampton was to divest local blacks of farms that they had been given by his predecessor, restoring the land to its former white owners. "It put them at the bottom of the ladder," he later explained; "it is not a bad thing for anyone to touch bottom early, if there is a good solid foundation under him and then climb from that."[9]

Armstrong is best known to history as the founder of Hampton Normal and Agricultural Institute, which opened in 1868. Underwritten by the American Missionary Association (an organization representing the same New England Congregationalists who had founded the Foreign Mission School at Cornwall half a century before), Hampton quickly became the nation's premier educational institution for African Americans (and, after 1878, for Native Americans and native Hawaiians as well). The regime at the school followed the industrial formula that Armstrong's father had developed in Hawaii. Students paid for their own educations by working in the institute's fields, workshops, and kitchens, a system that reduced the school's costs while instilling wholesome lessons about responsibility and work. (Fears that black people would revert to idleness once the compulsion of the lash was withdrawn were ubiquitous in the postbellum era.) Though most graduates were destined to careers as teachers, all students were required to study at least one manual trade. Moral philosophy, ancient and modern languages, history—the cornerstones of the classical curriculum still prevailing in white schools—found no place at Hampton. Nor did politics. For Armstrong, political participation was a trap, diverting the freedpeople from the true path of racial development.[10]

Samuel Chapman Armstrong introduced industrial education to the postbellum South; his protégé Booker T. Washington broadcast it to the world. Born a slave, Washington graduated from Hampton in 1875 and later returned to serve as Armstrong's assistant. In 1881 he opened a school of his own, the Tuskegee Normal and Industrial Institute, where he quickly earned acclaim for his conservative, "sensible" approach to racial matters. Washington's apotheosis came in 1895, at the Cotton States and International Exposition in Atlanta. Decrying "agitation of questions of social equality" as "the supremest folly," the Tuskegeean gave an apparent black seal of approval to the Jim Crow regime settling over the South. "In all things purely social, we can be as separate as the fingers," he famously declared, yet "one as the hand in all things related to our mutual progress."[11]

The "Atlanta Compromise" speech served not only to establish Washington's status as the "representative" black political leader in the United States; it also made him an international celebrity. Educators and politicians from around the world found their way to Tuskegee, seeking solutions to their own nations' racial and educational predicaments. *Up from Slavery*, Washington's 1901 autobiography, quickly became the most widely translated book in American history, with editions in Turkish, Zulu, and everything in between. Needless to say, different readers drew different conclusions about the significance of Washington's life. While many African Americans fastened on themes of autonomy and self-help—Marcus Garvey famously declared his dream of becoming "the Booker T. Washington of Jamaica"—whites focused on industrial education, a system that had seemingly accomplished the great desideratum of the postslavery Western world: enhancing black productivity and usefulness without awakening unhealthy aspirations for social and political equality. In the early years of the century, Washington worked with German imperial officials to create a short-lived mini-Tuskegee in Togo. British officials in Rhodesia and South Africa, where the discovery of diamonds and gold had created an insatiable demand for cheap, docile black labor, corresponded regularly with the Tuskegeean and even invited him to come and overhaul their systems of native education. One can only wonder what Opukaha'ia might have made of this unlikely legacy.[12]

By conventional historical standards, Opukaha'ia is not a significant historical figure. You will not find him in your textbook, except perhaps in Hawaii. Yet his story poses fundamental challenges to historians of the United States. Over the last generation, subjects like African American, Asian American, and Latino/a studies have entrenched themselves in university faculties and curricula, yet they are still typically treated as marginal or supplemental—subjects for the shaded sidebars of high school history texts. Opukaha'ia's story challenges this practice. Not only does it illuminate the experience of previously neglected groups—indigenous Hawaiians, Cherokees, southern freedpeople—but it also connects those experiences to one another and to the broader history of the nation.

Opukaha'ia's journey also challenges our understanding of historical boundaries, in two distinct but related ways. To trace his travels is to discover a universe in motion, a world in which people, commodities, and cultural forms ranged across national borders, creating novel connections and exchanges— Chinese silks for American sealskins, a republican constitution for the Cherokee, a Togolese Tuskegee. "Globalization" may be a recent coinage, but the processes it describes have gone on for centuries. Yet Opukaha'ia's story also reveals the erection of new kinds of boundaries, the emergence of new systems of racial classification and exclusion. Thus the Foreign Mission School at Cornwall ended with a white woman burned in effigy for the sin of marrying an Indian, while the Christian universalism and democratic optimism of the early Hawaii mission transmogrified, over the course of two generations, into a global regime for reducing the world's darker people to a state of permanent vassalage.

Race, Nation, and Empire in American History is a response to these challenges. At the most basic level, the book seeks to recapture the worlds of men and women like Opukaha'ia, to illuminate lives and struggles that too often slip through the cracks of more "mainstream" historical narratives. But it is also an attempt to rechart the historical mainstream. Opukaha'ia may be an obscure figure, but the processes that his story reveals are anything but minor: the global expansion of American merchant capital; the rise of an evangelical Christian mission movement; the dispossession (and subsequent erasure) of indigenous people; the birth of new identities, grounded in race, religion, gender, and nation, and the tensions within and between them; the endless struggles over the place of darker-skinned peoples in a nation that continues fundamentally to imagine itself as white. All of these themes resurface, in different contexts and combinations, in the essays that follow.

The book is also a meditation on boundaries. As Opukaha'ia's life suggests— and as a growing body of works in American history and American studies confirms—the United States is and has long been a robustly global nation, whose politics, economy, and culture have both shaped and been shaped by developments in the wider world. The essays that follow are full of transnational connections and cross-pollinations, of people popping up in unexpected places. Yet they are also stories of people being put, quite literally, in their place, of bitter struggles over the boundaries of race and nation. One of the central claims of this book is that these two seemingly contradictory processes, of boundary crossing and boundary making, are and have always been intertwined.[13]

One of the morals of Opukaha'ia's story—and, again, one of the main contentions of this book—is that boundary disputes are not new. On the contrary, they are as old as the republic. It is by now a truism that the Declaration of Independence, with its soaring invocations of human equality and "unalienable rights" to "life, liberty and the pursuit of happiness," was written by a slaveholder—a man who insisted not only on black people's inherent incapacity for citizenship but also on the impossibility of blacks and whites living together as free people in a common society. The struggle over boundaries was also exhibited in the 1790 Naturalization Act, a law that revolutionized modern understandings of citizenship by creating a procedure for "naturalizing" aliens as Americans but that also reserved the process for "free white persons." Passed by the very first American Congress and signed into law by George Washington, the Naturalization Act represents the wellspring of much of subsequent American history, including many of the problems and processes discussed in this book: the coming tides of European immigration, the reduction of native peoples to the status of domestic dependents, Chinese "exclusion," and the abiding aversion of most Americans to "foreign entanglements," even as they seek to broadcast their values, cultural forms, and commodities across the globe.

While such issues are not new, they possess particular salience today. By grim coincidence, the origins of this book trace to September 2001, as the editors entered a conversation about the direction of the ethnic studies program at our university. A few days later, the twin towers of the World Trade Center—symbol of both the global economic preeminence of the United States and of the complex fissures of race, ethnicity, and class within it—fell. The years since have brought a presidential declaration of a "war on terror" and a pair of shooting wars in Afghanistan and Iraq, both of which have now devolved into long-running counterinsurgency wars. We have also witnessed, as in previous eras of war and popular alarm, an assault on civil liberties at home, including detention without trial, suspension of the right of habeas corpus, and revelations of government wiretaps without the formality of warrants. We have had reports of a global network of secret American prison camps and been treated to gruesome photographs of the systematic humiliation and torture of Muslim detainees by American soldiers—photographs that evoke other images in the American archives, complete with bound bodies and leering bystanders. We have seen renewed debates over immigration control and the propriety of the "racial profiling" of dark-skinned travelers, as well as a sometimes rancorous debate over America's role in the world, including the question of whether the United States is or ought to be an "empire." Different readers will doubtless have different opinions about these matters. Some may object to the way in which we have represented them here. But all should agree that the current situation has invested the questions examined in this book with new interest and urgency.

8—James T. Campbell, Matthew Pratt Guterl, & Robert G. Lee

The essays that follow are arranged in five sections. Part I, "Who's Who: American Encounters with Race," examines the history of efforts to sort and classify America's diverse inhabitants. Joanne Pope Melish traces the emergence and transformation of "the native" as a racial category in New England in the colonial and early national periods, revealing the locally diverse, confusing, and sometimes contradictory conceptions that emerged as New Englanders tried to make sense of a complex and fluid reality. Vernon Williams reexamines the career of Franz Boas, a German Jewish immigrant and child of the European revolutions of the mid-nineteenth century, whose academic assault on prevailing ideas of fixed racial inheritance transformed American understandings of human variety. The section closes with George Hutchinson's essay on novelist Nella Larsen, one of the Harlem Renaissance's most enigmatic and misunderstood personalities. Moving between Larsen's own time and representations of her in scholarly work today, Hutchinson offers a meditation on Americans' persistent difficulty in imagining a subject that is at once white and black, European and American. Taken together, the three essays illuminate both the global scope and the local specificities of race making, while reminding us of the essential arbitrariness of any system of racial classification.

The essays in Part II, "Ironies of Empire," offer distinctly different perspectives on the global expansion of American cultural, economic, and political power in the nineteenth and twentieth centuries. Eric Love examines a familiar problem among historians of American empire—the annexation of Hawaii—but arrives at an unfamiliar conclusion. While most scholars have linked the onset of formal imperialism in the late nineteenth century with the era's increasingly rigid racial ideas, Love suggests that ideologies like Social Darwinism and "scientific racism" could also be impediments to empire, with at least some racists recoiling from the idea of trying to absorb hordes of unassimilable, dark-skinned folk into the body politic. Matthew Frye Jacobson examines the complex cultural, ideological, and political reverberations set off by two of the defining movements of the late nineteenth and early twentieth centuries: the quest for overseas markets for American manufactures and the surge in European immigration. To put the matter too bluntly, Jacobson reminds us that the debate over America's place in the world unfolded alongside a debate over the place of the world's people in the United States. Finally, James Campbell examines America's rise to globalism from the standpoint of South Africa—a country in which the imprint of the United States has been especially significant. He shows how a variety of American "goods," including not only commodities but also cultural forms, industrial techniques, and racial ideologies, found their way to South Africa, and how they were in turn taken up and refashioned by different groups of South Africans.

As its title suggests, the third section of the book, "Engendering Race, Nation, and Empire," examines the complex interrelationship between processes of race making, nation building, and imperial expansion through the prism of gender. Louise Newman examines the "new imperialism" of the late nineteenth century but complicates the story in two different ways: first, by setting the rise of overseas empire in the context of a longer history of American encounters with "backward" people; and second, by focusing on debates over the status and role of women. In a masterpiece of historical synthesis, Newman shows how ideas about the proper status of women provided a crucial ideological underpinning of empire, offering a justification for forcibly intervening in the lives of people—Native Americans, southern freedpeople, Filipinos—whose domestic affairs did not conform to "civilized" norms. Matt Garcia also examines social conflict through a gendered lens, but he focuses not on questions of womanhood but rather on struggles over the meaning of manhood. Specifically, he explores intraethnic conflict between Mexican American immigrants and Mexican *bracero* workers in the *colonias* of Southern California in the decades after World War II, showing how differences in experience and class position came to play themselves out on the terrain of masculinity. The section closes with Natasha Zaretsky's essay on the strange career of Delia Alvarez, whose status as the sister of the longest-held American prisoner of war in North Vietnam placed her at the complex conjunction of the Chicano movement, the women's movement, and the antiwar movement.

As the example of Opukaha'ia shows, life history represents one of the most promising vehicles for escaping the confines of narrowly national histories. The essays in Part IV, "Crossings," trace the experiences of three peripatetic American women whose travels not only carried them beyond the borders of the United States but also challenged assumed borders of individual, racial, and national identity. Matthew Pratt Guterl unfolds the story of Eliza McHatton, a southern slaveholder displaced by the Civil War, as she ventured from Louisiana to Mexico and eventually to Cuba, seeking to recover her "lost" life in the Old South. Historian Kevin Gaines examines the experience of African American civil rights lawyer Pauli Murray, as she struggled to reconcile the demands of racial loyalty and liberal universalism, as well as her own conflicted racial, national, and sexual identities, in the cauldron of decolonizing Africa. In the final essay in the section, Ruth Feldstein excavates a transnational black radical politics through a close reading of the life and work of jazz singer Nina Simone.

"End Times," the book's final section, offers a trio of reflections on the nation's recent past and near future, looking at struggles over the meaning of racial, cultural, and religious difference in a world defined by increasing global economic integration and by deepening global conflict. Prema Kurien turns the problem inside out by focusing on the predicament of Indian American scholars working in American universities. As Kurien shows, Indian American scholars working in such fields as postcolonial and subaltern studies have offered powerful critiques of Western (and specifically American) imperialism, only to find themselves assailed by conservative Indian American groups deriding them as captives of the West and demanding a return to "traditional" Hindu forms of knowledge and belief. Robert Lee offers a comparative exploration of the "Yellow Peril" of the nineteenth and twentieth centuries and fears of a militant "brown" Islam in American culture today, exposing a host of unexpected parallels and connections. The section closes with an essay by Melani McAlister examining the alleged "clash of civilizations" between the United States and the Islamic world from the perspective of Christian evangelicals—a community, she argues, that is far more variegated in its political attitudes than media stereotypes might suggest. Though the three essays offer very different understandings of the nation's present predicament, all highlight common themes and problems, from the power of prophetic belief to the role of modern media in the creation and perpetuation of racial, religious, and national chauvinism. They also remind us, yet again, of the complex, continuing entanglements between race, nation, and empire, between the assertion of American power abroad and struggles over identity and difference within America's borders.

All of which brings us back to where we began, to the story of Opukaha'ia and a weathered gravestone in a remote corner of northwestern Connecticut—a stone memorializing the life and death of "Henry OBOOKIAH, a native of OWHY-HEE." No body lay beneath the marker. After long years of obscurity, Opukaha'ia experienced something of a historical revival in the late twentieth century. A series of developments within Hawaiian society—the rise of a Hawaiian sovereignty movement, the continuing spread of evangelical Christianity on the islands, controversy over indigenous land claims and over the propriety and legality of separate schools for native Hawaiian children—sparked new interest in Opukaha'ia's life and legacy. Not surprisingly, different groups interpreted that life and legacy in different ways, but most agreed that the final resting place of Hawaii's first Christian convert was properly on the islands. In 1993 his body was exhumed and returned to Hawaii, where it was reinterred in Kahikolu cemetery in Napoopoo, on the big island of Hawaii. Located on the grounds of an early American Board mission church, the grave is just a few hundred yards from Kealakekua Bay, where Opukaha'ia made his original plunge and where tourists now frolic. It is a long way from Kealakekua Bay to Cornwall, Connecticut, though perhaps not as far as we once imagined.

NOTES

1. See E. W. Dwight, *Memoirs of Henry Obookiah: A Native of Owhyhee and a Member of the Foreign Mission School, Who Died at Cornwall, Connecticut, February 17, 1818, Aged 26 Years* (New Haven, Conn.: Office of the Religious Intelligencer, 1818).

2. Ibid., 5–7; Henry Obookiah, *A Short Elementary Grammar of the Owhihe Language* (1818; Honolulu: Manoa Press, 1993). On Mills, see Samuel J. Mills, *Communications Relative to the Progress of the Bible Societies in the United States* (Philadelphia: Philadelphia Bible Society, 1813); and Mills and Daniel Smith, *Report of a Missionary Tour through the Portion of the United States Which Lies West of the Allegheny Mountains* (Andover, Mass.: Flagg and Gould, 1815).

3. Lyman Beecher, *A Sermon Delivered at the Funeral of Henry Obookiah, a Native of Owhyhee, and a Member of the Foreign Mission School in Cornwall, Connecticut, February 18, 1818* (Elizabeth-Town, N.J.: Edson Hart, 1819). On the founding of the Foreign Mission School, see *Extracts from the Report of the Agents of the Foreign Mission School to the American Board of Commissioners for Foreign Missions, September, 1817* (Hartford, Conn.: Hudson and Co., 1818); Joseph Harvey, *The Banner of Christ Set Up: A Sermon Delivered at the Inauguration of the Reverend Harmon Daggett as Principal of the Foreign Mission School in Cornwall, Connecticut, May 6, 1818* (Elizabeth-Town, N.J.: Edson Hart, 1819); and Harmon Daggett, *An Inaugural Address, Delivered at the Opening of the Foreign Mission School, May 6, 1818* (Elizabeth-Town, N.J.: Edson Hart, 1819).

4. On the origins and history of the Hawaiian mission, see Bradford Smith, *Yankees in Paradise: The New England Impact on Hawaii* (Philadelphia: Lippincott, 1956); and Patricia Grimshaw, *Paths of Duty: American Missionary Wives in Nineteenth-Century Hawaii* (Honolulu: University of Hawaii Press, 1989). For contemporary accounts, see Hiram Bingham, *A Residence of 21 Years in the Sandwich Islands; or, The Civil, Religious, and Political History of Those Islands, Comprising a Particular View of the Missionary Operations Connected with the Introduction and Progress of Christianity and Civilization among the Hawaiian People* (Hartford, Conn.: Hezekiah Huntington, 1847); and Rufus Anderson, *Heathen Nation Evangelized: History of the Sandwich Islands Mission* (Boston: Congregational Publishing Society, 1870).

5. Mills's involvement with the American Colonization Society, including his ill-fated journey to West Africa, is discussed in Philip J. Staudenraus, *The African Colonization Movement, 1816–1865* (New York: Columbia University Press, 1961).

6. Theda Perdue, "Elias Boudinot," in *Encyclopedia of North American Indians: Native American History, Culture, and Life from the Paleo-Indians to the Present*, ed. Frederick E. Hoxie (Boston: Houghton Mifflin, 1996), 81. See also Thurman Wilkins, *Cherokee Tragedy: The Ridge Family and the Decimation of a People* (2d ed.; Norman: University of Oklahoma Press, 1986); and Edward Everett Dale and Gaston Litton, eds., *Cherokee Cavaliers: Forty Years of Cherokee History as Told in the Correspondence of the Ridge-Watie-Boudinot Family* (Norman: University of Oklahoma Press, 1939).

7. Perdue, "Elias Boudinot," 81. Boudinot's editorials are excerpted in Theda Perdue

and Michael D. Green, eds., *The Cherokee Removal: A Brief History with Documents* (Boston: Bedford Books, 1995).

8. James D. Anderson, *The Education of Blacks in the South, 1860–1935* (Chapel Hill: University of North Carolina Press, 1988), 38–42.

9. Donald Spivey, *Schooling for the New Slavery: Black Industrial Education, 1868–1915* (Westport, Conn.: Greenwood Press, 1978), 7.

10. On the origins of the "Hampton model" of industrial education, see Anderson, *Education of Blacks in the South*, 33–78. See also Samuel Chapman Armstrong, *Education for Life* (Hampton, Va.: Hampton Normal and Agricultural Institute, 1913); and Francis Greenwood Peabody, *Education for Life: The Story of Hampton Institute, Told in Connection with the Fiftieth Anniversary of the Foundation of the School* (Garden City, N.Y.: Doubleday, Page and Co., 1918).

11. The complete text of Washington's Atlanta speech, as well as a digest of contemporary responses to it, is included in Booker T. Washington, *Up from Slavery: An Autobiography* (1901; New York: Oxford University Press, 1995).

12. See Louis R. Harlan, "Booker T. Washington and the White Man's Burden," *American Historical Review* 71 (January 1966): 441–67. On the South African case, see James T. Campbell, "Models and Metaphors: Industrial Education in the United States and South Africa," in *Comparative Perspectives on South Africa*, ed. Ran Greenstein (New York: St. Martin's Press, 1998), 90–134.

13. For a sampling of recent efforts to recast American history and American studies in transnational perspective, see Thomas Bender, ed., *Rethinking American History in a Global Age* (Berkeley: University of California Press, 2002); Amy Kaplan and Donald Pease, eds., *Cultures of United States Imperialism* (Durham, N.C.: Duke University Press, 1993); John Carlos Rowe, ed., *Post-Nationalist American Studies* (Berkeley: University of California Press, 2000); and Reinhold Wagnleitner and Elaine Tyler May, eds., *"Here, There, and Everywhere": The Foreign Politics of American Popular Culture* (Hanover, N.H.: University Press of New England, 2000).

PART I

Who's Who: American Encounters with Race

The Racial Vernacular
Contesting the Black/White Binary
in Nineteenth-Century Rhode Island

JOANNE POPE MELISH

On August 8, 1843, at the end of a letter to Elisha Reynolds Potter Jr., of South Kingstown, Rhode Island, concerning unrelated matters, Governor John Brown Francis segued to an upcoming celebration of the Narragansett Indians, to be held in Potter's hometown in the southern section of the state: "What is this great Indian powow,'" he asked. "I thought the Tribe were Negroes."[1] More than a century and a quarter later, on February 22, 1970, the feature story in the Sunday magazine section of the *Providence Journal-Bulletin*, the major daily newspaper serving the state of Rhode Island, made essentially the same point. A bold, forty-eight-point footer running across two facing pages of the article read, "When is an Indian not an Indian? In South County, it's when he's a Negro."[2]

These two quotations illustrate the persistent characterization of the Narragansett Indians and other New England tribes as "black" beginning in the early nineteenth century, a development understood to be part of a rapid progression toward the relatively rigid black/white racial binary characteristic of the United States, often contrasted to the complex and fluid racial framework operative in Latin America. The movement toward a black/white binary occurred as a new racial order emerged in the northern United States after the American Revolution in response to resultant economic and social dislocations, the gradual emancipation of slaves, the assertion of new state authority over indigenous tribes, and the influx of increasing numbers of new immigrants drawn to the Northeast by the first phase of American industrialization. Under these conditions, categories of difference that previously had supported a hierarchy of statuses (for example, slave, bond servant, ward, citizen, slave owner), and thus had been understood to be mutable and shaped by environment and culture, hardened into a fixed framework of innate and permanent raced social identities coded by physiognomy and descent. Terms used in public records to characterize persons of indigenous descent—"Indian," "mustee," and "molatto"—gradually were replaced by "Negro," "black," and "coloured." The word "Indian" became more or less reserved to describe a people imagined to be close to extinction as a result of disease, defeat, and the race mixing and cultural conflation that the new terms implied.

Most of the pressure to consolidate differences into a black/white dyad came from the state in an attempt to "turn the heterogeneous into the manageable," in David Theo Goldberg's words.[3] But the relentless progression to the binary was not uncontested. It met considerable resistance, especially but not exclusively on the part of native people themselves. Contradictory positions were articulated even at the state level. A range of racialized identities was negotiated and deployed in resistance to or disregard of the binary. Local public officials and the common citizenry purposefully chose "negro," "black," and "coloured" as distinct terms with different meanings to account for an increasingly complex variety of differences in origins (in terms of both place and status), lineage, and culture. People of wholly or partly native descent continued to describe themselves as "Indian," an assertion of continuity of cultural practice, tradition, and, since mixed-race children were usually the offspring of Indian women and African men, their matrilineality.

Racial designations were locally inflected and relational, indexed by local readings of a host of different factors—cultural conventions, economic relationships, gender conventions, status relationships, national identities, citizenship status, religion, and perhaps others. Place and social context could give similarly descended people variant racialized identities; very specific circumstances could produce different racial identities for closely related people and could change either an official or a colloquial racial identity of the same person. Well into the antebellum period, an increasingly rigid set of abstract racial categories defined by the state sat uneasily upon a much more complex and contradictory set of racial characterizations in practice, reflecting not only local meanings of distinctions based on color, descent, and class among long-settled U.S. populations but also attempts to coin racialized social identities for a shifting matrix of new immigrants. Such a set of locally inflected, negotiated, complex, contradictory, and polymorphous racial characterizations may be called a "racial vernacular." People of color shaped the racial vernacular, deploying specific characterizations to establish sovereignty, support legal rights and claims, evade authority, gain sympathy, or appeal to patriotism. Anglo-American local officials, familiar in most cases with the actual lineage of their neighbors whose lives they regulated, classified them by terms that would accommodate their increasingly complex family trees yet place them in some sort of orderly (and implicitly hierarchical) matrix, and then applied the same vocabulary, sometimes uncertainly (as in "molatto or mustee"), to fit transient strangers into the matrix.

Rhode Island offers a useful case study of the evolution of this fluid and evolving language of racial difference in the nineteenth century, its collapse into a binary from which the Indians had officially "disappeared" by the end of the nineteenth century, and the impact of its legacy on twentieth-century struggles to reconstruct, repair, and celebrate the memory of slavery and emancipation in Rhode Island.

The context for these developments was the 1636 settlement by the English of a region they called "Rhode Island," whose native population was Narragansett, and the almost immediate importation of enslaved Africans. Africans and Indians were located quite differently in the English colonial order. Virtually all Africans were enslaved, and the concern of English authorities was at the outset and remained their control. The situation with respect to the Narragansett was different. Although many Narragansetts and other Indians were also enslaved (or bound for long terms), the principal concern of English authorities in dealing with the Narragansett as a *nation*, especially after the defeat and massacre of the tribe near the end of King Philip's War, was their "management" and protection, through formal state guardianship (out of self-interest, certainly, but also to stem the rapid depletion of their tribal lands in ill-conceived land transactions).

A particular racial vernacular evolved in colonial Rhode Island in this context. The first step, of course, was the collapse of specificity in the popular identification of ethnic groups: Bambara or Igbo into "Negroes" or "Africans," and Narragansetts into "Indians."[4] The particular ethnicity or place of origin of individual slaves, while sometimes a matter of initial interest to slaveholders in New England as elsewhere on the theory that some ethnic groups made "better" slaves than others, seldom remained a salient feature of an individual slave's identity except when expressed in a personal name such as Gambia. As specific ethnicity became something of an abstraction, the term "African" itself became for African slaves and slaveholders an ethnic term; for slaves, and later free persons of African descent, it also became a term expressing fictive national origin. The currency, through international trade, of Spanish and Portuguese terms, often in corrupted forms, such as "Negro," "Mollatto," and "Mustee," along with "black" in English and "African," provided the first glossary of classification.

By 1700, whites in Rhode Island were referring to the Narragansetts as simply "Indian" in most domestic contexts, local government records, private correspondence, and colony/state actions seeking to control social behavior; the popularity of the generic "Indian" was facilitated by the presence of some Pequots, Niantics, Wampanoags, Nipmucs, and other Indian peoples in Rhode Island communities. In official contexts, however—in land transfers, discussions of alliances and hostilities, and most legislation directly concerned with the tribe per se—Narragansetts remained "Narragansett" for the next 150 years.[5] In these contexts, "Narragansett" functioned as a national identity, within which remained encoded the notion of "native" connection to the land.

Although it is possible that the indigenous peoples of southern Rhode Island and west and central Africa encountered each other as "Narragansetts" and "Gambians," nonetheless, as David Eltis has pointed out, the effect of the slave trade was to "encourage an elementary pan-Africanism" among slaves of different African ethnicity;[6] to the Africans, "Narragansett" would have no particular meaning. Therefore, it was probably as generic "Indians" and "Africans" that the social lives of the two groups were policed and recorded by Europeans as they began to labor and live together in the Rhode Island countryside.

The immediate context for reshaping the language of classification of Indians and Africans by Europeans was their concurrent labor. Before 1750, nearly all Africans and Narragansett Indians who labored in white households were slaves or bond servants. Pequot and Narragansett captives had been sold as slaves or bound for long terms at the end of the Pequot and King Philip's Wars, many out of the colony but some, especially women and children, within New England.[7] The sale of Indian land had also forced many Narragansetts into service. As Tobias Shattock, a Narragansett, wrote to Colonel Joseph Hazard in 1768, "We have been threatened with ruin for a course of Years, by having our Land Sold from us; that we have greatly fear'd we must come into Bondage with our Children." Many had indeed bound their children and occasionally themselves to labor in white households.[8]

Africans and Indians in Rhode Island labored side by side. The 1774 Rhode Island census reveals that of the 17 percent of white Rhode Island families (1,503 households), spread across all but three of the twenty-eight cities and towns, that had slaves and/or bound servants of color in their households, nearly one-quarter employed Indians, and nearly half of those (46 percent) employed Indians and Africans together. By the eve of the American Revolution, an extensive subculture of family slaves and bound servants of color, many working together in fields and dairies, many more socializing together, had developed in Rhode Island, especially in King's County (later Washington County), where sizable plantations producing foodstuffs and horses for export to the West Indies required large numbers of workers.

Inevitably, contiguity in bondage resulted in some intermarriage, and a plurality of terms with reference to these people and their offspring—"Indian," "black," "negro," "mollato," and "mustee"—began to appear at the local level, in the records of town officials and in account books and diaries. The colony, on the other hand, maintained three classifications for Rhode Island residents:

"white," "Indian" and "black," resisting the popular plural vernacular but not yet imposing a black/white binary either.

As of 1774, hypodescent had not yet become a guiding principle in the formation of protoracial ideology with respect to African/Indian intermixtures. The 1774 Rhode Island census lists six independent families of color that have some members enumerated in the "Indian" column and others in the "black" column. Of the 188 independent Indian families listed, several have heads of household with the names "Sippeo," "Cuff," "Caesar," "Quom," and "Sambo"—all classical and West African day names common to African slaves. Among fifty-five independent "black" families listed, one has a head of household named "Mustee."[9] These listings demonstrate that Sippeo, Caesar, and Cuff were considered "Indians" even with African heritage; in 1774 the persistence of Indian cultural practices or language use apparently still outweighed considerations of status, phenotype, and so forth. (We know that as late as 1753 some Narragansetts still spoke no English, as evidenced by a deposition identified as having been made by "Sarah Tom an Indian Woman of Charleston in Kings County, Mr. George Babcock being the Interpreter.")[10]

But, by the late eighteenth century, the meaning of the terms "black" and "Negro" in English usage was changing. In one usage, "black" was becoming a physical descriptor, while "Negro" was at least sometimes used to convey the notion of mixed descent with African heritage predominating, often with a latent implication of enslaved origins as well. Hence, referring back to Rhode Island at the time of an earlier census in 1755, Ezra Stiles observed in 1773 that "the blacks were chiefly Negroes, excepting in the country of King's County, where are the Remains of the Narragansett Indians."[11] This wording suggests that, in that Rhode Island county, some of the "blacks" were *not* "Negroes," but Indians.

Another important implication of the 1774 census listings is that many "Indian" families listed by head of household apparently were living independently among whites, along with free African-descended families, as relatively assimilated (in English eyes) elements of the community, no longer living in the "native" manner. Quite likely, they had first lived in the households of whites as servants and slaves, and then had formed independent households, some of whose members perhaps still labored for local white families.

The census reports 494 "Indians" living in 106 independent families in Charlestown on parcels of land individually owned or held in common by the tribe. These, too, included some individuals of full or partial African descent. In 1765 Simeon Matthews petitioned the Rhode Island General Assembly for relief under the law excluding Indians living as members of the tribe from taxation, stating that he "acknowledges himself to be an Indian has taken a Wife that is part Indian & part Negro & *live together after the manner of the Indians.*" Simeon Matthews appears as "Simeon Marthers" in the census, the head of a household consisting of a male and a female over sixteen and a male and female under sixteen, all listed as "Indians."[12]

In the years that followed the Revolution, however, officials at the state and federal level began to document Indian "disappearance" as a consequence of race mixing. In December 1831, Dan King, chair of a committee appointed by the Rhode Island General Assembly to investigate the condition of the Narragansett tribe of Indians, reported, "The once powerful nation of the Narragansetts is found to be rapidly verging toward that state of complete extinction which has long since overtaken their less fortunate neighbors and that period appears to be fast approaching when they will be known only in history. . . . Of between one hundred and fifty and two hundred who are claimed as members of that tribe, . . . only five or six are genuine untainted Narragansetts all the rest are either clear or nearly Negroes. . . . Forty years ago this was a nation of Indians now it is a medly [*sic*] of mongrels in which the African blood predominates."[13]

The federal government, too, saw imminent extinction as the consequence of the decline in Indian "genuineness," a characteristic defined by what was termed "purity of blood." Jedidiah Morse, commissioned by the secretary of war in 1820 to visit and report on "the actual state of the Indian Tribes in our country," noted of the "remnants" of New England tribes that "very few of them are of unmixed blood."[14] In Rhode Island and elsewhere in New England, Indians were becoming extinct because, by the magic of hypodescent, they were becoming "Negroes."

Actual intermarriage was by no means the only rationale for moving Indians into other categories. Especially after 1780, local officials also reclassified many people, especially women, who had been previously classified as Indian. Undoubtedly debates about the advisability of ending slavery, debates that would result in the passage of a gradual emancipation act in 1784, heightened whites' awareness of the presence in their households and communities of African-descended people. Especially after 1780, anxiety about continuing to control—and *identify* in order to control—a population once at least nominally controlled by the formal structures of slavery also seems to have led local officials to "blacken" native people, most frequently women, who had been slaves or indentured servants, either redesignating them or introducing uncertainty into their classification. For example, the Warwick town clerk characterized Mary Carder as "Indian" in 1775 but "Negro" in 1784; the Providence town clerk described Sarah Hill as "Indian or Mustee" in 1784 but "Negro" in 1791. Ambiguous characterizations with two or more alternatives offered—"mustee or mo-latto," "molatto or Indian"—also began to appear with frequency.[15]

The passage of the *post nati* gradual abolition statute in 1784 directly affected only newborn children of slaves but had the effect of inspiring increasing numbers of emancipations of existing enslaved Indians and Africans. Thrown together in freedom as they had been in bondage, in cities and towns they formed additional mixed-race households and communities on the margins of white society—independent households like those enumerated in the 1774 census. But now, these households were increasingly characterized by whites as simply "negro." After 1790, the term most frequently used became "black," although "negro" remained in use as well. This progression seems to suggest a shift toward social identities emphasizing phenotype, as slavery moved into the ever more distant past and associations with enslaved status faded. Yet varieties of "mixture" proliferated, and the appearance of the terms "coloured" and "of colour" around 1800, and the steady increase in their use, alongside and appar-ently in distinction to "black," seem to reflect an effort to account for it. "African" continued to be used to describe ancestry.

At the same time, it is apparent that some of the slaves freed in the 1780s and 1790s who were partly or possibly entirely of African descent "went native" to live in Charlestown on Narragansett tribal land with relatives, joining mixed-race families formed earlier, like that of Simeon Matthews.[16] By the early 1800s, many people of mixed African and Indian (and European) descent, along with those solely of Indian descent, were living "after the manner of the Indians" on the remaining tribal land in Charlestown. While these people often were often described, as Dan King did in his 1831 report, in racialized terms intended to disparage ("a medly of mongrels in which the African blood predominates"), their social identity remained "Indian," at least in part because they were living on land still controlled by the tribe (and still coveted by whites). But in-creasingly, the state sought to curtail the participation of mixed-race people in tribal affairs by denying Indian "authenticity" on the basis of African descent; for example, in 1792 the State of Rhode Island in its guardianship position excluded Narragansett men with mothers of African descent from voting rights in tribal council elections.[17]

Narragansetts expressed a variety of feelings about the relationship between the African and European ancestry of some of them and their Indian identity. In most situations, Narragansetts of mixed descent living in the community in Charlestown appear to have continued to think of themselves as Indian. Many of them frequently insisted on their Indian identity when it was challenged, as when John Hammer of Hopkinton sought to invalidate a Hopkinton Justice

Court warrant issued to "John Hammer black man" because he was "an Indian man."[18] As one group, writing as "Members of the Narragansett Tribe of Indians," noted at the end of a restrained but insistent refutation of the King report addressed to the Rhode Island General Assembly in 1832, "And as to the Mixture of African and European Blood with that of the native Indians; It has been done, and cannot be undone by any Legislative Act."[19] These Narragansetts seemed to be arguing that "mixed blood" did not invalidate Indian identity or membership in the tribe.

But by this time, other Narragansetts had begun citing as "immemorial custom" the notion that "if any Indian woman or girl married a negro man or any one who had a mixture of negro blood, she forfeited all her rights and privileges as an individual of the Nation from which she and they descended and particularly all right and title to lands belonging to the tribe or Tribes to whom they belonged."[20] By the 1830s, this argument was being used strategically in situations of competing claims to land or leadership to weaken the case of the opposing party. For example, in 1822 Eunice Rogers, a Narragansett living on tribal land, petitioned the Rhode Island General Assembly to force the tribal council to give back a house and thirty acres of land originally belonging to Rogers that the council had leased to Roby Bacon, "a woman com into the town that was Neither Bred Born nor Brot up in nor tribe or town" who "has got a Clear Negro for her husband." While Rogers's objection was based primarily on her assertion that Bacon "never has brot any Satisfactory Certificate Evidence to the tribe that She is a lawful member of the said tribe—only her bare word— which is not agreeable to our Customs or Regulations," her characterization of Bacon as "this Negros wife" suggests that she felt a relationship with a "Negro" was a telling mark against the legitimacy of her claim—in a sense, against her own "Indianness."[21]

And some Narragansetts may deliberately have denied Indian descent and association with the tribe on occasion when that became desirable or necessary, for example, to evade the 1801 act passed by the Rhode Island General Assembly to prevent whites from making "contracts & securities . . . in consideration of a sale or sales of liquor" to "any of said Tribe or . . . any person of colour intermarried with one of said Tribe." This statute was widely interpreted as extending beyond the purchase of liquor to making loans to Narragansetts for any article or service illegal and uncollectible.[22] Eligibility of blacks but not Indians to vote in statewide elections after 1842 may have had a similar effect.

By 1820, there were three overlapping systems of racial characterization in play in Rhode Island. The first federal census reduced the matrix of social identity to two overlapping binaries: "free" and "enslaved," and "white" and "other." In its 1783 census, the State of Rhode Island had formally divided the population into four classifications: "White," "Black," "Indian," and "Mulatto"; "mulatto" recognized the continuing existence of Indians but collapsed all varieties of mixed lineage into one category that emphasized the salience of African descent. But ordinary people and local officials were still trying to account for variety, although in a slightly simplified set of terms. They used several terms: "white," "coloured" or "of colour," "black," "negro," "molatto" or "mulatto," and "Indian." The term "African" was disappearing, presumably because the legal slave trade had ended and the actual African origins of people of color were receding into the past. (Curiously, while spokesmen for the American Colonization Society who advocated the "return" of African descendants to Africa sometimes used the phrase "children of Africa" to characterize the targets of their interest, they seldom used the term "African," preferring "people of colour" or "coloured"; black leaders themselves avoided the term "African" in the belief that it heightened this association, although institutions such as "African" churches named by earlier generations retained those names.)[23] "Coloured" seems to have emphasized mixture (of African and Indian descent, with the possibility of European admixture) and often lighter skin. "Black" emphasized African descent and phenotype and seems to have been used frequently by officials to connote criminality or, for women, promiscuity. "Negro" suggested African descent, too, but seemed to emphasize servility and descent from people of enslaved status, with a possibility of European admixture. The term "molatto" was falling out of use, and "mustee" had virtually disappeared; whites seem to have decided that any African admixture obliterated the salience of Indian heritage implied by "mustee," while "molatto" suggested too strongly a European admixture. Political considerations described earlier made "mustee" unappealing to local people of mixed race themselves.

By 1820, mixed-race people with Narragansett ancestry were struggling to define themselves and seek a stable place in the society and polity of Rhode Island by negotiating raced social identities in terms of this racial vernacular. Place, class, and association worked to inflect their social identities differently.

People with African and Indian ancestry who lived on the margins of whites' communities distant from and connected weakly, if at all, to the tribe were considered by whites, and sometimes self-described, as "black," "coloured," or "Negro." While these communities were generally poor, some of their members were able to become relatively prosperous and successful; for some of them, emphasizing their connections to some of the "best (white) families" through their former enslavement as Africans was more socially useful than emphasizing their connections to a "declining" tribe. An example is William J. Brown, who was born in Providence, lived in the black community there, and identified himself proudly on the first page of his 1883 autobiography as the descendant of one of the slaves owned by Nicholas Brown and Company, of the prominent family of merchants, slave traders, and abolitionists who were instrumental in the establishment of Brown University. William J. Brown also stated that "my mother's relations were the Prophets, who belonged to the Narragansett tribe, and resided in Cranston"; however, besides noting his grandmother's burial "according to Indian custom," Brown devoted the bulk of his memoir to the struggles of his family to triumph over the discrimination they suffered as free blacks. After William Dorr's rebellion in 1842, it was Brown who negotiated the agreement by which black men in Rhode Island (but *not* Indians) became eligible to vote as a reward for their support of the Charter Government against Dorr. Brown clearly was understood by black and white communities in Providence, and by himself, to be an African American, his acknowledged Indian ancestry notwithstanding.[24]

Poorer, less successful people of Indian and Indian/black ancestry who lived in poor black communities, especially in urban areas, along with African-descended people, became targets of racism in response to what whites saw as the growing problem of social disorder and public expense presented by the growing free black population emerging out of slavery. It was claimed that the state of free blacks everywhere was one of "extreme and remediless degradation, of gross irreligion, of revolting profligacy, and, of course, deplorable wretchedness."[25] The power of this rhetoric was the notion that blacks were inherently foreign to the American continent. "Among us is a growing population of strangers," an American Colonization Society speaker declared in 1829; "Are they not . . . aliens and outcasts in the midst of the people?"[26] These arguments fueled an influential movement to remove them and send them to Africa. Roundups of people identified as blacks to warn them out, travel restrictions, bond requirements, and mob attacks were other removal strategies directed at people living in black neighborhoods—which included many Indian-descended people, identified in the estimation of the community, and often self-identified, as "black" or "coloured."

In sum, people of mixed Indian and African descent who did not maintain strong connections with the tribal lands and activities that took place there, whose parents and grandparents had lived in whites' households in bondage, and who lived in urban environments amid the black population, considered themselves "negro" or "coloured" with perhaps an awareness of Indian ancestry like William Brown's. Unlike him, they had achieved no economic and social standing as "exceptional" blacks in the larger community, and they became targets of antiblack violence and removal along with freed persons of African descent. As people of color, they, too, suffered the indignities and assaults by which whites signaled their desire to rid their towns and cities of what they considered to be a degenerate and eternally alien people.

Just as place and social context could give similarly descended groups of people variant or vernacular racial identities, even more narrowly defined circumstances could produce two different vernacular racial identities for closely related individuals. For an example of how place, class, and association operated to produce a vernacular black identity targeted for removal, we can look at the riot that took place in 1831 in Snow Town, the name given to the largest black community in Providence—"an area tenanted chiefly by idle blacks [the term invoking criminality] of the lowest stamp," in the words of a newspaper article about the event.[27] There, a dispute between "black" and white sailors in September 1831 erupted into four nights of mob violence in which some twelve houses occupied by "blacks" were destroyed or badly damaged and another five or six suffered broken windows. The militia was called, and in the melee, five whites died.

In hearings that followed, John Gardner, a "stout black man" born in North Kingstown, Rhode Island, was charged with being a rioter, and Langarthy (Langworthy) Weeden, a "black servant" who was his friend, was asked to testify. "Weeden" and "Gardner" are common names of people identified with the Narragansett tribe in Washington County, which has always been called "the Narragansett country" and which includes North Kingstown. Weeden signatures appear on tribal petitions to the Rhode Island General Assembly in the nineteenth century, and Indian Gardners are sprinkled throughout the public records of Washington County's towns; three Gardners and six Weedens were listed on the 1880 Narragansett Tribal Roll.[28] While not certain, it is extremely likely that these two men were Narragansetts; they had become "black" in the context of Snow Town.

Another incident of "black" disorder leading up to the Snow Town riot was the rape of a white woman, Hannah Cornell, by Joseph Nocake. Nocake had been identified as an Indian when he was warned out of Providence as a person of "bad fame and reputation" four years earlier. This was not a mistake; the name "Nocake" appeared repeatedly as a Narragansett name (sometimes as "Nokegg") on various documents throughout the eighteenth and nineteenth centuries, including a petition from members of the tribe in Charlestown to the General Assembly in May 1831, four months before the riot. But with an already "bad reputation" further blackened by his return to the city in defiance of the warning-out order and by his residence in Snow Town, Joseph Nocake was charged for the murder of Hannah Cornell as a "black man." Apparently in 1831, Nocakes (as well as Gardners and Weedens) were Indians in Charlestown at the same time that they were "blacks" in Snow Town.[29]

A dramatic murder case in northeast Rhode Island illustrates the impact of a different constellation of factors, including national identity, on vernacular racial identity. In 1831, the year of the Snow Town riot, three brothers named Thomas, Uriah, and Amasa Walmsley were each charged and deposed as "man of colour, laborer," in the murders of their aunt, Hannah Frank, and her lover, John Burke. The Walmsleys were members of a large African- and Narragansett-descended family whose name appeared regularly on tribal petitions and rolls, sometimes as "Wamsley," for three hundred years. These men lived in a "black" neighborhood called "Monkeytown" in the town of Burrillville in the northwest corner of the state. All three signed their depositions with an "X." Their aunt, widely known as "Black Hannah," was described as "part black and part white" by witnesses. (Hannah Frank and the Walmsleys' father were half brother and sister.) One witness testified that Amasa, in a conversation shortly after the murder, referred to the event as "the negro scrape," suggesting that both Amasa and the witness thought of Hannah's race as somehow distinct from Amasa's ("man of colour" in the indictment, but possibly Indian in his own mind), but also not "black." John Burke was a recent Irish immigrant. As the testimony in the trials makes clear, the Walmsleys did not approve of their aunt, Black Hannah, keeping company with Burke the Irishman. In the course of the altercation that apparently led to fatal beatings of Burke and Frank, Amasa was heard to exclaim that "if Burke did not go back to his own country he'd lick him if he saw him again."[30]

Here we can see how national identity, along with descent, culture, gender, and class, could operate to index vernacular "racial" identities. The Walmsleys, lower-class, illiterate residents of Monkeytown who were of mixed descent—part African and part Narragansett, living far from Narragansett tribal land and apparently maintaining little connection with the tribe—were officially "coloured." They saw their aunt as "negro," "blacker" than they, even though they shared her African lineage, and she, unlike them, was described as "part white" as well. We can speculate that Hannah's pattern of descent—part black and part white but apparently *not* part Indian—increased the salience of her "blackness." Her gender, if not her sexual behavior, may also have "blackened" her. Also significant is Burke's identity as an Irish immigrant, a member of a group already becoming the target of considerable hostility in New England. (An attorney in a different Rhode Island case involving an Irishman in 1832 wrote in his case notes, "These accursed Irishmen—This scum of another Country.")[31] Burke's status as an alien may have highlighted Amasa Walmsley's unimpeachable Americanness; that, together with Black Hannah's sexual promiscuity, may have cast his act, reprehensible as it was, in a certain "manly" and patriotic light. We cannot know for certain, but something, at any rate, allowed Amasa, charged as a "coloured" man, the dubious distinction of being convicted and hanged for the murders with the official designation "Indian." (Thomas and Uriah were not convicted.)

For Narragansett-descended people who remained near the Narragansett tribe's reserve and "lived in the manner of the Indians," the struggle to define themselves in opposition to a discourse of degeneration and redesignation as "negro" or "black" and nearing extinction took a still different path. These Narragansetts were described in John M. Niles's *Gazetteer* in 1819 as the remnants of a people who had "passed away like a dream and the places that knew them know them no more. . . . The remains of this tribe at this place amount to about 100, nearly all of whom are intermixed with the whites and Negroes. They are an abject race." Jedidiah Morse's 1822 report to the U.S. secretary of war on Indian affairs, assessing "the actual state of the Indian tribes in our country," offered the same rhetoric of "remnants" and "mixed blood." The 1831 King report similarly linked decline in "Indian blood" and the increase in "Negro blood" to a catalog of decay and social collapse in virtually all aspects of Narragansett life and culture.[32]

But while the disadvantaged condition of "negroized" Indians living in "black" communities on the margins of white cities and towns made them targets of mob attack and removal rhetoric, the tight tribal attachment of Narragansetts living on tribal land in Charlestown forced whites to regard them as indigenous, local—and thus not easily subject to discourses of removal. Their nativeness made claims of strangerhood impossible and talk of Africa irrelevant; at the same time, their "negritude" precluded talk of moving them west to live in "Indian country." Jedidiah Morse argued that New England Indians, "having intermarried with the lowest classes of white people and Negroes, and feeling no sympathy with Indians of pure blood, would not be comfortable, or happy, or of wholesome influence, if removed and planted among them."[33] The discourse of Narragansett racial degeneration, while it might rhetorically eradicate Indianness, could not easily erase nativeness as long as the Narragansetts remained closely connected to their ancestral land.

Over the ensuing century, however, the racial vernacular began to collapse in the face of state and federal pressure toward the black/white binary, and with it went the prospects for continued Narragansett sovereignty. The designation "Indian" disappeared completely from official records. In 1852, 1855, 1858, and 1866, successive committees of the Rhode Island General Assembly were appointed to explore detribalization of the Narragansett tribe and sale of their public lands. The Narragansetts were repeatedly described in press reports and by the succession of legislative committees as "nearing extinction." These reports emphasized not simply a reduction in numbers but also a diminution in "racial purity." The 1852 committee noted that "no Indians of whole blood remain." The 1855 committee reported that only 147 Narragansetts remained, of whom none were "full-blooded" and eleven were "half- or "three-quarters' blooded."[34]

The discourse of extinction was supported by a calculus of appearance and culture as well as blood. The Rhode Island Indian commissioner told the General Assembly in 1858 that the Narragansett no longer "look Indian" and lacked a "distinct Indian culture." His report included a consanguinity table that accounted for 122 recognized Narragansetts, of whom none were "full blooded," two were "three-fourths' blooded," ten "half-bloods," and the rest "one-fourth or less than one-fourth blooded."[35]

The popular discourse of disappearance mirrored the official reports. In 1870 a local historian argued that the remaining Narragansetts had become "mixed bloods and mongrels, with a large infusion of negro blood in their veins, . . . doomed to inevitable and speedy extinction."[36] During the whole century, news reports repeatedly lamented the death or imminent death of "the last Narragansett." For example, in 1859 the *Westerly Narragansett Weekly* noted that seven women of "genuine Narragansett blood" were still living, but "with their death, the last remnant of the original noble race [will have] ceased to exist."[37]

It was not until 1880, however, that the Rhode Island General Assembly finally took formal steps to detribalize the Narragansett and thus to extinguish Narragansett identity. Some of the uncertainty in earlier discussions regarding the wisdom of this plan may have been a consequence of the ambiguous political position of African Americans in the state. While many in the General Assembly may have wanted to conflate Indians with African Americans in order to undermine their authenticity as Indians, they did not necessarily want to establish their bona fides as "blacks" when William J. Brown had just negotiated the vote for Rhode Island's African Americans as a reward for their loyalty to the state during the Dorr Rebellion. But by 1880, after a long, weary, and violent post–Civil War period of southern Reconstruction, politicians in Rhode Island, as elsewhere, were tired of protective guardianships. A final Committee of Investigation was appointed to consider "the tribe and its extinction"—a charge that left the conclusion in little doubt, in a year when the census for Washington County, where most Narragansetts lived, included only three categories: "black," "mulatto" (for which no individuals were listed!), and "white."[38]

Various members of the Narragansett tribe gave extensive evidence at open hearings. They dealt complexly with their characterization as a "negro tribe." Several witnesses tried to lay claim to a mixed-race identity that did not demand either the forfeit of rights (sovereignty and land) inherent in its Indian component or the denial of cultural and lineal connections with Africans. For example, Samuel Congdon testified as a Narragansett that he was "a black republican and an abolitionist, clean to the backbone, every inch of me."[39] Others resisted characterization as anything but Indian.

But the committee's first finding of fact was "that there is not a person of pure Indian blood in the tribe, and that characteristic features, varying through all the shades of color, from the Caucasian to the Black race, were made manifest at the several meetings of the Committee. Their [the Narragansetts'] extinction as a tribe has been accomplished as effectually by nature as an Act of the General Assembly will put an end to the name."[40] The General Assembly agreed and passed an act to "detribalize" the Narragansett, sell their common lands, and disperse them into the surrounding community. Ironically, officially obliterating their collective identity as Indians once and for all necessitated enumerating them as Indians so that the proceeds of the sale of their land might be equitably distributed among them; 342 individuals with Narragansett ancestry stepped forward. (Others with equally credible Narragansett ancestry who opposed detribalization refused to register.) In this way, the state in its clarifying capacity authenticated its "tribe of Negroes" *as Indians* in order to transform them fully and completely into non-Indians; henceforth, the Narragansett tribe was to be formally regarded as extinct; its erstwhile members were to be viewed as simply "negroes."

The collapse of the racial vernacular into the state's formal black/white binary left the Narragansetts with very little room and few tools with which to reassert their Indian identity, but in the 1930s they began to wage a campaign to regain public, and also federal and state, recognition as "authentic" Indians. They obtained a state charter as the Narragansett Tribe of Indians, Inc., a nonprofit corporation; they inaugurated a tribal newspaper, the *Narragansett Dawn*; and they began inviting the public to their ceremonials, for which they carefully chose what white Americans by that time recognized as distinctively Indian (primarily Plains Indian) dress. But when, in the 1970s, they successfully sued the State of Rhode Island for the return of 3,200 acres of tribal land and obtained federal recognition as an Indian tribe, predictably their efforts sparked a new outburst of public skepticism about their authenticity as Indians. It was in this context that the 1970 *Providence Journal-Bulletin*'s Sunday magazine published the story with the forty-eight-point footer cited at the beginning of this essay— "When is an Indian not an Indian? In South County, it's when he's a Negro." This formulation demonstrates the inability of the rigid binary of racial terms to accommodate a multiracial heritage, in contrast to the more complex racial vernacular of the eighteenth and early nineteenth centuries, which had supported a more flexible array of social identities.

The disjuncture between eighteenth/nineteenth-century vernacular racial characterizations and the twentieth/twenty-first-century binary also poses problems for current efforts to acknowledge, explain, and celebrate so-called minority histories. This is illustrated by the struggle over the cultural ownership of an important historical event commemorated at a site called Patriots' Park in Portsmouth, near Newport, Rhode Island, site of one of the most famous battles of the American Revolution. There, on August 29, 1778, a Continental regiment composed entirely of men of color, the First Rhode Island, repelled three waves of Hessian assault in the battle of Rhode Island.[41] In 1974 the National Historic Landmarks Program selected the battleground as a historic site and placed a small monument and a boulder with a plaque commemorating "The Black Regiment" there.[42] Since then, ceremonies honoring the role of the "Black Regiment" in the battle of Rhode Island have been held there annually.[43]

For the last ten years, however, Patriots' Park has been the site of a very different kind of battle, a struggle over identity and representation. Who were the solders of the "Black Regiment"?

In 1994, when the Federal Highway Administration made funding available for "enhancement projects" to improve or preserve historic sites associated with highways,[44] the Newport City Branch of the National Association for the Advancement of Colored People (NAACP) and the Rhode Island Black Heritage Society spearheaded a proposal to improve the site.[45] Paul Gaines, an African American, chaired the Patriots' Park Improvement Project. In 1996 William F. Bundy, head of the Rhode Island Department of Transportation (RIDOT) and an African American former naval officer, selected "Patriots' Park Landscape Project" as Rhode Island's first "Enhancement Project" under the transportation funding bill. By 1999, a site plan and design for a new monument had been submitted to RIDOT, and Gaines, who shared them with his committee and members of the Newport County NAACP, reported "a very favorable and supportive atmosphere, a lot of excitement about this project."[46] The design was very simple, a platform with a wall with two doorways, engraved with the names of soldiers in the First Rhode Island. Louis Wilson, professor of Afro-American studies at Smith College, who had spent several years recovering and documenting the names of all men of color who had served as soldiers in the American Revolution, provided the names of all known members of the regiment, coded by various categories: city of birth, slave status, and racial characterizations, including "Black (people who are Black but not noted in record . . .)"; "Mulatto (Indian/Black/European)"; "African (West Africa/Guinea coast"; "Negro"; "Indian"; and "Mustee (Indian/Black)." Many of the names on the list were "Indian" and "Mustee (Indian/Black)."[47]

Since every transportation enhancement project funded by the Federal Department of Transportation requires that groups with a direct interest and involvement in the history of the project site be given an opportunity to comment on the design, in late 1999 RIDOT invited twelve groups, including a variety of Indian tribes and bands, African American organizations, and representatives of assorted local institutions and government agencies to participate as consulting parties.[48]

By February 2001, Louis Wilson had prepared a text explaining the creation of the regiment, to be installed on the front of the monument. This narrative, and another describing the actual battle itself, were forwarded to the various consulting parties.[49] While agreement was easily reached on the description of the battle after one revision, controversy erupted over the description of the formation and membership of the regiment.[50] The narrative stated that "the heroic events that brought this nation into being" had been "shared by a significant number of " 'blacks,' which at that time included Negroes, Mulattos, Mustees and Native Americans," and it went on to refer to the men of color in the regiment as "slaves," "blacks," and "free blacks."[51] The NAACP, through Paul Gaines and his committee, was delighted with the plan and the text.[52] John Brown of the Narragansett Indian Tribe Historic Preservation Office (NITHPO), however, was not; he wrote directly to the Advisory Council on Historic Preservation in Washington, D.C., to say that the text on the monument was "bad history," and in a letter to Paul Gaines he indicated his disagreement with its "false characterization and misinterpretations" of Indians as "blacks."[53] In the absence of a satisfactory revision, Brown requested that all textual references to Indians and the names of Indian enlistees be deleted from the wall.

It would take four years and eleven drafts before the parties finally reached a consensus on a text that would identify the soldiers who fought in the Rhode Island First to (almost) everyone's satisfaction. While there were also other issues having to do with the precise role and tribal affiliation of Indians who fought at the battle of Rhode Island, the most vexing problem was whether the regiment could or should be called "black" if there were Indians in it. Revisions and counterrevisions were proposed and rejected. In response to a proposal that the whole idea of a narrative be jettisoned in favor of simply listing soldiers' names, John Brown agreed—but only if the plaque bearing the words "Black Regiment" on the boulder erected in 1974 were removed. The NAACP was adamant that the original memorial remain in place.[54]

In April 2004—ten years after the Federal Highway Administration initiative to enhance Patriots' Park began—one last proposal achieved sufficient consensus for the Federal Highway Administration to direct RIDOT to finish the plans and send the project out to bid. The final text, headed simply "The Rhode Island First Regiment," reads, in part, "From the beginning of the war, there were blacks and Indians fighting alongside the white soldiers . . . . The rank and file were predominantly blacks and Indians, both free men and those recently freed. The majority of the soldiers in the First Rhode Regiment were believed to be of African descent, which has led to its being celebrated as the Black Regiment; regimental rosters reveal a significant number of the soldiers to be Indians."[55] It was agreed that the individual names of the soldiers of the First Rhode Island would also appear on the front panel of the monument, and that the boulder with the plaque engraved "The Black Regiment" would also remain on the site.

To most of the African Americans interested in Patriots' Park, calling the Black Regiment "black" was historically accurate because the soldiers of the First Rhode Island were "always" referred to as "black." This argument shifts an interpretation born in the mid-nineteenth-century collapse of vernacular racial identities backward almost a century to the Revolution. One could argue, however, that it reflects a reasonable investment in that interpretation as a source of solidarity, political recognition, and power for "blacks" today. "Indians," on the other hand, have no investment in a conception rooted an alien, patrilineal understanding of kinship that "Africanized" the Narragansett, erased their Indianness, radically disempowered their community, and still surfaces to challenge their sovereignty.

These irreconcilable positions illustrate the difficulties posed by the assumption that the set of terms used to identify racialized categories of difference in any given moment transparently corresponds to a fixed vocabulary of social meanings. Rather, as this essay has endeavored to show, the terms deployed in a given period reflect a point on the evolutionary arc of the struggle between individuals and communities on the one hand and the nation-state on the other to define how heritage and physical difference will be meaningful in negotiating social and political power.

NOTES

1. John Brown Francis to Elisha Reynolds Potter Jr., August 8, 1843, Elisha Reynolds Potter Jr. Papers, Rhode Island Historical Society, Providence, R.I.

2. *The Rhode Islander* (the *Providence Journal-Bulletin* Sunday magazine section), February 22, 1970, 12–13.

3. David Theo Goldberg, *The Racial State* (Malden, Mass.: Blackwell, 2001), 34.

4. While, as Michael Gomez has pointed out, some ethnic labels were undoubtedly artifacts of the slave trade, nonetheless slave traders and owners were aware of distinctions among language groups and regional origins of prospective slaves, as evidenced by orders specifying more and less desirable slaves in these terms, and often ethnic and

regional origins were reflected in slaves' names and the names they gave their children. Michael A. Gomez, *Exchanging Their Country Marks: The Transformation of African Identities in the Colonial and Antebellum South* (Chapel Hill: University of North Carolina Press, 1998), 7.

5. See, for example, Rhode Island Colony Records, 4:425, June 1729; Warwick Town Papers, June 1720, January 1725, July 1728, Rhode Island Historical Society; there are countless other examples.

6. David Eltis, *The Rise of African Slavery in the Americas* (Cambridge, U.K.: Cambridge University Press, 2000), 226. Eltis provides a fascinating and textured discussion of "the relatively slow development of a broader sense of Africanness or even blackness" among African ethnic groups in response to encounters with Europeans in Africa and the experiences of enslavement and transportation to the Americas in chapter 9, "Ethnicity in the Early Modern Atlantic World."

7. The question of Narragansett slavery is controversial. A Rhode Island law passed during King Philip's War in 1676 outlawing the lifetime enslavement of Indians (except for debt) is sometimes cited as evidence that Indians were only bound for a term, never enslaved. The issue is complicated further by the fact that some Indians explicitly called or bequeathed as "slaves" were in fact so-called Spanish Indians, or Tuscaroras enslaved in the Tuscarora War, and shipped to Rhode Island in the early 1600s. Nonetheless, on August 13, 1676, at the conclusion of King Philip's War, Narragansett warriors who had escaped the Great Swamp Massacre were sold into slavery at an average price of thirty-two shillings; many were shipped to the West Indies, but it is not certain that some did not remain in New England. Periodically, probate records in southern Rhode Island towns list "Indian man" or "Indian boy" with high values comparable to those of "Negro man" and "Negro boy," in contrast to entries for "the time of an Indian boy" at much lower value, suggesting that the former reflect instances of enslavement, the latter of indenture. William Almy's will leaving "one Indian Man Servant & his wife & Child to his heirs" in 1677 with no designation "Spanish" can be read as referring to a local (e.g., Pequot or Narragansett) slave. Inventory of William Almy, April 23, 1677, case of *Job Almy v. Mary Townsend and Job Almy*, Rhode Island Superior Court of Judicature, Record Book A, 248, Rhode Island Supreme Court Judicial Records Center, Pawtucket, R.I. For a discussion of this issue, see Margaret Ellen Newell, "The Changing Nature of Indian Slavery in New England, 1670–1720," in *Reinterpreting New England Indians and the Colonial Experience*, ed. Colin G. Calloway and Neal Salisbury (Boston: Colonial Society of Massachusetts, 2003), 106–36; and John A. Sainsbury, "Indian Labor in Early Rhode Island," *New England Quarterly* 48 (1975): 378–93.

8. Tobias Shattock to Joseph Hazard, 1768, Hazard Papers, Rhode Island Historical Society. For examples of binding out Indians, see the indentures of children Hannah George, 1719; John Newcomb, 1721; Elizabeth Pisquees, 1728; and the self-indenture of Simon George, 1731, in Rhode Island Historical Society Miscellaneous Manuscripts. See also the 1732 petition of John Potter protesting the fraudulent binding out and ill use of an Indian man named Grigry, Petitions to the General Assembly, 2:72, Rhode Island State Archives, Providence, R.I.

9. Manuscript Census of the State of Rhode Island, 1774 (microfilm copy), Rhode Island State Archives. The census was published, with significant errors and idiosyncratic combination of categories, in John R. Bartlett, *Census of the State of Rhode Island 1774* (Providence: Knowles, Anthony and Co., 1858).

10. Champlin Papers, 1:29, August 1753, Rhode Island Historical Society.

11. Franklin Bowditch Dexter, ed., *The Literary Diary of Ezra Stiles*, 3 vols. (New York: Charles Scribner's Sons, 1901), 1:380.

12. Petition of Simeon Matthews to the Rhode Island General Assembly (emphasis added), 1765, Narragansett Indians Miscellaneous Petitions, Rhode Island State Archives; Manuscript Census of the Inhabitants of the Colony of Rhode Island and Providence Plantation, 1774, Rhode Island State Archives.

13. Report of Dan King to the Rhode Island General Assembly, December 1831 (hereinafter cited as King Report), Committee Reports to the General Assembly, n.p., Rhode Island State Archives.

14. Jedidiah Morse, *A Report to the Secretary of War of the United States, on Indian Affairs* . . . (New Haven, Conn.: S. Converse, 1822), 24.

15. Warwick Town Council meeting, March 13, 1775, and June 14, 1784, Warwick Town Council Records, 3:39 and 3:161, Warwick Town Hall, Warwick, R.I.; Providence Town Council meeting, February 3 and 6, 1784, and May 30, 1791, Providence Town Council Records, 5:256–58 and 6:163, City Hall, Providence, R.I. For a detailed treatment of redesignation, including these and other instances, see Ruth Wallis Herndon and Ella Wilcox Sekatau, "The Right to a Name: The Narragansett People and Rhode Island Officials in the Revolutionary Era," *Ethnohistory* 44 (Summer 1997): 443–62.

16. While scholars have paid much attention to New England colonists' fear of the ever-present possibility of whites' "going native," the implications of the frequent resort of their African servants to just this possibility have not been fully considered.

17. "An Act for regulating the Affairs of the Narragansett Tribe of Indians, in this State," February 1792, *Records of the State of Rhode Island, 1784–92* (Providence, 1881), 10:476.

18. Hopkinton Justice Court Records, October 8, 1793, Hopkinton Town Hall, Hopkinton, R.I.

19. Narragansett File, 90, Rhode Island State Archives.

20. Sarah (Potteogue) Pendleton, September 26, 1796, Whitestown, N.Y., Brothertown Records, 1774–1804, folios 1–2: 11–13, Hamilton College Archives, Clinton, N.Y., cited in Ann Marie Plane, *Colonial Intimacies: Indian Marriage in Early New England* (Ithaca, N.Y.: Cornell University Press, 2000), 169–70.

21. Narragansett Indian Miscellaneous Petitions, Rhode Island State Archives.

22. Miscellaneous Petitions, October 1801, Rhode Island State Archives.

23. For two overlapping but contrasting arguments about the uses of these terms by black intellectuals, see Sterling Stuckey, "Identity and Ideology: The Names Controversy," in *Slave Culture: Nationalist Theory and the Foundations of Black America* (New York: Oxford University Press, 1987), 193–244; and Joanne Pope Melish, *Disowning*

Slavery: Gradual Emancipation and "Race" in New England, 1780–1860 (Ithaca, N.Y.: Cornell University Press, 1998), 248–52.

24. William J. Brown, *The Life of William J. Brown, of Providence, R.I.: With Personal Recollections of Incidents in Rhode Island* (Providence: Angell and Company, 1883).

25. John Hough, *Sermon Delivered before the Vermont Colonization Society at Montpelier, October 18, 1826* (Montpelier, Vt.: E. P. Watton-Watchman Office, 1826), 8.

26. Leonard Bacon, *A Plea for Africa, Delivered in New Haven, July 4, 1825* (New Haven, Conn.: T. G. Woodward, 1825), 13.

27. Unidentified clipping, Box 326, No. 1, Hay Rider Collection, John Hay Library, Brown University, Providence, R.I.

28. Depositions, Potter Papers; Petition to the General Assembly, 4th Monday in October, 1823, Narragansett Indian Miscellaneous Petitions, Rhode Island State Archives; Jamestown Town Council Records, August 28, 1759, and May 24, 1760, 1:100–102, Jamestown Hall, Jamestown, R.I.; Providence Town Papers, 10:148, Rhode Island Historical Society; Membership Roll of the Narragansett Tribe, Paul Campbell Research Notes, Ms. 369, Rhode Island Historical Society.

29. Box 13, Folder 127, Albert C. Greene Papers, Rhode Island Historical Society; Charlestown Land Evidence Records, 4:339; Petition to the General Assembly, October 1810, and May session, 1831, Narragansett Indian Miscellaneous Petitions, Rhode Island State Archives.

30. All of the material on the Walmsley case comes from the Walmsley case notes, Box 14, Folder 53, Greene Papers; and from *State v. Amasa Walmsley and Thomas J. Walmsley*, Rhode Island Supreme Court Judicial Records Center.

31. *State of Rhode Island v. William Walker et al.*, Box 14, Greene Papers.

32. John M. Niles, *A Gazetteer of the State of Connecticut and Rhode Island* (Providence, 1819); Morse, *Report to the Secretary of War*, 23–24; King Report, n.p.

33. Morse, *Report to the Secretary of War*, 24.

34. Committee's Handwritten Notes [on] Report to the General Assembly in October 1852, and Report of the Commission on the Narragansett Tribe of Indians, January 1855, both in Paul Campbell Research Notes, Box 2, Folder 17.

35. Report of the Commissioner of the Narragansett Tribe of Indians, Made to the General Assembly, January 26, 1858, Paul Campbell Research Notes, Box 2, Folder 17.

36. *New England Historical and Genealogical Register and Antiquarian Journal* 14 (April 1870): 192.

37. *Westerly Narragansett Weekly*, August 25, 1859.

38. *Narragansett Tribe of Indians Report of the Committee of Investigation: A Historical Sketch and Evidence Taken. Made to the House of Representatives at Its January Session, A.D. 1880* (Providence: E. L. Freeman, 1880), hereinafter cited as Detribalization Report.

39. Detribalization Report, 52.

40. Ibid., 6.

41. Anthony Walker, *So Few the Brave: Rhode Island Continentals, 1775–1783* (Newport,

R.I.: Seafield Press, 1981), 50–54; Sidney S. Rider, *An Historical Inquiry Concerning the Attempt to Raise a Regiment of Slaves by Rhode Island during the War of the Revolution. With Several Tables Prepared by Lt.-Col. Jeremiah Olney, Commandant* (Providence: S. S. Rider, 1880). This history is summarized in a paragraph headed "Historical Significance" in a letter from Edmund T. Parker Jr., chief engineer, Rhode Island Department of Transportation (RIDOT), to William F. Bundy, director, RIDOT, January 18, 1995. This and all correspondence on the project subsequently cited is archived at the Rhode Island Historical Preservation and Heritage Commission (RIHPHC), Providence, R.I.

42. Review of this history in Vincent J. Palumbo, principal civil engineer, RIDOT, to Edward F. Sanderson, executive director, RIHPHC, April 22, 1996.

43. Parker to Bundy, in a paragraph headed "Current Status," January 18, 1995. The most recent anniversary celebration, called "The 226th Anniversary of the First Rhode Island Regiment, 'The Black Regiment,'" was sponsored by the New Port County Branch of the National Association for the Advancement of Colored People (NAACP) on Sunday, August 29, 2004, at 3 P.M. at Patriots' Park. Announcement in mailer distributed by the Rhode Island Black Heritage Society.

44. Following the signing into law of the Intermodal Surface Transportation Efficiency Act of 1991 (ISTEA), RIDOT, early in 1992, began to formulate policy and prepare for implementation and administration of provisions of the act requiring expenditures for transportation enhancement activities. The ISTEA required that 10 percent of a state's Surface Transportation Program funds be spent on "transportation enhancements," emphasizing historical sites. Harold J. Neale, Charles R. Anderson, and Barbara M. Shaedler, "A Historical Review of the TRB Review Board A2A05 Committee: Landscape and Environmental Design Committee. Prepared for 70th Anniversary Celebration at the Mid-Year Meeting, Topeka, Kansas, August 2002," 11.

45. Parker to Bundy, January 18, 1995.

46. Paul L. Gaines, chair, Patriots' Park Development Committee, to Vincent J. Palumbo, principal civil engineer, RIDOT, June 30, 1999.

47. The list and an explanation of the coding, with parenthetical definitions included, is in Louis E. Wilson to Derek Bradford, June 27, 1999; Derek Bradford to Mike Hebert, Historical/Archaeological Office, RIDOT, July 19, 1999.

48. Section 106 Documentation Form, Patriots' Park Enhancement Project, Portsmouth, Rhode Island—RIC No. 99103, RIFAP No. STP-ENHR (203), May 1, 2001; individual letters from Vincent J. Palumbo, chief civil engineer, RIDOT, dated November 30, 1999, to John B. Brown III, tribal historic preservation officer (THPO), Narragansett Indian Tribe, and Matthew Vanderhoop, natural resource director and THPO, Wampanoag Tribe of Gay Head (Aquinnah); individual letters from Vincent Palumbo, dated December 16, 1999, to Maurice Foxx, tribal chairman, Mashpee Wampanoag; Linda Elderkin-Degnan, president, Pokanoket/Ampanoag Federation/Wampanoag Nation; Bela Joaquina Teixeira, executive director, Rhode Island Black Heritage Society; Paul Gaines, chair, Patriots' Park Development Committee, Newport County NAACP; Kevin O'Malley, regional manager, Colt State Park; Herbert Hall, president, Portsmouth Historical Society; and Robert G. Driscoll, Portsmouth town administrator.

49. Edward S. Szymanski, chief transportation projects engineer, to Edward Sanderson, March 9, 2001.

50. Redraft, July 5, 2001; agreement communicated to all parties by Edward S. Szymanski, chief transportation projects engineer, Office of Environmental Programs, RIDOT, in letters dated September 18, 2001.

51. "Patriots Park Dedication Wall Text," with attached memo from Edward Sanderson to Richard Greenwood, February 16, 2001.

52. Paul L. Gaines to Edward S. Szymanski, March 7, 2001.

53. John Brown to Paul L. Gaines, March 22, 2001, quoted in Edward Szymanski to Melisa L. Ridenour, division administrator, Federal Highway Administration, June 23, 2002.

54. John Brown to Edward S. Szymanski, October 4, 2002; Richard Greenwood memo recording telephone conversation with John Brown, May 1, 2003; Richard Greenwood interview with the author, August 19, 2004.

55. Excerpt of text headed "(NITHPO Revised copy): Front Panel, Patriots Park Monument," appended to letter from Edward F. Sanderson to Edward S. Szymanski, April 16, 2004.

What Is Race?

Franz Boas Reconsidered

VERNON J. WILLIAMS JR.

The notion that the United States' white, Anglo-Saxon, Protestant, hegemonic elites in the eighteenth, nineteenth, and early twentieth centuries incorporated Northern and Western European "scientific racism" into their racial theories is the subject of serious qualification in this essay. This piece seeks to demonstrate that a representative number of middle-class European immigrants to the United States thought that this nation violated the principles of liberty and equality—principles that they coveted in the liberal democratic revolutions that had swept Europe. For them, the United States had fallen short in the practice of those ideals—especially in reference to African Americans. In the not so distant past of the United States, Northern and Western European outsiders—men such as Alexis de Tocqueville, Franz Boas, and Gunnar Myrdal—made significant contributions to the understanding of race and racism in the American social order. For those commentators the most important issues centered around whether African Americans could attain equal civil and political rights without racial conflict and without the jettisoning of American democracy. For de Tocqueville, the nineteenth-century French politician and author of *Democracy in America* (1835), the issues were insurmountable. As the great historian of race and racism, George M. Fredrickson, has astutely observed, de Tocqueville was "fatalistic"—that is, he believed in the omnipotence of cultural and social processes. Put another way, de Tocqueville believed the prospects of changing the mores and social habits that separated blacks, whites, and red Indians were dismal.[1] Writing more than a century later, the Swedish political economist Gunnar Myrdal, who aimed his critical barbs at American social scientists for purveying a fatalism that rationalized a "laissez-faire" or "do-nothing" bias on the issues of race and race relations, was nevertheless unable to fully extricate himself from the labyrinth of pessimism. Historians Donald W. Southern and Walter A. Jackson have concurred in the argument that Myrdal's concept of the "American Creed"—that is, a system of general values that Americans adhered to in reference to race relations—was virtually a "deus ex machina" derivative of his severe bout with depression over the course of the Second World War and his revulsion against the pessimism of most European intellectuals.[2]

With both de Tocqueville and Myrdal, Franz Boas, the protean German Jewish immigrant and the father of modern American anthropology, shared a fatalism stemming from his embrace of physical anthropology. Boas, did not, however, eschew activism. During the course of his long life, he was intimately involved in or a commentator on virtually every major social movement for black liberation. It is true that Boas certainly believed—of course, with significant qualification—that African Americans had a defective ancestry as a result of having smaller brain cavities than those of European Americans. (Boas embraced the early physical anthropological assumption, which posited a direct relation between brain size or cranial capacities and intelligence, and on the basis of the data at hand, he argued that blacks were serially inferior to whites.) Boas, however, did not think that blacks' serial inferiority should be used to exclude them as individuals from participating, as much as their capacity allowed, in the community or nation-state. This essay tells an important part of that story, for it links Boas's German and Jewish pasts and his American present and locates him as a transnational figure in American racial thought.

Over the last two generations, Franz Boas has assumed a gargantuan stature in American intellectual history. A host of historians and historically minded social scientists have documented the role of Boas and his extraordinary stable of students—Melville Herskovits, Margaret Mead, Ruth Benedict, and Zora Neale Hurston, to name a few—in challenging biological understandings of human difference. For Boas, the different attributes of groups of people were not evidence of inherent superiority or inferiority but products of the distinct circumstances in which people lived. He played a particularly important role in challenging ideas about Negro inferiority, arguing that the conspicuous degradation of black Americans owed far more to the blighting effects of white prejudice than to any innate racial inferiority. A recent profile in the *New Yorker* put the case bluntly, describing Boas as the "rebel anthropologist [who] waged war on racism."[3]

Boas did indeed oppose prevailing racial ideas, helping in the process to usher in a profound revolution in American intellectual life. Yet his ideas were both more complex and more equivocal than is commonly acknowledged. While his antiracist stance was far ahead of its time, he never fully transcended the assumptions of physical anthropology laid down by the staunch racists of previous generations. Even as he exposed the folly of most existing measurements used to demonstrate Negro inferiority, he continued to accept the existence of slight differences in hereditary aptitudes between races, based on such factors as brain weights and cranial capacities; even as he insisted that African Americans were fully capable of responsible citizenship, he conceded that they were less apt to produce "men of high genius."[4] The tension between Boas's emphasis on cultural and historical determinants and his lingering attachment to scientific racial explanations represents one of the signature features of his work, as well as an important chapter in the wider history of American racial thought.

The father of modern American anthropology was born into a liberal Jewish household in Minden, Westphalia, Germany, on July 9, 1858, a decade after the liberal, democratic revolutions that had swept continental Europe. The leaders of those revolutions sought liberty—the expansion of individual liberties and the establishment of constitutional governments with representative bodies. Furthermore, they espoused democracy through the embrace of the universal vote. Finally, they sought to create nation-states through the unification of different and varied ethnic groups within their territorial boundaries. By the time of Boas's birth, these revolutions had failed. His parents—his father, Meier, was a successful merchant; his mother, Sophie, was the founder of the first Froebel Kindergarten in Minden—were close associates of many prominent "Forty-eighters," including Carl Schurz and Abraham Jacobi, who married Sophie's younger sister. This setting inculcated in Boas the liberal ideals to which he held firmly throughout his life. So intense was the fervor for revolutionary ideals in the Boas household that his Jewish background had few direct intellectual consequences for the young Franz. Although "raised an orthodox Jew," as Marshall Hyatt has pointed out, Boas later recalled that his religious education "was purely sop for his grandparents, who were orthodox"; his "parents had broken through the shackles of dogma." According to Boas, "My father had retained an emotional affection for the ceremonial of his parental home, without allowing it to influence his intellectual freedom. Thus I was spared the struggle against religious dogma that besets the lives of so many young people." Still, his ethnicity would have a decisive impact on his later anthropology and politics.[5]

After receiving his doctorate in physics in 1882 and spending an uneventful year at Berlin University and another year in the German army, Boas studied and waited for a teaching position in the increasingly conservative and anti-Semitic climate of Bismarck's Germany. Disappointed, he left for Baffinland in 1883 to write a book on "psychophysics." His experience there, working among Eskimos, compelled him to change disciplines to what was then called "ethnology." It also sharpened his belief in a common human nature, shared by "civilized" and "primitive" people alike.[6] "It was with feelings of sorrow and regret that I parted from my Arctic friends," he wrote after his return, while working at Berlin's Ethnological Museum. "I had seen that they enjoy life, and a hard life, as we do; that nature is also beautiful to them; that feelings of friendship also root in the Eskimo heart; that, although the character of their life is so rude as compared to civilized life, the Eskimo is a man as we are; that his feelings, his virtues and his shortcomings are based in human nature, like ours."[7]

Stymied in Germany, Boas immigrated to the United States in 1887. But there, too, he had difficulty securing steady employment in Anglo-dominated institutions. Virulent anti-Semitism pervaded the nation at the time of Boas's arrival, enflamed by the influx of large numbers of Eastern European Jews. It should be noted that the wave of German Jewish immigration of which Boas was a part had begun as early as 1830. Many of the German Jewish immigrants were successful in commerce, business, and finance, as well as the skilled trades and specialty farming.[8] Nonetheless, as the distinguished historian Leonard Dinnerstein has observed:

> They [German Jews] . . . knew that they were not well liked and were ex-
> cluded from general social intercourse with Christians of the same socio-
> economic status as their own. But they feared, correctly, that the presence of
> the east Europeans would create new tensions and that all Jews would be
> judged by the characteristics and deportment of the worst of them. On the
> other hand, they assumed a burden of extra responsibilities to help coreli-
> gionist immigrants acculturate. The behavior of established German Amer-
> ican Jews, therefore, reflected a mixture of fear, disgust, and responsibility
> in promoting the welfare of their coreligionists.[9]

Although Boas, according to his biographer Douglas Cole, was "prickly about his Jewishness and actively hostile to anti-Semitism when he encoun-tered it," he, nevertheless, as Leonard B. Glick has pointed out, "was in many respects a typical representative of that segment of late 19th century Jewry who had in effect abandoned the struggle to integrate Jewish identity with German nationality and had opted for an all-out effort to assimilate themselves out of existence." Although Boas thought that African Americans, like Jews, would eventually be assimilated, his indictment of African Americans was not mere camouflage for attacking anti-Semitism. In 1915 Boas would write, "The Negro of our times carries even more heavily the burden of his racial descent than did the Jew of an earlier period; and the intellectual and moral qualities required to insure success to the Negro are infinitely greater than those demanded from the white, and will be greater, the stricter the segregation of the Negro community." For Boas, the plight of African Americans in the United States was exceptional. Yet during his early career, Boas's post as geographical editor of *Science* was not funded in 1888; he was forced to resign a position as a docent in physical anthropology at Clark University in 1892; and he was dismissed from a temporary position as chief assistant of anthropology at the World Columbian Exposition in Chicago two years later. William Rainey Harper, president of the University of Chicago, refused to offer him a professorship in 1894, citing his inability to "take direction" as one reason. The unemployed Boas was left to fend off creditors even as he mourned the death of his young daughter.[10]

When Boas had returned to Germany in the spring of 1885, he had attempted to qualify for a position at the University of Berlin and studied with the ethnologist Adolph Bastian and the physical anthropologist Rudolph Virchow at the Royal Ethnographic Museum. Both of those scholars were prodigious figures in the history and institutionalization of German anthropology and important figures in the young Boas's intellectual maturation—especially his ideology, theoretical orientation, and methodological approach.

Boas followed the theoretical approach of Bastian—a person who, the recent scholar Matti Bunzl argues, attempted to unite "a sense of the universal with an appreciation of the particular." Like Bastian, Boas would later adopt the idea that ethnology's raison d'être was to capture the rich diversity of indigenous peoples and their cultures in the event that those peoples were lost to future generations. In short, according to Bunzl, Bastian, in part, prepared the way for "Boas' embracive anthropology."[11] Like Bastian, Rudolph Virchow—under whom Boas studied anthropometry—was a racial liberal. The recent scholar Benoit Massin has pointed out correctly that Virchow was a liberal who opposed anti-Semitism and was a leader of the anti-Bismarckian Progressive Party and a member of the Reichstag Party for more than thirty years before his death in 1902.[12] Nevertheless, despite Bastian's and Virchow's racial liberalism, their views on the issue of the mental capabilities of "savages" were expressed "negatively rather than positively." Thus, Massin has argued, Boas's earliest mentors, like most German anthropologists, held hierarchical assumptions in reference to race—albeit the case that they were not clearly defined—and often adhered to purely craniometrical points of view.[13] This orientation perhaps contributed to unevenness in Boas's later ideas in reference to the mental capabilities of blacks.

Ironically, Boas's very marginalization in the anthropological community may have helped him to challenge the dominant assumptions of the field. In 1894 he published "Human Faculty as Determined by Race," a long essay introducing the themes he would pursue through the rest of his career. To appreciate the significance of the essay, it is necessary to understand the racial climate of the time. In the 1890s Negrophobia pervaded every aspect of American life. The 1877 reconciliation between North and South inaugurated the lowest point in the history of white-black relations in the United States. The decades that followed brought disfranchisement, Jim Crow, and the horror of lynch law all across the South. In the North racism was less blatant and extreme, but there too the position of black people deteriorated. In such a context, rational discussion of the condition of African Americans was virtually impossible.[14]

Far from challenging the racist order, American social science endorsed it. As early as the 1840s, leaders of the "American School" of anthropology, such as Samuel George Morton, Josiah C. Nott, and George R. Glidden, had based a major part of their defense of slavery on comparative measurements of the cranial cavities of blacks and whites. Such ideas were elaborated by Boas's contemporaries, who supplemented brain weights and cranial cavities with a variety of other spurious qualities of the Negro. Daniel G. Brinton, a former medical doctor who was appointed professor of linguistics and folklore at the University of Pennsylvania, was typical. "The adult who retains the more numerous fetal, infantile or simian [characteristics]," he wrote in 1890, "is unquestionably inferior to him whose development has progressed beyond them. . . . Measured by these criteria the European or white race stands at the head of the list, the African or negro at its foot." Brinton's colleague at the University of Pennsylvania, Edward D. Cope, agreed, pointing to the Negro's flat nose, prognathous jaw, inferior facial angle, "deficiency of the calf of the leg, and the obliquity of the pelvis" to demonstrate the race's apelike nature.[15]

Late nineteenth-century racial science reached a climax of sorts in Frederick L. Hoffman's 1896 book, *Race Traits and Tendencies of the American Negro*. A German-born employee of the Prudential Insurance Company, Hoffman claimed to be "free from personal bias which might have made an impartial treatment of the subject difficult," but his book echoed all the conventional racial wisdom of the era. Indeed, he went further, predicting, in the Darwinian language of the time, the impending extinction of African Americans. Since emancipation, Hoffman argued, black people had deteriorated physically and morally. They were doing so, moreover, because of their "race traits and tendencies" rather than because of the adverse circumstances in which they were forced to live; as Hoffman put it, it was "not in the conditions of life but in race and heredity that we find the explanation." Persons of mixed ancestry were also allegedly subject to the same deterioration: "The mixture of the African with the white race has shown to have seriously affected the longevity of the former and left as heritage to future generations the poison of scrofula, tuberculosis and most of all, of syphilis."[16]

This was the context in which "Human Faculty as Determined by Race" was written. Rather than reject the significance of cranial capacities and brain weights outright, Boas stressed the great variation within particular groups, as well as the considerable overlap between them. While whites appeared, on average, to have slightly larger brains than blacks—hence their greater propensity for genius—the differences was statistically small, and in any case far less significant than the differences among whites. In such circumstances, there was no basis for making any a priori judgments about particular individuals. As George Stocking and others have noted, Boas's defense of black capacity was still tentative; he wrote "as a skeptic of received belief rather than a staunch advocate of racial equipotentiality." "The lower portion of the face assumes larger dimensions" among blacks, Boas conceded:

> The alveolar arch is pushed forward and thus gains an appearance which reminds us of the higher apes. There is no denying that this feature is a most constant character of the black races representing a type slightly nearer the animal than the European type. The same may be said of the broadness and flatness of the nose of the Negro and of the Mongol; but here again we must call to mind that prognathism, and low broad noses are not entirely absent from the white races, although the more strongly developed forms which are found among negroes do not occur. The variations belonging to both races overlap. We find here at least a few indications which tend to show that the white race differs more from the higher apes than [does] the Negro.

Nonetheless, applying the tools of science for all the anthropometric measurements he could obtain on the various races, Boas concluded, "We have no right to consider one [race] more ape-like than the other."[17]

Judged by today's standards, "Human Faculty" is striking for its tentativeness, as well as for its generous concessions to scientific racism, yet in its own time it represented a fundamental challenge to the reigning orthodoxy. The response of his fellow anthropologists bordered on hysteria. In 1895 Daniel Brinton devoted his presidential address to the American Association for the Advancement of Science to rebutting Boas's claims. "The black, the brown and red races differ anatomically so much from the white, especially in their splanchnic [visceral] organs, that even with equal cerebral capacity, they would never rival the results by equal efforts," he wrote.[18] But Boas refused to be dismissed. In 1896, he finally secured a permanent academic position at Columbia University, where he received tenure in 1899. In the years that followed, he forged close ties to the Smithsonian Institution, the American Folklore Society, the American Ethnological Society, and Brinton's own American Association for the Advancement of Science. By the early 1900s, Boas, the longtime outsider, had become a powerful member of the American anthropological fraternity. By 1920, he was the dominant figure in the field.

Even as Boas's prestige grew, his work continued to be characterized by a marked tension between liberal humanitarian sentiment and a lingering attachment to nineteenth-century physical anthropology. In a 1900 address before the American Folklore Society, Boas pursued the cultural determinist position, arguing that the mind of primitive man differed from that of civilized man not in its organization, as the advocates of the so-called comparative method had claimed, but rather in the character of experience to which it was exposed. The mental function—abstraction, inhibition, and choice—could all be found among primitive peoples; thus, there was no justification for the Spencerian argument that primitive peoples occupied a lower evolutionary stage. In the same address, however, Boas acceded to the argument of black inferiority: "A number of anatomical facts point to the conclusion that the races of Africa, Australia, and Melanesia are to a certain extent inferior to [those of] Asia, America, and Europe."[19]

"The Negro and the Demands of Modern Life," published a few years later, was similarly suffused with tension. While he once again pointed out that the "average" Negro brain was "smaller than that of other races," and that it was "plausible that certain differences of form of brain exist," Boas nevertheless emphasized that the data did not conclusively demonstrate differences in intellectual ability. "We must remember that individually the correlation [between brain weight and mental ability] . . . is often overshadowed by other causes, and that we find a considerable number of great men with slight brain weight." Such measurable differences as did exist between races, moreover, were "small as compared to the total range of variations found in the human species." The conclusion of the essay came with a strangely eugenic twist: "There is every reason to believe that the Negro when given the facility and opportunity will be perfectly able to fill the duties of citizenship as well as his white neighbor. It may be that he will not produce as many great men as the white race, and his average achievement will not quite reach the level of the average white race, but there will be endless numbers who will do better than the [white] defectives whom we permit to drag down and retard the healthy children of out public schools."[20]

Again, it is the tentativeness and qualification that strikes the modern ear, but in their own time Boas's ideas were profoundly subversive of existing racial ideas. Among those influenced by Boas was W. E. B. Du Bois, at the time a professor of sociology at Atlanta University. As early as 1898, Du Bois had noted the centrality of physical anthropology, much of it based "on the flimsiest basis of scientific fact," in buttressing the dominant discourse of race. Du Bois first wrote to Boas in 1905, requesting his help in identifying the best and latest works on the anthropology of the Negro and inviting him to participate in a forthcoming conference on "the health and physique of the Negro American." Boas was unable to accept the invitation, but the two met the following year, when Boas came to Atlanta to deliver the university's commencement address, initiating a friendship that lasted for more than three decades.[21]

The speech that Boas delivered in Atlanta was an amended version of an article that he had published two years before, entitled "What the Negro Has Done in Africa." The article represented the opening of a new front in the anthropologist's campaign against racial explanations of human difference and achievement. Rather than gauge the ability of the Negro by the "work he has accomplished as a slave" or under the "trying conditions" that followed emancipation, Boas suggested that "whites ought rather to look at the negro in his own home, and see what advances in culture he has made there." Drawing primarily on an inspection of African materials in European museums, he offered a long list of African achievements. Africans had contributed "more than any other [race] to the early development of the iron industry." They had worked out "strict methods of legal procedure," built up local trade, assimilated foreign cultures, and established powerful states. "The achievements of the negro in Africa, therefore," he concluded, "justify us in maintaining that the race is capable of social and political achievements; that it will produce here, as it has done in Africa, its great men; and that it will contribute its part to the welfare of the country."[22]

In assuming a direct relationship between Africa and African American character and potential, Boas was once again revealing his attachment to nineteenth-century racial science. He was also, once again, striking a devastating blow against it. For most American scholars at the time, the inferiority of Africa and Africans was axiomatic, offering one more proof of black Americans' limited potential. Daniel Brinton's comments in his 1890 book, *Races and Peoples*, were typical:

> The low intellectual position of the Austafrican [Negro] race is revealed by the facts that in no part of the [African] continent did its members devise the erection of walls of stone; that they domesticated no animal, and developed no important food-plant; that their religions never rose above fetishism, their governments above despotism, their marriage relations above polygamy. It is true that many of them practice agriculture and the pastoral life, but it is significant that the plants which they especially cultivate, the "durra" or sorghum, millet, rice, yams, manioc, and tobacco, were introduced from Asia, Europe or America.[23]

As for claims that Africans had created great empires, Brinton was frankly contemptuous. "The powerful monarchies which at times have been erected in that continent over the dead bodies of myriads of victims have lasted but a generation or two," he wrote in *The Basis of Social Relations*, a work published posthumously in 1902. "The natural limitations of the racial mind prevented it."[24]

In other disciplines, too, the allegedly backward character of Africa and

Africans was an article of faith. Sociologist Jerome Dowd, a North Carolinian who studied briefly at the University of Chicago, described the diverse West African people as "abnormal or retrogressive" in his influential two-volume work, *The Negro Races*. He based his claim on reports of physical anthropologists, who believed that the West African's brain was "so constituted that its sensorimotor activities predominate over his idio-motor activities; i.e., his passions and natural impulses are exceptionally potent and his inhibiting power exceptionally feeble."[25] Similar arguments informed historian Joseph Tillinghast's *The Negro in Africa and America*, published in 1902. A descendant of an old Rhode Island family and the son of a South Carolina slaveholder, Tillinghast stated emphatically that Africans had produced "no great industrial system, no science, and art," primarily because they were constitutionally incapable of exercising "foresight" or restraining their "sexual proclivities."[26] Needless to say, such arguments provided intellectual justification for the ongoing, violent exclusion of African Americans from every aspect of southern political and social life.

Boas's account of Africa flew squarely in the face of this orthodoxy. Far from being trapped in a state of timeless backwardness, Africans had made significant contributions to human civilization; "at a time when the European was still satisfied with rude stone tools," he told students in Atlanta, "the African had invented or adopted the art of smelting iron," the achievement from which all subsequent technological progress flowed. Far from feeling discouraged or inferior, the students should "confidently look to the home of your ancestors and say that you have set out to recover for the colored people the strength that was their own before they set foot on the shores of this continent." A generation later, W. E. B. Du Bois would still remember the effect the speech had on him: "I was too astonished to speak. All of this I had never heard and I came then and afterwards to realize how silence and neglect of science can let truth utterly disappear or even be consciously distorted." Du Bois would credit his own career as an African historian to the inspiration of Boas.[27]

Boas himself was acutely aware of the political implications of his argument, recognizing the way in which recognition of the achievements of blacks in Africa undermined the claims of white supremacists at home. Addressing fellow whites in 1909, he wrote:

> The essential point that anthropology can contribute to the practical discussion of the adaptability of the Negro is a decision on the question of how far the undesirable traits that are at present undoubtedly found in our Negro population are due to race traits, and how far they are due to social surroundings for which we are responsible. To this question anthropology can give the

decided answer that the traits of the African culture as observed in the aboriginal home of the Negro are those of a healthy primitive people with a considerable degree of personal initiative, with a talent for organization.

After further outlining Africans' achievements in the realms of politics, industry, and the arts, Boas returned to the predicament of black America: "The impression which we gain from the failure of the American Negro to manifest himself in any of these directions is due, not to native inability, but to the degrading conditions under which he has been placed for generations."[28]

By the 1920s—the decade that the late historian of immigration John Higham called "the decade of the tribes"—Boas, whose own ethnic group was being subjected to abuse by proponents of immigration restriction, anti-Semitic businessmen such as Henry Ford, supporters of 100 percent Americanism, and the Ku Klux Klan—was especially disturbed by the upsurge of both nativist and racist ideologies of both whites and blacks. Boas, however, never relented in his struggle for black liberation. (Although he opposed the racial chauvinism of the young black writers of the Harlem Renaissance, he nevertheless supported many of those same writers in their scholarly endeavors.)

In the decades that followed, Boas remained a skeptic of received wisdom about race, as well as a consistent advocate of black equality. He was one of the first American intellectuals to criticize the racial use of psychological testing and experiments. Early in his career, Boas had held out the hope that psychology would provide definitive insight into racial mental differences, but in "The Problem of the American Negro," published in 1921, he warned that many investigations into the mental abilities of black and white children were biased. "I am not convinced that the results that have been obtained are significant in regard to racial ability as a whole," he wrote. He took special aim at a much-publicized recent study by M. R. Trabue, based on results from U.S. Army Alpha and Beta tests that purported to prove the mental inferiority of southern blacks, accusing Trabue of using poor scientific method and of confusing signs of environmental deprivation with evidence of innate inferiority. "Anyone who knows the abject fear of the Southern negroes who are put under the control of an unknown white officer in foreign surroundings, anyone who knows the limitations of early childhood and general upbringing of negroes in the South, will accept these findings, but will decline to accept them as convincing proof of the hereditary inferiority of the negro race," he wrote.[29]

Another article that demonstrated Boas's maturing thought was "What Is Race?," which appeared in the *Nation* in 1925 and in which he sought to delimit the boundaries of the nature-versus-nurture controversy. Though the article mentioned blacks only once, its implications for the so-called Negro problem were obvious. Unlike earlier writings, this article argued that it was simply wrongheaded to try to "judge" an individual "by the size of his brain" or other physiological forms and functions, mainly because such forms and functions "vary enormously in each race, and many features that are found in one race are also found belonging to other races." In the absence of proof of distinct "hereditary mental traits" in different races, it was safe to infer that the "behavior of an individual is therefore not determined by his racial affiliations, but by the character of his ancestry and his cultural environment." One could "judge the mental characteristics of families and individuals but not of races."[30]

By 1928, when *Anthropology and Modern Life* was published, Boas expressed shock and dismay at how much supposedly scientific literature was still "based on the assumption that each race has its own mental character determining its cultural or social behavior." He stated unequivocally that the concept of racial types was "based on subjective experience" rather than science, and that there were, moreover, "no pure races." Yet it would be an overstatement to assert that Boas had completely rid himself of racist anthropological assumptions. He still maintained that "the distribution of individuals and of family lines in the various races differs." He still argued that white people possessed, on average, larger brains than black people, and he conceded the usefulness of comparative research on racial brain weights as long as "we avoid an application of our results to individuals." "It is not possible," he asserted, "to identify an individual as a Negro or White according to the size and form of his brain, but serially the Negro brain is less extremely human than that of the White."[31]

Boas spent his life as a fugitive of nineteenth-century physical anthropology, but he never quite escaped. As late as 1938, his "men of high genius" hypothesis reappeared in the highly revised edition of *The Mind of Primitive Man*, his classic 1911 text. The persistence of such ideas in American social science, and in Boas's own work, gives credence to George Fredrickson's statement that "history in general does not . . . provide much basis for the notion that passionately held fallacies are destined to collapse because they are in conflict with empirical reality." Yet one ought not stint Boas's contribution either. In challenging prevailing ideas about black inferiority, in insisting on the cultural and environmental rather than racial bases of human difference, Boas laid a solid antiracist foundation for future social scientists and activists.[32]

To sum up, although Boas was not naive about his own group's self-interest in discrediting antiblack racism and believed, as Hasia Diner has pointed out, his writings "could be employed as effective weapons to combat anti-Jewish sentiment," he, nonetheless also believed that blacks and Jews had a common bond of suffering.[33] In essence, Boas's writings on African Americans reveal the tension between his lifelong belief in inherent racial differences and his commitment to cultural explanations of human behavior, between his political and scientific commitments, and between the science of physical anthropology and his liberal values. De Tocqueville and Myrdal shared many of those same values. Unlike Boas, however, they were not immigrants. As a consequence, they were not themselves witnesses over long periods to the social structural changes and oppositional social movements in the United States that were sufficiently wrenching to compel Boas to reassess his positions on race and race relations. Put another way, the increasing migration of blacks from the southeastern states to New York, bringing what was thought to be a peculiar southern problem to the doorsteps of Boas and his students in the urban-industrial North, provided a context that even the most callous social scientists could not ignore. Fatalism was an option—one that even Boas increasingly flirted with after 1920.

NOTES

1. George M. Fredrickson, *The Comparative Imagination: On the History of Racism, Nationalism, and Social Movements* (Berkeley: University of California Press, 1997), 98–116.

2. Donald W. Southern, *Gunnar Myrdal and Black-White Relations: The Use and Abuse of an American Dilemma, 1944–1969* (Baton Rouge: Louisiana State University Press, 1987), 34; Walter A. Jackson, *Gunnar Myrdal and America's Conscience: Social Engineering and Racial Liberation, 1938–1987* (Chapel Hill: University of North Carolina Press, 1990), 135–64.

3. C. R. Pierpont, "The Measure of America: How a Rebel Anthropologist Waged War on Racism," *New Yorker*, March 8, 2004, 48–63.

4. Vernon J. Williams, *Rethinking Race: Franz Boas and His Contemporaries* (Lexington: University Press of Kentucky, 1996), 102.

5. Marshall Hyatt, *Franz Boas—Social Activist: The Dynamics of Ethnicity* (New York: Greenwood Press, 1990), 4.

6. George W. Stocking Jr., *Race, Culture, and Evolution: Essays in the History of Anthropology* (New York: Free Press, 1968), 143.

7. Melville Herskovits, *Franz Boas: The Science of Man in the Making* (New York: Scribner, 1953), 1.

8. Leonard Dinnerstein, *Anti-Semitism in America* (New York: Oxford University Press, 1994), 53.

9. Ibid.

10. Glick cited in Douglas Cole, *Franz Boas: The Early Years, 1858–1906* (Seattle: University of Washington Press, 1999), 280–83; Franz Boas, *The Mind of Primitive Man* (New York: Macmillan, 1911), 274–75; Harper cited in George W. Stocking Jr., ed., *A Franz Boas Reader: The Shaping of American Anthropology, 1883–1911* (Chicago: University of Chicago Press, 1974), 219.

11. Matti Bunzl, "Franz Boas and the Humboldtian Tradition: From Volksgeist and Nationcharakter to an Anthropological Concept of Culture," in *Volksgeist as Method and Ethic: Essays on Boasian Ethnography and the German Anthropological Tradition*, ed. George Stocking Jr. (Madison: University of Wisconsin Press, 1996), 17–19.

12. Benoit Massin, "From Virchow to Fischer: Physical Anthropology and 'Modern Race Theories' in Wilhelmine Germany," in *Volksgeist as Method and Ethic*, ed. Stocking, 82–91.

13. Ibid., 96–98.

14. Franz Boas, "Human Faculty as Determined by Race," in *Franz Boas Reader*, ed. Stocking, 223–27. See also Vernon J. Williams Jr., *From a Caste to a Minority: Changing Attitudes of American Sociologists toward Afro-Americans, 1896–1945* (Westport, Conn.: Greenwood Press, 1989), 34–57.

15. On the American School, see William R. Stanton, *The Leopard's Spots: Scientific Attitudes toward Race in America, 1815–1859* (Chicago: University of Chicago Press, 1960); and George Fredrickson, *The Black Image in the White Mind: The Debate on Afro-American Character and Destiny, 1817–1914* (New York: Harper and Row, 1972). Brinton and Cope are quoted in John S. Haller Jr., *Outcasts from Evolution: Scientific Attitudes of Racial Inferiority, 1859–1900* (Urbana: University of Illinois Press, 1971), 178 and 191; and in Stephen Jay Gould, *The Mismeasure of Man* (New York: W. W. Norton, 1981), 116.

16. Frederick L. Hoffman, *Race Traits and Tendencies of the American Negro* (Philadelphia: American Economic Association, 1896), preface and 188, 312.

17. Boas, "Human Faculty as Determined by Race," 230–32; Stocking, *Race, Culture, and Evolution*, 163–64, 189.

18. Daniel G. Brinton, "The Aims of Anthropology," *Proceedings of the American Association for the Advancement of Science* 44 (December 1895): 12.

19. Franz Boas, "The Mind of Primitive Man," *Journal of American Folk-Lore* 14, no. 1 (1901): 1–11.

20. Franz Boas, "The Negro and the Demands of Modern Life," *Charities*, October 7, 1905, 86–87.

21. W. E. B. Du Bois, "The Study of the Negro Problems," *Annals* 11, no. 1 (1898): 19.

22. Franz Boas, commencement address at Atlanta University, May 31, 1906, Atlanta University Leaflet, no. 19.

23. Daniel G. Brinton, *Races and Peoples: Lectures on the Science of Ethnology* (New York: N. D. C. Hodges, 1890), 191–92.

24. Daniel G. Brinton, *The Basis of Social Relations* (New York: Putnam, 1902), 71.

25. Jerome Dowd, *The Negro Races*, 2 vols. (New York: Macmillan, 1907), 1:432, 447–48.

26. Joseph A. Tillinghast, *The Negro in Africa and America* (New York: Macmillan, 1902), 96.

27. Boas, commencement address at Atlanta University, May 31, 1906; W. E. B. Du Bois, *Black Folk Then and Now* (New York: Henry Holt, 1939), vii.

28. Franz Boas, "Industries of the African Negroes," *Southern Workman*, April 1909, 25.

29. Franz Boas, "The Problem of the American Negro," *Yale Quarterly Review* 10, no. 1 (1921): 386–90.

30. Franz Boas, "What Is Race?," *The Nation*, January 28, 1925, 90–91.

31. Franz Boas, *Anthropology and Modern Life* (New York: Norton, 1928), 18, 38, 40.

32. George Fredrickson, *The Arrogance of Race: Historical Perspectives on Slavery, Racism, and Social Inequity* (Middletown, Conn.: Wesleyan University Press, 1988), 265. For discussions of the "minimal" racism of pre-1902 German physical anthropology and its aftermath, see Andrew Zimmerman, *Anthropology and Antihumanism in Imperial Germany* (Chicago: University of Chicago Press, 2001); and Gretchen E. Schafft, *From Racism to Genocide: Anthropology in the Third Reich* (Urbana: University of Illinois Press, 2004).

33. Hasia R. Diner, *In the Almost Promised Land: American Jews and Blacks, 1915–1935* (Westport, Conn.: Greenwood Press, 1977), 147.

An End to the Family Romance

Nella Larsen, Black Transnationalism, and American Racial Ideology

GEORGE HUTCHINSON

The linchpin of race and empire in American history is the articulation of race with family, the recruitment of familial intimacy, psychic formation, and social as well as financial inheritance to the reproduction of race and its inevitable companion, racial hierarchy. Recruiting "family" to the discipline of "race" has been crucial to sustaining the economic and political marginalization of African Americans, particularly. The gradual formalization and nationalization of racial definitions into their modern American forms did not precede but rather followed from the need to prevent the spread of families, and thus "identities," that threatened the institution of race and its discriminatory governance of properties and privileges and rights.[1] Women bore the greatest burden in the reproduction of that institution. So much is common knowledge: black women reproduced blackness regardless of the "race" of their mates (and not infrequently against their will); white women, under enormous threat if they were to break the rules of the color line, reproduced whiteness. The terrorism aimed at black men for interracial sexuality or "rape" (so often used as an excuse for lynchings even if the unstated crime was an economic or social transgression) was one expression of the centrality of women's sexuality to the reproduction of the racial order.

The consequences have been vast. We tend to think of races as extended families. The subordination of familial relationships to racial identity in American history has shaped the psychology of Americans of all races—but especially, I suspect, blacks and whites—so profoundly that it undergirds most theorizations of race and cultural identity in Americanist scholarship to this day, including, notably, theories of diaspora. Black transnationalism, as it is usually presented, opposes or transcends the confines of the national state with racial identities, and these racial identities have an irreducible genealogical component that is also presumptively familial and cultural. Without the genealogical component, the "political" identity and cultural affiliation cease to exist; with it, certain bonds of cultural affiliation and political identification are expected and others discounted. Such notions of black transnationalism may not be antidotes to American racial ideology and cultural colonialism so much as extensions of it. How might we ensure that the current notions of racial diaspora do not reproduce and extend a specifically North American ethos of race under a false guise of transnationalism?

The forms of repression, fetishization, and disavowal that continue to undergird the ethos of race in the United States will be most evident at the intersection of race and family. At issue here is not biological inheritance or "hybridity" (a term, as Werner Sollors has argued, that only makes sense within the discourse of race as species), nor even cultural hybridity, which also presumes an originary "purity" of some cultures, but the realm of intimacy and primary relationships in which human subjects take form—and all the forces of American society that help subordinate this realm to the rules of race.[2]

This essay focuses on Nella Larsen, best known as a novelist of the Harlem Renaissance, because the story of her life, literary career, and reputation demonstrates in a uniquely illuminating way the workings of color-line culture from the years of Jim Crow to the present day, and because Larsen's own fiction provides the most distinctive critique we have of that phenomenon. Moreover, she frames her critique in black feminist, transnational, and trans-"racial" terms that raise essential ethical challenges to the discourse of family that still informs the deep structure of American racial ideology.

My story begins with a fragment in the history of the Scandinavian diaspora. About 1886, a young woman named Marie Hansen left Denmark, displaced by the after-effects of the Dano-Prussian War, and settled in Chicago. Knowing little about the nature of her new environment except that she could not survive in it on her own, she became engaged to a man who could speak her language, a cook who had immigrated from what were then the Danish West Indies. His name was Peter Walker. That he was "colored" and she "white" would not have seemed to them the obstacle that most Americans considered it. In the Danish West Indies, racial classifications differed dramatically from those in the United States. Quite possibly, Peter never considered himself a "Negro." Nine and a half months after he and Marie (now "Mary") Hansen had applied for a marriage license, Nellie Walker was born on Armour Street near Twenty-second, in the heart of Chicago's most infamous red-light district.[3] Within a year her father was dead or gone. Mary, however, had managed to latch on to another working-class Danish man—this time white—and would give birth to a white daughter named Anna Elizabeth fourteen months after Nellie's entry into the world. Through this rather remarkable achievement she took on the surname "Larsen" and undoubtedly saved her colored daughter from the orphanage. It would prove a defining event of Nella Larsen's emotionally catastrophic life.

That Mary Larsen was able to keep and raise her first daughter within the context of marriage to a white man—particularly a working-class white man—was remarkable. By the same token, her mothering of her daughter came under almost unbearable stress. White women with "mulatto" daughters were routinely assumed to be prostitutes and braved catcalls in the streets when seen with their children. As she grew older, Nella Larsen would come to recognize that she was a burden to her mother and a blot on her existence, as well as a cause of constant tension in her home. Virtually as long as Nella lived with the family in Chicago, the Larsens lived in "mixed" neighborhoods either in or on the border of the vice district because they were unwelcome elsewhere during the very period that Chicago developed into a viciously segregated city.

Indeed, the neighborhood of Larsen's birth and of much of her childhood, known as "the Levee," was infamous on an international scale at the turn of the twentieth century. Brothels, peep shows, and burlesque houses were ubiquitous in the area. A guide to the city published in 1892 claimed that "the very scum of the population" lived in the area of Larsen's birth.[4] Here one came upon the brothels and bagnios "where depraved women, both white and black, pursue their avocations and carry on with males of their class, nightly orgies that are either unseen or unnoticed by the police."[5] The Levee was home to "the most depraved of men and women, black, white, and mixed."[6] This series of terms was repeatedly used to identify the Levee with sexual perversity. "Black, white, and mixed" signified a zone of abjection, unpoliced, bottomless in depravity. Such were the neighborhoods in which working-class interracial families were tolerated, though often singled out as the city's greatest shame.

Racially "Mulatto" and then "Negro," according to official designations, "Nellie" Larsen was Danish American as well. In a period when the vast majority of African Americans came from generations of people born in North America and traced their most personally meaningful line of descent to slaves in the South, Larsen had no southern ancestors, black or white. Her extended family was Scandinavian, a fact that was and is difficult to integrate with American assumptions about race, ethnicity, and culture—so much so that Larsen's first biographers concluded she had fabricated her connections to Denmark.[7] In adulthood, without having studied the language formally in school, Larsen could both speak and read Danish without the help of a dictionary.

A common experience for Danish Americans—an extended visit to "*det Gammel Land*" with her mother and half sister—both solidified Larsen's sense of ethnic connectedness to Denmark and exacerbated her feeling of racial difference. The trip may well have been an attempt to escape the difficulties besetting an interracial family in turn-of-the-century Chicago. In the mid-1930s, Larsen would tell the English author Bryher about a period of her childhood spent in small-town Denmark, where she was "the only dark child in the family and town, [and she] loathes music, because people always insisted that [as] a negro she must sing."[8] The particular version of one of the Danish games Larsen later described in her first publication was played specifically on the rural Jutland peninsula in the 1890s.[9] Such details place Larsen's childhood experiences not in the great capital city, the Scandinavian gateway to Europe and to Denmark's Caribbean colonies, but in a provincial town setting in which she would have felt even more intensely her "difference."

Living in such a town, Larsen would have been quite a sensation. Many villagers in such provinces lived and died without ever seeing a person of other than German or Scandinavian complexion and physiognomy. Yet they were not, of course, ignorant of the existence of the "darker races." The Danish colonies in the Caribbean were part of what made Denmark an empire in spite of its recent humiliations, and traveling entertainers from the United States were already the hit of Copenhagen in the field of popular culture. The cake-walk was taking the "*Klunker*" (haute bourgeois) aristocracy by storm. During the winter season, the Cirkus building in Copenhagen put on variety shows each year, the most popular of which in the 1890s was the "black opera" ("*Den sorte Opera*") with fifty African American performers. The musical comedian George Jackson taught Danes the latest American dance melodies.[10] Many country people in Denmark who had never seen a "colored person" before certainly had notions about them, to a great extent derived from American culture. If Nellie had been hoping to find acceptance among her mother's people, not as an exotic but as one of them, this would have been very disappointing.

It could not have been all bad, however, since Larsen would later return to Denmark for an extended period. In fact, Larsen's first two publications were translations of Danish riddles and games for an African American children's magazine. She not only remembered the games she had learned more than twenty years earlier well enough to write them out, but she even remembered the music central to one of them well enough to transcribe it, and she remembered the lyrics and rhymes to the games, which she translated. Larsen's brief introduction to her first contribution, published in the June 1920 number of *The Brownies' Book*, read, "Dear Children: These are some games which I learned long ago in Denmark, from the little Danish children. I hope that you will play them and like them as I did."[11] The next month she followed up with another group of games and riddles, under the title "Danish Fun." By suggesting that African American children would enjoy these games, was she attempting to "play up" her Danish background for social-climbing purposes, as some have charged, or was she nonchalantly countering racial patterns of expectation that begin taking hold in childhood, channeling individuals toward their respective "places" in the racial order? Larsen's contributions answered editor W. E. B. Du Bois's call to interested adults: "Tell us . . . what foreign countries you would like described, briefly what dark children—and white, too, for that matter, for we colored people must set the example of broadness—are doing all over the world."[12] Larsen was uniquely qualified to respond to this appeal, thus encouraging a cosmopolitan sense of black identity. And she had not, after all, been brought up on African or African American folklore and children's games.

Did her mother ever think of leaving Nellie with the family in Denmark? It is an unanswerable question, but it brings attention to the fact that Mary Larsen kept her black daughter by her side until Nellie was a young adult, despite the extraordinary pressures in Chicago on such family units. In Denmark, Nellie would perhaps always have been a curiosity, but this was not nearly as threatening as the situation she and her mother faced in turn-of-the-century Chicago, to which they nonetheless returned to rejoin Peter Larsen on the "white" west side in 1898. The years following this return were probably the most traumatic of Nella Larsen's life.

They were also the years in which Chicago developed into an overwhelmingly segregated city, establishing the basic pattern that would characterize it for the rest of the twentieth century. South-side Chicago, in fact, led the way in the racial segregation of American urban life that continuously accelerated from 1900 to 1970 and fundamentally shaped the racial culture of the United States as we know it—that shaped the racial awareness of most Americans alive today and served as a basic instrument of white supremacy.[13]

After Mary and her daughters returned to Chicago, the two girls began their formal education in a local school serving primarily Scandinavian and German immigrants, until the family moved back into the heart of the vice district at Twenty-second and State Streets, evidently driven out of the "white" neighborhood where Peter had been living in their absence. For the next eight years, while Nellie and Anna Larsen grew to puberty, Chicago experienced rising pressures for segregation and periodic waves of racial terror, with the storm center on the edges of the very neighborhoods in which the Larsens lived. The connection between the two half sisters had, insofar as was possible, to be hidden. Indeed, Anna Larsen did not attend the public school Nella attended in 1903 and for which both girls were zoned. Nor did she attend Nella's high school. The suppression and "disappearance" of interracial families are part of the background of the misunderstanding of Larsen with which we must struggle today.

After two years of high school, in 1907, Nella was sent away to normal school at Fisk. About the same time, her family took out a mortgage on a house in an all-white neighborhood. Notably, the house was only a few blocks from the Chicago Normal School, which readily accepted blacks, charged no tuition to city residents, and was the usual route to a teaching position in Chicago. Clearly, the family had decided Chicago was not the place for her. Her connection to the family could do her no good in attracting a mate or a job and could only harm fifteen-year-old Anna's prospects as both girls approached marriageable age.

Nella's half sister, like the vast majority of working-class girls, never even attended high school. The family had decided that precisely because she was black, Nella would need more education than Anna, a far better than average education for any girl of her class. She would have to learn to make her way in the Negro world, outside Chicago—a world in which she had no family connections to help protect or support her. To avoid a miserable destiny, she would need training for one of the few professional careers open to black women, primarily teaching, nursing, or social work. As one of the premier institutions of the race, and a place where aspiring teachers often found likely husbands in addition to prized credentials, Fisk was an excellent choice—and a significant one at a time when many whites believed blacks should be tracked into vocational education rather than the liberal arts. Yet Peter Larsen's pay as a streetcar conductor was insufficient to send Nella to Fisk and support the family at the same time. The cost of Fisk was almost certainly funded by Mary Larsen's work as a dressmaker. Notably, in adulthood Nella Larsen, whose formal education never included dressmaking, was an expert at making over dresses and was noted for her fashion sense. In her fiction, a woman's ability to dress herself in textures, styles, and colors of her own choosing is a prime index of a woman's personal agency.

Fisk provided Larsen's first experience of living in a nearly all-black environment, and one with almost no immigrants. Only one of her classmates was from the North, and most were devout Christians. It was in many respects a new world, and everywhere were the signs that blacks and whites did not belong together. If Mary had accompanied "Nellie" to Nashville, they would have had to move to separate cars when the train crossed the Ohio River and stopped in Kentucky. They could not have walked through Nashville's Union Station together, or sat together on the streetcar to campus, or slept in the same building there. Yet the records of Larsen's attendance at Fisk are the first in which her mother's first name appears as her own middle name, indicating a particularly strong identification with her mother at the very time the two were hurtling into different spheres. She would continue to use "Marie" or "Marian" as a middle name for the rest of her life.

In a period when white Nashville expressed its contempt for blacks by not only segregating them but also refusing to provide distinct facilities for "ladies" and "gentlemen" of the race, Fisk zealously embraced Victorian gender mores. Every race depended, as the catalog asserted, "upon the intelligence, frugality, virtue, and noble aspirations of its women."[14] The girls' and women's housing in Jubilee Hall, the architectural symbol of the university, guarded their sacred role in the race's progress. Much of that role centered on sexual discipline, which was closely supervised by female faculty. The discipline was well expressed in the uniforms required of all women, consisting of a white shirtwaist suit with no trimmings and a navy blue suit. No silk or satin was allowed on any clothing or accessories, and jewelry was discouraged.[15]

Restrictions on women's dress at Fisk became a source of intense conflict in the course of the 1906–7 school year. By the spring of 1907 a student rebellion was brewing against the old-fashioned policies of the nearly all-white, aging, and Christian fundamentalist administration, which students interpreted as racist. Most insultingly, a new rule had been passed "restricting the wearing of jewelry by young ladies to one ring, and requiring them to wear uniform on all social occasions, because a few have dressed in a manner contrary to the wishes of several of the faculty."[16] Notably, in the one known photograph of Larsen from about the time she attended Fisk, she is wearing an attractive necklace with a jeweled pendant and a delicate white blouse with a plunging neckline, trimmed beautifully in fine lace. Shortly after detailing the student complaints and reaffirming the current policies "regarding extravagant and expensive dress and jewelry," the faculty minutes of June 1908 list Nellie Larsen as one of eight girls who would be told not to return in the fall.[17]

The expulsion put Larsen's future in grave doubt and her family in an excruciating position. Whites in their neighborhood were openly hostile to black would-be residents, and in 1909 they would force a white man to resell after learning that his wife was black. With few options, Nella Larsen turned next to her family in Denmark. She would come of age in Copenhagen, returning to the United States at the age of twenty-one.[18]

Once again, familial self-protection in the face of the American color line motivated Larsen's extended residence in Denmark. In contrast to Nella, Anna Larsen never visited Denmark after the early childhood trip, and she had little memory of that country in adulthood. The older girl's affiliation with Danish culture and ethnicity, then, was decisively reinforced as a consequence of her blackness. At the same time, her experience in Denmark would profoundly affect her sense of racial difference and of the meaning of race as such.

There is every reason to believe that this second journey to Denmark was considered a possible permanent move. When Larsen left for Denmark in 1908, she was seventeen years old—approximately the same age her mother had been at the time of her immigration to the United States. If she came home for a visit in the winter of 1909 (when a ship manifest lists her "race or people" as "Scandinavian") and then returned for at least two more years, which seems likely, then she spent a crucial period in the formation of her mature personality in Scandinavia, years in which she would have been expected to be attracting a husband. That she had affectionate contact with relatives in this period is suggested by the fact that her grandmother gave her a pair of silver candlesticks as a keepsake.[19]

Larsen's renderings of Copenhagen and of Helga Crane's experiences there in *Quicksand* are detailed and subtle enough in themselves to prove that the author had lived there for several seasons at least. Most significant for the purposes of this argument, Larsen repeatedly brings attention to the differences in racial culture between Denmark and the United States; her novel may be the only source through which one can recover some sense of what an African American's experience was like in Scandinavia at the time:

> Her dark, alien appearance was to most people an astonishment. Some stared surreptitiously, some openly, and some stopped dead in front of her in order more fully to profit by their stares. "Den sorte" dropped freely, audibly, from many lips. The time came when she grew used to the stares of the population. And the time came when the population of Copenhagen grew used to her outlandish presence and ceased to stare. But at the end of that first day it was with thankfulness that she returned to the sheltering walls of the house on Maria Kirkplads.[20]

Some passages in *Quicksand* are as vivid as any documentary history could be. In many cases they dramatize the differences between Danish and American perceptions of racial identity, differences Larsen could not have learned about in any books at the time: "There was also the Gammelstrand, the congregating-place of the vendors of fish . . . where Helga's appearance always roused lively and audible, but friendly, interest, long after she became in other parts of the city an accepted curiosity. Here it was that one day an old countrywoman asked her to what manner of mankind she belonged and at Helga's replying: 'I'm a Negro,' had become indignant, retorting angrily that, just because she was old and a countrywoman she could not be so easily fooled, for she knew as well as everyone else that Negroes were black and had woolly hair."[21]

Helga Crane is conscious of a significant difference between the kind of interest her racial markings aroused among a variety of classes in Denmark and the kind of contempt they aroused in the United States. Her sense of racial shame, moreover, Larsen presents as a specifically American shame, even while attending to the special contours of racism in Denmark.

For example, Helga goes with a number of friends to a vaudeville show in the winter at the Circus, and after being bored by the first several acts, she is embarrassed by the sudden appearance of an African American duo who perform out-of-date ragtime songs and dance: "And how the enchanted spectators clapped and howled and shouted for more! Helga Crane was not amused. Instead she was filled with a fierce hatred for the cavorting Negroes on the stage. She felt shamed, betrayed, as if these pale pink and white people among whom she lived had suddenly been invited to look upon something in her which she had hidden away and wanted to forget."[22] The cylinder-shaped "Cirkus" building in Copenhagen, which had opened in 1886 and would burn down in 1914, to be rebuilt thereafter, held vaudeville and variety shows in the winter months, the "off-season" for circuses; and these shows not infrequently featured black entertainers in song and dance routines.[23] The team of Johnson and Dean, for example, appeared there during their seven-year tour of European cities, from which they returned to the United States in September 1909. A review in *Variety* in October of that year, consonant with Helga Crane's critique, complained that they had fallen off in quality while abroad and had been spoiled by European adulation; and though "high class," they were still doing "coon songs." Out of date by American standards—those of State Street in Chicago, especially—they were nevertheless the most acclaimed "colored" act in Europe at the time.[24]

In some documents, chiefly employment and school applications—beginning with one to the school of the New York Public Library, which normally required a high school diploma and preferred a college degree, Larsen claimed that she audited classes at the University of Copenhagen or took its "open course." Although she never officially enrolled in the university, she may well have attended lecture series there that were the equivalent of what the New York Public Library School termed its "open course" and that required no formal registration. In various documents and published works, she indicated considerable familiarity with Scandinavian modernism, and while living in Copenhagen, she read the left-wing, rather highbrow newspaper *Politiken*, which followed general artistic and cultural developments with great avidity, devoting front-page feature articles to lectures at the university, artists or exhibitions, literary figures, and the like. An original feature of *Politiken* was the "Chronique," in which intellectual celebrities would comment on modern social problems, science, literature, and art criticism.[25] One could get a fair education in Scandinavian early modernism merely by following this newspaper.

Allusions and references to European and Scandinavian modernists figure frequently in Larsen's fiction and other documents of her reading. Henrik Ibsen, Knut Hamsun, and Jens Peter Jacobsen, for example, were all important points of reference for her. And yet no one has made a concerted effort to investigate the relationship between her work and Scandinavian modernism. One is driven to wonder by what reasoning we automatically align Larsen with an African diaspora rather than a Scandinavian one. The notion of diaspora, after all, usually implies not simply a "blood" connection to a particular geography but a cultural and psychological one. My point is not to impugn Larsen's relationship to a black diaspora but to put in question the emphasis on African origins and dispersal in theorizing that diaspora, with Africa as "motherland." It seems likely, in fact, that the difficulty in understanding, even crediting, Larsen's relationship to Denmark—let alone thinking of her as a (black) Scandinavian American writer—derives from the conflict between her life and American assumptions about the nature of diasporic black identity as such.

Scandinavian American immigrant fiction with American-born protagonists regularly dwells on a protagonist's feelings of being "betwixt and between" —going to Scandinavia in hopes of finding a sense of belonging that she lacks in America, only to discover that she does not, after all, fit in.[26] As a black or biracial woman, Larsen experienced such difficulties in unique ways, giving her an unusual perspective on the intersection of race, ethnicity, nationality, and gender. The Copenhagen scenes in *Quicksand* reveal the differences between the position of a young "mulatto" woman in Copenhagen and that of one in New York—or Chicago, or the black South, for that matter—finally coming to focus on the relationship between race, reproduction, and women's sexuality.

Plagued by fears of interracial marriage because of what it might mean for her children, Helga decides that she cannot marry a white man. She carries a profound dread of racism's power over relations of intimacy and family belonging, a dread her Danish relatives and suitor find incomprehensible. From this point her residence in Denmark seems doomed, for she has no future there outside of marriage; she would remain not only an outsider to Danish society but also a permanent dependent of her aging aunt and uncle. She tells her aunt that she does not believe in mixed marriages because they bring "only trouble— to the children—as she herself knew but too well from bitter experience."[27] Fru Dahl responds:

> Because your mother was a fool. Yes, she was! If she'd come home after she married, or after you were born, or even after your father—er—went off like that, it would have been different. If even she'd left you when she was here. But why in the world she should have married again, and a person like that, I can't see. She wanted to keep you, she insisted on it, even over his protest, I think. She loved you so much, she said.—And so she made you unhappy. Mothers, I suppose, are like that. Selfish. And Karen was always stupid. If you've got any brains at all they came from your father.[28]

The aunt's thinking pointedly contrasts with stereotypical white American views that "mulattoes" inherit their intelligence by way of their white ancestry. Fru Dahl also specifies that Helga's feelings about "mixed" marriages would be different if she had stayed in Denmark from childhood. Helga echoes this judgment in a moment of ironic identification with her mother after returning to New York. Contemplating why she could not return to Copenhagen and marry a white man, she concludes bitterly, " 'Because I'm a fool.' "[29] And, one might add, because she has grown up American with a mother who paid dearly for transgressing the color line. Helga will not make the mistake her mother did.

Another feature of Helga's growing alienation from her aunt and uncle and their Danish environment involves the position of women. The Danish custom of matchmaking, indeed of teaching girls to use their sexuality in order to enhance the family class status, both determines the Dahls' treatment of Helga and initiates her feeling of insecurity with them.

For Helga Crane, adult female sexuality seems cruelly bound to "race" and class interests that truncate women's lives. Larsen could never make peace with women's compulsory role in racial reproduction. When Helga Crane returns to New York from Denmark, she is confronted once again with a kind of bourgeois black nationalism that vilifies interracial intimacy and in relation to which her recent extended residence among "Nordics" makes her suspect. Among her Harlem friends, she must keep her family background a secret. This racial imperative also articulates with sexual "responsibility," whereby educated African Americans feel a duty to marry and produce children to offset the reproductivity of the more "unfit" members of the race. Racial survival, as Helga's former fiancé, for example, sees things, depends on eugenic "hygiene" and the proper discipline of sexuality. Appalled by the interracial socializing between blacks and whites in New York, he awakens in Helga Crane feelings of "polite contempt." Although she cannot bring herself to consider marrying a white man, Helga does not share the notion that such relations are inherently traitorous. After an aborted attempt at an affair with a married man, Helga, full of self-loathing, seeks refuge in black Christianity, marriage to a preacher, and uplift in the rural South—following the pattern of embracing the race as "family" and finally integrating into the racially divided pattern of American life. It is at this point that *Quicksand* veers most radically away from correspondence with the author's own life story, and from the essentially realistic method of development she had used for the bulk of the novel.

After giving birth in rapid succession to four children, and nearly dying in the fourth childbirth, Helga Crane loses all faith in Christianity and all interest in her husband. She recognizes her temporary interest in "uplift" as both presumptuously wrong-headed and unsatisfying. Scarcely has she recovered from the birth of her fourth child when she becomes pregnant again. Bedridden, her life endangered by the new pregnancy, she asks her nurse to read to her Anatole France's story "The Procurator of Judaea." As I have argued elsewhere, "The Procurator of Judaea" reveals how concepts of racial difference connect with patrician practices of empire-building, slavery, and national chauvinism, contributing to the oppression of women and the repression of sexuality except for purposes of producing racial subjects for the state—a theme that pertains equally to Helga Crane and her white mother. Racial ideology, as Larsen presents it, requires the sacrifice of boundary figures, whose symbolic victimage is formally demanded by a thoroughly racialized social order and its constitutive discourse. Correlatively, the self-integration of the racial subject entails the abjection of whatever destabilizes, by evading, the racial order, so that the "interracial" position (for lack of a better term) becomes a zone of incomprehensibility, compulsive fetishization, and disavowal.

In *Quicksand* Helga Crane's black fiancé, though committed to racial eugenics and contemptuous of "miscegenation," feels an intense erotic attraction to her that seems in part provoked by his knowledge of her interracial origins. We are told that she is a "despised mulatto" and that her "lack of family" disconcerted his own family.[30] "She was, she knew, in a queer indefinite way, a disturbing factor. She knew too that something held him, a something against which he was powerless."[31] Similarly, Helga's friend Ann Grey (from whom Helga keeps her "white" background a secret) fulminates endlessly against white people and blacks who maintain relations with them, and yet she "ape[s] their clothes, their styles, their gracious ways of living" and prefers European classical music to jazz and spirituals.[32] Her name likewise suggests an abject "whiteness" or interraciality at the core of her identity, "Miss Anne" being a derogatory term for a white woman and "Grey" an obvious signifier of black-white mixture.

In *Passing*, her next novel, Larsen would explore such psychological dynamics even more intensively. If *Quicksand* focused on the life and consciousness of a woman "neither white nor black" in the words of the novel's epigraph, *Passing* concerns the anxieties aroused by a woman both white and black. Clare Kendry is literally white in appearance, with blond hair and alabaster skin, and she lives as a white woman married to a white businessman, John Bellew. Yet she is "black" according to American racial norms, having been raised by her "mulatto" father before being taken in following his death by white aunts on Chicago's west side. As her aunts kept her race a secret, she had been able to "pass" into the white world and (to their horror) "marry white," her passage into the black bourgeoisie having been blocked by her suspect origins and class status. When the novel opens, as a white woman Clare Kendry is effectively excluded from the Negro world with which she longs to reconnect, and she has latched on to her childhood friend Irene Redfield as the conduit of her reconnection, provoking a deep disturbance in Irene's psyche, a phobic defense against the dissolution of racial and sexual boundaries upon which Irene's "identity" depends.

Irene places the highest value on a sense of security that requires racial, sexual, gender, class, and national boundaries. She is thus determined to prevent Clare from returning to the "the race." One cannot go freely back and forth; nor, once one has decided to pass, should one be allowed back across the line. The immense attraction Irene feels for Clare alternates, as Samira Kawash has emphasized, with repulsion.[33] Clare becomes an eroticized, fetishized element in Irene's fantasy life, a woman of occult powers, mysterious and magnetic, uncanny, "almost too good looking," and at the same time not to be endured. She represents precisely what Irene attempts to banish psychologically in order to secure her identity.[34]

Irene's anxieties about racial difference parallel those of Clare's husband, who abhors the specter of "race-mixing." In fact, after making his fortune on business ventures in Brazil, John Bellew had decided to move back to the United States because Brazil had too many "niggers" and allowed a blurring of racial boundaries that repelled him. Yet his very repugnance for "miscegenation" coincides with a fetishistic attraction to racial difference, revealed in his pet name for his wife, "Nig." Bellew needs his "Nig," as Judith Butler has argued, as the "spectre of a racial ambiguity that he must subordinate and deny" to sustain his racial identity.[35] The same can be said of Irene, whose phobic insistence that Clare remain "white" expresses her need for absolute difference.[36]

If John Bellew has moved back to the United States because of the racial indeterminacy signified by "Brazil," Irene's husband, Brian Redfield, wants to move to Brazil precisely because he believes that country has no color line, and he could practice medicine without regard for his clients' color. His desire to move to Brazil, however, conflicts with Irene's fierce attachment to both American nationality and racial identity as defined in the United States.

A correspondence develops between Brian's desire to move to Brazil and Clare's determination to move freely between the white and black worlds, even it if should mean the dissolution of her marriage. These two threats to Irene's psyche ultimately merge when she becomes convinced that Brian and Clare have fallen in love—a conviction the text refuses to authorize. Whether Clare is really trying to seduce Brian Redfield is not at all clear; what is clear is that Irene identifies Clare with aspects of Brian's desire that are growing outside Irene's control, and outside North American notions of identity. Clare Kendry is the moral equivalent of "Brazil" in Irene's mind. In a very different way than in

Quicksand, then, Larsen has thematized the articulations between American nationality, the color line, and sexuality.

Deriving from the invisible crossroads between blackness and whiteness, upper and lower classes, a place "out of bounds" in social terms, Clare inhabits a symbolically central position in the psyches of both her husband and Irene, who are the most insistently "American" characters in the novel. In contrast, Clare is presented, like her handwriting on Italian stationery, as "out of place and alien." She dies at the hands of Irene at the end of the novel, pushed out of a black Christmas party in a sixth-floor apartment, just as her husband breaks into the apartment where it is being held and accuses her of being a "damned, dirty nigger." According to the narrator, Irene's panicked response to Bellew's discovery is a determination that she cannot have Clare "free."[37]

Notably, the text never tells us explicitly how Clare "fell" from the window, because Larsen has ingeniously used a third-person limited point of view to filter all of our knowledge of events through Irene's consciousness, and Irene will not allow herself to remember what happened the moment after she rushed toward Clare at the open window and put a hand on her. When the black/white woman who threatens the racial boundary is done away with, no one will be to blame; her disappearance must remain a mystery, an absence on which the racial order depends.

The dynamics of racialization that Larsen's fiction probed helped shape the very reading practices through which it—and she, the "mystery woman of the Harlem Renaissance"—would later be read.[38] Her mere use of "mulatto" characters provoked accusations of trying to appeal to racist whites for acceptance on their terms, or for dealing with the trivial concerns of a tiny sector of the light-skinned elite. Biographical speculation about her was often wildly inaccurate, and Larsen's European experience raised questions about her relationship to "blackness." In his introduction to the Collier Books paperback edition of *Passing*, the classroom standard from the early 1970s through 1986, Hoyt Fuller recalls the initial reception of the novel and informs the reader that, like her main characters, Larsen "had gone off to Europe for a try at rejecting her Blackness, only to return in the end to wrap it closely about her again."[39] In fact, Larsen went abroad on a Guggenheim fellowship (the first black woman so honored) in order to write a novel "laid partly in the United States and partly in Europe. The theme will be the difference in intellectual and physical freedom for the Negro—and the effect on him—between Europe, especially the Latin countries Spain and France." Larsen was not rejecting her "blackness" but exploring its meaning in different contexts: "I have never been in these countries and therefore feel that I am not prepared without visiting them to judge attitudes and reactions of my hero in a foreign and favorable or more unfavorable environment."[40] Larsen was an exemplar of the kind of cosmopolitanism Ross Posnock has located in black intellectual culture.[41]

When black feminist critics and others began revisiting Larsen's novels for alternative visions of black female authorship in the African American canon, the position of biracial and "passing" characters would still be considered trivial, but now it seemed beside the point in coming to grips with Larsen's "real" concerns. While the masculinist biases implicit in Fuller's introduction would be repudiated, Larsen would be fit into a "sisterhood" or black matrilineage extending from Phyllis Wheatley to Alice Walker. In this project of reclamation, Larsen's exploration of the zone between the races, and its suppression both socially and psychologically—for which "black aesthetic" critics had dismissed her—came to seem merely a "mask," a ruse forced on her by white expectations and stereotypes about black sexuality. Larsen's allegedly superficial emphasis on "mulatto" characters or "passing" had, in this view, prevented her from more boldly investigating her real theme—black female sexuality—and compromised her worth as an author.[42] Through a failure of nerve, Larsen sabotaged her own novels.[43] But she had at least anticipated later, more explicit and satisfying treatments of black female sexuality by authors such as Toni Morrison, Alice Walker, Gloria Naylor, Gayl Jones, and Ntozake Shange. Subordinating Larsen to her proper racial line of descent entailed a discounting, even dismissal, of crucial features of her experience and beliefs, which can be said equally of the major attempt at biographical reclamation soon to follow in the same spirit.

Yet had it not been for her reclamation under precisely such auspices, who knows how long we would have had to wait for serious consideration of Larsen's achievement? Just as Larsen, after returning from Denmark in 1912, could only have been accepted by a black nursing school, so in the late twentieth century could she only have been "rescued" for the literary canon by scholars making a place for her in a specifically "black" canon defined by racial expectations formed out of the whole history of racial segregation in American life. It is not coincidental that her place was defined in familial metaphors with profound psychological resonances. In the United States, after all, we assume that race and family are joined at the mother's hip. Ultimately, however, Larsen refuses to be domesticated. The "mysteries" of her life and the problems to be found in reconstructions of it, as well as in accounts of her position in literary history, constitute a remarkable reflection of the continuing effect of the color-line culture in which she was entrapped.

Just as Larsen, in the course of childhood, was traumatized by the particular ways in which the color line affected interracial families, attempting (very successfully for the most part) to quash such families out, so has the understanding of her life and work been determined by the later intellectual and institutional effects of that very phenomenon. This does not have meaning merely for that still small minority of people sometimes termed "biracial." The subordination of "family" to "race," the attempt to ensure that families would always serve to reproduce race, is one of the great constants in the legal, social, cultural, and spiritual history of the United States.

One of the most important black authors of the interwar period, Larsen did not "inherit" her feminist consciousness or fictional technique through a collective tradition rooted in black culture but developed it out of diverse resources in response to a specific social and cultural position. Far from detracting from the relevance of her work for black feminism (or, indeed, world feminism) generally, this fact only enhances it. Larsen denies centrality to the metaphor of family descent on which American culture built its racial formations—in the process mortgaging women's bodies to the reproduction of race and subordinating all intimate relations to that invidious abstraction—while nonetheless acknowledging the political and social valence of black racial consciousness as a critical, and highly diversified, feature of modernity.

NOTES

1. See, especially, A. Leon Higginbotham Jr. and Barbara A. Kopytoff, "Racial Purity and Interracial Sex in the Law of Colonial and Antebellum Virginia," *Georgetown Law Journal* 77 (August 1989): 1967–2029.

2. Werner Sollors, *Neither White Nor Black Yet Both: Thematic Explorations of Interracial Literature* (New York: Oxford University Press, 1997), 129.

3. All biographical information used in this article derives from my book, *In Search of Nella Larsen: A Biography of the Color Line* (Cambridge, Mass.: Belknap Press of Harvard University Press, 2006).

4. John J. Flinn, *Chicago, the Marvelous City of the West: A History, an Encyclopedia, and a Guide* (2d ed.; Chicago: Standard Guide Co., 1892), 577.

5. Ibid., 578.

6. Ibid., 577.

7. I have discussed some of the problems with these studies in "Nella Larsen and the Veil of Race," *American Literary History* 9, no. 2 (1997): 329–49. The current biographies of Larsen are Thadious Davis, *Nella Larsen, Novelist of the Harlem Renaissance: A Woman's Life Unveiled* (Baton Rouge: Louisiana State University Press, 1994); and portions of Charles R. Larson, *Invisible Darkness: Jean Toomer and Nella Larsen* (Iowa City: University of Iowa Press, 1993).

8. Bryher to H.D., December 13, 1936, H.D. Papers, Yale Collection of American Literature, Beinecke Rare Book and Manuscript Library, Yale University, New Haven, Conn.

9. "*Kat efter Mus*" ("Cat and Mouse," as Larsen calls it) was recorded in three versions

in Evald Tang Kristensen's pioneering collection, *Danske Börnerim, Remser og Lege* (Copenhagen: Karl Shønberg, 1896), 498. Only the version that matches Larsen's had been recorded from Jutland, and it was not noted elsewhere. The other games Larsen wrote up, though obviously authentic, are not represented in Kristensen's work, although one or two of them seem to be related to games Kristensen's informants identified.

10. Steffens Linvald and Knud Sandvej, *København har moret sig* (Copenhagen: Politikens Forlag, 1966), 118.

11. Nella Larsen Imes, "Three Scandinavian Games," *The Brownies' Book*, June 1920, 191.

12. Quoted in Dianne Johnson-Feelings, "Afterword," *The Best of the Brownies' Book*, ed. Dianne Johnson-Feelings (New York: Oxford University Press, 1996), 346.

13. Douglas S. Massey and Nancy A. Denton, *American Apartheid: Segregation and the Making of the Underclass* (Cambridge, Mass.: Harvard University Press, 1993), 31. See also Allan H. Spear, *Black Chicago: The Making of a Negro Ghetto, 1890–1920* (Chicago: University of Chicago Press, 1967).

14. *Catalogue of the Officers and Students of Fisk University, 1907–1908* (Nashville, Tenn.: Fisk University, 1908), 13.

15. Ibid., 18.

16. Letter to President and Prudential Committee of Fisk University, in College Faculty Minutes, June 8, 1908, Special Collections, Fisk University Library, Nashville, Tenn.

17. College Faculty Minutes, June 13, 1908, Special Collections, Fisk University Library.

18. Nella Larsen, author's statement; Marion L. Starkey, "Negro Writers Come into Their Own," unpublished manuscript, Alfred A. Knopf Collection, Harry Ransom Humanities Research Center, University of Texas at Austin; Nella Larsen Imes, Application for Admission to the Library School of the New York Public Library, Box 30, New York Public Library Library School Collection, Rare Book and Manuscript Library, Columbia University, New York, N.Y.; Nella Larsen Imes file, John Simon Guggenheim Memorial Foundation, New York, N.Y.

19. Davis, *Nella Larsen*, 46.

20. Nella Larsen, *Quicksand*, in *"Quicksand" and "Passing,"* ed. Deborah E. McDowell (New Brunswick, N.J.: Rutgers University Press, 1986), 73.

21. Ibid., 76.

22. Ibid., 82–83.

23. Linvald and Sandvej, *København har moret sig*, 134.

24. Henry T. Sampson, *The Ghost Walks: A Chronological History of Blacks in Show Business, 1865–1910* (Metuchen, N.J.: Scarecrow Press, 1988), 341, 474, 478; postcard of Johnson and Dean, postmarked Copenhagen, August, 18, 1907, photograph number 6293/1966, in collection of the Bredemuseet of the Nationalmuseet, Brede, Denmark.

25. *Politikens Historie set indefra 1884–1984*, vol. 2 (Copenhagen: Politikens Forlag, 1983), 72. See also issues of *Politiken* for 1908–12.

26. Dorothy Burton Skårdal, *The Divided Heart: Scandinavian Immigrant Experience through Literary Sources* (Lincoln: University of Nebraska Press, 1974), 105–6.

27. Larsen, *Quicksand*, 78.

28. Ibid.

29. Ibid., 97.

30. Ibid., 18, 8.

31. Ibid., 7–8.

32. Ibid., 48.

33. Samira Kawash, *Dislocating the Color Line: Identity, Hybridity, and Singularity in African-American Literature* (Stanford, Calif.: Stanford University Press, 1997), 159.

34. Larsen, *Passing*, 156. Ann duCille's interpretation of the novel parallels mine in important respects. DuCille sees Clare as a kind of "alter libido" to Irene, who is bent on denying her in order to preserve her middle-class existence. DuCille cites Lauren Berlant's insight that Irene wants to wear Clare's way of wearing her body, " 'like a prosthesis, or a fetish' "—a point that strongly influences my understanding of the novel. See Ann duCille, *The Coupling Convention: Sex, Text, and Tradition in Black Women's Fiction* (New York: Oxford University Press, 1993), 104–5; and Lauren Berlant, "National Brands/National Body: *Imitation of Life*," in *Comparative American Identities: Race, Sex, and Nationality in the Modern Text*, ed. Hortense Spillers (New York: Routledge, 1991), 111.

35. Judith Butler, *Bodies That Matter: On the Discursive Limits of "Sex"* (New York: Routledge, 1993), 173. My own approach to the concepts of abjection, transgression, and fetishism derives chiefly from Butler; Julia Kristeva, *Powers of Horror: An Essay on Abjection* (New York: Columbia University Press, 1982); Laura Mulvey, *Fetishism and Curiosity* (Bloomington: Indiana University Press, 1996); and Peter Stallybrass and Allon White, *The Politics and Poetics of Transgression* (Ithaca, N.Y.: Cornell University Press, 1986). See also Henry Krips, *Fetish: An Erotics of Culture* (Ithaca, N.Y.: Cornell University Press, 1999). Helena Michie suggests that Larsen creates an "erotics of passing" in *Sororophobia: Differences among Women in Literature and Culture* (New York: Oxford University Press, 1992). Merrill Horton, in "Blackness, Betrayal, and Childhood: Race and Identity in Nella Larsen's *Passing*," *CLA Journal* 38 (September 1994): 31–44, builds on this view to argue that Irene secretly desires to pass, accounting for an erotics Freud identified with the adult's desire to feel the joy of childhood play.

36. Kawash, too, has emphasized this symmetrical relationship between Irene Redfield and John Bellew in their responses to Clare, in *Dislocating the Color Line*.

37. Larsen, *Passing*, 143, 238, 239.

38. The term comes from Mary Helen Washington, "Nella Larsen: Mystery Woman of the Harlem Renaissance," *Ms.*, December 1980, 45.

39. Hoyt Fuller, "Introduction," in Nella Larsen, *Passing* (New York: Collier/Macmillan, 1971), 12.

40. Nella Larsen Imes, fellowship application for 1930–31, John Simon Guggenheim Memorial Foundation, New York, N.Y.

41. Ross Posnock, *Color and Culture: Black Writers and the Making of the Modern Intellectual* (Cambridge, Mass.: Harvard University Press, 1998).

42. The case was made forcefully in the introduction to what instantly became the standard classroom edition of Larsen's novels. Deborah E. McDowell, "Introduction," in Larsen, *"Quicksand" and "Passing,"* xxx.

43. Ibid., xxx–xxxi.

PART II

Ironies of Empire

White Is the Color of Empire

The Annexation of Hawaii in 1898

ERIC LOVE

On June 15, 1898, two months into the war with Spain, the U.S. House of Representatives passed by an overwhelming margin, 209 to 91, a joint resolution for the annexation of Hawaii. On July 6, the Senate gave its approval, 42 to 21. It took a week for this news to reach Honolulu, a strange and ironic sign of the islands' peculiar isolation. The majority of native Hawaiians—royalists, others loyal to the deposed queen, Liliuokalani, and their sympathizers—mourned, for the second time since 1893, the loss of their country. But the Americans in the islands, in the words of an eyewitness, received the news "with unbounded enthusiasm," with the ringing of bells, the blowing of factory whistles, with joyous shouts and fireworks. The *Pacific Commercial Advertiser* ran a one-word headline, "ANNEXATION," and beneath it, "Honolulu, H.I., USA." A newspaperman named Henry Whitney responded with patriotic verse:

> And the Star-Spangled Banner
> In triumph shall wave
> O'er the isles of Hawaii
> And the homes of the brave.[1]

Reactions in the United States were more cautious; and insofar as they were divided, far greater numbers celebrated annexation than did not. "The America of the twentieth century," the *New York Sun* declared, "has taken its first and most significant step towards the grave responsibility and high rewards of manifest destiny." For the *Boston Transcript*, "The Rubicon has at last been crossed. This country," it said, "now enters upon a policy that is entirely new. It has thrown down its former standards, cast aside its old traditions, has extended its first tentacle two thousand miles away, and is growing others for exploration in southern and eastern seas."[2] However divided by philosophy and reaction, both the celebrants and skeptics of 1898 shared in the recognition that this event, and others that took place during and in the aftermath of the war, marked an extraordinary and unprecedented moment in the nation's history.

Historians of the period can clearly relate as they continue to debate one another over the events of that year and their significance. Why the war with Spain began and why it ended with the acquisition of an empire on two oceans are questions on which consensus has been elusive. However, on one question of great significance—what effect did race ideology have on U.S. imperialism?— they have reached a remarkable level of consensus. Put simply, they argue that race ideology advanced empire: that in the aftermath of the war, ascendant racial ideas—essentially an array of white supremacist convictions: Anglo-Saxonism, Social Darwinism, manifest destiny, benevolent assimilation, and the "white man's burden"—armed imperialists with an impenetrable rationale for seizing Cuba, annexing Puerto Rico, Guam, Hawaii, and the Philippines, and extending American dominion over all of their inhabitants, more than 10 million people of color, whom the majority of Americans dismissed as alien, inferior, incapable of self-government where they lived and impossible to assimilate into the republic. According to this common interpretation, the United States took these places and their populations because the logic of market-capitalist expansion, hemispheric security, missionary-humanitarian obligation, manly honor, and white supremacy demanded it.

The first premise of this essay is that the received historiography is significantly flawed. What follows, then, attempts to demonstrate several things that are contrary to what is now the dominant narrative on race and American imperialism at the end of the nineteenth century: first, that the imperialists' relationship with the racist structures and convictions of their time was discordant, not harmonious. This point, by itself, has immediate effects on the shape and nature of the narrative: it ceases to be about the ways in which the imperialists manipulated racist ideas in order to achieve their goals and becomes, instead, one in which racism is a problem of power; or, put another way, one in which empire is achieved only after a hard struggle against the traditions, demands, and expectations of the racist social order of their time.

The case of Hawaii's annexation presents the best demonstration of what such a narrative might look like: it turns the most revealing light on the complexities, contingencies, and ironies of the dynamics of race, racism, and empire. Most general accounts of race and late nineteenth-century U.S. imperialism focus on the war of 1898 and the Philippines. But for our purposes, Hawaii is the superior case study for several reasons: it evolved and unfolded over more than half a century, whereas the Philippines went from being virtually unknown to the vast majority of Americans to annexed territory in the space of eight bewildering months of war, electioneering, and peacemaking. It is a fact not often acknowledged that even the "large policy" visionaries were caught off guard by the consequences of Dewey's dramatic victory over the Spanish in Manila. Alfred Thayer Mahan and Theodore Roosevelt both expressed awe and uncertainty over what should be done with the Philippines; Henry Cabot Lodge wanted them, at first, only to trade them for island possessions closer to the United States. The Philippines debate, however dramatic, is in many ways merely an echo of the ones that took place over Hawaii. Considered on a wider historiographical landscape, any understanding of the place that race occupied in the story of American imperialism is incomplete if it does not comprehend the full significance of Hawaii.

It can be said that U.S. relations with Hawaii began in 1820, the year that the American missionaries first arrived on the islands. Formal relations, however, began twenty-two years later when King Kamehameha III sent a pair of diplomats to Washington, D.C., to secure formal diplomatic recognition from the United States. From these meetings came the Tyler Doctrine, which became the framework for U.S. policy toward Hawaii from the moment of its announcement until annexation. The doctrine claimed that the United States had a unique set of interests in, and therefore a special relationship with, the island kingdom; that Hawaii's continued independence was in the "true interest" of all the commercial powers who had a presence there; and that the United States would be "dissatisfied" by any attempt by another power "to take possession of the islands, colonize them, and subvert the native government."[3] The Tyler Doctrine was utterly silent on granting diplomatic recognition. To some, this was an indication of Hawaii's remoteness, not just geographically but beyond the nation's foreign policy horizon (here it is important to recall that the Tyler Doctrine came in being years before the Mexican War extended the nation's borders to the Pacific; those acquisitions would significantly reorient policy vision). John Quincy Adams suspected that the secretary of state, Daniel Webster, withheld recognition from the Hawaiians for one very specific reason, "which is that they are black."[4] Whether the accusation was true at the time need not concern us; what it points to, however—that racism would be a vital force in the evolution of U.S.-Hawaiian relations—establishes a vital arc in the narrative.

The Ariadne's thread of U.S. policy was to strengthen and maintain its special relationship with Hawaii, through culture, commerce, immigration and settlement, and the protection of the islands' sovereignty according to the Tyler Doctrine. Each element was affected over time by race, annexationist sentiment especially. Over the half century from 1842 to the revolution of 1893, annexation was considered a perilous option by Democrats and Republicans alike—a strategy that the United States would turn to not out of any sense of fulfilling its "manifest destiny," but to keep the islands out of the hands of rival powers. Central to what made annexation the policy of last resort was race. In 1854, in response to deteriorating political conditions in the Hawaiian government and

British threats, the U.S. minister stationed in Honolulu, David L. Gregg, negotiated an annexation treaty and sent it to Washington. It was a standard document of its type except for three remarkable provisions: the first, article 2 of the agreement, promised that Hawaii would be admitted "into the American Union as a State, enjoying the same degree of sovereignty . . . all the rights, privileges, and immunities . . . on a perfect equality with the other States of the Union"; the second declared that all Hawaiians—the king, "his chiefs and subjects of every class"—would receive "all the rights and privileges of citizens of the United States, on terms of perfect equality, in all respects, with other American citizens"; the third required the United States to appropriate $75,000 annually for ten years "for the benefit of a college or university" and common schools, to educate native Hawaiians and "enable them the more perfectly to enjoy and discharge" the duties of citizenship.[5] Although his was the party of expansionism; although New York Democrats celebrating his victory in 1852 raised their glasses to this toast: "Cuba and the Sandwich Isles [Hawaii]—may they soon be added to the galaxy of States"; although he stacked his cabinet with men well known for their expansionism; and although he said in his inaugural address that his administration would "not be controlled by any timid forebodings of evil from expansion," President Franklin Pierce rejected the annexation treaty.[6] His secretary of state, William Marcy, wrote afterward that the president objected strongly to the content and implications of article 2: "There is in his mind strong objections to the immediate incorporation of the islands in the present condition into the Union as an Independent State." Both men believed that the Hawaiians should have left questions of citizenship, statehood, and full and "perfect equality" to the United States, so that the administration could push ahead with annexation untroubled and "unembarrassed by stipulations on that point."[7] Annexation soon was abandoned.

Reciprocity had been attempted twice prior to the passage of the pivotal treaty of 1875. Both initiatives were turned down despite the clear advantages that would come by way of closer commercial relations: stronger ties between the two countries; enhanced economic and commercial development on the Pacific coast; and for some, the hope that it might bring annexation about more quickly. Others, a noisy and important hive of politicians, voted for reciprocity for the exact opposite reason: because, as Congressman James A. Garfield declared during the debate over this treaty, "it would obviate any necessity for annexing the islands." His feelings did not rise from any philosophical aversion to expansion: he approved of it entirely for his nation so long as it occurred within the temperate zone. He objected to expansion into the tropics—toward lands "inhabited by people of the Latin races strangely degenerated by their mixture with native races . . . occupying a territory that I earnestly hope may never be made an integral part of the United States." Strategic and economic concerns moved Garfield to support the letter of the treaty, but to his reckoning the spirit of it, the basis of the special relationship it embodied, arose out of racial sympathy that bound the United States to the islands through the presence of its white population. It was fortunate, he told the assembled congressmen, that Hawaii was "dominated in all its leading influences by Americans, our own brethren. Their hearts warm toward us as their first choice in forming alliances." The phrase "our own brethren" is significant in several ways: for how it justified the support of a commercial treaty; for how it erased native Hawaiians, Chinese, and other peoples of color as a presence having any consequence —no talk of engagement for the purpose of uplift, mission, or benevolent assimilation here; and, for our purposes, how it anticipated the ways in which whiteness shaped policy formation over the two decades that followed. "They [the islands] are ours in blood and sympathy," Garfield said, "and in this treaty they offer us the first place, an exceptionally favorable place, in their relations to the world."[8]

The great and dramatic shift that took place in U.S.-Hawaiian relations over the two decades that preceded annexation did not come from reciprocity but grew out of a demographic calamity. Diseases common to the West but unknown in the islands before 1778—cholera, influenza, measles, smallpox, and syphilis—cut down the native Hawaiians at a rate faster than natural increase. Census figures compiled over more than half a century confirm the devastation (table 1).

The population collapse threatened to break apart the social, political, cultural, and economic integrity of the kingdom. King Kamehameha IV's principal concern was how to rescue his people from extinction; the planter class, specifically the sugar growers, was losing its most proximate and inexpensive source of labor. All agreed that the solution was immigration, but there they parted ways. A previous labor shortage had been addressed by importing Chinese workers. Kamehameha believed that this had been a mistake; they worked but refused to assimilate—"they seem to have no affinities, attractions, or tendencies to blend with us, or any other race," he observed. The king, therefore, asked the Hawaiian legislature to recruit labor from what he called more "compatible" Polynesian groups, from "a class of persons more nearly assimilated with the Hawaiian race." Such a population, he said, would serve everyone's purposes: "besides supplying the present demand for labor," they "would pave the way for a future population of native born Hawaiians."[9] Over the king's pleas, however, labor was again brought in from China. Eventually a wider net

TABLE 1. Decline of the Native Hawaiian Population, 1832–1890

1832	130,303
1850	84,165
1853	71,091
1860	69,800
1872	56,896
1884	40,014
1890	34,436

Sources: Ralph Kuykendall and A. Grove Day, *Hawaii: A History* (New York: Prentice-Hall, 1948), 298; House Ex. Doc. no. 1, pt. 1, app. 2, *Affairs in Hawaii*, 53 Cong., 3d sess. (Washington, D.C.: Government Printing Office, 1895), 321; *Foreign Relations of the United States, 1894* (Washington, D.C.: Government Printing Office, 1895), app. 1, 256.

was cast, and Japanese workers began to enter the islands; Indian "coolies" and Portuguese would come, too, in significant numbers, but far larger numbers, tens of thousands in fact, poured in from Asia.

From about 1880 to the eve of the Hawaiian revolution in 1893, the rising Asian presence emerged as the single-most urgent and daunting concern for American policymakers. On February 14, 1881, James Comly, U.S. minister to Hawaii, informed Secretary of State James Blaine that over the previous three weeks "about 1,700 adult male Chinese immigrants had been added to the population." Fifteen hundred more were rumored to be on their way, thus a "majority of the adult male population of the islands is now Chinese." He warned Blaine that there would be no end to this movement so long as the "chief demand of the islands shall continue to be *more laborers*."[10] Blaine's reply was significant in at least two ways: first, although he was fully committed to keeping Hawaii in the American sphere, he rejected annexation as a solution. He told Comly that although the islands were "the key to the maritime domination of the Pacific States," the United States did not want "material possession" of them "any more [than the nation wanted] Cuba." The second important element of Blaine's reply was the solution he proposed, a "less responsible alternative" to acquisition: Americanization—in other words, "a replenishment of the vital forces of Hawaii" through, Blaine wrote, a "purely American form of colonization." The strategy he pondered would reverse Hawaii's descent into the Asian sphere of influence by pushing back the Chinese workers, replacing them with people who Blaine believed were already prepared for the rigors of laboring in tropical climates (it was commonly believed that Hawaii lay in the tropical zone), men and women "trained in the rice swamps and cane fields of the Southern States."[11] However indirect, Blaine was clearly proposing that

African Americans be sent to Hawaii. The plan never came to fruition, but once again we see the dynamics of race and empire taking peculiar turns.

By 1890 concerns about the Chinese were being eclipsed by more urgent and immediate fears of the Japanese. Between 1885 and 1894, over 30,000 Japanese immigrants entered Hawaii. By 1896, Japanese nationals accounted for 60 percent of the islands' labor force. This fact helped set into motion, in 1897, the annexation movement that finally succeeded; that episode will be addressed shortly. We must first take account of the events that immediately preceded and followed the Hawaiian revolution of 1893. In November 1892 the American minister in Honolulu, John L. Stevens, cabled Secretary of State John Foster to warn him of the growing magnitude of the Asian threat he was witnessing. The situation had reached a critical point where, he said, the islands would be pulled decisively "to Asia or . . . America"; the numbers coming in were making Hawaii into "a Singapore, or a Hongkong," suitable for foreign domination but "unfit to be and American Territory or an American State under our constitutional system." Stevens saw no other course than annexation and laid out a plan to "Americanize the islands." He proposed that the United States intervene immediately, "assume control of the 'Crown lands, dispose of them in small lots for . . . [American] settlers and freeholders." Hawaii would be transformed by the creation of a "permanent preponderance of a population and civilization which will make the islands like southern California . . . bringing everything here into harmony with American life and prosperity." Hesitation or delay, he said, would only "add to present unfavorable tendencies and make future possession more difficult."[12] The note does more than simply repeat anxieties expressed by his predecessors in Hawaii or echo Americanization strategies similar to Blaine's. It reveals the thoughts of the man who two months later sided with white revolutionaries who overthrew Hawaii's Queen Liliuokalani. Without Stevens's intervention, ordering marines from the USS *Boston* ashore in a critical and intimidating show of force at a key moment, the coup would probably have failed.

Once the revolutionaries took over the capital, they declared the establishment of a provisional government and immediately sent a delegation to Washington, D.C., to negotiate the terms of Hawaii's annexation to the United States. The treaty that resulted was put together under extraordinary circumstances. The president, Benjamin Harrison, had been defeated for reelection the previous fall by Grover Cleveland. He would leave office on March 4, 1893. The representatives of the provisional government had only arrived in the capital on February 3. This left less than a month to make the treaty and then persuade the Senate to ratify it. Foster wanted the islands. He also understood that all parties had to work with great care to produce an agreement that would not antagonize Congress. This meant that certain things the Hawaiians asked for would not be received: tariff protection for sugar, dollars to fund improvements in Pearl Harbor, an oceanic cable from Honolulu to the United States. Most important, Foster dismissed the delegates' request for a provision that would have protected both Hawaii's contract labor system and the immigration policy that brought tens of thousands of Chinese, Japanese, and Portuguese "coolie" workers to the islands. The secretary of state understood that cheap labor was indispensable to the islands' sugar industry, but he also understood the mood of Congress and the nation. Only months earlier, Congress had renewed the Chinese Exclusion Act. Any part of the treaty that appeared either to favor Chinese labor or undermine the exclusion law, Foster said, "would have the same effect upon the [treaty's] opposition that a red flag would have upon a bull."[13] This was left out, but the treaty did include a special article that prohibited all future immigration from East Asia into Hawaii and from the islands into the United States. Foster's message was clear: annexation would not endanger the Chinese exclusion law or any other part of the domestic racial order.

Despite the best efforts of Foster and Harrison, the treaty did not come to a vote before Cleveland's inauguration, and five days after taking office the new president withdrew the treaty from the Senate "for purposes of re-examination." Again, details of the investigation of Stevens's unlawful role in the coup and the treaty's defeat need not detain us. For our purposes, two facts are far more relevant. First, during the few weeks that the treaty was before the public, race emerged as the most contentious issue. The *Nation* warned its readers that annexation meant eventual statehood and citizenship for the motley races of the islands. The result would be a population "of natives recently emerged from savagery, speaking foreign tongues, Japanese, Chinese, and Portuguese," voting and "deciding our Presidential elections in case of a close division of the Electoral College."[14] The *Chicago Herald* predicted that Hawaii would form a "pigmy State of the Union" and called its annexation "ridiculous."[15] The *Chicago Evening Journal* declared that by "annexing this sugar plantation with its mixed population we risk all in case of war. On this continent we are supreme; in the midst of the Pacific Ocean we would be at the mercy of the Chinese population of Hawaii."[16] In an article titled "Manifest Destiny," Carl Schurz attacked the policy of acquiring regions in the tropical zones, "inhabited by a people so utterly different from ours in origin, in customs and habits, in traditions, language, morals . . . in almost everything that constitutes social and political life." To his reckoning, "Climatic influences . . . made them what they are and render an essential change of their character impossible."[17]

The second fact is that around the time of the defeat of this treaty, imperialists started to piece together a strategy that allowed them to exploit race to their advantage: not by invoking Social Darwinism, benevolent assimilation, or the "white man's burden," or by overwhelming the racist outcries of anti-imperialists with their own racial rhetoric. They, instead, focused on whiteness. From 1893 until annexation was confirmed five years later, the imperialists in their sundry speeches and writings diminished the importance of the islands' nonwhite majority—cast it as irrelevant to the true purpose of acquiring the islands. Annexation, they argued, was necessary, just, and correct, a duty that Americans were obligated to fulfill, not to uplift and Christianize savage natives or Asian coolies, but for the sake of the whites.

This discourse came together in stages. The first insisted that Hawaii was, in theory and praxis, a white civilization and justified the revolution on that single premise. Just weeks after the coup, Sereno Bishop, a white Hawaiian and leading annexationist, explained in the *New York Evening Post* that the revolution was instigated by the queen's hostility. Liliuokalani, he said, aided by "a reactionary heathen element," was determined to "destroy the white share of influence in the government, and put the forty millions of white capital and all *our* beautiful civilization which has created this Paradise under the boot of ignorance and brutality."[18] Many in the United States swallowed Bishop's version of events whole. "The Queen simply went from bad to worse," declared the *New York Herald*, "and the white population rebelled against further degradation. Hence her disposition."[19] The next stage called for annexation in order to defend and maintain white civilization in the islands from the Asian threat. In a letter to the *New York Times* published on January 31, 1893, shortly after the coup, Alfred Thayer Mahan returned to the issue of the Chinese threat. He saw it as a crucial element in the revolution, "evident from the great number of Chinese, relative to the whole population, now settled in the islands." The question that remained for the United States was whether Hawaii would "in the future be an outpost of European civilization, or of the comparative barbarism of China."[20] The final stage to emerge in 1893 emphasized racial sympathy between whites in the United States and Hawaii. Senator John Tyler Morgan of Alabama, a reluctant imperialist in this instance, told the *New York Times* that unless the alternative was their acquisition "by some foreign power," he preferred that the islands remain "under an independent form of government." What made annexation to the United States palatable, he said, was that the revolutionaries represented "the best class of Hawaii," men in the best position to voice "the desires of the intelligent and enterprising portion of the Hawaiian population," by which he certainly meant the whites.[21] Samuel Chapman Armstrong, the son of Presbyterian missionaries who was born on Maui in 1839, wrote in the *Southern Workman* of his concern for his white brethren who were "seek[ing] annexation and . . . vigorously courting the United States for that purpose." He feared that they would fail, that "the American policy of refusing new territory seem[ed] likely to prevail." Nevertheless, he held out hope. The islands' remarkable progress, he said, was due solely to "the control of its affairs by white people," mostly Americans, and that "the conquest by American missionaries of the Hawaiian Islands . . . gives the United States both a claim and an obligation in the matter—a claim to be considered first in the final disposition of that country, an obligation to save decency and civilization in that utterly broken-down monarchy."[22]

A separate but nonetheless connected development that occurred in Hawaii fixed whiteness at the center of state building and, as events progressed, all future discussions of annexation. In March 1894 the leaders of the provisional government and elected delegates assembled to draft a constitution. From the beginning, Hawaii's new political order contained racial exclusions. The majority of the native Hawaiians, all Asians, and the Portuguese were disfranchised by the new constitution. The white leadership justified this move on the grounds that these groups were ignorant of the principles of republicanism and therefore were a "menace to good government." The final version of the constitution, proclaimed on the auspicious date of July 4, 1894, succeeded in converting the principle of control by the "responsible" element into an actual frame of governance. In *American Expansion in Hawaii*, historian Sylvester Stevens detected something else significant: a connection between the local racial agenda and annexation. "The obvious purpose being the establishment of a conservative Republic," wrote Stevens, "was the organization of such a government as would hold the turbulent racial and other forces in Hawaii in check until better relations could be established in the United States." The link to annexation is clearly implied in the constitution. Delegates placed in it an article that "expressly authorized and empowered" the president and his cabinet "to make a treaty of political and commercial union" with the United States. Despite this power, the task would be a formidable one.[23]

Both the political and racial climates of the 1890s were hostile to imperialism, particularly when policymakers reached out toward places like Hawaii: distant, unfamiliar, and exotic places occupied by a conglomeration of "inferior" races. Worse still for the expansionists, annexation was inevitably tangled up in questions of statehood and citizenship. The effect on policies and treaties was always devastating. Whitelaw Reid, editor of the *New York Tribune*, a devout Republican, and imperialist, complained bitterly of how difficult it was "to get anybody in Congress to admit the possibility of dealing with [the Hawaiian islands] in any other way than by making them a state in the union." He observed that the same presumption tied policymakers' hands in the Caribbean: "Everybody seemed to consider it natural, as well as certain, that Cuba would come in some day as a state." Reid's convictions regarding race and nationalism told him, just like they told millions of other Americans, that making states out of distant territories and granting citizenship rights to incompatible races was foolishness, "humanitarianism run mad, a degeneration and degradation of the homogeneous, continental Republic of our pride." Reid the imperialist understood that popular racist attitudes, laws, and structures conspired to hinder expansionism.[24]

Reid's imperialist cohorts knew this as well. This is why, even as the Republican Party committed itself to an expansionist foreign policy, its approach was constantly marked by hesitation and conservatism. For example, while some supported an aggressive naval building program, others asked who would pay for it. And although leading Republicans attacked Democrats for practicing a "policy of retreat" and for "taking down the American flag" in Hawaii, the best and strongest language they could muster up for their national platform in 1896 declared that the islands should be "controlled" by the United States—a far cry from "annexed." The vague language of this plank most likely indicated that the party was divided over the issue. Regardless, soon after William McKinley won the presidency, the issue was again forced on the party, and the nation.

A week after his inauguration, McKinley was pounced on by annexationists from both Hawaii and the United States. Representatives of the Republic of Hawaii and their American sympathizers made their case with great urgency. The new government had shown itself to be conspicuously ineffective at controlling immigration into the islands. Japanese workers were entering at a rate of roughly 1,000 per month. By the spring of 1897 they had become the second-largest population on the islands, behind only the native Hawaiians. Worse still, these workers, supported by official pressure from Tokyo, had begun to demand voting rights. The white minority, severely alarmed by these developments and too weak to resist them for much longer, turned to the United States. Their minister to the United States, Francis Hatch, wrote to the State Department, detailing the magnitude of the threat and predicting calamity. The specter of the "yellow peril," now represented by Japan instead of China, reenergized the annexationist movement. Americans were told that predatory Japan threatened the Tyler Doctrine, their nation's predominant position in the islands, and white civilization in general and their fellow white Americans in particular. McKinley was asked to consider the worst possibilities: the unraveling of America's dominant position in the islands and the prospect of a powerful and hostile enemy in Hawaii, jeopardizing the peace and security of America's Pacific coastline. In June 1897 the president ordered the assistant secretary of state to reopen negotiations and draft a treaty of annexation. Within days the agreement was done, signed on June 16, 1897, and sent to the Senate the very same day.

The summer and fall of 1897 witnessed a back-and-forth public debate over annexation in which race was, once again, a central issue. Imperialists perfected the line of argument that justified annexation on the basis of whiteness. In May of that year, the Hawaiian branch of the Sons of the American Revolution published an address to their compatriots in the United States. In it, familiar themes were repeated: that the islands were an "advanced outpost of American civilization in the Pacific"; that the dominant character of the republic was not native Hawaiian but white and American; that what they were facing was an "irrepressible contest between the Asiatic and American civilizations"; that annexation did not "per se confer" citizenship rights to the inferior races present in the islands; and that once the islands were annexed, federal immigration and naturalization laws would force the Asians out, creating wide fields of opportunity for "white workers from the United States."[25] Another white Hawaiian, Lorrin Thurston, in his *Handbook on the Annexation of Hawaii*, injected a different element into this discourse, the imagery of familial bonds, to complement white racial sympathy. Over the previous half century, he said, the relationship between the two countries had become "like that of an indulgent and protecting elder brother toward a little sister." Hawaiian civilization, he wrote, was not only "the direct product of American effort" but also "a child of America."[26]

Thurston's *Handbook* was significant in another way. He did not simply repeat that Hawaii was a white civilization in need of rescuing, nor did he just practice the common rhetorical tactic of reducing or ignoring the nonwhite elements of the population (which outnumbered the whites by a factor of almost twenty to one). He attempted to argue that two groups, the native Hawaiians and the Portuguese, were in fact fit for citizenship and completely assimilable. He described the natives as "conservative, peaceful, and generous . . . not Africans, but Polynesians. They are brown," he explained, "not black." Thurston was even bolder with the Portuguese, adding them to a cluster of European groups who could be considered white. Seven thousand, he said, had been born in Hawaii and educated in the public schools "so that they speak English as readily as does the average American child." He described their collective character in terms meant to communicate their assimilability, if not their essential whiteness. They were, Thurston wrote, "a hard-working, industrious, home-creating and home-loving people, who would be of advantage to any developing country."[27]

Opposition reacted with fierce intensity during this period also. The *Baltimore Sun* asked its readers to ponder what could be done with such a "mixture of races" as existed in Hawaii. If the islands were annexed, "are the Portuguese to retain the ballot and outvote the Americans? If we make them into a State," it continued, "shall we consent to receive at Washington two senators evolved from this mass of Asiatic ignorance?" To the *Philadelphia Record*, the nation's racial order was in immediate danger from imperialism. It was a "mockery to build up a rampart of anti-immigration and quarantine laws on the one hand," it said, "and on the other to take in at one gulp the whole mass of diseased and depraved serfs who constitute the greater part of the population of the Hawaiian islands."[28] Labor brought to the debates its specific objections. The *American Federationist* dismissed the native Hawaiians as "semi-civilized, with no conception of the privileges, much less the rights, hopes, and aspirations of a republican form of government." The Japanese, to their reckoning, were worse: "coolie laborers" who toiled without complaint "under conditions wholly at variance with any conception of American manhood." Of the Portuguese and Chinese "coolies and others equally low in the economic, social, and civilized scale," the *Federationist* asked, "Who can honestly assert that they will become under any form of government, congenial, or assimilate to an enlightened homogeneity[?]"[29]

Labor saw Hawaii's annexation through this optic, tinted dark by decades of practicing anti-Chinese racism and making what began as a local movement into a national policy. Policymakers were pragmatic men—politicians, partisans, and most of all vote-counters—who knew that they had to reckon with the exclusion acts. The intelligent policymaker would not undertake any project that might violate them and, as a result, alienate a constituency as powerful and potentially volatile—the strikes of 1877, Haymarket, Pullman, and dozens of other conflicts, less infamous, were still fresh memories—as labor. In short, the demands of the racial social order of the 1890s would not allow the imperialists to speak and act in the ways presented in the dominant historiographical narrative. If the imperialists tried at the outset to justify annexation on the grounds that it was the nation's duty to uplift, civilize, and carry out a plan of benevolent assimilation on tens of thousands of Japanese and Chinese workers, organized labor would have revolted against the Republicans and fled to the Democrats, and the effects on the party would have been disastrous. The president's actions in December 1897 indicate that at least one leading politician considered this possibility.

In his annual message, McKinley reaffirmed his support for the treaty and prodded Congress to act on it. The Hawaiian senate had ratified the treaty unanimously in September, he said, "and only awaits the favorable action of the American Senate to effect the complete absorption." The president was, by this time, clearly aware of the obstacles that stood in the policy's way, particularly those that involved the islands' Asian, native Hawaiian, and Portuguese majority. He told the legislative branch that it was up to it to determine the "political relation [of Hawaii] to the United States," the "quality and degree of the elective franchise of the inhabitants," and the "regulation of the labor system."[30]

These were perilous questions that McKinley was content and probably wise to leave at Congress's doorstep. The president cast the maneuver in a more flattering light, basing it, he said, on his faith in "the wisdom of Congress" and his confidence in its ability to ratify the treaty and, at the same time, address the race question: to—as McKinley put it—"avoid the abrupt assimilation of elements perhaps hardly yet fitted to share in the highest franchises of citizenship." Whatever Congress's plan might turn out to be, McKinley insisted that it provide Hawaii with "the most just provisions of self-rule in local matters with the largest political liberties as an integral part of our Nation" because, he said, "no less is due to a people who, after nearly five years of demonstrated capacity to fulfill the obligations of self-governing statehood, come of their free will to merge their destinies with our body-politic."[31]

Two points emerge from these statements; both reveal what had become the preferred strategy of the imperialists with regard to race. First, throughout this part of the address, we see that McKinley's first concern and greatest sympathy were with the white minority. As a politician, an imperialist, a Republican, and president of the United States, he knew that the whites' integrity, character, achievements, and racial identity provided the best case for annexation. Second, on nearly every key point McKinley attempted to remove the nonwhite majority from the debate. He knew that their presence would only be a source of trouble and injury to his cause. In asking Congress to bar the largest parts of the islands' population from "the highest franchises of citizenship" while allowing the Hawaiian government to maintain control over local matters, the president sought to sustain white dominance and the racial status quo in Hawaii. In calling on Congress to adjudicate the troublesome issues that touched on race, McKinley in effect asked it to ratify the treaty and annex the islands, while keeping the nonwhite majority at bay: while denying them, in other words, the rights of equal citizenship, the vote, and access to the domestic labor market. His reference to "nearly five years . . . of self-governing statehood" negated decades of native governance and erased the history and the presence of the native Hawaiians. Given the facts of the revolution, the Americans' role in it, and what followed, McKinley would not have counted the native people among those who came to the United States seeking annexation "of their free will." It was clear to everyone that only the whites had done this; indeed, at the time, they would have been considered the only group on the islands capable of pursuing such a goal. Only whites had "demonstrated the capacity" for self-government. Here was the critical distinction between the capable and the incapable, the assimilable and the incongruous. The president had all but declared that white rule was the necessary prerequisite for annexation.

Congress reconvened in January 1898 and debated the treaty in executive session. The imperialists believed that they were only a handful of votes short of the sixty that were needed for ratification.[32] This was too optimistic. Deliberations dragged on, and in February no signs were emerging that would indicate that any more senators were persuaded by the treaty's alleged virtues to move into the imperialist column. It was then that the events that took the United States into the war against Spain stole attention from Hawaii: the DeLome letter ridiculing President McKinley and the explosion of the USS *Maine* in Havana Harbor, Cuba, which killed more than 250 American sailors. Resistance in the Senate and the imminent war left the annexationists with little hope that they could win a two-thirds vote; as a result, they altered their strategy. Rather than press ahead with the treaty, changes were made so that the islands could be acquired by a joint resolution, a method that required only a simple majority in both houses of Congress to pass.

On March 16, 1898, the Senate Committee on Foreign Relations issued its report, supporting the joint resolution and recommending annexation.[33] All of the old and well-explored justifications appeared in the committee's report, with one significant difference. The Japanese threat had been moved to the top of the list of the committee's "reasons in favor of the annexation of Hawaii," ahead of justifications based on military and strategic advantages and the role they would play in advancing American trade in East Asia. The report was blunt in this respect: acquisition, it said, would "prevent the establishment of an alien and possibly hostile stronghold in a position commanding the Pacific coast and the commerce of the North Pacific." Further along it became more emphatic. The United States, it said, must act "NOW to preserve the results of its past policy, and to prevent the dominancy in Hawaii of a foreign people."[34] Here was the confluence of national defense and fear of the "yellow peril."

Easily the most remarkable aspect of this document arose out of the committee's attempt to confront the inescapable race issue, the questions that surrounded what it called "the character of population we will acquire from those islands." The committee followed the trajectory established by McKinley and others and justified annexation on the grounds of racial sympathy. The report proclaimed, "In all respects the white race in Hawaii are the equals [*sic*] of any community of like members and pursuits to be found in any country. The success they have achieved in social, religious, educational, and governmental institutions is established in results that are not dwarfed by a comparison with our most advanced communities."[35]

Whiteness was the critical motif of the Foreign Relations Committee's support. It stated that the islands' whites—the conjunction of Americans, Britons, Norwegians, Germans, French, and other nationalities—made up 22 percent of the total population: a minority but a significant one, in terms of numbers but in other ways as well. "These white people are so united in the support of good government," said the report, "that there is no political distinction of nationalities among them, and harsh differences of opinion on public questions are seldom found."[36] Whiteness was, then, their great common bond and at the same time the solvent that obliterated all less profound distinctions—nationality, religion, culture, ethnicity, language, and history.

Like Thurston, with whom it shared motivations and goals, this Senate committee counted the Portuguese in with the 22 percent, asserting that they "*are also recognized as white citizens*" (a judgment that would have certainly amazed and distressed Sanford Dole). The evidence of this was to be found in what the committee presented as the Portuguese's decidedly Anglo-Saxon qualities. The Portuguese, the report said, "are thrifty and law-abiding people," who had "intelligent conceptions of the value of liberty regulated by law." Also, their aesthetic sensibilities fit them into the category of white. Readers were told that "their homes are uniformly comfortable, and usually vine-clad and tasteful in their surroundings." Furthermore, according to the report, "their advancement in education and in the acquisition of substantial property is very marked since their arrival in Hawaii, and their desire to become citizens of the 'Great Republic' is very earnest."[37] Thus, whiteness had become so vital to the imperialists' cause in 1898 that they would invent it where, at another time in another place with another agenda, the Portuguese would have been cast—as they had already been in Hawaii—as the most debased of peoples and anything but "white."

This emphasis on the virtues of the white minority was only magnified by the comparisons the report made between them and the Asians and native Hawaiians. The Japanese were merely "coolies . . . collected from the lower classes," a "community of ignorant people" and a "dangerous element." Unlike the Portuguese, the Japanese, according to the committee report, were "not trustworthy as laborers, nor honest in their dealings as merchants." The committee was patronizing toward the Chinese, who were called "the most industrious and thrifty race that has come to Hawaii." The soft touch evidenced here—particularly when compared with what had been said about the Chinese previously in the Congress and in the popular and labor press—probably arose from the committee's perceiving them as relatively powerless and unthreatening, with respect to the aggressive Japanese and because, the report declared, they "evince[d] little desire to use the ballot, from which they are excluded." The native Hawaiians occupied the very bottom of the committee's regard.[38]

To its reckoning the only race capable of governing the islands and worthy of admission was the white, but its members required immediate aid, meaning annexation. "It is beyond question that, as a factor in government, the united white race is indispensable to the safety of the people of Hawaii," said the report. But then it continued, the whites "could not control the islands without the frequent presence, if not the constant attendance, of the warships of the United States and of the European powers," to hold the Japanese at bay. The absence of American control, the committee predicted, would undoubtedly lead to one of two catastrophes: the first would be the beginning of "civil strife and bloodshed . . . and would result in the rule of some white man as dictator"; the second, the more fearful, involved "a Japanese man-of-war . . . stationed at Honolulu" and "the capture of the islands by Japan."[39]

The committee dismissed the arguments put forth by the opponents of annexation as "minor objections" that had no "appreciable value" in comparison to the great advantages that would be gained by taking the islands. The benefits the committee referred to were not simply material, according to the report; annexation, it said, was "an imperative duty that we owe to Hawaii." The duty was an urgent one, made so by the "sudden influx of Asiatics," whose "increasing numbers [are] an ever present peril to Hawaii." Here, as before, America's obligations were portrayed in the language of family. Protecting the islands and annexation, the report said, "is a duty that has its origin in the noblest sentiments that inspire the love of the father for his children, or a country from its enterprising and honorable citizens, or a church for its missions and the heralds it has sent out with messages of deliverance to those pagans in darkness, or our Great Republic to a younger sister that has established law, liberty, and justice in that beautiful land that a corrupt monarchy was defiling with fraud . . . and dragging down to barbarism. We have solemnly assumed these duties and cannot abandon them without discredit."[40] The consequences of inaction or refusal were too great to disregard. "If we do not interpose to annex Hawaii or to protect her from the influx of Asiatics," the report concluded, the islands' whites "will soon be exterminated."[41]

The Foreign Relations Committee pushed for annexation by conjuring up an image of a Hawaii without Asians and free of native influence: a place both preserved and reserved in the future exclusively for the prosperity of whites. It imagined this picture quite vividly. The report spoke of the islands' fertility "and its abundant fisheries" being great enough to "insure a comfortable living to more than tenfold the present population." Indeed, it said, the "effort of the Republic to fill up the public domain with white people from the United States" had induced "a strong tide of such immigrants." "The climate, soil, and the agricultural products," the report insisted, "invite such immigrants." The last point would soon become a point of contention between the rival parties supporting and opposing annexation.[42]

On May 1, 1898, the U.S. Asiatic Squadron led by Commodore George Dewey attacked an outgunned and antiquated Spanish fleet in Manila Harbor, the Philippines. Dewey's victory was swift, complete, and cost only one American life. For the Hawaiian annexationists, the conflict came at a fortuitous moment, for the groundswell of nationalism, patriotism, and support for the war effort gave them a long-awaited and precious opportunity to secure their prize.

Three days after the battle, Congressman Francis Newlands of Nevada presented a resolution, almost identical to the one that had floundered so badly in the Senate, providing for the annexation of Hawaii. Two weeks later it emerged from the Committee on Foreign Affairs with the endorsement of the majority of its members. Politicians on both sides of the question realized that popular enthusiasm for the war and the people's intense desire to help American forces, regardless of the cost, gave the annexationists the upper hand. The resolution would pass easily in the House of Representatives if only it could come to a vote. When the anti-imperialist Republican Thomas B. Reed, the Speaker of the House and chairman of the Committee on Rules, tried to stop the resolution, fellow congressmen, party leaders, and the McKinley administration pressured him for three weeks until he finally bowed.[43] On June 2 newspapers published polls that revealed that majorities in both the House of Representatives and the Senate favored the resolution. Annexation would be a fact, they said, before Congress adjourned for the summer.[44]

The debates in the House of Representatives and the Senate were remarkably similar in language, content, and tenor. Both were run through with cliché, naked appeals to patriotism, speculations on the economic benefits of annexation and the need to uphold the Tyler and Monroe Doctrines, and the constitutionality of acquiring the islands. Neither debate broke much new ground. The *Congressional Record* reveals senators restating many of the arguments and observations that had been made by congressmen only days earlier. Indeed, in the majority of their often lengthy speeches, politicos in both houses repeated points made in 1870 and 1893, both for and against annexation.

The one unprecedented element in these deliberations was the war. The annexationists did everything they could to exploit the resurgence of patriotic feelings and the new "war spirit." References to the righteousness of the nation's cause, its humanitarianism, and the bravery of America's fighting men consistently drew applause in both chambers. Invoking Commodore Dewey had a similar rousing effect, and his name quickly became a metaphor for national defense, a strong navy, duty, and patriotism. Congressman Robert Hitt favored Hawaii's annexation because the war had showed the people the vulnerability of the Pacific coast. "There is no one in our country so recreant in his duty as an American," he said, "that he would refuse to support the president in succoring Dewey after his magnificent victory, lying in Manila Bay, holding in control the Spanish power there, but unable to land for want of reinforcements and surrounded by millions of Spanish subjects." "Yet," he declared, "it is impossible to send support to Dewey to-day without taking on coal and supplies at Honolulu in the Hawaiian Islands."[45]

In the Senate, John T. Morgan chastised his colleagues whose "fine, silken, glossy arguments about the Constitution" prevented the nation from effectively prosecuting the war. Morgan's first concern, he said, was with the welfare of the soldiers, and Hawaii was essential in order to provide them with both a supply line and a safe haven. "We shall presently be having wounded men and men sick with all manner of tropical diseases coming back from the Philippines . . . and Senators here on this floor [are] filibustering to prevent those men from having a friendly welcome and a landing under their own flag and their own country in Hawaii."[46] Voting against annexation was by implication unpatriotic, a betrayal of Dewey and thousands of American soldiers battling Spanish tyranny half a world away. The opponents of annexation protested what the imperialists were doing by conflating war and empire, by misleading the people, but it was an inadequate response.

Their opponents' best weapon was to play on the nation's racism and focus their attacks on the facts of the islands' racial composition. Congressman Hugh Dinsmore of Arkansas pointed to the "forty-two percent of the population of the island[s]" that was "Mongolian, Chinese, and Japanese." He accused the annexationists of doing violence to the Chinese Exclusion Acts with their resolution. "Are you to take into full citizenship the Chinese whom your laws exclude from coming to this country?" he demanded to know. "Are you going to confer upon them the immunities and privileges and sovereignty of American citizenship, when you say that they are not good enough even to come among us upon our own territory temporarily?"[47] Congressman Champ Clark of Missouri scolded the imperialists for, as he put it, laboring "under the delusion that in the twinkling of an eye any sort of human being, no matter how ignorant, vicious, or degraded, can be made worthy of American citizenship."[48]

The prospect that annexation would grant equal citizenship to "degraded" races and overwhelm the nation's racist structures and social status quo was the vital theme that ignited the anti-imperialists. Senator Justin Morrill of Vermont despised the chance of his nation being infected by the "undesirable character of the greater part of [the islands'] ill-gathered races of population." They were too many, said Morrill, and the whites—"less than 3 per cent of the present number of inhabitants of Hawaii are American in origin"—too few, "not enough to dominate or to boss the 97 per cent of other nationalities." The mass, he warned, though they were unacceptable, would expect to become "full-fledged citizens . . . entitled to share in governing the United States in both Houses of Congress." "To this," he declared, "I am irrevocably opposed."[49] Morrill, too, thought it absolutely necessary that the United States control Hawaii, but the racial obstacle was serious enough to make him call for a solution other than annexation, one that involved fewer burdens and would not imperil the United States. "We can be a friend," he said, "without taking them into our family."[50] Senator William Roach of North Dakota chose to taunt his rivals. To justify their stand the resolution's supporters must have convinced themselves, he said, "that the civilization of the United States would be improved by the infusion of . . . the Kanakas; that none of the lepers of that unhappy land would ever scatter leprosy in this country; that rescued from their poverty, they would make us all rich; the brightest star in the blue field of our flag would be that represented by the country of dusky ex-cannibals."[51]

Stephen White of California discoursed in the Senate chamber for four days against annexation; race was the point of departure for his most provocative objections. The nation's great strength, he said, was the result of the "homogeneity of the American people," a population uncorrupted by "the ignorant, venal, and savage, living far removed and alien to us in language and ideas." What, he inquired, could be gained by absorbing the Hawaiian majority? The native peoples, who were on the path toward extinction, he said, would make poor citizens: "Obliteration would come before [the Hawaiian] is qualified to be one of us. " Not only should the Hawaiians never be "elevated to the position of American citizenship," he said, "no country tenanted by incompetents should ever be acquired for permanent occupancy" by the United States. "Not every clime," he said, "not under every sun, not in the home of every race can the American citizen be found."[52]

White expanded on his racial objections by linking "the character of the population we will bring in by annexation" to the interests and prejudices of America's working classes. The Japanese population in the islands, numbering about 24,000, was not excluded under the imperialists' resolution, he said, and their numbers would certainly grow. "We exclude Chinese laborers," he said, "but we do not drive away those already there. Therefore the Asiatics in the islands will remain and Chinese and Japanese 'cheap labor' will be incorporated."[53] White was speaking to several constituencies here—unions and workers in all parts of the nation that had supported Chinese exclusion in the past—but he spoke especially to his fellow westerners. He wanted to persuade them of the dangers of annexation, to revive their anti-Chinese prejudice and impress it on Congress. "We assume to be fond of our laborers," said White, "and yet we design importing or forcing into this country, by extending our boundary, an element of competition with which our kindred can not possibly hope to compete."[54] He spoke most directly to his fellow politicians, Democrats and Republicans, who wanted labor's votes. White reminded them that "not very long ago the people of this country agitated the question of the restriction of immigration. It is but a few weeks since it was the subject of discussion in this Chamber. It is but a few years ago when it was almost provocative of a revolution upon the western coast of this country. We then objected to importing Mongolians by the shipload, and now, as remarked to me by a distinguished Senator, we propose to bring them in by the continent load."[55]

The annexationists did not engage their opponents directly on these arguments, nor did they contradict their foundational assumption—that Hawaii's nonwhites were unwanted in the United States both as workers and as citizens— nor did they speak, in the main, of the "white man's burden." The imperialists kept to their best arguments, beginning with the war. The nation was fighting on two oceans, and the resolution's friends believed, rightly, that their most powerful argument was that Hawaii must be taken as a war measure. Operations in the Philippines, they said, required that men and materials be transferred through those islands, an assertion that only magnified their strategic value. After the war, with the fear of the Asian "menace" all but proven, Hawaii would be the nation's first outpost in the defense of the Pacific coast. The imperialists knew from history, distant and recent, that racism acted on policies such as this one like a poison. So they ignored the taunts and refused to be bound to any rationale that would place a mass of humanity universally deemed undesirable at the center of their policy.

They did not, however, surrender the race issue to their adversaries. Whiteness and white racial brotherhood became a vital leitmotif of pro-resolution debate. Congressman Frederick Gillett of Massachusetts confessed to feeling "a special sympathy with these islands." Much of it had been engendered by memories of the first generation of missionaries who had gone there, men and women from his state. "After many days the bread they cast upon the waters is returning to us again," he proclaimed. Their descendants, declared the congressman, had rescued the islands for civilization, overthrew the "debauched monarchy," and built "a republic modeled on our own." This made annexation correct and just, according to Gillett, because Hawaii's white minority, who were asking "to return to our allegiance" and "share in the honor and protection of our flag," had beyond any doubt "show[n] their love for their native country."[56]

Congressman Robert Hitt raised his arguments from the same ground. He demanded to know from his colleagues: "Are you not as Americans proud of that little colony, the only true American colony, the only spot on earth beyond our boundaries in the wide world where our country is preferred above all others?" The chamber answered with thunderous applause.[57] Annexation was justified, to his reckoning, by the similarities—cultural, political, institutional, and racial—that bound the two countries together. Hawaii should be annexed for the sake of the "Caucasian element," Hitt said, that "strong intellectual and industrial force on the island . . . men sprung from our blood who have borne themselves with . . . enlightenment, courage, and energy . . . [applause], whose only fault is that they love our flag more than their own."[58]

Hitt and others demanded quick action from Congress through pleas that "the rapid growth of the Japanese element" threatened the islands' fundamentally white civilization. Hitt maintained that Tokyo was demanding equality for its citizens on the islands, pressuring Hawaii's government to allow it to "pour" in thousands more Japanese and "the right to demand for all Japanese any privileges or rights . . . which could include the right to vote or hold office." Tokyo's success would mean the end of white rule and civilization. Hawaii, he said, "would be converted into a Japanese commonwealth immediately."[59]

De Alva Alexander of New York ignored the nonwhite majority in his speech; it was, he said, the "Anglo-Saxon residents and their supporters" who were offering the islands to the United States "an extent of territory larger than Connecticut and Rhode Island combined." White racial sympathy made annexation desirable, to his reckoning, for the great extent of land he mentioned was "owned as well as governed," he said, "by a people who are bone of our bone and flesh of our flesh."[60] The alleged Japanese threat weighed on Alexander as heavily as anyone. The question, he said, was not only, "Shall we annex Hawaii[?]" but also, "Are we willing to allow some other nation to annex it[?]" Throughout 1896 and 1897, he observed, "the Japanese entered Hawaii at a rate of 2,000 per month, until now they number 25,000, or nearly one-quarter of the total population." If this went on unchecked, meaning if annexation failed, Alexander predicted that "soon the supremacy of Japan will be completed."[61] To Alexander's mind, then, racial duty in the name of preserving white civilization left no other option to the United States than to annex Hawaii.

The transformation of Senator George Frisbie Hoar of Massachusetts from staunch anti-imperialist, to imperialist, and back again to fierce anti-imperialist in the case of the Philippines further reveals the power of racial sympathy in the case of Hawaii. In his *Autobiography of Seventy Years*, Hoar recalled a meeting with President McKinley and a conversation that changed his mind about annexation. When Hoar told the president that he did not favor annexation, McKinley was taken aback. "I don't know what I shall do," the president said. "We cannot let those islands go to Japan," he told the senator; "Japan has her eye on them. Her people are crowding in there. I am satisfied that they do not go there voluntarily, as ordinary immigrants, but that Japan is pressing them in there in order to get possession before anybody can interfere. If something is not done, there will be before long another revolution and Japan will get control." That rival and predatory nation, he said finally, "is doubtless waiting for her opportunity."[62]

The exchange struck Hoar and compelled him to rethink his position. Thoughts of Hawaii's white founders and the predicament of their descendants had a peculiar effect on the senator's mind. They were, to Hoar, people much like himself, men and women from his state, more like neighbors than strangers living in a besieged paradise on the other side of the world. "American missionaries had redeemed the [native] people from barbarism and Paganism," he wrote; "Many of them, and their descendants, had remained on the Islands." Their efforts alone, Hoar believed, had created the government that he recognized as honorable and capable of creating a legitimate political contract with the United States. "By the Constitution of Hawaii, the Government had been authorized to make a treaty of annexation with this country," he said, while ignoring the tens of thousands who were disfranchised by that same document. Racial and cultural sympathy mattered more to this senator, who loathed the prospect of the islands falling into the orbit of Japan "not by conquest, but by immigration." The United States had to annex the islands, Hoar reasoned, out of duty, both racial and national, and "deliver them from this oriental menace."[63]

By pushing whiteness to the center of their case, congressional annexationists took up a disingenuous strategy, imitating Thurston by overinflating the white population's numbers and inventing whiteness around the Portuguese. Francis Newlands of Nevada was most blunt: "The whites in Hawaii consist of Americans, English, and Portuguese, all of whom can be easily assimilated." Similarly, when Congressman Hitt held up the "twenty to twenty-five thousand . . . people of European or American origin" as the best justification for seizing Hawaii, he proclaimed that the group was composed of "a good many Germans, British, and a large number of Portuguese."[64]

Those who wanted to make the Portuguese white insisted that their decades on the islands had worked a transformation. They had learned American ways, embraced its culture, and adapted to its institutions. More than half of the population counted in the 1896 census had been born on the islands and educated in the schools there, which, Hitt told his fellow congressmen, "are similar to the schools here." The children had leaned to speak "English as an ordinary American child." They had also picked up other "white" qualities, such as the aversion or immunity to certain diseases. Leprosy, supposedly brought to the islands by the Chinese, was, said the congressman, "a malady that rarely affects people of the Caucasian race of the better class, who use an abundance of soap and water." Hitt announced that there was "little or no leprosy" among the Portuguese, which made them like other "clean, [and] highly civilized people anywhere."[65] Congressman Alexander counted 21,000 "Anglo-Saxons, Germans, Scandinavians, and Portuguese" among those groups "with whom we are familiar, to whom we do not object, and among whom we live and associate, without a thought that they are not homogeneous and desirable."[66] Charles Pearce of Missouri declared that, by joining the Portuguese to the islands' British, German, and American communities, "the percentage of intelligence at the present time among these elements is as large as that which exists in any of the new sections of our country."[67]

The annexationists pressed their cause further by arguing that the passage of time would certainly witness the increase of the white population and expansion of white control over the islands. They maintained that the objectionable elements of the present population would only decrease, that some would disappear utterly, making only more room for white settlement. The "Kanakas" were "gradually becoming extinct," said Congressman Newlands, and the Chinese and Japanese had come there only as contract laborers. The overwhelming majority of these emigrants were men, few had brought their families, and most of them, Newlands assured the country, remained "devoted to their own country" and intended to return someday. "The existing Mongolian population, therefore, will necessarily be withdrawn," he said, "and under wise exclusion laws there will be none to take its place." Hitt asserted that the "Asiatics would rapidly disappear in numbers under the operation of our laws," eliminating contract labor and enforcing the restriction acts.[68] Congressman Alexander suggested that the Chinese would probably leave Hawaii voluntarily since they were only there "to accumulate . . . a few hundred dollars" while looking forward to the day when "the steamer shall return them to their own people and homes." Within ten years, he continued, there would be just a handful of Asians left on the islands, and the few who remained would be found "washing the dirty linen of a superior and more prosperous people."[69]

The enemies of annexation rejected these predictions: first, out of their own prejudices; and second, because they, like many others, thinking Hawaii tropical, embraced the ancient conviction that whites withered in hot places. Champ Clark said that if any valuable lands had escaped the sugar barons' greed, "they are not fit for our children and other white people of our breed, for the all-sufficient reason that they can not endure outdoor work in that sultry climate." John Bell of Colorado asserted that there was not one example in all of history where a white civilization thrived in a tropical zone. "The American civilization, the European civilization, is an incarnation of the temperate zone. It cannot exist anywhere else," he contended. Bell concurred that the white race was incapable of laboring successfully in Hawaii: "It will take two or three generations before you get one [white man] that will stand that climate. And when you get that type you will get a type but little better than the native himself." Bell continued, "I want to say that the entire cultivation of Hawaii today is [done] by Asiatic labor. You may speculate about the American people Americanizing Cuba, Americanizing Puerto Rico, Americanizing the Philippine Islands, but it is a mere dream. It can never be. And I hope to God the day will never come when we shall have a single foot of tropical climate within the bounds of the exemplary Government." In the Senate, Richard Pettigrew of South Dakota said that because of its tropical temperatures Hawaii was no place for Americans, as history had already proven. He observed that although the islands had been open to the United States since 1875, very few Americans had been drawn to them. "The population of Americans in the islands [had] not increased materially under this wonderful influence," he said, referring to reciprocity, because "the climate had no attraction for them."[70]

For many, the emergence of the United States as an imperial power was a moment for celebration unfettered by conscience. For others, the events that led up to the acquisition—the years of nasty inter- and intraparty battles, rumors of corruption, back-room politics, and eccentric diplomatic maneuvers —would, as the *Boston Transcript* predicted, "soil the pages of American history." But the newspaper also held out hope that the nation's honor might still be restored "by stopping where we are and dealing with our new and strangely acquired trust in a spirit of highest patriotism, altruism, and honesty." Many, like this newspaper, feared that Hawaii was not the end but rather the precursor to more, and even more distant, annexations, "a powerful fulcrum for our insatiate world lifters." The *Springfield Republican* saw lying beyond the joint resolution a "larger plan of imperialism, of which the taking of Hawaii forms only a part, and a comparatively small part." The first step was important, said the *Republican*, because "it lends an easiness to the next," but the newspaper was hopeful and certain "that the second line of defense [against imperialism] . . . will prove stronger than the first line." Several leaders in the Senate who had supported Hawaii's annexation had announced, directly after that vote, and anticipating a movement to seize the Philippines, that they would not go further. "The senior Massachusetts senator [Hoar] voted for the Hawaiian resolution, but declares his opposition to further distant annexations. The senior Alabama senator [Morgan] has been a leader in the Hawaiian scheme, but says he is opposed to going so far as the Philippines. Other examples can be cited to the same effect," said the newspaper. "It is accordingly with great hope of success that the anti-imperialists fall back into their second line of intrenchments [sic]."[71]

At first the *Republican*'s optimism appeared sound and well reasoned. It noted correctly that there were what it called "peculiar influences bolstering up the Hawaiian conspiracy which will be absent from the support of other schemes of annexation."[72] The accrual of history, policy, religion, commerce, and institutions that, over the course of a half century, justified and rationalized annexation did not exist for the United States and the Philippines. There were no sugar interests whose representatives would lobby interested (and occasionally corruptible) senators, nor was there an annexation commission from Manila rushing to Washington, D.C. There was certainly no racial sympathy, shared Anglo-Saxon blood, or "outposts of American civilization" in jeopardy to be romanticized. Nevertheless, the war was still on. Politicians, the press, and the people would speculate about the future all through the summer of 1898, but nothing could be known for certain until the conflict was over. Only then would the nation decide what would be done with the Philippines.

NOTES

1. Ethel M. Damon, *Sanford Ballard Dole and His Hawaii* (Palo Alto, Calif.: Pacific Books, 1957), 332.

2. "Hawaii Annexed," *Public Opinion*, July 14, 1898, 41.

3. *Foreign Relations of the United States, 1894* (Washington, D.C.: U.S. Government Printing Office, 1895), app. 2, 39.

4. Charles Francis Adams, ed., *Memoirs of John Quincy Adams*, 12 vols. (Philadelphia: J. B. Lippincott and Co., 1874–77), 11:275.

5. William Marcy to David L. Gregg, April 4, 1854, *Foreign Relations of the United States, 1894*, app. 2, 128.

6. Ralph S. Kuykendall, *Hawaiian Kingdom* (Honolulu: University of Hawaii Press, 1938), 410; James D. Richardson, ed., *Compilation of the Messages and Papers of the Presidents*, 11 vols. (New York: Bureau of National Literature, 1897), 6:2731–32.

7. Larry Gara, *Presidency of Franklin Pierce* (Lawrence: University Press of Kansas, 1991), 147; Roy Franklin Nichols, *Franklin Pierce* (Philadelphia: University of Pennsylvania Press, 1931), 393–99; Henry Barrett Learned, *William Learned Marcy, Secretary of State* (1929), 6.

8. Burke A. Hinsdale, ed., *Works of James Abram Garfield*, 2 vols. (Boston: James R. Osgood and Co., 1893), 2:320, 322; *Congressional Record*, 44th Cong., 1st sess., 2273.

9. Kuykendall, *Hawaiian Kingdom*, 75, 76.

10. James Comly to James G. Blaine, February 14, 1881, in *Foreign Relations of the United States, 1882* (Washington, D.C.: Government Printing Office, 1893), 620.

11. Blaine to Comly, December 1, 1881, in *Political Discussions*, ed. James G. Blaine (Norwich, Conn.: Henry Bill Publishing Co., 1887), 395; *Foreign Relations of the United States, 1894*, app. 2, 1159–60.

12. John L. Stevens to John Foster, November 20, 1892, in *Foreign Relations of the United States, 1894*, app. 2, 377, 381.

13. Thomas J. Osborne, *"Empire Can Wait": American Opposition to Hawaiian Annexation, 1893–1898* (Kent, Ohio: Kent State University Press, 1981), 2; Julius Pratt, *Expansionists of 1898* (Gloucester, Mass.: Peter Smith, 1959), 119; Sylvester Stevens, *American Expansion in Hawaii* (Harrisburg, Pa.: Archives Publishing Co., 1945), 232–34. All terms brought to the negotiations by the Hawaiian delegation appear in *Foreign Relations of the United States, 1894*, app. 2, 235–36; see also Michael J. Devine, *John W. Foster* (Athens: Ohio University Press, 1981), 66–67; and George W. Baker, "Benjamin Harrison and Hawaiian Annexation," *Pacific Historical Review* 33 (August 1964): 295–316.

14. *The Nation*, February 9, 1893.

15. A survey of newspapers appears in the *New York Times*, February 2, 1893.

16. A survey of newspapers appears in the *New York Herald*, February 8, 1893.

17. Carl Schurz, "Manifest Destiny," *Harper's New Monthly Magazine*, October 1893, 742.

18. *New York Evening Post*, February 8, 1893.

19. *New York Herald*, February 16, 1893.

20. *New York Times*, January 31, 1893.

21. "Senator Morgan's Views," *New York Times*, February 3, 1893.

22. *Southern Workman*, February 22, 1893.

23. Stevens, *American Expansion in Hawaii*, 271–72.

24. David Healy, *U.S. Expansionism* (Madison: University of Wisconsin Press, 1970), 53.

25. Sons of the American Revolution, *An Address by the Hawaiian Branch of the Sons of the American Revolution, Sons of Veterans, and the Grand Army of the Republic to their Compatriots in America Concerning the Annexation of Hawaii* (Washington, D.C.: Gibson Brothers, 1897), 5–8.

26. Lorrin Thurston, *A Handbook on the Annexation of Hawaii* (St. Joseph, Mich.: A. B. Morse, 1897), 3–8.

27. Ibid., 3–8.

28. *Public Opinion*, June 24, 1897, 771–73; July 1, 1897, 5–6.

29. "Should Hawaii Be Annexed?" *American Federationist* (March 1897): 216.

30. Richardson, *Compilation of the Messages and Papers of the Presidents*, 10:38, 39.

31. Ibid., 10:39.

32. Stevens, *American Expansion in Hawaii*, 293.

33. U.S. Senate, Committee on Foreign Relations, *Annexation of Hawaii*, Senate Report no. 681, 55th Cong., 2d sess., 1897–99.

34. Ibid., 27–31.

35. Ibid., 10.

36. Ibid.

37. Ibid., 11.

38. Ibid.

39. Ibid., 12, 13.

40. Ibid., 15.

41. Ibid.

42. Ibid.

43. Ernest R. May, *Imperial Democracy* (Chicago: Imprint Publications, 1991), 243.

44. William Robinson, *Thomas B. Reed, Parliamentarian* (New York: Dodd, Mead and Co., 1930), 366–67.

45. *Congressional Record*, 55th Cong., 2d sess., 5772.

46. Ibid., 6344.

47. Ibid., 5778.

48. Ibid.

49. Ibid., 6144.

50. Ibid., 6141.

51. Ibid., 6357.

52. Ibid., 614.

53. Ibid., 617.

54. Ibid.

55. Ibid.

56. Ibid., 5783.

57. Ibid., 5773, 5774.

58. Ibid., 5773.

59. Ibid., 5774.

60. Ibid., 5786.

61. Ibid., 5785, 5786.

62. George Frisbie Hoar, *Autobiography of Seventy Years*, 2 vols. (London: Bickers and Son, 1904), 2:306, 307, 308,

63. Ibid., 2:308.

64. *Congressional Record*, 55th Cong., 2d sess., 5775.

65. Ibid., 5774, 5775.

66. Ibid., 5778.

67. Ibid., 5896.

68. Ibid., 5775.

69. Ibid., 5787.

70. Ibid., 5789, 5883, 6260.

71. "Hawaii Annexed," *Public Opinion*, July 14, 1898, 41.

72. Ibid.

Annexing the Other

The World's Peoples as Auxiliary
Consumers and Imported Workers, 1876–1917

MATTHEW FRYE JACOBSON

A turn-of-the-twentieth-century advertising card for Singer sewing machines depicted a grass-skirted Pacific "native" busily working a modern sewing machine inside a grass hut. Here was the American reverie in its crystalline form: the foreigner as both a reliable consumer and an industrious worker. Throughout the period from the 1870s to World War I, American politicians and manufacturers feared that the engines of industry could not be slowed without undermining the nation's stability, but also that, at its accustomed pace of production, the nation risked outstripping its own capacities to absorb its goods. This dual anxiety cast foreigners in a corresponding dual role: foreign peoples would keep the American economy afloat as both auxiliary consumers in a vast, worldwide export market and as auxiliary workers in an ever-expanding domestic labor market. National well-being depended on the grass-skirted native's willingness both to purchase the sewing machine and take up the needle trades.

The two sides of this economic saga—the necessary export of goods and the necessary import of workers—generated a strange, Janus-faced ideology of dependency and scorn that profoundly influenced the temper of American nationalism and indeed the very notion of "Americanness" in this period. Various "natives" and "savages" abroad were blithely tarred as inferiors and identified as prime candidates for a brand of "uplift" that entailed, among other things, a strict lesson in modern modes of desire and habits of consumption. They were also reviled for their failure to need U.S. products—shoes, clothing, textiles, machinery—quite as much as the U.S. economy seemed to need their business. Similarly, the soaring numbers of diverse immigrants at home were welcomed for their labor power and yet resented for the economic competition they represented, as well as for the element of "difference" they introduced to the society. In both cases, the deep American dependence on these foreign peoples seems to have fueled the animus against them. Americans may have been wont to hold the Pacific native, the African or Latin American savage, the East European greenhorn, or the Chinese sojourner at arm's length, but emergent economic circumstances had set the nation in a rather tenacious embrace of precisely these unassimilated peoples. Their engagement in U.S. economic growth as theoretical consumers and as actual workers had much to do with the kind of industrial society the United States was becoming; their perceived backwardness and inferiority had everything to do with the way American identity had come to be understood.

The United States' spectacular economic growth at the turn of the twentieth century was attended by an equally spectacular pattern of downturns and failures: nearly half of the years between 1870 and World War I were depression years: 1873–79, 1882–85, 1893–97, 1907–8, and 1913–15. One mainstay of economic discussion throughout these years was fevered talk of "overproduction" and the need to secure foreign markets. Economic depression, in this formulation, was a sign not of capitalism's failure but of its stunning and unabsorbed success: the wheels of industry were simply churning out more goods than Americans could hope to consume themselves, and so other markets would have to be sought and secured. In the 1870s Commander Robert Shufeldt, long interested in opening the "Hermit Kingdom" of Korea to American interests, had put the matter most starkly: "At least one-third of our mechanical and agricultural products are now in excess of our wants, and we must *export* these products or *deport* the people who are creating them."[1] "Our manufacturers have outgrown or are outgrowing the home market," concurred the National Association of Manufacturers (NAM) in an atmosphere of crisis in the mid-1890s; "expansion of our foreign trade is the only promise of relief."[2]

But whether or not "overproduction" was the proper frame for understanding the boom and bust of the Gilded Age and Progressive Era economy (many economists today question it), whether or not foreign markets indeed held the key to national prosperity, it is true that this period marked a dramatic shift in the balance of U.S. trade. The years 1876 through 1880 represented the first time in U.S. history when the country had a positive balance of trade for five consecutive years. This was not an aberration but a watershed: before 1876, there were only fourteen years in which the nation's exports exceeded its imports; between 1876 and the 1970s, there were only three years (1888, 1889, and 1893) in which they did not. As a quick measure of the rise in U.S. productivity in these years, the nation's gross national product for the five-year period 1869–73 was $9 billion; for the five-year period 1897–1901, it was over $37 billion. Gross farm product, too, nearly tripled between the Civil War and the turn of the century.

Agricultural products and textiles led the way in the United States' significant shift toward becoming an exporting rather than an importing nation. New technologies of cultivation and harvest and the opening of new lands after the 1860s dramatically increased the nation's overall agricultural production. Cotton production nearly doubled between 1870 and 1890, for instance; wheat production increased by over 30 percent in the decade of the 1870s alone. Both crops accounted for a huge proportion of the nation's exports. But by the 1890s, even manufactured goods ran in this direction. In 1880 agricultural items accounted for 84 percent of all U.S. exports; just after the turn of the century, that figure had fallen to about 67 percent, as minerals, ore, and manufactured goods gained ground. Interest in the export market was especially sharp among oil producers: by the mid-1880s, Standard Oil shipped over 90 percent of its kerosene abroad (70 percent to Europe, and another 21 percent to Asia). U.S. exports overall climbed by fits and starts throughout this period, from $526 million in 1876 to over $1 billion per year by the late 1890s; exports continued to climb steadily, reaching $2 billion for the first time in 1911, and jumping to $5, $6, and $7 billion per year during the war years of 1916–19. Although the export market continued to receive only a fraction of the foodstuffs and goods that the domestic market absorbed, the trends were still impressive. As of 1893, only Great Britain's exports exceeded those of the United States.

Notwithstanding the dissent of some labor leaders and others, over the later decades of the nineteenth century a formidable consensus did develop on the overproduction thesis and the need for foreign markets. A series of articles by economist David Wells in 1887 and 1888 (later published under the title *Recent Economic Changes and Their Effects on the Production and Distribution of Wealth and the Well-Being of Society*) presented a cyclical economic theory and analysis whose chief solutions included market penetration abroad. Charles Arthur Conant, Washington correspondent for the *New York Journal of Commerce* and a financial editor of *Banker Magazine*, also concluded that sustained domestic productivity and global expansion were the only means to maintain both labor's wages and capital's profits. Industrialists like Andrew Carnegie quickly agreed that export to foreign markets was the only feasible way of alleviating the surplus.

Business and financial organs and organizations like *Banker Magazine*, *Bradstreet's*, the American Banking Association, and the National Association of Manufacturers all became outspoken advocates of export trade as the new panacea for the nation's woes of overproduction. The constituency that coalesced around the overproduction thesis ultimately included not only business and finance but also the conservative press and importantly placed politicians and State Department figures. President Grover Cleveland emphasized the need to "find markets in every part of the habitable globe"; William Day, assistant secretary of state under William McKinley, commented enthusiastically on the "vast undeveloped fields of African and the Far East."[3]

The policy implications of the overproduction thesis were clearly spelled out by military and economic theorists like Alfred Thayer Mahan and Brooks Adams. In *The Influence of Sea Power upon History* (1890), Mahan linked the nation's growing agricultural and industrial productivity to the need for a modern navy that could protect the commercial fleet and control the waterways. The only choices the United States faced, in his view, were either to absorb American products at home through some "socialistic" mechanism or to find new markets for American goods across the seas. Mahan anticipated Frederick Jackson Turner's notion of a new national order in the post-"frontier" era. The seas now constituted the frontier, a vast safety valve to drain off the nation's surplus production. In Mahan's view, production, shipping, and colonization (in that order) constituted the mainsprings of historic activity among powerful, seagoing nations. Control of the seas was the key to controlling the nation's economic fate in a period of overproduction.

Brooks Adams, too, started with the premise of overproduction and, like Mahan, ended with a dramatic series of policy initiatives. As he put it in *America's Economic Supremacy* (1900), the United States "stands face to face with the gravest conjuncture that can confront a people. She must protect the outlets of her trade, or run the risk of suffocation." Without significant changes in economic and administrative arrangements, the United States could conceivably suffer gluts "more dangerous to her society than many panics such as 1873 and 1893." In a frankly Darwinian discussion under the subhead "The New Struggle for Life among Nations," Adams warned, "On the existence of this surplus hinges the future." He thus advocated a policy of territorial expansion and administrative concentration ("for governments are simply huge corporations in competition"), including consolidating the West Indies under U.S. control, vigorously maintaining "Asiatic markets," and building an isthmian canal as a key to traffic and communication within this emergent trade empire. "If America is destined to win this battle for life," he argued, "she must win because she is the fittest to survive under the conditions of the twentieth century."[4]

The newly energetic quest for markets would not only cast the American government in an increasingly active role but would also have tremendous implications for those regions that represented the target of such economic aspiration. According to Africa enthusiast Henry Sanford, for instance, President Chester A. Arthur was "influenced by the idea of covering those unclad millions [in Africa] with our domestic cottons." In 1883 Sanford cultivated interest in

Washington in the notion of an African International Association under the sponsorship of Belgium's King Leopold II, and the United States did participate in the Berlin Conference on the development of the Congo in 1884–85.[5] Finally, the African market proved far less important for American exporters than either Latin America or Asia—or, indeed, than the cherished image of those naked millions might have promised—but it is no small matter that, as early as the 1880s, the United States had joined the colonial powers of Europe at the conference table on the topic of "developing" the Congo. Increasingly, whether by informal means of economic penetration or by more overt methods of territorial aggrandizement by conquest or treaty, the American quest for new markets would lead down the road of empire.

Taken together, China and Latin America nicely demonstrate two distinct dimensions of the imperial imagination that necessarily attended the "overproduction" thesis of American economic health and stability. The story of the United States in China illumines the realm of imperialist fantasy, as the fondest hopes of exporters reduced the whole of Chinese history and culture to a series of "wants" whose particulars were as easily discerned by the Western eye as they were fulfilled by Western industry. The story of the United States in Latin America, on the other hand, illumines the realm of pure imperial power and its deployment, as policymakers annexed entire nations, not only as consumers of North American goods, but as elements in a strategic infrastructure for an export economy whose requirements included canals, harbors, coaling stations, and naval bases all beyond the proper borders of the nation itself.

The China clipper was our Parthenon, wrote historian Samuel Eliot Morison. The idea that China and the China market held some special significance for the United States has a long and varied history. As early as 1791, Alexander Hamilton had declared that India and China together represented an "extensive field for the enterprise of our merchants and mariners [and] an additional outlet for the commodities of the country." In 1882, as he vetoed congressional immigration measures, Chester Arthur noted that, though continued Chinese immigration posed a hazard to the republic, it was linked to American opportunity in the East, "the key to national wealth and influence," and therefore forbearance was required on Americans' part. By the time the United States had annexed Hawaii and was asserting hegemony over the Philippines (the "stepping-stones to China") at the turn of the twentieth century, it had become axiomatic among manufacturers, economic theorists, diplomats, and politicians that China was crucial to America's future. When they spoke of attaining foreign markets as a salve to the crisis of overproduction, that is, it was often China that they had in mind.[6]

Indeed, once continental expansion was complete, the idea of China, if not the vast country itself, became annexed to American dreams of continued territorial "progress." As one cotton manufacturer put it in an 1899 address, the government should protect and extend "our interests in what was once the old Far East or what is now our new Far West."[7] The intertwining themes of American expansiveness and the China market constituted a powerful formulation. As Brooks Adams observed in 1900, "From the earliest times, China and India seem to have served as the bases of human commerce; the seat of empire having always been the point where their products have been exchanged against the products of the West."[8] The Chinese question was no less than "the great problem of the future," and East Asia, "the prize for which all energetic nations are grasping."[9]

American interest in the boundless China market peaked in the 1890s. This rise owed in part to domestic events and the nation's psychic economy during the decade. The Census Bureau's announcement that the nation's western frontier had "closed," a demographic interpretation endorsed and popularized by historian Frederick Jackson Turner in "The Significance of the Frontier in American History" (1893), lent new urgency to the decades-old web of concerns regarding overproduction, stagnation, discontent, radicalism, and the cure-all of foreign markets. The severe depression of 1893, moreover, along with the precipitant increase in labor agitation and class violence in places like Homestead, Pennsylvania, heightened anxiety and raised the stakes of discovering an economic salve, which, for many, could only mean finding new markets for American goods of all sorts.

It was in the 1890s, too, that Americans cast an eye nervously to China to keep watch over the increasingly aggressive activity of their economic rivals in the region. If domestic unrest and the symbolic blow of the closing of the frontier seemed to increase the stakes of capturing the China market, the international scene added urgency. In the Sino-Japanese War of 1894, Japan triumphed in its bid to wrest control of Korea from a terribly overmatched and outgunned Chinese army. The German seizure of Kiaochow and a scramble among Japan, Germany, France, Great Britain, and Russia for railroad and mining concessions in China throughout the late 1890s—culminating in the Russo-Japanese War in 1904—quickly gave shape to a "spheres of influence" arrangement that threatened vivisection of historic Chinese territories. Though many Americans did not at all regret the modernizing influence this would have over China, they did tend to worry over the prospect of securing their own "sphere." In this context, organs like the *Journal of Commerce* urged the State Department to devote more energy and resources to the protection of U.S. interests in China.

Around the same time that the specialized interests of the *Journal of Commerce* and the American Asiatic Association (AAA) were making their wishes known, the China question entered popular American consciousness through the back door, as it were, during the Spanish-Cuban-American War and the subsequent U.S. war in the Philippines. In the spring of 1898, few Americans would have guessed that a war with Spain in the Caribbean over the political fate of Cuba would end with a heightened U.S. military presence in the Pacific and East Asia. But when Admiral George Dewey routed the Spanish fleet in the Philippines, in what began as a more modest effort to impede its progress to the Caribbean theater, new questions suddenly arose regarding U.S. interests and rights in Asia itself. What would become of Spain's former colonies—not only Cuba and Puerto Rico, but the Philippines, too—in the wake of U.S. victory? What would be the relationship between U.S. "liberators" and members of the Filipino independence movement, who, like their counterparts in Cuba, had been fighting Spain side by side with American forces?

The heady glow of victory in this "splendid little war," as Secretary of State John Hay termed it, and the long-standing interest in capturing Asian markets sealed the question in American debate. Despite a vocal anti-imperialist movement in the United States, and despite the Filipinos' resolve to drive their American "liberators" from the archipelago by force of arms if necessary, the drift of American opinion and the direction of administration policy favored a continued and powerful U.S. presence in Asia and the Pacific. The United States now annexed Hawaii, too, after decades of raising and dropping the plan. But China and the China market provided motive for all of this: interest in the Philippines themselves was rarely held up in American discussion as the chief motive for Philippine conquest. Rather, the archipelago would serve as a "stepping-stone" to the China market, just as Hawaii would be a critical way station for U.S. naval traffic.

Even with an outpost in the Philippines, however, the United States lacked the geographical advantages of Japan and Russia. And compared with the colonial powers of France, Germany, and Great Britain, the United States was coming to Asia rather late in the game. The solution to such practical problems was announced in September 1899, in John Hay's so-called Open Door Notes: "Earnestly desirous to remove any cause of irritation," the Unites States here proposed to "the various powers claiming 'spheres of interest' that they shall enjoy perfect equality of treatment for their commerce and navigation within such 'spheres.'"[10] In this spirit, Hay requested formal assurances from the interested powers that they would not interfere in treaty ports or leased territories, that the Chinese government would continue to levy and collect duties in all ports, and that harbor dues and railroad charges would be consistent for all nations operating in the region. The "Open Door Notes" thus represented no mere codification of long-standing U.S. policy in China: in enlisting support for that policy among the other leading powers, Hay sought to turn U.S. foreign policy into international policy. The Open Door was particularly well suited to U.S. needs and to the existing balance of power in the area: it precluded a direct confrontation with the other powers and yet did away with the economic disadvantages the United States might have suffered by lacking a "sphere" to call its own. The notes thus represent an imperialistic economics in the guise of anticolonialism. (In true colonial fashion, it is worth noting, Hay neglected to consult with China before issuing the notes.) In conversation with an adviser some years later, he insisted on the anticolonial dimension of the Open Door policy, even as his language and his syntax betrayed its imperialist assumptions: "We have done the Chinks a great service," he declared, "which they don't seem inclined to recognize."[11]

If a potential confrontation with Japan and the European powers was one problem the United States faced in its quest for a piece of the China market—and one that, for the time, Hay was able to finesse—monumental Chinese "ingratitude" was yet a second. Like the other colonizers in Chinese territories, whose missionary activities and scramble for spheres and concessions were exerting great force on Chinese society, the United States confronted powerful currents of antiforeign sentiment among the Chinese themselves and a stubborn Chinese insistence on adhering to familiar ways. The greatest single outburst of Chinese antiforeignism in the period was the Boxer Uprising, the dramatic armed rising of a patriotic society devoted to driving unwanted foreigners out of China. Among the symbols of the foreign presence singled out for attack were missionaries and mission properties, foreign legations, and tokens of the Western technological presence like railroads and telegraph lines. The Boxers tore up segments of the Tientsin-Peking Railway, downed communication lines, isolated Peking from outside communications and contact, killed the German minister and a member of the Japanese legation, and held the foreign legations under siege for three weeks in the summer of 1900. An allied force, including several thousand U.S. soldiers, was dispatched to relieve the legations and to put down the rising. The siege ended on August 14, after twenty-five days.[12]

Through all of this, the Americans' overriding aim was to "preserve Chinese territorial and administrative entity, protect all rights guaranteed to friendly powers by treaty and international law, and safeguard for the world the principle of equal and impartial trade with all parts of the Chinese Empire"—in short, to keep the Open Door ajar, notwithstanding the fierce antiforeignism of some of the Chinese themselves.[13] This powerful antiforeignism found further outlet in the revolutionary activities of leaders like Sun Yat-sen in the early years of the new century. The growing Chinese nationalist sensibility was one among many factors that caused American interest in the China market to cool considerably after the turn of the century.

Many businessmen, however, had begun to recognize the limitations of the market in other respects—regardless of the hundreds of millions of potential customers involved—due to the actual purchasing power of the Chinese, their inclinations as consumers, and the difficulties presented by the country's weak commercial infrastructure. As the U.S. consul general in Hong Kong had written in 1899, "99 percent of China is still closed to the world. When the magazine writer refers in glowing terms to the 400,000,000 inhabitants of China, he forgets that 350,000,000 are a dead letter so far as commerce is concerned."[14] Some American politicians, too, now questioned earlier myths of the China trade. In a 1907 article titled "The Awakening of China," Teddy Roosevelt lauded the strides in modernization and education, and the increased commercial and industrial activity, in China, but in general he was unwilling to challenge Japanese hegemony in the region after the Russo-Japanese War of 1904. Unlike many of his predecessors, Roosevelt concluded that China did not rank as terribly significant among the many foreign interests of the United States.[15]

Still, propaganda as to the vast potential of the China market would not abate altogether in some quarters. Although the 1890s may have been the high-water mark of U.S. interest in and hope for the export trade in China—the myth at its most potent—such interest did not vanish altogether. The NAM retained a vivid interest, as did the AAA, which even in the wake of the Boxer Uprising saw the U.S. thrust into East Asia as being "in obedience to the call of manifest destiny."[16] Throughout this entire period, from William Seward's early vision of ushering China into the "modern" world to the AAA's tenacious view that the Far East should properly represent the United States' Far West, the magic that the China market worked on the American imagination owed largely to the sheer numbers involved. "In China there are four hundred millions of people," exclaimed one business journal, "more than five times as many as exist in the United States. The wants of these four hundred million people are increasing every year. What a market!"[17] The notion of feeding, clothing, and otherwise outfitting those millions was enough to drive decades-long discussions of China's economic significance, even in the face of the contrary realities of actual trade figures and Chinese people's actual indifference to American habits of consumption and modes of dress. *If only* they could be converted to wheat instead of rice. *If only* they could be persuaded to adopt middle-class American standards of attire and a civilized sense of the requisites of a proper, well-appointed wardrobe.

But if their numbers were too impressive for American manufacturers and merchants to get out of their minds, the Chinese themselves—with their customs and habits, their way of life, and their apparent pride in "isolation" from the civilized West—posed a real problem as potential customers. Ultimately, the question of the China market would rest not on the number of zeros in the country's population figures but on the people's desires—their "wants," not as the likes of Josiah Strong defined them, but as they themselves defined them. And if missionaries and other Western observers frequently commented on how much the Chinese seemed to need, so did they rather humbly acknowledge how little the Chinese seemed to *want*.

As far back as the early nineteenth century, American traders had complained of Chinese traditionalism and the culture's consequent disregard for Western styles and goods. The Chinese were "hostile to all improvement," merchant Ebenezer Townsend had concluded. "If the world were like the Chinese, we should yet have worn fig-leaves."[18] Among the traits commonly attributed to the Chinese in early merchants' and missionaries' accounts were torpidity, a remarkable fondness for stasis, whose underside was an equally remarkable resistance to innovation and change, and a stubborn scientific and technological backwardness. These secular traits corresponded roughly to what missionaries meant by the phrase "children of darkness." Among the traits cataloged in the missionary Arthur Smith's chapter-by-chapter summary of *Chinese Characteristics* (1900) were "Economy," "Conservatism," and "Indifference to Comfort and Convenience"—none of which boded particularly well for merchants or manufacturers hoping to entice the Chinese with a cornucopia of modern conveniences. Indeed, it was symptomatic, as far as Smith was concerned, that Chinese clothing had no pockets—no natural place to carry "a pocket-comb, a folding foot-rule, a cork-screw, a boot-buttoner, a pair of tweezers, a minute compass, a folding pair of scissors, a pin-ball, a pocket-mirror, . . . a fountain pen," or other such appointments that any middle-class Victorian would likely require. He also noted darkly that the merchandise in Chinese shops seemed never to move.[19] That the rising culture of consumption could not engulf and colonize China as easily as it could the American hinterland became proof of Chinese inferiority and backwardness.

Thus, if U.S. hopes for China were never realized, if U.S. influence in the region was never what diverse actors like William Seward, John Hay, or the businessmen of the NAM had dreamed of, the history of the United States in China in this period—and the history of China in the popular American imagination—is still a history of imperialist ideology par excellence. It involved the impulse to reform a population to suit U.S. needs (or, short of that, to dismiss that population as inferior); it involved making decisions that affected huge numbers of people on the ground in Asia on the basis of American and European ideas; and it involved exerting influence over secondary regions like Hawaii and the Philippines, again with less attention to the immediate consequences for those peoples than for the requirements of the distant United States. In popular estimation, China may have represented an ancient but now decadent "civilization," not a "barbarous" or "savage" land. But U.S. designs and conduct in "the new Far West" were not altogether inconsistent with the lessons that Teddy Roosevelt had drawn from the old: the globe was covered with mere "waste spaces" eventually to be overrun by the English-speaking peoples of Europe and North America.[20]

Whereas U.S. attitudes toward China generally combined an awe at the size of the potential market with an arrogant aspiration to move this "decadent" civilization into the modern era, attitudes toward Latin America derived from the twin convictions that, first, Latin Americans were mostly savages and, second, destiny had provided lands south of the border as a mere extension of the North American "frontier." Latin America was, as the Monroe Doctrine had declared in 1823, the United States' backyard—a region that was off-limits to the expansive ambitions of the European powers, to be held in reserve for the pleasures of the United States.

"The savage is over the border," announced one popular song during the Mexican War of the 1840s, "Ready for fight and mischief, / So frontier men—to arms!" The key elements here are portentous: "savage," "mischief," "frontier," "arms." That the peoples of Central and South America and the Caribbean were so many "savages," that their meager capabilities ran primarily to mischief, and that the stewardship of the more civilized United States would benefit these savages whether or not they recognized it were points of such impressive consensus that, from the mid-nineteenth century onward, the border ceased to have much meaning when it came to determining the national interest and the right to pursue it. "Frontier men," that is, continually and rather routinely answered the call to arms, crossing into one or another of these nations in the North American backyard in order to enforce the North American will. If an occasional gunboat patrolled the Yangtze to protect American traders and missionaries or to back up American wishes with force, military coercion became the very way of life in U.S. dealings south of the its border. If the principle of "territorial integrity" governed American thinking on the China question, the very opposite determined U.S. conduct in its own hemisphere.

Latin America and the Caribbean had long occupied the imagination of expansive American nationalists. Way back in 1823, John Quincy Adams had described Cuba as subject to a kind of political "gravitation" that would bring it—like an apple falling from a tree—ineluctably toward the North American Union. For many southern businessmen—and, not incidentally, their northern associates—the dream died hard, even after Appomattox. Latin American trade "is ours by *natural laws*," argued one southern journal in the late 1880s.[21] There was thus a rich fund of precedent in U.S. thinking and conduct for the imperialist designs in the region in the late nineteenth century and after—as when the United States resolved a conflict over the placement of the Venezuelan boundary without bothering to consult with officials of Venezuela itself; or when, by the terms of the Platt Amendment, the Senate retained the United States' "right of intervention" in Cuban affairs in order to protect "life, liberty, and property"; or when, by fiat, the Supreme Court declared Puerto Rico to be "appurtenant and belonging to the United States" without granting Puerto Ricans the status of U.S. citizens; or when, in his corollary to the Monroe Doctrine, Teddy Roosevelt assigned the United States sole responsibility for policing the hemisphere; or when, *twenty times* between 1898 and 1920, U.S. marines landed in Caribbean countries to establish "stability" on U.S. terms. (When asked what exactly would constitute "stability" in Cuba, General Leonard Wood replied, "When money can be borrowed at a reasonable rate of interest and when capital is willing to invest in the Island, a condition of stability will have been reached.")[22]

Whatever the precise calculus by which the McKinley administration entered the war between Spain and its colony in revolt, the United States emerged from the war not only with a newly invigorated economic power in the region but also with a military presence and the unmistakable beginnings of an administrative empire. Earlier on, as Cuban rebels struggled against Spain and some had pondered the benefits of an alliance with the United States, rebel leader José Martí had wondered, "Once the United States is in Cuba, who will get her out?" A prescient question.[23] If the "splendid little war" brought the United States a stepping-stone to China in the form of the Philippine archipelago, results in the Caribbean were more dramatic still. Chief legacies of the United States' "humanitarian" intervention in behalf of the Cuban rebels included the Platt Amendment, a unique legislative solution to the dilemma of how to control newly liberated Cuba without going so far as to annex it. After two years of U.S. military occupation of the island without any solid consensus on the proper political disposition of the former Spanish colony (Cuba was partially protected from unbridled U.S. acquisitiveness by the Teller Amendment, by which Congress had denied designs for U.S. sovereignty over the island), Secretary of War Elihu Root sketched out a series of provisions under which, he felt, Cuba could be governed in a kind of limited independence. These provisions, the basis of the Platt Amendment, included the United States' "right of intervention" in Cuban affairs for the sake of protecting property and restoring order, a proscription of Cuba's treaty-making rights as a sovereign nation, and the right of the United States to acquire and maintain naval bases and coaling stations on the island. As tight as the U.S. grip would remain on Cuba under the terms of the Platt Amendment, Root frankly asserted that these provisions represented "the extreme limit of [U.S.] indulgence in the matter of the independence of Cuba." (That self-determination was an "indulgence" in this case speaks volumes about U.S. views of the region and its peoples.)[24]

A second, similar formula came to define the fate of Spain's other major Caribbean colony, Puerto Rico. By an article of the Treaty of Paris between Spain and the United States, Spain ceded "the island of Puerto Rico and the other islands now under Spanish sovereignty in the West Indies." Significantly, however, the treaty contained no specific language regarding the terms of Puerto Rico's eventual incorporation. Rather, it simply stated, "The civil rights and political status of the territories hereby ceded . . . shall be determined by the Congress."[25] Such determination came initially in the form of the Foraker Act in 1900, a bill whose original provisions included extending the U.S. Constitution to the island and granting American citizenship to its inhabitants. It was a much watered-down bill that actually passed, however, because Puerto Ricans' "fitness for self-government" was deeply questioned in some quarters. The gutted version of the bill provided that the island's inhabitants would be "citizens of Puerto Rico," not of the United States (this would be reversed only in 1917, by the Jones Act), and yet important aspects of their political life and fate would be decided in Washington, where a Puerto Rican resident commissioner with neither voice nor voting rights acted as the island's liaison in Congress.

Latin America occupied a different niche in U.S. economic thinking than did China, although assessments of white Americans' superiority to Latin American peoples were not altogether different. Like the Chinese, by long-standing tradition the peoples south of the border were seen as requiring "uplift" and a proper introduction to "progress," and yet—also like the Chinese—their prospects for assimilating to modern civilization seemed to some to be slender indeed. At the heart of white American assessments of Latin America was the issue of race. "If the United States as compared with the Spanish American republics has achieved immeasurable advance in all elements of greatness," the U.S. chargé d'affaires in Central America had remarked in the 1850s, "that result is eminently due to the rigid and inexorable refusal of the dominant Teutonic stock to debase its blood, impair its intellect, lower its moral standards, or peril its institutions by intermixture with the inferior and subordinate races of man. In obedience of Heaven, it has rescued half a continent from savage beasts and still more savage men."[26]

Such logic was still current decades later. In 1889 New England patrician Charles Francis Adams Jr. lauded a policy of extermination as the only alternative to becoming "a nation of half-breeds." Upon the U.S. invasion of Veracruz,

General Hugh Scott judged that "firmness is essential in dealing with inferior races."[27] And as sociologist Edward A. Ross surveyed the region in *South of Panama* (1915), he had to conclude that South America was "the victim of a bad start. It was never settled by whites in the way that they settled the United States." Rather, "the masterful whites" exploited the natives without either assimilating them or winning their allegiance. The result, in his view, was a politically stultifying combination of pride, contempt for labor, social parasitism, caste hierarchy, and pronounced authoritarian strains in both church and state, which, though attributable to historical circumstance rather than to race per se, by now seemed to run in the very blood of these peoples.[28]

The temper of U.S. Latin American policy was best summed up in Roosevelt's annual message to Congress in 1904, his "corollary" to the Monroe Doctrine. "Chronic wrongdoing," he warned, "or an impotence which results in a general loosening of the ties of civilized society, may in America, as elsewhere, ultimately require intervention by some civilized nation. . . . If every country washed by the Caribbean Sea would show the progress in stable and just civilization which with the aid of the Platt Amendment Cuba has shown since our troops left the island, . . . all question of interference by this Nation with their affairs would be at an end."[29]

European powers like Spain may have had their shortcomings, and the European presence in Latin America and the East may have been a source of some discomfort. But "chronic wrongdoers" of the sort who required the administration of Roosevelt's "big stick" were exclusively and always peoples identified in the American imagination as nonwhite. Like Leonard Wood, the governor general of Cuba, Roosevelt implicitly mingled economic notions such as "stability" (the atmosphere that a people was able to create for the safe conduct of trade) and "civilization" (a people's full participation in modern material progress) with ideas of "racial development" (a people's innate capacity for modernization or for "progress" in general). As these overlapping languages were applied in the U.S. quest for markets abroad, they gave name to the regions whose "backwardness" seemed to cry out for U.S. goods, and they provided justification for whatever action or intervention the United States deemed necessary to exert its will outside of its own borders. It was through this portentous marriage of a hierarchic worldview and sheer military might that the nation's destiny would become manifest.

But the foreigner abroad constituted only half of the sociopolitical equation under this regime of industrial progress and aggressive export; the resettled foreigner here at home was the other. While the Centennial Exposition in Philadelphia in 1876 represented a grand unveiling of the nation's new wares and its new thinking on the importance of securing a world market, it also hinted at one of the peculiar social dynamics that this global trade would create: in their economic affairs Americans were set on becoming more and more engaged with the world's peoples, but in their social outlook they were not necessarily becoming any less parochial than they had ever been. Foreigners at the fair found themselves very much out of favor among the American throngs. Turks, Egyptians, Spaniards, Japanese, and Chinese, according to one observer, "were followed by large crowds of idle boys and men, who hooted and shouted at them as if they had been animals of a strange species instead of visitors who were entitled to only the most courteous attention."[30] Such strains of xenophobia would become increasingly important in American civic life in the years between 1876 and World War I, as the successful export of American goods to all the world's peoples would also entail a massive import of the world's people—as workers—to take up places tending the nation's factories and machines. World labor migration was a natural twin to the phenomenon of the world commodity market; and since their own superiority to most of the world's peoples was a powerful current in American thought about illimitable foreign markets, Americans were decidedly uneasy about the growing presence of these inferior foreigners, either within the gates of the American factory or within the bounds of the domestic polity.

"The ebb and flow of the labor market is like the ebb and flow of the commodity market," wrote labor sociologist John R. Commons in 1919.[31] A whole range of forces—famines, earthquakes, ethnic violence, indebtedness and the vagaries of small farming, unbearable tax burdens—could unsettle people from their homelands, but the labor market and the laws of supply and demand dictated where they were likely to go. Americans then as now liked the pretty story of Emma Lazarus's teeming millions "yearning to breathe free"; and American political mythology has long relied on the icon of the freshly disembarked immigrant to give a human face to the grand but hazy ideal of "liberty." But the truth is more prosaic: as even the Congressional Commission on Immigration (the Dillingham Commission) concluded in its massive investigation early in the twentieth century, "With comparatively few exceptions the emigrant of to-day is essentially a seller of labor seeking a more favorable market."[32] Weekly earnings for laborers in the United States were estimated at $8.82 in 1890, $8.94 in 1900, and $10.68 in 1910. Laborers in Ireland, by contrast, could expect about $2 per week during this period; Italians in the Mezzogiorno most often worked for well under $2 per week; and field hands in the rural areas of turn-of-the-century Hungary could expect roughly $22 *per year*.

Even despite its depressions and downturns, then, and notwithstanding American trade unionists' fears that the labor market had become saturated, the United States represented "a more favorable market" to people from all over the world for a very long time. Immigration from Italy first began to reach appreciable numbers in the 1880s, and nearly 4 million Italians arrived between 1880 and World War I (though as many as 60 percent may have returned to Italy at one point or another). Migration from Russia—and particularly Jewish migration—mounted in the wake of the czar's anti-Semitic May Laws and a rash of violent pogroms in 1881; by 1915, the U.S. Census had tabulated over 3 million arrivals from Russian lands. Even despite the passage of the Chinese Exclusion Act in 1882, Asia sent nearly a half million immigrants between 1880 and 1915, including almost 200,000 from Japan. At the southern border, Mexican immigration began to mount in the first decade of the new century, and the years 1906 to 1915 witnessed 127,000 Mexican arrivals. The same ten-year period saw a total of over 650,000 arrivals from the rest of the Americas, including over half a million from Canada and another 125,000 from the West Indies. From Northern and Western Europe—the countries that accounted for what was inaccurately called the "old immigration"—Scandinavia sent well over a million and a half between 1876 and 1915; Germany sent over two and a half million; and even Ireland, whose statistical bell curve had peaked way back in the 1840s and 1850s, sent well over a million and a half immigrants during this period, over 50,000 per year during the 1880s alone. This was an astonishing movement of populations, no matter how one looked at it.

The flow of immigrants continued at impressive rates up to World War I, partially managed and directed by various middlemen and labor agents in the sending countries. Labor contractors and agents, known in various local vernaculars as "labor czars," *padroni*, or *reganchistas*, steered their compatriots toward specific work in specific regions of the United States—Chinese or Japanese laborers toward the western railroads, Hungarians toward Pennsylvania mines, Mexicans toward the Texas smelter industry, Greeks toward the western copper mines, or Italians toward the city-building projects of the eastern seaboard and the Midwest. The Alien Contract Labor Law (the Foran Act) of 1885 forbade the importation of "contract laborers"—that is, anyone who had contracted to do a particular job before immigrating—yet employers routinely circumvented the spirit of the law by drawing not on contracts per se, but on the existing, informal ethnic networks and family ties of their workers. As the Japanese consul in Tacoma, Washington, reported in 1898, the continued arrival of impoverished Japanese laborers in the Pacific Northwest could be attributed directly to the railroad contractors who were abetting them: "For a small sum, they get some of their workers to send letters to friends at home telling them of the benefits of railroad construction work, thereby persuading many unknowing Japanese to come to this region. Some of these unknowing ones cannot even afford lodging when they reach an open port, and the contractors or their agents advance them money for clothing and travel expenses. In some cases, the contractors or their agents also temporarily loan the thirty dollars people must have at the time they enter the country."[33] "The real agents who regulate the immigration movement," another observer concluded in 1912, "are the millions of earlier immigrants already in the United States."[34]

Thus, many immigrant groups were concentrated not only in certain geographic locales but also in certain occupational niches. In 1911, the Dillingham Immigration Commission devoted sixteen volumes of its monumental forty-volume study to *Immigrants in Industries*. The commission's compendium of statistics speaks not only to the immense presence of foreign workers in American industry in general but also to the clustering of particular groups within particular industries. In American clothing manufacture, to take one of the more striking instances, 72 percent of the workforce was foreign-born, and another 22 percent were children of immigrant fathers (the commission did not record the nativity of workers' mothers). In New York City's garment industry, the figures were even higher: 87 percent and 10 percent, respectively—or 97 percent immigrants and children of immigrants. Although Austrians, Germans, Poles, and other groups worked in the industry in significant numbers nationwide, fully three-quarters of the garment workers in New York were either East European Jews or Italians. In Chicago meatpacking, the numbers were nearly as dramatic: 78 percent foreign, and 14 percent children of foreign fathers, or all together 92 percent immigrants and their children. Poles and Lithuanians constituted fully 39 percent of this polyglot workforce. Nor were these industries anomalous. The statistics were remarkably consistent: from coal mining to the cotton factories, immigrants and their children constituted the vast majority of the workforce. Indeed, throughout this period some industries were impossible to conceive without their chief labor imports—Mexicans in the southwestern mining, the Chinese in railroad construction, Slavs in meatpacking, or Jews in the needle trades. As one Bureau of Labor report in Maine remarked, in that region "it would be difficult at the present time to build a railroad of any considerable length without Italian labor."[35]

The growing presence of foreigners on American soil raised many questions —among them, the very questions of "civilization," "barbarism," and "virtue" that attended the American quest for markets abroad during the same period. As one congressman complained during a debate in the 1880s over immigration, the new immigrants from Southern and Eastern Europe "do not know to purchase any of the luxuries which tend to elevate and enlighten people." As with the tribes of the plains or the Chinese in China, then, immigrants' status was not altogether independent of their habits of consumption.[36]

The most powerful outburst of working-class nativism was the anti-Chinese movement. The racially based, vigorously prolabor agitation had escalated in California and other regions of the West in the 1870s and had captured the federal political machinery by the 1880s, when Congress passed the first bill for Chinese exclusion. Even as early as the 1850s, when some 50,000 Chinese immigrants arrived on the West Coast, a Committee of Vigilance had appeared in California to protest the attempts of capital to flood the state with coolies and "degraded Asiatics."[37] Sporadic anti-Chinese violence broke out, and the state legislature passed a Foreign Miners Tax—enforced primarily against the Chinese—as a means of stemming the tide. In 1855 the California State Assembly declared, "We want the Chinese *trade*, but we do not want her surplus *population*," a sentiment that aptly summed up the dominant American stance for the balance of the century and beyond.[38] Over the next several decades, the political landscape of California, Oregon, Washington, Idaho, Wyoming, and Colorado became dotted with anticoolie clubs, Leagues of Deliverance, and other anti-Chinese organizations.

Anti-Chinese sentiments among white workers both intensified and became nationalized after 1869, when the completion of the transcontinental railroad stoked the flames of anti-Chinese race hatred in two distinct ways. First, as many mines dried up and as the railroad reached completion, Chinese laborers who had largely worked in these two industries began to drift into other sectors of the economy, particularly manufacturing enterprises, that by custom had been "white." The overpopulation of San Francisco and the newly pronounced Chinese presence in occupational niches in cigar manufacture and shoemaking, for instance, heightened white workers' alarm over their own potential displacement by Chinese contract labor. By 1873, Chinese labor was producing over half of California's boots and shoes; Samuel Gompers later recalled the feeling among cigar workers that, "unless protective measures were taken, it was evident the whole industry would soon be 'Chinaized.'" Indeed, the Chinese presence prodded cigar makers toward a national organization of labor unions, because "the help of all wage earners was needed in support of Chinese exclusion."[39]

Since the completion of the transcontinental railroad nationalized the market for these western goods, it also nationalized the perceived threat posed by Chinese labor. Not only did the Chinese presence threaten to depress wages in California's cigar-making industry, but the opportunities for distribution afforded by the railroad now brought western and eastern workers into direct competition with one another. If the Chinese drove wages down in the West, the argument went, they would also drive them down in the East, as California cigar manufacturers made a bid for the national market. The peril was registered more directly still in shoemaking when, in 1870, 500 striking white workers in the newly formed Knights of St. Crispin were replaced by Chinese strikebreakers in North Adams, Massachusetts. The year 1870 was thus marked not only by an anti-Chinese convention in California but by anti-Chinese labor rallies in eastern cities like New York and Boston as well.

The link in white workers' minds between the unsavory practices of monopoly capital, on the one hand, and the unfair competition of degraded Chinese labor, on the other, was forged during the early 1870s. At a Boston meeting of the Knights of St. Crispin, shoemakers denounced "Chinamen" as "ignorant tolls in the hands of oppressive capitalists." Labor leaders and theorists like Henry George now denounced Chinese immigrants as "long-tailed barbarians," complaining that "in every case in which Chinese come into fair competition with white labor, the whites must either retire from the field or come down to the Chinese standard of living."[40] Resolutions passed at an anti-Chinese demonstration in New York's Tompkins Square in July 1870 likewise combined antimonopoly rhetoric with a racial logic familiar from the discourses of overproduction and export: capital, by these lights, had imported "the lowest and most degraded of the Chinese barbaric race" to compete with "those whose more advanced intelligence and improved tastes have generated in them a proportionately greater number of wants and desires."[41]

Like employers themselves, these white workers saw something natural in the degraded state of Chinese labor—yet it was a degradation that could ultimately affect even the superior "white" worker unless, as this assembly urged, Congress put an end to "the importation of coolies." "The Chinamen labor for such pitiful wages that they undermine Caucasians," commented the *Atlantic Monthly* in 1871; "no white labor can live with any decency or self-respect" at such wage levels.[42] As E. A. Ross summarized the argument in retrospect years later, whites could compete favorably with the Chinese under normal conditions, but not under bad conditions. His pithy formula: "Reilly can *outdo* Ah San, but Ah San can *underlive* Reilly."[43]

Because so many of the imperiled "white" workers were actually immigrants themselves (hence Ross's use of the Irish "Reilly"), race became increasingly important in this formulation. As A. Oakey Hall argued at the Tompkins Square rally, the American people could not object to immigration per se, only to the capitalist venture to overrun labor with "another kind of tawny slave labor." Another orator, speaking in German, asserted that the country owed its greatness to "the laborers that had come from Europe."[44] The Joint Congressional Committee to Investigate Chinese Immigration in 1877 also drew careful distinctions along the color line separating Asian from European immigrants. Unlike Europeans, "there is not sufficient brain capacity in the Chinese to furnish the motive power for self-government," the committee declared. "Upon the point of morals, there is no Aryan or European race which is not far superior to the Chinese as a class."[45] Just as whiteness gathered European immigrants into the American fold in the legal framework of naturalization law (whose key phrase defining eligibility since 1790 was "free white persons"), so whiteness in the cauldron of labor competition naturalized European newcomers as honorary Americans, as against the *truly* foreign "Mongolian" immigrants—at least for a time.

But whereas racialism provided the venom of an anti-Chinese campaign (and, indeed, the "free white persons" clause in naturalization law had left the Chinese ineligible for citizenship and hence uniquely vulnerable), the driving logic of the movement was economic. Even the Joint Congressional Committee, whose concern was largely for the safety of American institutions, adopted labor's anti-Chinese argument wholesale. "The Chinese have reduced wages to what would be starvation prices for white men and women," ran the report; "this distinctive competition in some branches of labor operates as a continual menace, and inspires fears that . . . these ruinously low rates will . . . degrade all white working people to the abject condition of a servile class."[46]

Although a "California thesis" of the anti-Chinese movement rather too neatly exonerates the rest of the country, it is true that the movement was nowhere more militant than on the famous "Sand Lot" in San Francisco, where labor leader Dennis Kearney spewed anti-Chinese invective, where organized anti-Chinese agitation mounted throughout the late 1870s, and where, increasingly, anti-Chinese violence originated. In April 1877 an organization appeared in California calling itself the Order of Caucasians for the Extermination of the Chinaman; its announced aim was to "drive the Chinaman out of California" by a regime of harassment that, as spelled out in the bylaws, included the policy to "pursue and injure" not only Chinese immigrants themselves but also any white persons who "countenance their existence in any way." Members pledged to oppose the Chinese "to annihilation by every manner and means within the thin gauze of the law."[47]

Misgivings about the Chinese presence on the grounds of their religion or "civilization" were frequently aired, but the laborite strain of the movement was predominant in the tenor of the anti-Chinese argument. "We declare that the Chinaman must leave our shores," ran one Workingmen's Party manifesto. "We declare that white men, and women, and boys, and girls, cannot live as people of the great republic should and compete with the single Chinese coolies in the labor market. . . . To an American, death is preferable to life on par with the Chinamen." And "life on par with the Chinamen" was all that the future of

California held for the white working class, unless the swarm of Asian new-comers could be turned away.[48]

Both major political parties in California carried anti-Chinese planks from 1871 onward; and the Workingmen's Party, the first Marxist political party in the United States, garnered roughly a third of the vote in state elections during the decade behind the no-nonsense slogan "The Chinese Must Go!" Thanks largely to the influence of California labor, the state's second constitution (ratified in 1879) included an article prohibiting any corporation's employing, "directly or indirectly, in any capacity, any Chinese or Mongolian"; prohibiting the employ of Chinese "on any state, county, municipal, or other public work, except in punishment for crime"; and mandating that the legislature "delegate all necessary power to the incorporated cities and towns of this state for the removal of Chinese without the limits of such cities and towns, or for their locations within prescribed portions of those limits, and it shall also provide the necessary legislation to prohibit the introduction into this state of Chinese after the adoption of this Constitution."[49]

In the late 1870s western delegations of the U.S. Congress also brought the Chinese question to the national agenda. A congressional report submitted in 1877 (by a committee that happened to be dominated by Californians) urged legislation "to restrain the great influx of Asiatics to this country."[50] Several bills calling for the termination of Chinese immigration were introduced in 1878 and 1879, culminating in the Fifteen Passenger Bill (1879), which provided that no ship could take aboard more than fifteen Chinese passengers for transport to the United States. At a time when Chinese immigration was running toward 10,000 per year, such limitations would have had a tremendous impact. President Rutherford B. Hayes vetoed the bill, however, largely out of sensitivity to diplomatic and commercial relations with China and the treaty protections affecting American nationals and interests in Asia.

But by now the talk of exclusion was not to be quieted. "Every country owes its first duty to its own race and citizens," opined the *San Francisco Examiner* in 1880. "This duty properly observed on this Coast will cause much riddance of the Chinese pest."[51] In 1882 Senator John F. Miller of California introduced the first bill to suspend Chinese immigration—in this version, for a period of twenty years. The bill won vigorous support among western and southern congressmen, passing the Senate by a vote of 29 to 15, and the House by a vote of 167 to 66 (55 abstaining). Like his predecessor, Chester Arthur vetoed this bill, for his part on the grounds that the twenty-year suspension was too long and that such a draconian law would damage the U.S. image among trading partners in Asia. But in the spring of 1882, he did sign a revised bill that reduced the suspension to ten years (subject to renewal), and the Chinese Exclusion Act became law. So portentous was this triumph for American labor perceived to be that its possible repeal became the stuff of science fiction: offering a horrific vision of American life a hundred years hence in *Caesar's Column* (1890), populist Ignatius Donnelly projected that the industrial "underworld" would include, among myriad other races and nations, "even Chinese and Japanese; for the slant eyes of many, and their imperfect, Tartar-like features, reminded me that the laws made by the Republic, in the elder and better days, against the invasion of the Mongolian hordes, had long since become a dead letter."[52]

Still despised (as Donnelly's comments indicate) and now newly vulnerable, the Chinese immigrants who had already entered the United States suffered a series of violent attacks in the long wake of exclusion. Indeed, historian Shih-Shan Henry Tsai has identified fifty-five anti-Chinese riots in the West during the late decades of the nineteenth century, including thirty-four in California, nine in Washington, and four in Nevada. Though the residents of Wyoming perpetuated only one anti-Chinese riot, the outrage at Rock Springs (1885) was among the most spectacular in its fury: twenty-eight Chinese miners were killed, fifteen others injured, several hundred driven out of town, and Chinese property estimated at $147,000 was destroyed. Rock Springs stands out only for the scale of violence; the distinction from other anti-Chinese outrages across the West was in degree, not in kind. Like the upheaval in Tacoma in 1885, many of these riots were regarded as serious enough even by an avowedly anti-Chinese federal government to provoke the intervention of federal troops.[53]

Anti-Chinese agitation is unique in the history of American nativism for the consistency of its violence, for its success in capturing the major workers' organizations as well as both national political parties, and ultimately, for its success in winning legislation that singled out one national group for total exclusion. Indeed, since some of the movement's key participants were immigrants themselves, it is only with major qualifications that we can consider this "nativism" at all. But the argument against the foreign worker that began with the Chinese was broadly applied in ensuing years, in both its racialist and its economic dimensions—even to those European newcomers whose perceived "whiteness" initially shielded them during the Sand Lot tumult of the 1870s. By the turn of the century, it was not at all unusual to hear that any number of groups—whether Bohemians, Italians, Japanese, or Jews—were fundamentally "like the Chinese."

Asians, of course, were not the only immigrants to run afoul of American labor and its allies in government. Armenians in California, for instance, though exempted from the prohibitions imposed by the Alien Land Law, did suffer discrimination in housing and in the social organization of cities likes

Fresno, whose color bars, by local custom, placed them on the nonwhite side of the divide; and Armenian farm workers were sometimes terrorized by violent night riders in the state's orchard lands. Likewise, in the 1910s members of the American Federation of Labor (AFL) decried Mexican immigrants as a "torrent of peon poison" and lamented that able-bodied American men were forced to sit idle without work while "slim-legged [Mexican] peons with tortillas in their stomachs" performed construction work in their full view.[54] "Cheap labor," spat the AFL *Advocate* in a 1915 piece on Mexican labor in the Southwest, "—at the cost of every ideal cherished in the heart of every member of the white race, utterly destroyed and buried beneath the greedy ambitions of a few grasping money gluttons, who would not hesitate to sink the balance of society to the lowest levels of animalism, if by so doing they can increase their own bank account."[55] Like the Asians before them, Mexican workers were seen not as potential fellows in a common cause, but as dangerous tools in the hands of monopoly capital, whose innate racial degradation threatened to degrade even the noblest of American laborers.

For some, it was neither an illogical nor a terribly long leap from the necessary exclusion of the inferior Chinese to the necessary exclusion of the inferior European races. As the U.S. consul at Budapest remarked in the early 1890s, "These Slovacks are not a good acquisition for us to make, since they have so many items in common with the Chinese."[56] Immigration restrictionists like Senator Henry Cabot Lodge readily concurred: the new immigration, composed of "races most alien to the body of the American people," now threatened the prized homogeneity that was presumed to ensure the smooth governance of the republic; and not only were they different, but their difference itself hardly recommended them as fellow citizens. The new immigrants in general, wrote Lodge, "do not promise well for the standard of civilization of the United States." Citing a State Department report on the "almost revolting" character of many of the new immigrants, Lodge elsewhere declared that not only was "our immigration changing in point of race," but that it was in fact "deteriorating."[57] Such reasoning would gather force in the Immigration Restriction League in the 1890s and the emergent eugenics movement of the first decade of the 1900s, finally cresting with the racially based and highly restrictive legislation of 1917 and 1924.

Just as in the case of transpacific and Latin American expansion, then, Americans' inevitable economic contacts with the world's peoples—in this case as an imported labor force—carried with them an immense undercurrent of anxiety, lest the nation, however superior, somehow become contaminated. As the majority opinion in the case of *Chae Chan Ping v. United States* (1889) asserted, it is the "highest duty of every nation to preserve its independence, and give security against foreign aggression and encroachments . . . no matter in what form such aggression and encroachment come, whether from the foreign nation acting in its national character or from the vast hordes of its people crowding in upon us."[58] The court in *Fong Yue Ting v. United States* (1893) reaffirmed "the right to exclude or to expel all aliens or any class of aliens, absolutely or upon certain conditions, in war or in peace, being an inherent right of every sovereign and independent nation, essential to its safety, its independence and its welfare."[59] Like the Platt Amendment and other legal mechanisms by which the United States held at arm's length the Caribbean or Pacific peoples whose territories it had grasped, immigration and naturalization decisions like *Fong Yue Ting* or the later restriction bills expressed a deep American ambivalence toward the peoples to whom, economically, the nation had become inexorably yoked.

In their profound foreignness in popular American views, immigrant workers shared a niche with the overseas "natives" and "savages" whose lives were to be transformed by the modern wares issuing from American factories. This period of tremendous productivity had brought Americans into unprecedented levels of engagement with diverse peoples both at home and abroad on terms that, from the American perspective, were bound to cast the foreigner as an inferior —as a barbarian whose customs screamed out for revision to an approximation of the American norm; as a relic of some earlier epoch, inexplicably evading the natural laws of "progress"; as a human draft animal whose brawn could be enlisted to carry out the designs of the Anglo-Saxon intellect; as a visitor from the premodern, whose accustomed deprivations threatened to bid down American standards of living; or as an Old World incendiary, reared amid the inequities of a semifeudal regime and now importing dangerous doctrines that had no proper place in a self-governing republic.

   The confrontation with such peoples both at home and abroad left powerful traces on the texture of American nationalism, providing new narratives of national grandeur and new idioms of national superiority—and new depths of xenophobic antagonism. In both nativist and imperialist discourses, mere ethnocentrism shaded toward rage, in part because of the peculiar dependence of the "superiors" on their "inferiors" in this instance: precisely by their staggering economic successes, Americans had become bound to the foreign market and the foreign worker, and yet the peoples of the world did not proceed faithfully along the script provided them by American wishes in either case. When an orator like Josiah Strong railed against the incoming hordes or promised an Anglo-Saxon conquest of the world, his very confidence in Anglo-Saxon superiority gave voice to a fear for the well-being of the republic. As historian John

Higham has written, "Not all jingoes were nativists or all nativists jingoes, but both the aggressive psychology of the one and defensive reaction of the other provided instinctive rallying points for a society dubious of its capacity to compose its conflicts."[60]

The historic American encounter with foreign peoples thus took place in intricate relation to the ambivalent American *idea* of foreign peoples: images and stereotypes of the foreigner—by turns menacing, cowed, aggressive, vanquished, needy, or defiant—framed the social and political relations between the United States and its economic participants from around the globe; and these relations, in their turn, had the power to generate a new round of images or to put a new tint on old ones. The confrontation between American merchants with the peoples of Asia, Africa, and Latin America, then, like the confrontation between American factory owners and their immigrant hires, cannot be understood fully apart from the acres of verbiage and imagery produced by the nation's flourishing print culture and its emergent information industries. Gilded Age and Progressive Era magazines, newspapers, novels, travel books, reformist tracts, and academic treatises established the ideological conditions for these encounters by standardizing various preconceptions of the foreigner and by representing the encounters themselves as unshakable demonstrations of this or that ethnological truth about the character of this nation and the nature of the world's diverse populations.

NOTES

1. Charles S. Campbell Jr., *The Transformation of American Foreign Relations, 1865–1900* (New York: Harper and Row, 1976), 109.

2. James Lorence, "Organized Business and the Myth of the China Market: The American Asiatic Association, 1898–1937," in *Transactions of the American Philosophical Society* 71, pt. 4 (1981): 10.

3. Thomas McCormick, *China Market: America's Quest for Informal Empire, 1893–1901* (Chicago: Quadrangle, 1967), 37, 38.

4. Brooks Adams, *America's Economic Supremacy* (New York: Macmillan, 1900), 72, 89, 133, 131.

5. Campbell, *Transformation of American Foreign Relations*, 101.

6. Michael Hunt, *The Making of a Special Relationship: The United States and China to 1914* (New York: Columbia University Press, 1983), 12, 90.

7. Lorence, "Organized Business and the Myth of the China Market," 25.

8. Adams, *America's Economic Supremacy*, 72.

9. McCormick, *China Market*, 129.

10. Thomas Paterson, ed., *Major Problems in American Foreign Policy: Documents and Essays* (Lexington, Mass.: D. C. Heath, 1978), 298.

11. Richard Drinnon, *Facing West: The Metaphysics of Indian-Hating and Empire Building* (Minneapolis: University of Minnesota Press, 1980), 277.

12. On the Boxer rebellion, see especially Hunt, *Making of a Special Relationship*; and Walter LeFeber, *The American Search for Opportunity, 1865–1913*, vol. 2 of *The Cambridge History of American Foreign Relations* (Cambridge, U.K.: Cambridge University Press, 1993).

13. Paterson, *Major Problems*, 299.

14. Paul A. Varg, *The Making of a Myth: The United States and China, 1897–1912* (East Lansing: Michigan State University Press, 1968), 38.

15. Theodore Roosevelt, "The Awakening of China" (New York: Board of Foreign Missions of the Reformed Church in America, 1908).

16. Lorence, "Organized Business and the Myth of the China Market," 43.

17. Charles Soutter Campbell, *Special Business Interests and the Open Door Policy* (New Haven, Conn.: Yale University Press, 1951), 12.

18. Stuart Creighton Miller, *The Unwelcome Immigrant: The American Image of the Chinese, 1785–1882* (Berkeley: University of California Press, 1969), 35.

19. Arthur Smith, *Chinese Characteristics* (London: Oliphant, Anderson, and Farrier, 1900), 128.

20. Theodore Roosevelt, *The Winning of the West*, 4 vols. (Lincoln: University of Nebraska Press, 1995), 1:1.

21. LeFeber, *American Search for Opportunity*, 26.

22. Lloyd Gardner, "A Progressive Foreign Policy, 1900–1921," in *From Colony to Empire: Essays in the History of American Foreign Relations*, ed. William Appleman Williams (New York: John Wiley and Sons, 1972), 217.

23. Philip Foner, *The Spanish-Cuban-American War and the Birth of American Imperialism* (New York: Monthly Review Press, 1972), xxx.

24. Louis Pérez Jr., *Cuba: Between Reform and Revolution* (New York: Oxford University Press, 1995), 187.

25. José Trías Monge, *Puerto Rico: The Trials of the Oldest Colony in the World* (New Haven, Conn.: Yale University Press, 1997), 27.

26. Frederick Pike, *The United States and Latin America: Myths and Stereotypes of Civilization and Nature* (Austin: University of Texas Press, 1992), 147.

27. Ibid., 146, 211.

28. Edward A. Ross, *South of Panama* (New York: Century, 1915), preface, n.p.

29. Paterson, *Major Problems*, 329–30.

30. Robert Rydell, *All the World's a Fair: Visions of Empire at American International Expositions, 1876–1916* (Chicago: University of Chicago Press, 1984), 14.

31. John R. Commons, *Industrial Goodwill* (New York: McGraw-Hill, 1919), 1.

32. Mark Wyman, *Round-Trip to America: The Immigrants Return to Europe, 1880–1930* (Ithaca, N.Y.: Cornell University Press, 1991), 34.

33. Yuji Ichioka, *The Issei: The World of the First Generation Japanese Immigrants, 1885–1924* (New York: Free Press, 1988), 63.

34. Oscar Handlin, ed., *Immigration as a Factor in American History* (Englewood Cliffs, N.J.: Prentice-Hall, 1959), 56.

35. Thomas Kessner, *The Golden Door: Italian and Jewish Immigrant Mobility in New York City, 1880–1915* (New York: Oxford University Press, 1977), 58.

36. Gwendolyn Mink, *Old Labor and New Immigrants in American Political Development: Union, Party, and State, 1875–1920* (Ithaca, N.Y.: Cornell University Press, 1986), 109.

37. Elmer Sandemeyer, *The Anti-Chinese Movement in California* (Urbana: University of Illinois Press, 1973), 42.

38. Ibid., 42.

39. Mink, *Old Labor and New Immigrants*, 71.

40. Ibid.

41. *New York Times*, July 1, 1870, 1.

42. *Atlantic Monthly*, November 1871, 598.

43. E. A. Ross, *The Changing Chinese: The Conflict of Oriental and Western Cultures in China* (New York: Century Co., 1911), 47.

44. *New York Times*, July 1, 1870, 1.

45. *Congressional Record*, 44th Cong., 2d sess., 2005.

46. Ibid., 2004.

47. *New York Times*, April 3, 1877, 4.

48. Mink, *Old Labor and New Immigrants*, 82.

49. Roger Daniels, *The Politics of Prejudice: The Anti-Japanese Movement in California and the Struggle for Japanese Exclusion* (New York: Atheneum, 1977), 18.

50. Shih-Shan Henry Tsai, *The Chinese Experience in America* (Bloomington: Indiana University Press, 1986), 59.

51. Alexander Saxton, *The Indispensable Enemy: Labor and the Anti-Chinese Movement in California* (Berkeley: University of California Press, 1971), 147–48.

52. Ignatius Donnelly, *Caesar's Column: A Story of the Twentieth Century* (1890; Cambridge, Mass.: Belknap Press of Harvard University Press, 1960), 38.

53. Shih-Shan Henry Tsai, *China and the Overseas Chinese in the United States, 1868–1911* (Fayetteville: University of Arkansas Press, 1983).

54. Neil Foley, *The White Scourge: Mexicans, Blacks, and Poor Whites in Texas Cotton Culture* (Berkeley: University of California Press, 1997), 48.

55. Mario T. Garcia, *Desert Immigrants: The Mexicans of El Paso, 1880–1920* (New Haven, Conn.: Yale University Press, 1981), 104, 103.

56. *North American Review*, January 1891, 30–31.

57. Ibid., 32, 35; *North American Review*, May 1891, 608.

58. *Chae Chan Ping v. United States* 130 U.S. 581 (1889), at 606.

59. *Fong Yue Ting v. United States*, 149 U.S. 698 (1893).

60. John Higham, *Strangers in the Land: Patterns of American Nativism, 1865–1925* (1955; New York: Atheneum, 1978), 76.

The Americanization of South Africa

JAMES T. CAMPBELL

An American arriving in South Africa today can scarcely help but be struck by how familiar it seems. South Africans, black and white, drink Coca-Cola, eat Kentucky Fried Chicken, and spend exorbitant sums on Nike shoes and sportswear. They shop in sprawling suburban malls, modeled on American prototypes and offering a dizzying array of American commodities. The local cineplexes carry the latest Hollywood blockbusters, while television, which the apartheid state prohibited until 1976, serves up an endless stream of American commercial programs. The same process is evident in the realm of politics. While South Africa's history as a British colony is reflected in the country's parliamentary system and its renewed membership in the Commonwealth, many of the controversial political issues debated in South Africa today—federalism, judicial review, minority rights, affirmative action—revolve around concepts appropriated (some might say misappropriated) from American political discourse.

Examples could be multiplied almost indefinitely, but the point is clear. When the Union of South Africa was established in 1910, its political, economic, and cultural metropole was Great Britain. Today, Britain's role has been usurped by the United States. This essay examines that process.

Before proceeding, it may be useful to anticipate a few objections. To highlight the American presence is not to imply that the United States is the sole foreign influence on South Africa. Nor is it to suggest that American influence is somehow universal or evenly spread across the country. In a society as riven by racial, class, ethnic, and generational cleavages as South Africa, the process of "Americanization" has inevitably been uneven and contested. Manifestly, U.S. influence has been most marked in urban areas, preeminently in Johannesburg, which is, in a more than figurative sense, a product of American knowledge and inspiration. American influence has typically spread along generational lines, with young South Africans, black and white, appropriating American music, fashion, and even slang as a means to distinguish themselves from their more conservative, more Anglicized elders. Last but not least, the process has been distinctly racialized. While both black and white South Africans have proved extraordinarily receptive to American culture, they have typically embraced different aspects, while entertaining profoundly different ideas about the nature of the American experience and its relevance to South Africa.

This qualification prompts another. An inquiry like this one invites a kind of argument by accretion, of trying to prove one's case through an endless catalog of "Americanisms" in South African life. Such data, however, represent the beginning rather than the end of the analytical problem. The enduring popularity of American jazz, for example, is obviously a significant datum, but it tells us nothing in itself about the mechanisms by which such music was introduced in South Africa or what it meant to different audiences. The same might be said about Hollywood westerns, Tuskegee-style "industrial education," or *The Cosby Show*, which had the bizarre distinction of being the highest-rated television show in South Africa during the twilight of apartheid. In short, "Americanization" involves processes of reception—of selection and interpretation—as well as of transmission. While the vast differences in national scale and power have often made it difficult for South Africans to resist American penetration, it would be misleading to portray them as helpless victims of American hegemony. In many cases, they have actively sought out American goods, images, and ideas, incorporating them into their own lives to yield new ways of understanding and acting upon their worlds. One of the chief challenges of transnational history is to take into account these myriad moments of cultural exchange, without succumbing to the simplifications of "cultural imperialism" on one hand or of unfettered agency on the other. In today's brave new world of globalization, Marx's hoary dictum is more pertinent than ever: people make their own history, but not exactly as they choose.

One other potential criticism should be noted. Put simply, why pick on South Africa? What country today is not plagued by Coca-Cola, Nike, CNN, *Baywatch*, and other manifestations of Generica America? Fair enough. But even if one concedes the point, the historical particularities of the process in different societies are surely worthy of careful analysis. As it happens, South Africa is something of a special case. In few, if any, societies in the world did the process of Americanization begin so early; in few, if any, has it been so replete with irony or of such central historical significance. When the 1939 Mixed Marriages Commission convened (to take a singularly obnoxious example), its first act was to dispatch a representative to the U.S. Library of Congress to study American precedents. (For the record, the search uncovered well over a hundred antimiscegenation statutes, in thirty-seven different states.)[1] American experience was likewise invoked, implicitly or explicitly, in the elaboration of segregation, in the beginnings of radio and television broadcasting, in the establishment of the first suburbs, in changing fashions in music, dress, and interior decoration, in conservation policy, in the creation of Bantustans, in the political struggles against apartheid, and in innumerable ongoing debates about apartheid's legacy. In short, "Americanization" is a deeply rooted, complex, contested historical process with profound significance for South Africa's past, present, and future.

Commerce between North America and South Africa reaches into the eighteenth century. Merchants in New England and Cape Town conducted a lively trade, often in defiance of both British mercantilist and Dutch East India Company regulations. New England slave ships, en route from Madagascar, routinely stopped at the Cape to take on provisions, leaving a portion of their human cargoes as payment. In the years after American independence, upward of two dozen American ships per year put in at Cape Town; today's Victoria and Alfred Waterfront, a tourist mecca modeled on San Francisco's Fisherman's Wharf, stands near the site of what Capetonians two centuries ago called "the American wharf." Settlers in the Cape ate American grain, built homes out of American timber, and aged wine in American-made barrels, some of which was later quaffed in New England taverns. With the outbreak of the Napoleonic Wars, transatlantic commerce swelled still further, to the point that the United States briefly stood as South Africa's largest trading partner.[2]

British annexation of the Cape in 1806 ended this early boom, but the traffic recommenced in the 1830s, as America's industrial revolution created a robust demand for South African primary products. The wool boom that transformed the Cape economy in the mid-nineteenth century was propelled by American manufacturers, who purchased over a third of local output. The burgeoning U.S. shoe industry provided an insatiable market for South African skins and hides. A single firm, the G. S. Holmes Company, the first American firm to open a branch in South Africa, shipped over 200,000 hides per year from the Cape to Boston in the 1850s. Many Union soldiers in the American Civil War wore boots made from South African leather and slept beneath blankets woven from South African wool. The Confederate raider *Alabama* did a booming business in South African waters, seizing one Union vessel right off Cape Town, an episode memorialized in an enduring folksong, "Daar Kom Die Alabama."[3]

Some of the United States' surging industrial output found its way back to South Africa. The U.S. farm implement industry, one of the bellwethers of the American industrial revolution, quickly cornered the local market. Cyrus Mc-Cormick's reapers were available in South Africa in the early 1850s, within a few years of their introduction in the United States. The market for plows was likewise dominated by American imports, sold through local agents and sporting such brand names as the Yankee, the Eagle, and the American Planet, Jr. Barbed wire, at once the most prosaic and most profound symbol of colonial rule, was likewise imported from the United States, beginning in the 1870s. By century's end, Americans supplied virtually all of South Africa's sewing machines, typewriters, bicycles, cash registers, cameras, and canned meats. American dominance was perhaps most conspicuous—and certainly most enduring —in fuel oils, initially in kerosene and later in gasoline or "petrol." If late nineteenth-century South Africa had an equivalent to today's ubiquitous Coca-Cola can, it was the bright red five-gallon tin with the Standard Oil logo.[4]

As significant as these early linkages may have been, the process of "Americanization" began in earnest only with the mineral revolution. The discovery of diamonds at Kimberley, followed a decade and a half later by the opening of the Witwatersrand goldfields, ignited in southern Africa the most compressed and ferocious industrial revolution in the history of the world. Significantly, this revolution coincided with sweeping changes in American economic life. Consolidation, abetted by new organizational and management techniques, radically transformed the character and scale of economic activity. Among the industries most affected was mining. Throughout the American West and later the world, the pick-wielding digger was displaced by vast, highly capitalized mining operations, overseen by professional mining engineers. Educated at new institutions like Yale's Sheffield School and the Colorado School of Mines, these new "scientific" miners possessed expertise in engineering, chemistry, mineralogy, metallurgy, and what we today would call management, all with an eye to extracting the greatest possible amount of ore at the least possible cost.[5]

By the late nineteenth century, American mining engineers were spread across the globe, from Colorado to Australia to Peru. Southern Africa drew them like a magnet. Kimberley was home to at least a thousand Americans, the most famous of whom, Gardner Williams, doubled as U.S. consul and chief operating officer of Cecil Rhodes's De Beers Company. Easily twice as many Americans found their way to the goldfields of the Witwatersrand, which posed many of the same technical problems as the hard rock mines of Nevada. By the mid-1890s, over half the mines on the Rand were managed by Americans, and a chain of new cities had sprouted along the reef with names like Denver, Cleveland, and Florida. In the wake of the engineers came a motley collection of American journalists, entrepreneurs, and adventurers, eager to sample life in the world's latest, greatest boomtown. Americans established Johannesburg's first hotel, its first steam laundry, and its short-lived horse-drawn tram system. One U.S. expatriate made a handsome living importing used stagecoaches from California. Americans even dominated the Rand's criminal underworld: the so-called Bowery Boys, a network of Eastern European Jewish pimps expelled from their base on New York's Lower East Side in 1894, relocated to Johannesburg and quickly cornered the local prostitution market.[6]

It is no exaggeration to say that Americans built South Africa's gold industry.

It was an American, John Hays Hammond, chief engineer of Rhodes's Consolidated Gold Fields, who first persuaded skeptical Randlords that the unprecedented investments required for deep-level mining could be made to pay, notwithstanding the low grade of ore. Hammond's judgment was confirmed by Hamilton Smith, an engineer from the Nevada silver fields who was brought out by the Rothschilds in 1893 to assess the Witwatersrand, and by George Becker, head of the U.S. Geological Survey, who produced the first comprehensive survey of the Witwatersrand complex three years later. The list goes on and on. As Mark Twain, an old digger who passed through Johannesburg in 1895, put it, "South Africa seems to be the heaven of the South African scientific mining engineer. He gets the choicest places and keeps them."[7]

It is important, of course, to maintain a sense of proportion here. The flood of people and products from the United States was focused on the Witwatersrand and obviously not characteristic of South Africa as a whole. Great Britain still outstripped the United States in the total value of exports to South Africa and, with occasional brief exceptions, would continue to do so for the next eighty years. Finance capital remained emphatically British, thanks to a tangle of British, U.S., and Cape laws that prevented American banks from opening branches in South Africa. More surprisingly, mining capital remained almost exclusively European, despite the enormous contributions Americans made to the industry in terms of technical and management expertise. No American mining house arose on the Rand, a fact that sharply distinguishes the South African case from, say, Rhodesia, Zambia, or the Congo, where American mining capital would come to wield enormous economic and political power. The obvious exception, the massive Anglo-American Corporation, which was launched in 1917 with the help of J. P. Morgan and future U.S. president Herbert Hoover (himself a mining engineer who had spent time on the South African goldfields), is more apparent than real: by 1930, most of the American interests in Anglo had been bought up by De Beers's Ernest Oppenheimer.[8]

Yet even admitting these qualifications, there is no gainsaying the growing U.S. presence in South Africa. Indeed, so prominent had American influence become that curtailing it would emerge as one of the chief objectives of the imperial officials sent out to "reconstruct" the Transvaal after the South African War of 1899–1902. Under the new "imperial preference" policy, U.S. trade with South Africa plummeted; American grain sales, a staple of the transatlantic trade for a century, were wiped out almost completely. To be sure, the policy was not airtight. Several U.S. companies qualified for imperial preference by incorporating themselves in Canada. American firms continued to dominate the oil and farm equipment industries, as well as the emerging automobile market. Unquestionably, however, the policy slowed the process of Americanization, while drawing a newly unified South Africa firmly into the orbit of the British Empire.[9]

If the aftermath of the South African War marked the end of the first phase of South Africa's "Americanization," the aftermath of World War I marked the commencement of the second. With the British economy mired in depression, it was left to American exporters to answer pent-up wartime demand. In 1920 the total value of U.S. exports peaked at over $60 million; for a brief moment, the United States stood yet again as South Africa's largest trading partner. So enticing was the South African market that some Americans began to consider direct investment. "There are splendid openings here for energetic men with sufficient capital to finance the undertaking and employ the large forces of cheap native labour found in most parts," the American consul in Cape Town reported in 1921. Two years later, the Ford Motor Company launched Ford, South Africa. (The venture was technically sponsored by Ford, Canada, to ensure that the new enterprise qualified for imperial preference on imported components.) By the end of 1923, the first Model T had rolled out of the company's new assembly plant in Port Elizabeth.[10]

The entrance of American capital was facilitated, paradoxically, by the 1924 election of the Nationalist-Labour "Pact," an Afrikaner-dominated, anti-impe-rialist government committed to enhancing South Africa's economic independence. The Pact's 1925 Tariff Act raised customs and duties on imports to unprecedentedly high levels, in a bid to nurture local manufacturing, curtail the political influence of British-dominated mining capital, and provide jobs for "civilised labour"—the poor and working-class whites who had voted the party into office. In most particulars, the act succeeded: the manufacturing industry grew spectacularly, eventually outstripping mining in its contribution to national gross domestic product; hundreds of thousands of white workers, male and female, secured decently paid jobs in match factories, canning works, automobile plants, textile mills, and later in the embryonic steel and chemical industries. Whether the act enhanced South Africa's autonomy, however, is a different question. As historian Richard Hull has shown, the new tariff regime essentially forced overseas firms with an interest in South Africa either to abandon the local market or to establish their own manufacturing subsidiaries inside the country. Dozens of U.S. corporations chose the latter course. For the first time, American capital began to enter South Africa on a significant scale.[11]

In 1926 General Motors's (GM) new South African subsidiary broke ground for an assembly plant in Port Elizabeth, just down the road from that of its chief rival, Ford. Within a year, Chevrolets, Pontiacs, Oldsmobiles, and Buicks were rolling off the line. International Harvester opened an assembly plant in Durban in 1928, consolidating U.S. dominance of the local agricultural implements market. The influx of American capital was especially pronounced in toiletries and health and beauty aids, perhaps the fastest-growing consumer industry in the United States at the time. Bristol-Myers, Johnson & Johnson, Colgate-Palmolive, and Gillette all launched local subsidiaries in the years between 1925 and 1931. Once unleashed, the flow of American investment continued, undeterred by the onset of depression or by a series of major political realignments in South Africa. The economic boom that followed South Africa's withdrawal from the gold standard in 1933 prompted another spurt of investment, as U.S. corporations raced to enter what *Businessweek* called "one of the most spectacular markets in the world." In 1936 Firestone established South Africa's first tire factory in Port Elizabeth. Coca-Cola, quintessential symbol of American consumer culture, arrived two years later.[12]

Though total U.S. direct investment in South Africa continued to lag behind investment from Great Britain, it had a disproportionate impact, concentrated as it was in manufacturing, the most dynamic sector of the economy. Like their predecessors on the diamond and gold fields, the American engineers and managers who came to South Africa in the years after 1925 brought with them a wealth of new, "scientific" techniques. Assembly-line production, time and motion studies, and other techniques of so-called scientific management were all introduced in South Africa by Americans. These innovations in production were accompanied by even more revolutionary innovations in the realm of consumption, or marketing. Someone, after all, had to buy the output of all these new, prolific factories. Particularly in a society like South Africa, where extreme maldistribution of wealth radically reduced the size of the aggregate local market, the future of manufacturing capital hinged less on productivity than on persuading people to consume.[13]

The devices employed by American capital in the 1920s to close the widening gap between production and consumption are familiar enough to historians: installment plans; the introduction of "yearly models"; the endless elaboration of superficial differences in functionally similar products. Advertising blossomed as a professional industry, complete with its own associations and journals, as well as its own vernacular, cribbed from the developing science of psychology. (The doyen of the new industry, Edward Bernays, was a nephew of Sigmund Freud.) Ultimately, of course, such initiatives did not forestall the Great Depression, but they did help to consolidate a culture of consumption, in which individuals' status, personal happiness, and even identity came seemingly to hinge on possessing this or that commodity.[14]

Given South Africa's elaborate tradition of labor repression, scholars have naturally focused their attention on production, leaving consumption as something of a historiographical orphan. Yet even a cursory glimpse at the sources suggests that South Africa, too, experienced a significant shift in the nature and meaning of consumption in the interwar years, with American capital and techniques playing central roles in the process. A professional advertising industry emerged, serviced by its own trade journal, *South African Business Efficiency*, launched in 1934. Dozens of local ad agencies emerged, all faithfully following American practice by striving to endow particular commodities with airs of distinction, leisure, youth, or sex appeal. At risk of overstating the point, one can see in South Africa in the 1920s and 1930s the emergence not only of a culture of consumption but also of an enduring association of Americanness with certain forms of consumption and display. The auto industry offers perhaps the best example. Given South Africa's size and the considerable distances between cities, the country's love affair with the automobile was probably foreordained, but it was American automakers that first fueled the romance. Like their American parents, the South African subsidiaries of Ford and General Motors used advertising to associate their products with wealth, sophistication, and personal freedom, encouraging buyers to express their individuality by choosing particular models, colors, and features. (In GM's case, advertising was also used to associate the company with the Pact's "civilised labour" policy: all GM ads included the legend, "100 per cent. White Labour.") Advertisements routinely cited the latest U.S. sales figures for particular models, to assure South Africans that they were obtaining the best that America had to offer. Through such techniques, U.S. auto manufacturers soon controlled over 90 percent of the local market.[15]

Needless to say, this new consumer ethic was not uniformly embraced; on the contrary, its spread was uneven, contested, and shaped by all of South Africa's myriad racial, class, and ethnic fault lines. Not surprisingly, early mass-marketing campaigns focused on English-speaking whites, a population that was, by South African standards, not only cosmopolitan but also disproportionately urban and affluent. The premier medium for reaching this market was *Outspan*, the most prominent of a new generation of mass-circulation weekly magazines that appeared in South Africa in the years after World War I. Like the American *Saturday Evening Post*, on which it was modeled, *Outspan* was a lavishly illustrated affair, offering wholesome, general interest articles, along with a solemn pledge "to introduce no politics." Designed to appeal to the entire family, the magazine included features on health, fashion, golf, music, movies, and dancing, as well as an endless stream of articles on automobiles ("Motoring Etiquette," "When an Engine Lacks Power," "Motoring Days of Yesteryear"). Each issue also included literally hundreds of advertisements, for everything from American "Frigidaires" (". . . truly modern. It saves work, worry, money and time . . . with every corner of every compartment chilled to the scientifically correct degree") to Odo-Ro-No underarm deodorant for women ("Dancing, tennis, riding—why should your enjoyment of them be spoiled by that horrid, nagging doubt—the doubt of your personal daintiness . . . ?"). Taken as a whole, *Outspan* conjured a vision of the South African good life, American-style—a vision of material progress, ample leisure, and domestic comfort, unruffled by financial insecurity or political dissension.[16]

Among African readers, *Umteteli wa Bantu* played a broadly similar role, though in radically different circumstances. Founded by the Chamber of Mines in the early 1920 to wean "responsible" African opinion away from militant organizations like the Industrial and Commercial Workers' Union, *Umteteli* targeted an emergent urban black middle class. The problem for the paper, and indeed for the target group itself, was how to distinguish members of this class from other Africans. Given the reality of urban segregation, entrenched in the 1923 Natives' (Urban Areas) Act, as well as the ongoing political assault against all forms of African accumulation and autonomy, members of this aspirant elite lived cheek by jowl with the working class and urban poor, often in equally parlous circumstances. In such a context, consumption acquired enormous personal and political significance. Dress, hairstyles, leisure activities, furniture, even the bric-a-brac that cluttered one's sitting room, all became coveted markers of difference, purchased even at risk of falling perilously into debt. In keeping with the priority of consumption, *Umteteli* devoted considerable column space to advertisements, peddling pianos, patent medicines, and everything in between. The influence of the United States, mostly implicit in *Outspan*, was utterly explicit in *Umteteli*. Not only did the paper carry regular columns on the achievements of African Americans; it also routinely invoked black America in its advertisements, presenting this record or that beauty treatment as the "latest" thing from the United States.[17]

Afrikaners presented an even more complex case. Over the first quarter of the century, Afrikaners poured into cities, driven from the land by the accelerating capitalization of the countryside. While many, indeed most, of these first-generation urbanites were poor, they also represented a substantial potential market. Developing this market became one of South African manufacturing capital's most urgent priorities. This priority, however, ran afoul of another. As Isabel Hofmeyr has shown, the first decades of the twentieth century represented a pivotal period in the history of Afrikaner Nationalism. The Second Language Movement, the emergence of Malan's National Party, and the 1914 Rebellion all reflected and advanced a growing sense of "*volkskap*," of shared nationhood and identity. Like nationalists in other places and times, Afrikaner Nationalist ideologues viewed commerce with a jaundiced eye. The comments of *Die Huisgenoot*, the largest-circulation Afrikaans weekly, were representative: "Our biggest daily papers, the cinemas, the school system, the language of our courts, the shops with their fashions and merchandise, the furniture in our houses are all bastions and agents of a foreign culture which claims for itself the right to overrun and conquer the world." In the years that followed, Afrikaner Nationalists would coin a revealing neologism for this alien plague: "*bioskoop-beskawing*," the culture of the movies.[18]

Fortunately for *Die Huisgenoot* (which, like *Outspan*, was sustained by advertising revenues), the imperatives of *volkskap* and consumption could be reconciled. The solution, as Hofmeyr suggests, lay not in resisting commerce but in incorporating it, by identifying certain forms of consumption and leisure as authentically Afrikaans. *Die Huisgenoot* itself led the campaign, helping to establish through its advertisements, articles, and illustrations the boundaries of legitimate consumption in everything from meat to movies, furniture to fashion. A "*regte*" Afrikaner would not eat marmalade, but he would eat "Gold Reef Konfyt" or, to take a slightly more contemporary example, "Ouma" Rusks (still allegedly made according to grandmother Grayvenstein's old Karoo recipe). Thus did the process of Americanization infiltrate those quarters that were most overtly hostile to it. Indeed, one might even suggest that Afrikaner intellectuals had, for a brief moment, outrun the wizards of Madison Avenue, who, in their rush to sell tomorrow's product today, had yet fully to grasp the vast commercial possibilities of yesterday.

As the lament of *Die Huisgenoot* suggests, the development of an American-inflected consumer culture was intimately related to the rise of mass media. In the quarter century that followed the creation of union in 1910, South Africa was transformed by powerful new forms of mass communication, from advertising and mass-circulation weekly magazines to gramophone records, radio, and Hollywood movies. Each of these media emanated from the United States; each carried a host of American associations and images.

Consider the world of music and entertainment. Even before the mineral revolution, South Africans, black and white, had already begun to exhibit an apparently insatiable appetite for American performance styles. The most popular form of mass entertainment in the nineteenth century, save perhaps for the circus, was the minstrel show, an American import, in which performers in blackface aped the antics and music of an imagined slave South. With the opening of the Witwatersrand, a host of new musical idioms, from ragtime to Tin Pan Alley, found their way to South Africa, borne on a tide of inexpensive American sheet music. The 1890s tours of Orpheus McAdoo's Virginia Jubilee Singers, an offshoot of the celebrated Fisk University Singers, created an enduring taste for African American spirituals, especially among African Christians. Vaudeville made its appearance in the early twentieth century, serving in South

Africa, as in the United States, as a way station between minstrelsy and movies. South Africa even hosted a touring Wild West show, run by a man named Texas Jack and featuring a young cowboy named Will Rogers. By ironic coincidence, this visit by a man who "never met a man I didn't like" overlapped with the visit of another who rarely met a man he did like—W. C. Fields, who arrived with a touring American vaudeville troupe.[19]

The cultural traffic accelerated in the 1920s, thanks to the gramophone, Thomas Edison's inexpensive, mass-produced device for reproducing recorded sound. Periodicals such as *Outspan* and *Umteteli wa Bantu* carried regular advertisements for dozens of different models, most American-made and all available on convenient installment plans. Initially, the industry ran on an agency business, with local outlets carrying a particular line of machines— Columbia and "His Master's Voice" were the most popular—along with that company's catalog of 78 rpm records. Weekly bulletins alerted customers to the latest American recordings to reach South African shores, from Louis Armstrong and his Hot Five to "Dixie" pioneer Jimmy Rogers, whose yodeling style hearkened back to the slave "hollers" of his native Mississippi even as it laid the foundations of country and western. Columbia opened a South African subsidiary in the late 1920s, enhancing access to American music while creating new recording opportunities for local artists. Tragically, many vintage South African records have been lost, but those that survive almost universally betray American, especially African American, influence. Mbaqanga, for example, the "African jazz" tradition that dominated urban African music in the 1930s and 1940s, was a self-conscious blending of "marabi," an urban proto-jazz of the early twentieth century, and American swing. Its most celebrated exponents—groups like the Jazz Maniacs and the Harlem Swingsters—expressed their affiliation with black America not only in their music but also in their names, their dress, their swagger. For such groups, comparison with the American original became, in the words of musicologist Christopher Ballantine, "the ultimate stamp of approval."[20]

The swelling popularity of American music was intimately connected to the rise of another, even more emphatically American medium: movies. As early as 1895, exhibitors from Europe and the United States had introduced South Africans to the wonders of the "kinetoscope." In the years after the South African War, moving pictures—typically single-reel affairs, lasting perhaps a minute—became a regular attraction in vaudeville programs and later in dedicated theaters. In an industry with no uniform specifications, different exhibitors relied on slightly different technologies, one of which—the "bioscope"— became South Africa's generic term for the cinema.[21]

The history of South African cinema is, to an extraordinary extent, the story of one man: Isadore W. Schlesinger. A dapper, diminutive man, Schlesinger was born in the old Austro-Hungarian Empire in 1871, one of nine children of Jewish parents. He arrived in the United States in 1884, settling on New York's Lower East Side, the cradle of so many future film industry moguls. While his father, Abraham, scratched his way up to own a cigar store and, later, an immigrant bank, I. W. established himself as a "merchant," peddling everything from hair combs to insurance policies. In the 1890s, for reasons that remain unclear, he embarked for South Africa. He arrived, inevitably, in Johannesburg, finding his way to an American-owned bicycle shop, where he asked for a job. "I'm good at selling things," he is alleged to have said. To test the proposition, the owners entrusted Schlesinger with a consignment of American chewing gum, an unfamiliar novelty that they had found impossible to sell. He returned a few days later having sold the lot, an achievement noted in passing by the visiting Mark Twain. From chewing gum, he graduated to life insurance, yet another American novelty, accumulating a small fortune as a traveling agent for the Equitable Insurance Company of New York. Schlesinger left the Transvaal during the South African War, but he returned afterward to launch a series of enterprises of his own. By the time of his death half a century later, this astonishingly neglected figure had built the Schlesinger Organisation, an empire of ninety companies embracing insurance, banking, real estate, advertising, agriculture, hotels, newspapers, radio, and most important, cinema.[22]

Schlesinger's genius lay in applying in South Africa methods and techniques perfected in the United States. His African Realty Trust, for example, developed the first of South Africa's leafy white suburbs, including Mount Pleasant in Port Elizabeth and Orange Grove, Parkhurst, and the "prestige" suburb of Killarney in Johannesburg. Following a method pioneered by American developers a generation before, African Realty sold lots on a monthly installment plan, promising buyers all the comforts of country living combined with proximity to the city. In 1926 Schlesinger launched the African Broadcasting Corporation (ABC), South Africa's, and indeed the continent's, first radio network. (ABC was amicably taken over in 1936 by the newly established South African Broadcasting Corporation.) He even revolutionized South Africa's citrus industry through the introduction of time and motion studies, assembly-line packing, and U.S. refrigeration technology. The list of Schlesinger's American-inspired innovations goes on and on, from South Africa's first amusement parks to an abortive attempt to introduce commercial aviation, from a chain of American-style "drugstores" to the creation of the Miss South Africa pageant.[23]

It was Schlesinger's career as a movie mogul that best exhibited his distinctively American genius. In 1913 he bought the Empire, a failing vaudeville house in Johannesburg. In the space of just a few years, he parlayed that initial stake into African Consolidated Theatres, which, with its sister company, African Film Productions, dominated South Africa's cinema industry until 1956, when the Schlesinger Organisation sold its movie interests to Twentieth Century Fox. Like his counterparts in Hollywood, Schlesinger was quick to recognize the value of vertical integration, of bringing production, distribution and exhibition all under one roof. Indeed, he went further than most American studios, creating companies to oversee theater catering, film advertising, even the production of newsreels that accompanied features. The heart of Schlesinger's domain was Johannesburg's Commissioner Street, South Africa's "Great White Way," which featured Broadcast House, headquarters of the ABC radio network, and three massive movie theaters, the Empire, His Majesty's, and the Coliseum, which between them seated more than 6,000 patrons. Like the contemporary "picture palaces" of New York and Los Angeles, Schlesinger's theaters pandered to dreams, offering not only movies and fine dining but also sumptuous appointments, from arches and classical statuary to the Coliseum's famous vaulted ceiling, painted to resemble the night sky. For generations of white South Africans, the "evening out" for dinner and a movie became a cherished weekly ritual—a ritual that, with the delayed advent of television, persisted far longer in South Africa than the United States. Needless to say, the movies that locals flocked to see were predominantly—by the 1930s, almost exclusively—American. Westerns, swashbucklers, gangster films, MGM musicals: all did robust business in South Africa, among both black and white audiences.[24]

In South Africa as in America, the emergence of cinema sparked controversy, with critics bewailing the medium's baleful effects on the individual, family, and nation. In substance and tone, such attacks were similar to those directed at the American film industry, but they were inflected in distinctively South African ways. How could the superiority and reputation of "white civilisation" be upheld when Hollywood filmmakers insisted on representing white people in the worst possible light—as gangsters and adulterers, prostitutes and thieves? Would impressionable "natives" be capable of distinguishing reality from what they saw on the silver screen? Faced with such questions, South African officials lurched instinctively toward censorship. As early as 1910, authorities prohibited the screening of the Jack Johnson–Jim Jeffries fight, on the grounds that it had provoked race riots in the United States. For the next eighty years, South African censors would continue to monitor movies, in a vain quest to prevent the infiltration of "dangerous" and "inappropriate" ideas from the United States.[25]

Afrikaner Nationalists were particularly uneasy with "*die bioskoop*," focusing not only on its moral corrosiveness but also on its tendency to dissolve divinely ordained differences between nations. In the late 1930s leaders of the Broeder-bond commissioned an investigation, later published by Nasionale Pers, into ways to harness cinema's extraordinary power, to make a medium that was "*volksvreemde*" (alien to the people) "*volkseie*" (the people's own). Largely at the instigation of Afrikaner Nationalists, a succession of South African govern-ments from the 1930s to the 1970s maintained a lucrative subsidy system for South African films, particularly for films in Afrikaans, essentially guaranteeing a profit for anyone with a movie camera. Yet while the system did help to sustain a small local industry, it did not upset the dominance of Hollywood. As late as 1969, a full 98 percent of South African films were imported from overseas, the vast majority from the United States. Ironically, most of the dozen or so low-budget features produced annually by South African filmmakers were bound for that most American of venues, the drive-in theater.[26]

There was an even deeper irony here. The same Afrikaner Nationalists who decried "*bioskoopbeskawing*," who warned of the poison of America's commer-cialized, mongrelized culture, would, on acceding to power in 1948, pursue policies that drew South Africa even further into the American embrace.

On the surface, the years after World War II marked a period of sharp divergence between the United States and South Africa. In the United States, the war ushered in a period of unprecedented economic advance for African Americans, while laying the seeds of a political realignment that would bring the civil rights agenda into the center of the Democratic Party agenda. The situation in South Africa could scarcely have been more different. While the war years produced many of the same structural transformations—accelerating urbanization, the large-scale movement of black workers into secondary indus-try, increasing black political assertiveness—the result was not civil rights but the triumph of Daniel Malan's National Party on a platform of apartheid. The years that followed brought population registration, the Immorality and Mixed Marriages Acts, group areas, separate amenities, Bantu Education, intensified urban influx control, rural labor bureaus, forced removals, separate develop-ment, and a violent assault on all political opposition. Yet paradoxically, these years of divergence produced a dramatic intensification of economic, cultural, and political links between the United States and South Africa.

Like their predecessors in the Pact government a generation before, the Afrikaner Nationalists who came to power in 1948 set out to promote local manufacturing, which promised both to reduce the nation's economic depen-dence on Great Britain and to provide employment for the white working-class voters who were the new government's chief constituents. New import restric-tions, including high tariffs and local content rules, sharply reduced the flow of imports into the country. By 1950, the value of American exports to South

Africa had fallen by more than 75 percent. This loss was more than compensated, however, by the opportunities the new government created for American capital. Eager to acquire new technology and management techniques, the apartheid regime set out to entice American investors, offering generous policies on taxation and repatriation of profits, while waiving tariffs and license fees on companies with local subsidiaries. In effect, the Nationalists in 1948 did deliberately what their predecessors in the Pact had done half-wittingly in the 1920s, compelling companies with an interest in South Africa's expanding market to set up operations locally.

The result was a torrent of new American investment. Virtually overnight, U.S. direct investment in South Africa increased threefold. By the end of the 1950s, it had more than doubled again, until it represented over half of American investment in Africa. More than forty American firms, including such giants as Timken Bearings, Dow Chemicals, John Deere, Kellogg, Quaker Oats, and 3M, established local subsidiaries in the years after 1948. A host of others, most notably General Motors and Johnson & Johnson, dramatically expanded operations. In 1953 Mobil Oil built South Africa's first oil refinery, enabling the country to process more than a quarter of its annual fuel requirements. The investment surge was most dramatic in pharmaceuticals, an industry dominated before the war by German firms; no fewer than thirteen American pharmaceutical companies opened South African subsidiaries in the late 1940s and early 1950s. So conspicuous was the influx that the U.S. Department of Commerce began to issue an annual report on South Africa, touting the country's commitment to "capitalism and individualism," as well as its political stability and quiescent labor climate.[27]

As in the 1920s, the postwar investment surge had profound cultural consequences. Birdseye Corporation, for example, introduced South Africans to frozen food, an innovation made possible by the explosion in the American-dominated home refrigerator industry. The whole phenomenon of processed food, which swept across South Africa in the postwar decades, was quintessentially American, enshrining values of consumption, convenience, and speed. Equally significant was the arrival of IBM, which established a South African subsidiary in 1953 and began to market its then state-of-the-art 700 series computer a year later. As a recent class-action lawsuit has revealed, the machinery of apartheid was erected on an IBM platform. In the decades that followed, American computers would revolutionize the working lives of South Africans as fundamentally as American mining and manufacturing engineers had transformed the lives of previous generations.[28]

From the perspective of investors, of course, such considerations were secondary to profits. And make no mistake: investments in apartheid South Africa paid off spectacularly, generating rates of return that were consistently the highest in the world. In 1950 alone, the percentage rate of return on U.S. direct investment in South Africa was 27 percent. In the mid-1960s, it still hovered around 20 percent, more than half again higher than in Japan, which ranked second in the world, and nearly three times higher than in Canada, which ranked third. Even in the early 1980s, as apartheid crumbled and economic growth stagnated, U.S. companies still reported an average rate of return of 18 percent.[29]

The United States' deepening economic involvement in apartheid South Africa was accompanied by a profound change in the political relationship between the two countries, to the point that one can begin meaningfully to speak of the United States as South Africa's political metropole. This process was inseparable from the Cold War. Where previous American administrations had tended to view relations with South Africa through the prism of Great Britain, the Truman administration and its successors saw them unequivocally in East-West terms. By those lights, South Africa represented a vital ally. Not only did it command the Cape sea routes, but it also produced thirteen of the twenty-four minerals listed in the U.S. strategic stockpiling program, some of which were available nowhere else outside the Soviet bloc. Many of these minerals—vanadium, platinum, manganese—were vital to American military production. Most important of all, South Africa possessed vast supplies of uranium, conveniently embedded in the gold-bearing conglomerates of the Witwatersrand. And uranium, as historian Thomas Borstelmann has shown, was regarded as the key to national survival in the Atomic Age.

As the Cold War unfolded, the Truman administration was determined not only to exploit the Witwatersrand uranium deposits but also to ensure that they remained securely in Western hands. In June 1948—one month after the National Party's accession—negotiations commenced between the South African government, the local mining industry, and the "Combined Development Trust" of the United States and Great Britain. The eventual agreement, signed in November 1950, guaranteed the Western alliance (in practice, the United States) a uranium monopsony. In exchange, the United States committed to design, finance, and build six uranium-processing plants. The deal also included several less explicit quids pro quo. In February 1951 Secretary of State Dean Acheson announced that the United States would henceforth give "the most sympathetic consideration" to South African requests for military equipment, despite a confidential Central Intelligence Agency report that stated that "South African military planning, to a degree unknown in North Atlantic Treaty states, focuses on the basic requirement of internal security." At the same time, the United States used its considerable influence in the United Nations (un) to shield South Africa from international censure, by forestalling and, on occasion, vetoing anti-apartheid resolutions. (This policy, as Acheson himself conceded, served the dual purpose of defending an ally and denying a precedent to those who wished to introduce the subject of American race relations on the floor of the un.) Thus did one of the most unfree nations on the planet become a bastion of the "Free World."[30]

The new political entente gave South Africa unprecedented access to American capital, some of it from commercial banks but the bulk of it channeled through the Export-Import (Ex-Im) Bank, a government body, or the World Bank, an international agency dominated by the United States. It is worth looking closely at this process, if only to contrast the largesse of the American government and its international proxies during the early apartheid years with their extraordinary stinginess today, when a democratically elected government struggles to redress apartheid's legacy. In January 1951, two months after the uranium agreement, the World Bank announced a $50 million loan to the South African government, including $30 million for escom, the state-owned electricity supplier, and $20 million to modernize the country's transportation network. Lest there be any doubt that the loan signaled a deliberate shift in American policy, a consortium of eight American commercial banks unveiled a $30 million loan to the South African government on the very same day. A $35 million loan from the Ex-Im bank soon followed. Once the floodgates had been opened, American capital poured into South Africa. Of the nearly $200 million in Ex-Im grants, loans, and credits to Africa between 1945 and 1955, roughly $150 million—75 percent—was directed to South Africa. Over 60 percent of World Bank investment in Africa over the same period likewise went south of the Limpopo. (Most of the balance went to neighboring Rhodesia.) World Bank and Export-Import Bank money overhauled South Africa's road network, modernized its harbor facilities, funded new rail lines and rolling stock, and vastly increased the productive capacities of escom and iscor, the state-owned steel producer. South Africa's vaunted "modern infrastructure" was built with American dollars.[31]

The importance of American capital was vividly illustrated in the aftermath of the Sharpeville massacre in March 1960, when South African police fired on unarmed African protesters, killing sixty-nine and wounding over two hundred. The massacre provoked an international outcry and massive capital flight. Over a quarter billion Rands in investment left the country; gold and foreign exchange reserves fell by nearly 60 percent. All of this is familiar enough to historians. What is less often observed is the American role in containing the panic. In late 1960 a consortium of American investors, led by Charles Engelhard, a mineral and chemical industry baron with close links to the Kennedy administration, arranged a $150 million loan for the South African government. A few weeks later, the World Bank and the International Monetary Fund stepped in with loans totaling more than $40 million, pumping up South African reserves and reassuring skittish investors. American corporations also helped to calm the waters. In May 1961 the South African government funded a twenty-page insert in the *New York Times*, targeting potential investors. The insert included lavish testimonials from the managing directors of Coca-Cola and General Motors, both of whom announced substantial new investments. "My corporation does not idly play with this kind of money," the director of Coca-Cola declared, referring to the opening of a new bottling facility. "We believe in South Africa and the new plant is a demonstration of faith on our side." Buoyed by such support, the South Africa economy weathered the crisis and embarked on a decade of unprecedented economic growth. Direct American investment surged anew, topping $1 billion by the end of the 1960s.[32]

Given the constraints of space, this essay can only touch briefly on the more recent history of "Americanization." Three themes merit mention. The first and most obvious is the introduction of television, launched by the state-owned South African Broadcasting Corporation in January 1976. Historian Rob Nixon has described Afrikaner Nationalists' long refusal to admit this quintessentially American medium and the combination of circumstances that caused them eventually to relent. Suffice it to say that much of what they feared—an avalanche of American commercial programs, promoting values foreign to "the South African way of life"—came quickly to pass. Between the high cost of local production and the boycott of South African television by the British union Equity, an ever-increasing percentage of the shows on South African screens were American. The most successful—*Rich Man, Poor Man*, *Dallas*, and *Dynasty*—were not only American in origin but also served further to entrench South African (and especially white South African) assumptions about American wealth and power. Even the vaguely countercultural shows that began to appear in the 1980s—*Miami Vice* (dubbed into Afrikaans as "*Misdaad in Miami*") and *The Cosby Show*—portrayed an America of astonishing glamour and material comfort.[33]

The second process is spatial. The erection of the first shopping malls in the 1970s—malls modeled on American prototypes and, in several cases, designed by American firms—heralded a profound spatial reorganization of South Africa, a suburbanization of economic life, embracing commerce, consumption, and work. The process, which obviously mirrors developments in the postwar United States, accelerated in the 1980s and 1990s with the collapse of group areas and influx control, which had previously barred Africans from settling in urban areas. The result, in geographer Keith Beavon's apt phrase, is the birth of the "neo-apartheid city," an eerily American landscape of decaying, predominantly black inner cities, ringed by a white world of shopping malls and cluster housing, interspersed with fast-food outlets and landscaped corporate office parks, all bound together by a network of multilane roads.[34]

The third process is financial or, more accurately, political-financial. Facing slowing growth rates, continuing capital outflows, a massive increase in state spending (defense spending alone increased more than 1,000 percent in the 1970s), and a dangerously low level of domestic savings (itself an artifact of American-influenced consumption patterns among white South Africans), the Nationalist government did what any government would do in the circumstances: it borrowed money. Large-scale government capital projects were increasingly funded through short-term loans from American commercial banks, which offered far lower interest rates than those available locally. In 1974–75, for example, Citicorp lent $150 million to ISCOR, the steel parastatal, and another $30 million to ESCOM, to aid in the development of nuclear power. The need for short-term money increased after the Soweto uprising of 1976, which prompted another bout of capital flight. By the early 1980s, more than forty U.S. banks had made substantial loans to the South African government, the total value of which peaked at $4.7 billion in 1984. One ironic consequence of this dependence on American commercial loans was that South Africa found itself vulnerable to the swelling pressure for disinvestment in the United States. Facing growing political pressure at home, New York banks refused to roll over South African loans in 1985, precipitating a run on the Rand and forcing the South African government temporarily to suspend all foreign exchange transactions. When the definitive history of the end of apartheid is written, this chapter will loom large. For present purposes, the episode is significant as perhaps the final step in the century-long process by which the United States displaced Great Britain as South Africa's economic metropole.[35]

Which brings us to the present. Perhaps not surprisingly, the years since 1994 have accelerated the process of Americanization, while introducing a raft of new ironies and paradoxes. The privatization of the television industry, for example, has dramatically increased the predominance of American programming. The post-apartheid years have also seen another surge in American investment. Perhaps the most significant new arrival is the McDonald's Corporation, not only because of McDonald's status as a low-wage, low-skill employer, but also because of what the McDonald's regime implies in terms of speed, standardization, and the structure of domestic life. Post-apartheid South Africa has also provided fertile ground for American management consultants. Like the "scientific" mining engineers of the late nineteenth century or the "time and motion study" experts of the interwar years, consultants from

Arthur Andersen, Deloitte Touche, McKinsey and Company, and other U.S. agencies offer South African firms the latest in American management expertise. While the reports and recommendations of such consultants rarely circulate publicly, most have clearly emphasized trimming employment rolls. Whether slashing jobs will produce the long-term increases in competitiveness and national growth rates that American consultants promise remains to be seen. There is no question, however, that such policies exacerbate a national unemployment rate that already hovers, depending on one's figures, somewhere between 25 and 50 percent.

Last but not least, the post-apartheid years have brought increased political traffic with the United States. The African National Congress's election campaign in 1994 was managed by President Bill Clinton's house pollster, Stanley Greenberg, himself the author (back in his academic days) of an important comparative history of the United States and South Africa. Deval Patrick, Clinton's adviser on race relations, played a central role in helping South Africa's Ministry of Labour to draft affirmative action codes, even supplying the computers needed to interpret incoming data. (Embattled defenders of affirmative action in the United States might be forgiven for wondering whether such computers were available because of the dwindling home market.) President Clinton himself arrived in early 1998, finding in the august presence of Nelson Mandela a welcome respite from domestic scandal. During his visit, Clinton extolled open markets and stressed that the future of U.S. relations with the country and the region lay in "trade, not aid." Americans, he opined, wished South Africans well but owed them "nothing." What, one wonders, do South Africans owe the United States?

NOTES

1. Union of South Africa, *Report of the Commission on Mixed Marriages in South Africa* (Pretoria: Government Printer, 1939), 41–49.

2. Richard W. Hull, *American Enterprise in South Africa: Historical Dimensions of Engagement and Disengagement* (New York: New York University Press, 1990), 2–15; Eric Rosenthal, *The Stars and Stripes in Africa* (2d ed.; Cape Town: National Books, 1968), 13, 39–48; Robert Kinloch Massie, *Loosing the Bonds: The United States and South Africa in the Apartheid Years* (New York: Doubleday, 1997), xii–xiv. On Cape Town's Waterfront, see Nigel Worden, "Unwrapping History at the Cape Town Waterfront," *Public History* 16, no. 2 (1994): 33–50.

3. Hull, *American Enterprise*, 25–27; Massie, *Loosing the Bonds*, xix.

4. Hull, *American Enterprise*, 38–39, 69–77, 119–20; Rosenthal, *Stars and Stripes*, 222–24. Perhaps the most influential of these American commodities was the Singer sewing

machine, which revolutionized working and domestic life in countries all over the world; see Robert B. Davies, *Peacefully Working to Conquer the World: Singer Sewing Machines in Foreign Markets, 1854–1920* (New York: Arno Press, 1976).

5. Clark C. Spence, *Mining Engineers and the American West: The Lace-Boot Brigade, 1849–1933* (New Haven, Conn.: Yale University Press, 1970). Probably the best example of this new class of professional mining engineer was John Hays Hammond, who studied at Yale and Freiberg, before making his fortune in the American West and in South Africa; see Hammond, *The Autobiography of John Hays Hammond*, 2 vols. (New York: Farrar and Rinehart, 1935). On the transformation of American life in the late nineteenth century, see Robert H. Wiebe, *The Search for Order, 1877–1920* (New York: Hill and Wang, 1967); and Alfred DuPont Chandler, *The Visible Hand: The Managerial Revolution in American Business* (Cambridge, Mass.: Harvard University Press, 1977). On the wages of South Africa's mineral revolution, see Charles van Onselen, "The World the Mineowners Made: Social Themes in the Economic Transformation of the Witwatersrand, 1886–1914," in *New Babylon*, vol. 1 of *Studies in the Social and Economic Transformation of the Witwatersrand, 1886–1910* (London: Essex Publishers, 1982), 1–43.

6. For contemporary portrayals of Kimberley from an American perspective, see "Life on the Diamond Fields," *Harper's New Monthly Magazine*, February 1873, 325–26; and Gardner Williams, *The Diamond Mines of South Africa* (New York: Macmillan, 1902). See also G. R. Bozzoli, *Forging Ahead: South Africa's Pioneering Engineers* (Johannesburg: Witwatersrand University Press, 1997), 49–54, 59–73; Hull, *American Enterprise*, 67–69, 89–90; Rosenthal, *Stars and Stripes*, 121–28, 131–35 (Rosenthal includes an appendix listing American place-names in South Africa; see 228–29); and Enid De Waal, "American Black Residents and Visitors in the S.A.R. before 1899," *South African Historical Journal* 6, no. 1 (1974): 52–55. On the "Bowery Boys," see Charles van Onselen, "Prostitutes and Proletarians, 1886–1914," in *New Babylon*, 118–35.

7. The fullest account of American mining engineers in the period is Hammond, *Autobiography*, 291–429. See also Thomas J. Noer, *Briton, Boer, and Yankee: The United States and South Africa, 1870–1914* (Kent, Ohio: Kent State University Press, 1978), 21–68; Shula Marks and Stanley Trapido, "Lord Milner and the South African State," in *Working Papers in Southern African Studies*, ed. Patricia Bonner (Johannesburg: Witwatersrand University Press, 1981), 65–67; Hull, *American Enterprise*, 63–77; Bozzoli, *Forging Ahead*, 49–54, 62–73; and Rosenthal, *Stars and Stripes*, 121–28, 131–35, 141–48. Twain's comment is quoted in Massie, *Loosing the Bonds*, xxi.

8. Rosenthal, *Stars and Stripes*, 137–40; Hull, *American Enterprise*, 24–25, 36–37, 65–66, 77–82, 218. On the origins of Anglo-American, see Duncan Innes, *Anglo: Anglo-American and the Rise of Modern South Africa* (New York: Monthly Review Press, 1984), 75–96.

9. Noer, *Briton, Boer, and Yankee*, 91–110; Hull, *American Enterprise*, 120–23.

10. Hull, *American Enterprise*, 138, 153, 365.

11. Ibid., 132–34. On the Pact, protection, and the growth of South African manufacturing capital, see D. Hobart Houghton, *The South African Economy* (3d ed.; New York: Oxford University Press, 1973), 116–42, 236–39; and Robert H. Davies, *Capital, State and*

White Labour in South Africa, 1900–1960: An Historical Materialist Analysis of Class Formation and Class Relations (Atlantic Highlands, N.J.: Humanities Press, 1979), 177–244.

12. Hull, *American Enterprise*, 138–40, 182–89, 369. On GM see Eric Rosenthal, *The Rolling Years: Fifty Years of General Motors in South Africa* (Johannesburg: Felspar, 1976). On Coca-Cola, see Affiliated Advertising, *Brands and Branding in South Africa: Key Success Stories* (Johannesburg: Affinity Advertising and Publishing Co., 1993), 68–69. The comment in *Businessweek* is quoted in Thomas Borstelmann, *Apartheid's Reluctant Uncle: The United States and Southern Africa in the Early Cold War* (New York: Oxford University Press, 1993), 49.

13. See Belinda Bozzoli, *The Political Nature of a Ruling Class: Capital and Ideology in South Africa, 1890–1933* (Boston: Routledge and Kegan Paul, 1981), 190–200.

14. On advertising and the rise of a consumer culture in the United States, see Roland Marchand, *Advertising the American Dream: Making Way for Modernity* (Berkeley: University of California Press, 1985); and Richard W. Fox and T. J. Jackson Lears, eds., *The Culture of Consumption: Critical Essays in American History, 1880–1980* (New York: Pantheon, 1983). On Freud's nephew Edward Bernays, see Edward Bernays, *Biography of an Idea: Memoirs of Public Relations Counsel Edward L. Bernays* (New York: Simon and Schuster, 1965).

15. The GM ads appeared regularly in *Outspan* magazine throughout the 1920s.

16. For the disavowal of politics, see *Outspan*, March 4, 1927, 3. The quoted advertisements are from March 4, 1927, 46, and December 19, 1930, 60.

17. I pursue these themes further in Campbell, "T. D. Mweli Skota and the Making and Unmaking of an African Petty Bourgeoisie," paper delivered to the History Workshop conference, Johannesburg, February 1987. On urban areas legislation and its impact on elite accumulation, see Rodney Davenport, "African Townsmen? South African Natives (Urban Areas) Legislation through the Years," *African Affairs* 68, no. 1 (1969): 95–109; and Davenport, "The Triumph of Colonel Stallard: The Transformation of the Natives (Urban Areas) Act between 1923 and 1937," *South African Historical Journal* 2, no. 1 (1970): 77–96.

18. See Isabel Hofmeyr, "Building a Nation from Words: Afrikaans Language, Literature, and Ethnic Identity, 1902–1924," in *The Politics of Class, Race, and Nationalism in Twentieth-Century South Africa*, ed. Shula Marks and Stanley Trapido (London: Longman, 1987), 110.

19. Veit Erlmann, *African Stars: Studies in Black South African Performance* (Chicago: University of Chicago Press, 1991), 21–53, 59–68, 112–55; David Coplan, *In Township Tonight: South Africa's Black City Music and Theatre* (New York: Longman, 1985), 37–41, 94–110; Thelma Gutsche, *The History and Social Significance of Motion Pictures in South Africa, 1895–1940* (Cape Town: H. Timmins, 1972), 1–40, 149 n. 3, 327; Rosenthal, *Stars and Stripes*, 157, 168–73. On the origins of minstrelsy, see Robert C. Toll, *Blacking Up: The Minstrel Show in Nineteenth-Century America* (New York: Oxford University Press, 1974). On the sheet music industry, the global impact of which is still underappreciated by historians, see R. Charles Hamm, *Yesterdays: Popular Songs in America* (1975; New York: W. W. Norton, 1983).

20. Christopher Ballantine, *Marabi Nights: Early South African Jazz and Vaudeville* (Johannesburg: Ravan Press, 1993), 3–7, 12–28. On marabi and mbaqanga, see Coplan, *In Township Tonight*, 94–110, 113–39. To sample the eclecticism of the period, listen to "Aubuti Nkikho," recorded in London in 1930 by jazz impresario Griffiths Motsieloa and included in the musical sampler accompanying *Marabi Nights*. While the tune preserves elements of marabi, it also utilizes "Dixie" yodeling and Hawaiian guitars, apparently played by two Afrikaner musicians working in the same studio.

21. On cinema's origins, see Robert Sklar, *Movie-Made America: A Cultural History of American Movies* (2d ed.; New York: Vintage Books, 1994), 3–64. For the introduction of the medium to South Africa, see Gutsche, *History and Social Significance of Motion Pictures*, 1–95.

22. For a person of his stature—he was, by some calculations, the largest private employer of labor on the African continent—Schlesinger is a remarkably elusive figure. This account is culled from John R. Shorten, *The Johannesburg Saga* (Johannesburg: Voortrekkerpers Beperk, 1970), 365–66, 631–38; W. J. De Kock and D. W. Kruger, eds., *Dictionary of South African Biography* (Cape Town: H. Timmins, 1972), 2:632–33; and L. E. Neame, *City Built on Gold* (Johannesburg: Central News Agency, 1960), 181–82, 207–8, 227.

23. Shorten, *Johannesburg Saga*, 342–46; Neame, *City Built on Gold*, 229–30, 236. On the citrus industry, see A. P. Cartwright, *Outspan Golden Harvest: A History of the Citrus Industry* (Cape Town: H. Timmins, 1977); and Rosenthal, *Stars and Stripes*, 195–99. On the beginnings of radio broadcasting, see Eric Rosenthal, *"You Have Been Listening . . .": The Early Years of Radio in South Africa* (Cape Town: H. Timmins, 1974).

24. Gutsche, *History and Social Significance of Motion Pictures*, 199–231; Neame, *City Built on Gold*, 181–82; Trevor Philpott, "The End of an Innocent Age," *The Listener*, July 8, 1976, 4.

25. On censorship, see Gutsche, *History and Social Significance of Motion Pictures*, 283–306; and Keyan Tomaselli, *The Cinema of Apartheid: Race and Class in South African Film* (New York: Lake View Press, 1989), 9–28. For parallel developments in the United States, see Sklar, *Movie-Made America*, 161–74. Despite censorship, black South Africa soon blossomed into a major cinema market—a market, moreover, with distinctly American tastes; see Peter Davis, *In Darkest Hollywood: Exploring the Jungles of Cinema's South Africa* (Johannesburg: Ravan Press, 1996), 9–11, 20–59.

26. H. Rompel, *Die Bioskoop in Diens van die Volk*, 2 vols. (Bloemfontein: Nationale pers Beperk, 1942). On the subsidy system, see Tomaselli, *Cinema of Apartheid*, 29–51.

27. See U.S. Department of Commerce, Bureau of Foreign Commerce, *Investment in Union of South Africa: Conditions and Outlook for United States' Investors* (Washington, D.C.: State Department, 1954). On American investment, see Rosenthal, *Stars and Stripes*, 223–25; Massie, *Loosing the Bonds*, 76–78, 112; Borstelmann, *Apartheid's Reluctant Uncle*, 96–97; and William Minter, *King Solomon's Mines Revisited: Western Interests and the Burdened History of Southern Africa* (New York: Basic Books, 1986), 73–83.

28. Hull, *American Enterprise*, 212; Affiliated Advertising, *Brands and Branding*, 115.

29. Massie, *Loosing the Bonds*, 274; Hull, *American Enterprise*, 209–13, 250, 319.

30. Borstelmann, *Apartheid's Reluctant Uncle*, 164, 187–88. See also Rosenthal, *Stars and Stripes*, 212–15; Hull, *American Enterprise*, 213–17; and Minter, *King Solomon's Mines Revisited*, 105–10, 130, 138.

31. For a pioneering analysis of the role of American grants and loans in Africa, and in South Africa in particular, see W. Alphaeus Hunton, *Decision in Africa: Sources of Current Conflict* (2d ed.; New York: International Publishers, 1960), 76–90. See also Borstelmann, *Apartheid's Reluctant Uncle*, 165; Hull, *American Enterprise*, 204; and Rosenthal, *Stars and Stripes*, 215.

32. On the United States and South Africa in the aftermath of Sharpeville, see Minter, *King Solomon's Mines Revisited*, 187–203; Hull, *American Enterprise*, 245–55; and Massie, *Loosing the Bonds*, 88–89, 169–70, 214–15. (The statements by Coca-Cola and General Motors managers are quoted in Massie, *Loosing the Bonds*, 88–89.) For the post-Sharpeville economic boom, see Houghton, *South African Economy*, 209–29.

33. On the television debate, see Union of South Africa, *Report of the Commission of Inquiry into Matters Relating to Television* (Pretoria: Government Printer, 1971); Rob Nixon, *Homelands, Harlem, and Hollywood: South African Culture and the World Beyond* (London: Routledge, 1994), 43–76; and Trevor Philpott's four-part series in *The Listener*, July 8–29, 1976.

34. Keith Beavon, "Nearer My Mall to Thee: The Decline of the Johannesburg Central Business District and the Emergence of the Neo-Apartheid City," paper presented to the Institute for Advanced Social Research seminar, Johannesburg, October 1998. See also Nigel Mandy, *A City Divided: Johannesburg and Soweto* (New York: St. Martin's Press, 1984), 68–76.

35. Hull, *American Enterprise*, 266–67, 297–309, 349; Massie, *Loosing the Bonds*, 93, 170, 204, 368, 500, 591–93. In 1986, as in the aftermath of Sharpeville, a South African deputation hastened to the United States, visiting the State Department, the International Monetary Fund, and nineteen commercial banks to plead for new investment capital, as well as for patience in repaying existing loans. In contrast to the earlier period, they received no satisfaction.

PART III

Engendering Race, Nation, and Empire

Women's Rights, Race, and Imperialism in U.S. History, 1870–1920

LOUISE M. NEWMAN

The worldwide advancement of women's issues is not only in keeping with the deeply held values of the American people; it is strongly in our national interest.
—Secretary of State Colin L. Powell, 2004

Although the primary reasons for the U.S. invasion of Iraq were initially formulated in terms of protecting U.S. national security, in 2004 it was also commonplace to hear high-ranking politicians laud the U.S. presence in Afghanistan and Iraq in terms of its benefit for advancing women's interests. The State Department proclaimed on its website: "Twenty-five million women and girls [in Iraq and Afghanistan] are now free to go to school, vote in elections, and play an active role in their societies."[1] George W. Bush began his third presidential debate on October 14, 2004, by reporting that a nineteen-year-old girl had recently won an election in Afghanistan. And Colin Powell announced the appropriation of $10 million for the Iraqi Women's Democracy Initiative, designed "to prepare women to compete in Iraq's January 2005 elections, encourage women to vote, train women in media and business skills, and establish resource centers for networking and counseling."[2]

In other words, changing the status of women in Afghanistan and Iraq has become central to the United States' effort to democratize these countries. The wearing of a veil, the resistance to sending girls to school, the exclusion of women from public life and economic ventures—these things have, in U.S. political discourse, become synonymous with unfree and undemocratic societies. To bring freedom and democracy to Afghanistan and Iraq, the United States has declared it essential to "ensure women's rights." As one State Department official explained, "Ensuring women's rights benefits not only individuals and their families, it also strengthens democracy, bolsters prosperity, enhances stability, encourages tolerance and builds a more peaceful and stable world. Respect for women is central to building a law-abiding, civil society, which in turn is an indispensable prerequisite for functioning democracies."[3]

Justifying the U.S. occupation of Iraq in such terms raises interesting problems for feminists in the United States, particularly for those who are opposed to the war. How can American feminists oppose U.S. funding of women's centers in Iraq, or refuse to support programs designed to educate girls and empower women to reform patriarchal political institutions? On the other hand, what response should U.S. feminists make to the charge that the United States' attempts to promote the education of Iraqi women and girls is an imperialist act?

These dilemmas are not new to U.S. feminists who support antipatriarchal struggles across the globe. (Whether democracy is the best political system for ensuring women's rights is a question that U.S. feminists would do well to investigate, but that subject lies outside the purview of this essay.) Nor is the Bush administration the first to make use of feminist sentiment to advance U.S. interests. Rather, U.S. feminists have long faced such ideological challenges, as debates over women's rights have been implicated in the history of race and imperialism for more than a century. Examining portions of this history may deepen our understanding of why no ideologically pure position is currently available to U.S. feminists who are committed to advancing women's interests around the globe—why feminism cannot today be easily exported to Iraq, separable from the national interests of the United States. Equally important, we may come to appreciate some of the tragic ironies contained within this history—ironies that stem from the ways in which white women's past efforts to "advance women" were integral to extending democracy to purported racial inferiors, including the "assimilation" of African Americans during Reconstruction, the "civilizing of Indians" in the 1880s, and the colonizing of Filipinos in the late 1890s.

By the late nineteenth century, demands for women's rights in the United States had developed in conjunction with, and had also offered a response to, the United States' extension of its authority over so-called primitive peoples both at home and abroad. This new ideology grew out of and replaced the ideology of republican motherhood of an earlier generation. During and after the Revolutionary War, white elite women had stressed their unique roles as "republican mothers," responsible for raising and educating sons to become the virtuous citizens of a new republic.[4] As the franchise was extended to the freedmen and naturalized male immigrants, white women argued that the future of civilization (and the future of "the race") depended on the inculcation of white middle-class gender norms into those peoples purported to be their racial inferiors. This responsibility (of modeling gender norms and teaching democratic values) required that white women venture outside the home, the family, and the private sphere into a realm that was decidedly public. Therefore, one of the main achievements of women during the antebellum period in U.S. history was the creation of a legitimate role for white women as political actors and agents of the state—despite cultural assumptions about sexual differences that characterized them as unsuited for these civic roles.

After the Civil War, white women vastly expanded their public presence and political activities.[5] The combination of social anxiety about the presence of nonwhite groups needing to be incorporated into the body politic, along with newly emerging Social Darwinian theories, helped make possible new social and political roles for white women in the 1870s and 1880s. White women garnered unprecedented public visibility and social status from their roles as special government agents (Alice Fletcher), as appointed state commissioners on boards dealing with urban problems (Josephine Shaw Lowell), as leaders of the settlement house (Jane Addams) and temperance (Frances Willard) move-ments, as well as missionaries both at home and abroad (Helen Montgomery). New associations and institutions emerged, including the Women's National Indian Association (WNIA), the Woman's Christian Temperance Union (WCTU), Hull House and other settlement houses, and domestic and foreign missions— all of which enabled white women to serve as exponents of civilization, carrying the ideals of Christianity to "less advanced" or "primitive" peoples, whether they lived within or outside the borders of the United States. The woman's foreign mission movement eventually became the largest movement of white women in the United States, attracting more than 3 million women as members by 1915, far exceeding in size even Frances Willard's popular WCTU (160,000 members).[6]

From the 1870s through the 1890s, the white women's movement grew to unprecedented heights at precisely the moment that Social Darwinism as a worldview was in its ascendancy. Social Darwinism provided a hospitable intel-lectual environment for the emergence of a vital women's movement, in part by strengthening long-standing beliefs in white women's moral superiority and by linking the advancement of civilization with a specific understanding of sexual difference. According to the theory, all human societies advanced from savag-ery to barbarism to civilization; during the progression, sexual differences between men and women supposedly became more and more significant. As historian Gail Bederman explains, "Savage (that is, nonwhite) men and women were believed to be almost identical, but men and women of the civilized races had evolved pronounced sexual differences. Civilized women were womanly— delicate, spiritual, dedicated to the home. And civilized white men were firm of character, self-controlled, protectors of women and children."[7]

This was not a new ideology. For generations, Westerners believed that the supposedly elevated condition of women under Christianity had marked Christian nations as superior to non-Christian ones. The purity, chastity, and moral goodness of (white Christian) womanhood had long served to symbolize the righteousness of the United States as a civilized nation. What was new to the discourse in the 1870s, however, was its explicitly racialized and gendered claims: civilization was understood as a racial trait, something that was inherited by the white race. Moreover, the advancement of civilization and racial progress were now defined in terms of specific gender norms: the domesticity, piety, purity, and submissiveness of white women and the intelligence, independence, and self-restraint of white men were hailed as the touchstones of advanced civilization and white racial superiority.

However, what was particularly unsettling for American men was the public role that white women were advocating for themselves in promoting democracy. What made white women's own transgression of separate spheres ideology more palatable was the way in which their actions and beliefs simultaneously buttressed existing racial hierarchies. Their public work to extend democracy was carefully couched in an argument that their efforts in behalf of purported racial inferiors would ultimately reinforce the superiority of white Christian civilization, strengthen the nation, and contribute to the United States' role as an imperial power.

For the ruling elite of the United States, then, sexual difference, racial progress, and national power were all interconnected. The superiority of the United States as a civilized nation was not just symbolized by the status of its most privileged women but also was understood to be a direct consequence of its patriarchal gender system. Conversely, the relative powerlessness of uncivilized peoples was construed as the result of an inferior and perverted gender system. The primitive woman was presumed to lack the sexual differentiation and moral development of the civilized woman, due to her centuries-long oppression by the men of her own race. Whether the "primitive" woman was embodied in the white imagination as the Indian squaw, an Oriental harem girl, an African savage (or a modern-day Iraqi woman), she became the symbolic yardstick by which whites in the United States measured the social development and political power of the people/nation in question.

After the Civil War, the construction of a national citizenry had to be newly imagined because of the recent emancipation of 4 million slaves and the ratification of the Fifteenth (1868) and Sixteenth Amendments (1870), which affirmed in principle freedpeople's rights of citizenship. The overarching problem for white elites, however, was how to assimilate a people whom they considered to be racially inferior and thus a grave danger to the ongoing "progress" of U.S. civilization. For middle-class white women, one answer lay in becoming schoolteachers and educating freedpeople for democracy. Their notion of education included literacy but also the inculcation of Protestant religious values and normative gender roles. In particular, white women believed that black women needed to be taught domestic skills so that they would be able to maintain clean and well-ordered homes (to the benefit of the black race, as well as for prospective white employers who might desire well-trained domestic servants). Black men needed to be taught various "industrial" skills, such as carpentry, so that they could, as a landless people, still find ways to earn their livings and support their families. After the war ended, 4,000 white women went south to teach in schools set up for freedpeople. Thousands more played a vital role in the freedmen's aid movement by lobbying the federal government for financial support, raising private money, and founding freedmen's relief societies to help alleviate the destitution of former slaves. Many of the white women who went south were single, newly accustomed themselves to earning a living. Most of these women had supported themselves before the war by working for antislavery societies. In their own lives, industry and thrift had promoted their financial independence and civic-mindedness, and their view of what needed to be done for black women was filtered through this worldview.[8]

As historian Carol Faulkner has argued, the work of white women in the freedmen's aid movement was both radical, in terms of existing cultural norms at the time, and radicalizing for the white women involved. Women like Julia Wilbur (1815–95) and Josephine Griffing (1814–72) urged the federal government to hire more women as agents for the Freedmen's Bureau, knowing how badly "self-sacrificing earnest workers" were needed. They resisted the mainstream view that giving direct aid to blacks would promote laziness, and they lobbied for such assistance long after the government gave up on this policy. They stood up to criticism that their appeals for direct aid were counterproductive, and they empathized with freedwomen's vulnerability in the labor market.[9]

At the same time, white female reformers often proposed economic solutions that were deeply problematic, such as separating children from their mothers in an attempt to boost family income. For example, Griffing, acting as an agent for the Freedmen's Bureau, advocated sending young black girls to work as domestic servants in white families in the North, in an attempt to alleviate black families' poverty and provide an alternative to southern field labor.[10] White reformers interpreted freedpeople's resistance to such propositions in terms of laziness and immorality, even when the primary motivation was to keep their families together. As Faulkner has pointed out, such propositions reiterated the worst abuses of slavery, leading to complaints by freedpeople that agents (both white and black) were trafficking in blacks. The irony was both painful and profound: white women championed black women's economic independence through paid labor, but they also, as Faulkner notes, "exacerbated the crisis of family disruption and recapitulated pre-emancipation domestic arrangements."[11]

By the mid-1870s, with the end of Reconstruction, most northern white women who had gone south to educate the freedpeople had returned north again. But their conviction that blacks as a race could achieve progress through education had taken hold for a successive generation of white women, who took up the "Indian problem" in the 1880s. Northern white women understood that whites had a shameful past to overcome in their relation to the Indians, and they were highly critical of white administrators of Indian reservations who personally profited from the distribution of government rations. They were also critical of white settlers and railroad developers who appropriated reservation land for themselves. They knew that the U.S. government routinely made treaties that it did not honor and that it used its military power to squelch resistance. They had just witnessed what had been one of the most violent periods in white-Indian relations to date, including the Modoc War of 1872–73, the Red River War of 1874–75, and ongoing battles with the Sioux, Nez Perces, Utes, Apaches, and others. Helen Hunt Jackson's exposé *A Century of Dishonor* (1881) laid out this history in detail, and Jackson's premature death in 1885 only strengthened other female reformers' resolve to continue in her stead. They believed that they could play an important role in civilizing Indians, who had been recently relegated to reservations, and they thought of themselves as a benevolent force, counterdistinction to the U.S. government's brutality.[12]

For example, in 1884, at a Lake Mohonk conference, Alice Cunningham Fletcher recommended that a fund be started to build homes for young Indians returning from the boarding schools at Carlisle and Hampton Institutes. The idea was picked up by Sara Kinney, president of the Connecticut chapter of the WNIA, which helped build roughly forty new homes on reservations over the next four years.[13] White women's commitment to building physical structures that resembled white residences was both the symbolic and physical embodiment of their idea that civilizing Indians had to begin with inculcating a "proper" domestic life among Indian women. As Kinney later explained, "If we could excite . . . in [Indian women and children] a desire for home-life which should have in it the elements of decency and comfort and progress, we need have no fear for the men. Indian men are curiously like their white neighbors, they can be influenced through their affections, and may be led towards better ways of living by the women and children whom they love."[14]

Frances Willard, head of the Woman's Christian Temperance Union, also urged white women to expand their activities in behalf of women so as to include in their purview the rescuing of Indian women from the patriarchal abuses of Indian men. In an address to the National Council of Women, a gathering that included the heads of most of the major women's organizations from around the country, Willard tried to enlarge white women's understanding of the woman question by relating the story of a temperance worker on an

Indian reservation in Florida, who "saw oxen grazing and a horse roaming the pasture, while two [Indian] women were grinding at the mill, pushing its wheels laboriously by hand. Turning to the old Indian chief who sat by, the temperance woman said, with pent-up indignation, 'Why don't you yoke the oxen or harness the horses and let them turn the mill?' The 'calm view' set forth in his answer contains a whole body of evidence touching the woman question. Hear him: 'Horse cost money; ox cost money; *squaw cost nothing.*' "[15]

The scenario that Willard described reinforced white women's long-standing beliefs that Indians remained in a state of barbarism because they refused to allocate labor along acceptable gender lines. Indian societies, white women believed, needed to adopt individualist, capitalist understandings of property ownership; Indian men needed to shelter their women in monogamous family structures. White women were convinced that the successful assimilation of Indians could not be attained without the emancipation of Indian women from the oppression and mistreatment they experienced within Indian societies. White women thus took it upon themselves to mediate between what they defined as a brutal primitive male and his exploited female subject.

At the base of such views, however, lay a deep ambivalence about Indian women's capacity for civilization.[16] On the one hand, white women argued that all women, civilized and primitive, could be educated for civilization, made to embody the feminine and domestic qualities deemed necessary for any race's advancement—hence the insistence on sending Indian girls to schools like Hampton in Virginia and Carlisle in Pennsylvania to train them to become homemakers, teachers, and missionaries. On the other hand, white women considered Indian women, especially the ones who "return to the blanket," as the main impediment to the racial progress of the Indian race, as well as to the future of the United States.[17] White women reformers measured their success at assimilating Indians by the degree to which Indian women rejected their former habits of dress and self-presentation. As one observer of Hampton students commented, "They have fallen out with their old ways of doing things. The hair must now be arranged becomingly, the colors that adorn their persons must correspond, and there is a certain dignity exhibited in their carriage."[18]

Probably the most influential woman in the Indian reform movement was Alice Cunningham Fletcher (1838–1923), who was to become the intellectual architect of what later became known as the Dawes (severalty) legislation. Fletcher grew up in New York City and was educated in private schools. She became a governess in the family of a school friend and was supported with a large salary for many years. In the early 1870s, in her young thirties, she moved to Manhattan, joined Sorosis, and became active in the Association for the Advancement of Women, planning its annual congresses from 1873 through 1881.[19]

In 1879, when Fletcher was forty-one years old, she met Standing Bear, Thomas Tibbles, and Suzette and Francis La Flesche while they were on a speaking tour in the East to raise money for the Poncas who had been dispossessed of their land. By this point Fletcher had become a serious student of ethnology, studying under Frederick Ward Putnam, the director of the Peabody Museum at Harvard University. When Suzette La Flesche and Thomas Tibbles returned to Boston in early 1881, Fletcher approached them about the possibility of visiting their reservation. They arranged for her to spend several weeks during the summer camping in Dakota Territory, among the Sioux, a tribe known to whites for its defeat of General George Custer at Little Bighorn on June 25, 1876, and for the recent surrender and imprisonment of Sitting Bull and his followers at Fort Randall.[20]

This trip made an indelible impression on Fletcher, who was deeply moved by how much work Indian women did, admitting that "never before . . . did I realize the power of woman's work and how she is indeed the mother of the race."[21] Although it was clear to her that Indian women controlled their own property and that their labor was fundamental to the economic well-being of their families, Fletcher would nonetheless later argue that Indian women would have to give up much of their traditional work in order for their race to progress from barbarism to civilization.

In 1885, in response to a request from the Senate, Fletcher drew up a lengthy, 693-page compendium of U.S. policies, entitled *Indian Education and Civilization*, a document that solidly established her as a foremost expert on Indian affairs and contained her thinking on the reforms needed to assist Indians in assimilating into U.S. civilization. For Fletcher, the most important thing was to eliminate Indians' understanding of collective land tenure and to replace tribal authority with the patriarchal authority of individual Indian men. "Tribal control," Fletcher had written elsewhere, "which ignores the individual and the family (as established in civilized society) must be overturned, and this can only be effected surely, by giving individual ownership of the land, and thus setting up the legal homestead. Until these changes are made, all labor in behalf of the elevation, education and civilization of the Indian will be but partially effective."[22]

Fletcher thus concluded that Indians' traditional beliefs and practices about self-government, land, property ownership, family, and gender could not be accommodated. The most needed reforms, in her view, were individual ownership of land; monogamous family structures; male support of women and children through farming; traditional log cabins instead of Native American dwellings; Indian women's assumption of domestic duties; learning of English; conversion to Christianity; education of children in missionary, common, or industrial training schools; and adoption of white styles of dress and appearance.

The Dawes Act, when it was passed by Congress in 1887, followed the outlines of Fletcher's thinking and made the granting of U.S. citizenship conditional on Indian conformity to the economic, religious, and gender practices of Christian capitalistic, patriarchal civilization. First, it provided for allotments of land to individuals, as an initial step toward granting U.S. citizenship. (Heads of families received 160 acres; single persons over eighteen, of both sexes, received 80 acres each, and children under eighteen received 40—provisions similar to the Homestead Act.) In accordance with whites' customs, wives were not given their own allotments. Second, in specifying different amounts of land to be granted to married and unmarried individuals, the Dawes legislation provided incentives to Indians to relinquish traditional forms of kinship relations and to adopt white forms. Third, and most important, the Dawes Act deprived tribal authorities of unallotted land, specifying that all "surplus" lands would be sold to the government and opened to white settlement. Since the targeted Indian population was under 200,000, and reservations included 123 million acres—or more than 6,000 acres per person—this provision had tremendous significance. In the end, the Dawes legislation provided for a forced transference of a huge portion of Indian land from tribal control to the U.S. government. Since the policy was mandatory, tribal authorities could not vote to decline the provisions, and individual Indians could only decide between accepting or refusing the allotments—to refuse meant they would be left landless and deprived of citizenship rights in the U.S. polity.[23]

A few observers were vehemently critical of severalty legislation: a decade earlier, an unidentified editorialist called severalty bills a "sham disguise. . . . They ought to be entitled bills for annihilating the Indian nations, in order to steal their lands."[24] But Fletcher lent her unqualified support to the Dawes Act, arguing that the vast landholdings were not "fully utilized" by Indian tribes and actually impeded the "advance of the Indian by isolating him from the industries that teem throughout the length and breadth of our land." She thus praised severalty legislation for opening the way "for the legal release of the Indian from his hitherto anomalous position in our midst. . . . The Indian may now become a free man; free from the thralldom of the tribe; free from the domination of the reservation system; free to enter into the body of our citizens."[25]

A decade later, in the 1890s, Fletcher grew disillusioned with the results of the severalty policy that had, by this time, successfully broken down tribal/community loyalties and had empowered individual men, just as it intended. In 1891 Fletcher offered a new reading of the overworked and exploited squaw, whom Frances Willard had conjured in her attempt to mobilize the troops on the Indian woman's behalf. Unlike Willard's depiction, which had emphasized the degradation of the traditional Indian squaw, Fletcher's analysis stressed the Indian woman's importance and value to her community. "Under the old tribal regime woman's industries were essential to the very life of the people," Fletcher explained, "and their value was publicly recognized. . . . Her work was exalted ceremonially. . . . Her influence in the growth and development of tribal government, tribal ceremonies, and tribal power, shows that her position had always been one of honor rather than one of slavery and degradation."[26]

Fletcher knew that her outlook would seem to her white audience "to run counter to ordinary observation," but she also knew herself to be the better judge, and she cautioned her colleagues in the women's movement against making "superficial observation[s] from a foreign standpoint."[27] Fletcher felt the irony poignantly: Indian women, who had traditionally been honored by Indian tribal culture for their work, were now being relegated to the status of ordinary housewives.

It was an irony that white women of Fletcher's generation could never fully appreciate. The labor of Indian women, and the respect it was accorded in their own cultures, presented a potential opening for white women's rights activists who were already critical of their own dependency on men and confinement within the domestic sphere. Had Christianity and Social Darwinian forms of thinking not been so powerful, white women might have been able to reexamine their belief in the absolute superiority of white civilization. They might have been able to use the example of the Indian woman to challenge the strictures of civilizationist discourse that attributed racial progress to patriarchal gender relations, as well as to protest their own relegation to the domestic sphere. However, Social Darwinism's construction of sexual differentiation as the basis for white racial progress was a hegemonic ideology in this period. Not until Margaret Mead's examination of primitive sexuality in *Coming of Age in Samoa* (1928) would white feminists rethink the relation of the civilized to the primitive in ways that would attribute something positive to primitive societies that white civilizations could emulate.[28]

In the intervening decades, from 1900 to 1920, feminists like Charlotte Perkins Gilman (1860–1935) and Mary Roberts Smith Coolidge (1860–1945) would not be able to look to primitive societies as a model (the racism in social evolution was too blinding), but they did appreciate that primitive women maintained a measure of economic independence and personal autonomy that civilized women had lost.[29]

Moreover, Gilman drew important lessons from the racial assimilation of primitives as she formulated a new ideology that she and others explicitly identified as "feminist." Gilman, who had been five years old when the Civil War ended, thought that Reconstruction and its aftermath had demonstrated the possibilities for an enlarged assimilationist program. Unlike many of her predecessors, Gilman reviewed her country's recent treatment of African Americans and came to an optimistic conclusion: education and assimilation of freedpeople had worked. "The African race," Gilman declared, ". . . has made more progress in a few generations than any other race has ever done in the same time, except the Japanese."[30] If freedpeople could be so improved within such a short time, Gilman believed, then so could white women.

Whereas white women in the WNIA had understood sexual differences as a positive feature of Anglo-Saxon civilization, and the measure of whites' racial advancement, Gilman identified whites' sexual differences as a negative vestige of their primitive past—something that had to be expunged from civilization if further racial advancement was to be attained. Gilman's key contributions to feminist theory were to assert the social benefit of white women's racial similarity with white men—and to recast existing sexual differences as a "primitive survival" within Christian civilization, a detrimental vestige of less-evolved societies that blocked the ongoing social evolution of whites' civilization.

In short, Gilman primitivized the white woman as part of a critique of U.S. gender relations, arguing that altering her prescribed social activities—to eliminate her dependence on men and the home—would improve the biological/racial/cultural inheritance of white women. The "woman problem," as Gilman redefined it, was that civilized women had been denied time, place, and opportunity to manifest those race characteristics that were part of every white woman's common racial inheritance with white men.

In the late 1890s, the emergence of a strong imperialist sentiment, along with efforts to establish the United States as an empire with colonies overseas, fundamentally influenced the content of social evolutionary theory, and thus the direction of feminist thought that emerged out of this intellectual tradition. The Spanish-American-Filipino War of 1898–1902 was a crucial event for Charlotte Perkins Gilman and her contemporaries because it challenged them to rethink the impact that imperialism could have on both civilized and primitive men's characters, as well as to reflect on the international role the United States as a democratic republic might play in response to the weakening of European imperialism. As historian Kristin Hoganson has noted, the Spanish-American War was initiated as a "chivalrous crusade to . . . liberate the Cubans from Spanish oppression" but quickly turned into a "self-aggrandizing war . . . end[ing] in a bloody colonial war in the Philippines that involved over 126,000 American soldiers, more than 4,000 of whom lost their lives."[31]

Economic and military motives lay behind the United States' occupation of the Philippines. Because of its physical proximity to China, the Philippines represented the military base that the United States needed if it were to have any chance of securing a share of the lucrative China trade. But equally important, with the relegation of Indians to reservations and the Plains Wars largely over, U.S. politicians perceived a need to find new ways for civilized men to exercise their martial skills, now that the U.S. Census of 1890 had declared the domestic frontier closed.[32]

For Theodore Roosevelt, and other ardent supporters of the Filipino war, occupation of the Philippines offered white American men the racial crucible they needed to forge their manly character. As Hoganson explains, "imperialists were driven by . . . the conviction that holding colonies would keep American men and their political system from degenerating," and "they thought that the experience of holding colonies would create the kind of martial character so valued in the nation's male citizens and political leaders."[33]

The Filipino phase of the war also precipitated vociferous debates within the United States about the morality and wisdom of trying to civilize and bring democracy to a primitive (nonwhite, non-Christian) racial group living outside the boundaries of the country. Anti-imperialists argued that assuming the government of foreign territories was in violation of the Monroe Doctrine and went against democratic principles. This debate often revolved around the question of whether policies that had been created in the years following the Civil War to deal with so-called primitive groups within the United States— blacks, Indians, and the Chinese—would be effective in addressing the situation of "savages" in foreign lands, where colonizers would be subject to the enervating effects of tropical climates. In essence, anti-imperialists believed that the colonization of the Philippines was indefensible because they thought that attempts to civilize Filipinos were unlikely to succeed. Benign forms of colonization would be ineffective and harsher forms too brutal to have the desired effect of uplifting savages. These opponents of annexation often invoked the domestic "Negro problem" to warn the United States against embarking on the "deluded" mission of trying to govern foreign primitives. The outlook of Mrs. Jefferson Davis was characteristic: "The President probably has cogent reasons for conquering and retaining the Philippines. For my own part, however, I cannot see why we should add several millions of Negroes to our population when we already have eight millions in the United States. The problem of how best to govern *these* and promote their welfare we have not yet solved. . . . The question is, What are we going to do with these additional millions of Negroes? Civilize them?"[34]

Furthermore, anti-imperialists, like Carl Schurz, worried that the enervating effects of tropical climates and cultures would be too great for Anglo-Saxon men to withstand so far from home.[35] In the process of trying to civilize Filipino savages, white men could lose their own distinctive racial and gender traits (they would become lazy and dissolute), with the result that the Protestant work ethic would disintegrate, adherence to democratic principles would deteriorate, and most worrisome of all, sexually restrained Christian men would be in danger of becoming sexually profligate.

From the late 1880s through the early 1900s, new theoretical developments occurred within social evolutionary thinking to make these new imperial projects (in the Philippines, Cuba, and Puerto Rico) appear safe and effective for whites who were concerned about the possible devolution of themselves as individuals and as a race. Psychologist G. Stanley Hall (1844–1924), sociologists Lester Ward (1841–1913) and Edward Ross (1866–1951), and economist Thorstein Veblen (1857–1929) all helped to reconceptualize the gender-race traits of white masculinity so that Anglo-Saxon men could claim access to the energy, strength, and aggressiveness previously deemed to characterize primitive men, without endangering their own civilized traits of manliness.[36]

Furthermore, Ward's theories helped to assure others that Anglo-Saxon men were not as transmutable as once believed. He helped reconceptualize white women as the "racial conservator" of the white race so that for the first time the Anglo-Saxon woman was imbued with a critical evolutionary-racial function: her biological stability was revalued as being essential to enabling the white race to pass on its civilized traits. Accepting evolution as we must, Ward wrote in 1888:

> Recognizing heredity as the distinctive attribute of the female sex, it becomes clear that it must be from *the steady advance of woman* rather than from the uncertain fluctuations of man *that the sure and solid progress of the future is to come. . . . The way to civilize the race is to civilize woman.* And now thanks to science, we see why this is so. Woman is the unchanging trunk of the great genealogic tree; while man, with all his vaunted superiority, is but a branch, a grafted scion, as it were, whose acquired qualities die with the individual, while those of woman are handed on to futurity.[37]

Although they were to stay behind in the United States while white men occupied the Philippines, white women would nonetheless provide the necessary social insurance that white racial progress would continue. Even if white men degenerated or miscegenated while they were gone, white women would still ensure the advancement of civilization by passing on their own race traits to offspring they had at home. This meant, of course, that it was even more imperative that white women fulfill their primary social function of having children. Falling birth rates, which had been occurring for more than fifty years, took on new meaning in the context of U.S. imperialist ventures, which is why, at the turn of the twentieth century, even a small decline in white women's fertility was treated with great alarm, as potentially leading to "race suicide."[38]

Because of the ways in which civilized femininity and masculinity were being reconstituted in an imperialist era (white women have babies for the race; white men fight wars for the race), Charlotte Perkins Gilman faced a difficult theoretical task in her attempt to dislodge the supposedly natural sexual dichotomies constructed by social evolutionary theories. Yet, Gilman ingeniously built her own conceptualizations of white women's evolutionary development on an aspect of Ward's work that she called his "gynaecocentric" theory, in which he posited that early on in human history, women had controlled the process of sexual selection, choosing their mates and thereby determining the racial traits that would appear in offspring.[39] In Gilman's articulation, women in these matriarchal societies had had this power of sexual selection because they had been self-sufficient laborers, the primary economic producers in their own societies. But in civilized societies, white women had lost the power of sexual selection because they no longer "worked," having instead become economically dependent on men. For Gilman, so long as civilized women remained economically dependent on men, men would retain control over sexual selection. And because "the male did not select for points of racial superiority, but for such qualities as pleased him," the "future development of the race" would remain in jeopardy. Thus, Gilman's response to those who blamed whites' racial degeneration on the declining birth rates of white women was to argue that white women should be allowed to become economically independent of men so that they could once again resume control over sexual selection.[40]

Gilman also rebutted the notion, espoused by Roosevelt, Ross, and others, that warfare was of evolutionary benefit to whites by denying that warfare served the same evolutionary function for civilized societies that it had served for primitive societies. According to Gilman, in primitive societies, in which women had been able to care for themselves and their children without men's assistance, combat had served the interests of human progress—by leaving only the strongest men as sexual mates for women. In modern civilized societies, however, in which women were dependent on men for their economic survival, warfare had disastrous effects: the strongest men were likely to die in combat, leaving their wives and children destitute, while those men who were "too old or too young, [or were] the sick, crippled [or] defective [would be] left behind to marry and be fathers."[41] As "civilization advances and monogamy obtains," Gilman argued, "whatever eugenic benefits may have sprung from warfare are completely lost, and all its injuries remain."[42]

Thus for civilized societies, warfare would lead only to a further weakening of the white population, exacerbating the problem of "race suicide" and producing what Gilman called "surplus" women who lacked husbands and so by necessity remained single and childless. Refusing to accede to explanations that attributed declining birth rates to white women's selfishness or ambition, Gilman railed, "All this talk, for and against and about babies, is by men. One would think the men bore the babies, nursed the babies, reared the babies. . . . The women bear and rear the children. The men kill them. Then they say: 'We are running short of children—make some more.' "[43]

But Gilman clearly did not intend her theories to challenge the civilizationist hierarchy of social evolution. Although Gilman posited that "human labour comes by nature from the woman [and] was hers entirely for countless ages," still she believed that it was a good thing that savage men usurped savage women's labor. "Well it was for the human race," Gilman declared, "that the male savage finally took hold of the female's industry . . . [for] in the hands of the male [formal, capitalistic forms of] industry developed."[44] The solution to the woman problem, as Gilman saw it, was for civilized women now to embrace cooperative forms of labor and free themselves of their economic dependence on men.[45]

Like Alice Fletcher, Gilman believed that the key to primitive peoples' racial advancement lay in their adopting the gender practices (cult of domesticity, separation of spheres, and the ideals of true womanhood) that she, as a feminist, found oppressive in her own life and was determined to abolish from whites' civilization. Yet the contradiction so apparent to us was not visible to Gilman, who understood social evolution as an inevitable, normative, and unilinear progression. As each race proceeded from savagery through barbarism to civilization, the matriarchal structures of primitives would have to be replaced by the patriarchal structures of civilization. Only after industrial civilization had been attained could a race become fully egalitarian in its treatment of women.

One of the most profound ironies of this history, then, is that at the very moment that the white women's movement was engaged in a vigorous critique of patriarchal gender relations in the United States, it called for the introduction of patriarchy into those societies deemed "inferior" precisely because they did not manifest the supposedly civilized gender practices of the United States. In other words, white women's critique of the cult of domesticity—as restrictive and oppressive when applied to themselves—went hand in hand with their defense of domesticity as necessary for the "advancement" of primitive women.

The implications of this paradox were far-reaching. First, it limited the critiques white women could offer of the racism and sexism within their own society because in the end they had to acknowledge that patriarchy had been key to their own racial advancement. As I have argued, Indian women's labor, and the respect it was accorded in their own cultures, presented a potential opening for women's rights activists who were critical of their own dependency and confinement within the domestic sphere. But social evolution's construction of racial progress prevented them from proceeding down this road.

Second, the intellectual hold of evolutionary discourses prompted white women to view other cultures with condescension, delegitimizing dissent from nonwhite and non-Christian women who had no authority to speak if they could not lay claim to being civilized themselves. White women's belief in the superiority of white civilization enabled them to overlook the ways in which they were implicated within the systems of oppression that governed the lives of nonwhite women. White women often scapegoated the purportedly less enlightened men of primitive cultures as personally responsible for the worst cases of abuse when the problems were far more complex. For example, a Sinophile like Donaldina Cameron, who lived happily among the Chinese women she "rescued" from prostitution in San Francisco, lamented that "the Chinese themselves will never abolish the hateful practice of buying and selling their women like so much merchandise, it is born in their blood, bred in their bones and sanctioned by the government of their native land."[46] What Cameron ignored in her analysis was that U.S. immigration laws made it difficult for Chinese men to bring their wives and families into the country, and that states forbade intermarriage between Chinese men and white women.

Evolutionary discourses of civilization also had profound significance for women of color, who had to demonstrate that they too were "true women" (pious, virtuous, chaste, refined, respectable, good housekeepers) in order to certify that their race already was or would soon become civilized. Black women reformers offered themselves as models of true womanhood to prove to whites that there was nothing inherently inferior about the black race. Josephine St. Pierre Ruffin, a leader in the National Association of Colored Women, declared in 1895, "Too long have we been silent under unjust and unholy charges [that black women are immoral and unchaste]. We cannot expect to have them removed until we disprove them through *ourselves*."[47]

Inherent in black women's notion of racial uplift was an acceptance of patriarchal precepts, notwithstanding the challenge to black male leadership articulated by black women such as Anna Julia Cooper, Ida B. Wells, and Mary Church Terrell. For example, Cooper, agreeing that civilization was measured by the status of women, formulated a powerful corollary: black women's status and treatment were key to the race's progress. For Cooper that status was dependent on a notion of black women's purity, chastity, and essential moral goodness, as normatively defined but denied by whites. And to ensure that black women would be able to manifest these qualities, Cooper insisted that black men needed to protect and defend the women in their families from the sexual abuses of white men. What was progressive in this claim was the insistence that black women were not sexually promiscuous but sexually unprotected. Yet Cooper's call for protection was still a call to black men to act as manly men and to black women to embody the characteristics of true womanhood.[48]

Scholars have analyzed how black women resisted various aspects of these hegemonic discourses of race and gender to empower themselves as political actors. Glenda Gilmore, for example, argues that black women reformers in North Carolina often encountered the ideology of separate spheres in prescriptive literature and from white northern teachers but did not themselves advocate the cult of southern ladyhood. Rather, they articulated "an evangelically driven ethos of 'usefulness'" that gave them a "middle space between the spheres into which they might venture on the business of the race."[49]

In a similar vein, Patricia Schechter describes what she calls the "authenticating strategies" of Ida B. Wells's autobiography, *Crusade for Justice*, which enabled Wells to downplay the threat and transgression of a powerful black woman. According to Schechter, Wells framed her political actions in terms of a religious commitment, describing herself as an "instrument of justice," and was able to move beyond the private sphere of domesticity—wife, mother, daughter —by drawing on the long-standing protest traditions of southern black women. Nonetheless, as Schechter points out, Wells was careful to "mask passion and feeling in order to avoid the appearance of unrestraint or immortality that so easily attached to African American women."[50] Although Wells clearly transgressed the sexual politics of the postbellum South in her antilynching writings, both she and Cooper argued for the inclusion of black women in civilization's construct of femininity (as virtuous and pure), even as they struggled against the constraints of that discourse, which elevated white women to the extent to which they adhered to the Victorian ideologies of separate spheres and true womanhood.

What is imperative to grasp in this history is not simply the cultural ethnocentrism of early feminist thought but also the historical relationship between women's rights discourse, Social Darwinian discourse, and policies advocating racial assimilation. Gilman's feminist vision (and that of May French Sheldon, Mary Roberts Smith Coolidge, and others) was historically and discursively intertwined with the assimilationist/imperialist policies of the late nineteenth and early twentieth centuries.[51] To put this point another way, feminism, assimilation, and imperialism were historical siblings, the offspring of a marriage between democratic ideals and social evolutionary beliefs: equal citizenship was possible only for those who conformed to the racialized and gendered precepts of (white) civilization.

The irony that they were training others for the franchise, while still denied the vote themselves, was not lost on white women's rights activists in the second half of the nineteenth century. But whether they were proponents of woman suffrage or not, white female reformers never doubted that they were qualified for the type of public work and nation building in which they were engaged. White women who participated in the freedmen's aid movement, the Woman's Christian Temperance Union, the settlement house movement, and in domestic and foreign missions were combating virulent forms of racism that had denied whole groups of people the right to U.S. citizenship. They sympathized and identified with such groups because they, too, were denied their rights as citizens—denied the franchise, excluded from most political offices, prevented from serving on juries, and the like. In their efforts to extend democracy to those who could demonstrate their capacity for civilization, these women ultimately came to see themselves as exemplary civilizers—true and useful citizens of the United States, with socially valued civic roles.

In the years leading up to World War I, the wctu expanded its provenance to lobby on behalf of colonized women around the globe in an effort to repeal the Contagious Disease Acts, which permitted and regulated prostitution and were still in force in British and American colonies. As historian Laura Briggs has explained, both those who supported the acts and those who wanted the legislation repealed "deployed a language of women's rights." Defenders of the acts justified the registration of prostitutes as a "progressive measure" that prevented indentured servitude and other forms of forced prostitution, protected innocent wives against contracting infections from husbands who frequented prostitutes, and provided medical treatment to prostitutes who otherwise would not receive any. On the other side, advocates of repeal wanted to outlaw prostitution altogether, blaming the social evil on predatory men who seduced innocent women.[52] Offering arguments similar to those that called for the prohibition of alcohol, the wctu took the side of repeal, arguing for the "rescue" and "reform" of the victims.

After 1917, when the Jones Act awarded U.S. citizenship to Puerto Ricans, the United States, with the strong support of the wctu, decided to bring Puerto Rican law in line with the U.S. mainland's, where prostitution was illegal. Prostitution was thus outlawed in Puerto Rico, and the wctu began working with the U.S. government in earnest, organizing a "Police Women's Reserve Corps," a women's group that would help the police identify and arrest prostitutes. The government wanted to control the spread of venereal disease among the newly drafted Puerto Rican/American soldiers training on the island; the wctu invoked its obligation as the "evolutionary-civilization superiors" "to aid and guide" prostitutes.[53] New laws mandated the imprisonment of convicted prostitutes for six months, during which time they were forced to undergo painful and humiliating treatments for venereal disease: repeated blood tests, pelvic exams, vaginal irrigations, and so forth.

In these debates over what to do about prostitution on the island, no side had the moral high ground. The WCTU's discourse embraced the prostitutes it desired to reform, representing them as daughters and enlisting the support of elite Puerto Rican women to assist with the clean-up campaign. But it also supported aggressive and violent treatments, which ultimately led to mass riots on the part of imprisoned women. The involvement of elite Puerto Rican women in the antiprostitution campaign drew opposition from Puerto Rican men, who found the activities "very far from a lady's place."[54] But Puerto Rican men also spoke out on behalf of the prostitutes ("innocents, with no greater crime than to protect their own lives and those of their children who are dying of hunger") and against the United States, criticizing the policies that led to imprisonment, starvation, and invasive medical treatment.[55]

In sum, the history of women's rights has involved much more than a struggle over gender roles and has been intertwined with the United States' efforts to promote its imperial visions, couched in a language of democratic liberalism, both at home and abroad. In the nineteenth century, women's rights meant that freedpeople, Indians, Filipinos, Chinese, and others were to be judged by whether they had normative, nuclear, monogamous families, contained their sexuality within heterosexual marriages, and exhibited a specific, acceptable gendered division of labor. In 1917–18 women's rights discourse was invoked by both U.S. colonialists and WCTU members to call for the "protection" of innocent women and girls from the sexual threat of men of their race.

The discourse of women's rights has also justified the U.S. presence in and control over foreign territories. In the case of Puerto Rico, it helped give articulation to a struggle between U.S. colonial officials and Puerto Rican elites over the management of the sexuality of working-class women. For Afghani and Iraqi women a century later, women's rights is again helping to justify U.S. occupation and is being employed in an effort to articulate what it means be a democratic nation (both for the United States—in that U.S. women have a visible military presence—and for Iraq, as the rights of Iraqi women are being debated). As different as these cases are, what they have in common is the way in which claims about women's rights have been, and are still being, used to define democracy and freedom for nations whose gender norms and practices differ from our own.

Is the United States doing good by fostering women's rights in Iraq? Perhaps. But it is worth noting that the implementation of women's rights involves repression as much as liberation. If there is a lesson in the past that might be applicable to women in Iraq today, it lies in how women's rights continue to function as an authorizing discourse, obscuring the violence of occupation and celebrating instead a heroic vision of the United States as a nation committed to freedom and democracy for all.

NOTES

1. "Afghan and Iraqi Women: Looking to the Future with Renewed Hope," September 28, 2004, <http://www.state.gov/r/pa/ei/rls/36585.htm> (January 22, 2007).

2. George W. Bush, September 2004, <http://www.state.gov/documents/organizati on/36690.pdf> (2004–2005); Colin Powell, September 27, 2004, <http://www.state.gov/ secretary/rm/36496.htm> (2005).

3. "Respect for Women: The Bush Administration's Firm Commitment," March 27, 2003, <http://www.state.gov/g/wi/19423.htm> (March 3, 2007); "Afghan and Iraqi Women: Looking to the Future with Renewed Hope," September 30, 2004, <http://www.state.gov/documents/organization/36690.pdf> (January 22, 2007).

4. See Linda K. Kerber, *Women of the Republic: Intellect and Ideology in Revolutionary America* (Chapel Hill: University of North Carolina Press, 1980).

5. Historians have argued that the postbellum explosion in women's organizations was precipitated by the radicalizing influence of the Civil War, which brought women into public view in record numbers and resulted in a temporary breakdown in the ideology of separate spheres. Catherine Clinton, *The Other Civil War: American Women in the Nineteenth Century* (New York: Hill and Wang, 1984), 81, 90. Also see Louise Michele Newman, *White Women's Rights: The Racial Origins of Feminism in the United States* (New York: Oxford University Press, 1999), 26.

6. See Newman, *White Women's Rights*, 53.

7. Gail Bederman, *Manliness and Civilization: A Cultural History of Gender and Race in the United States, 1880–1917* (Chicago: University of Chicago Press, 1995), 25.

8. Carol Faulkner, *Women's Radical Reconstruction: The Freedmen's Aid Movement* (Philadelphia: University of Pennsylvania Press, 2004), 6–7, 50–51.

9. Ibid., 87–88, 58, 98.

10. Ibid., 117.

11. Ibid., 127.

12. Alice C. Fletcher, "The New Orleans Exposition," *Southern Workman* 14 (July 1885): 79; Helen Hunt Jackson, *A Century of Dishonor: A Sketch of the United States Government's Dealings with Some of the Indian Tribes* (Williamstown, Mass.: Corner House Publishing, 1881).

13. Joan Mark, *A Stranger in Her Native Land: Alice Fletcher and the American Indians* (Lincoln: University of Nebraska Press, 1988), 105.

14. Sara Kinney, *Home Building Report* (1890), 7, cited in Deborah A. Kallina, " 'There's Nothing a Woman Can't Do If She Undertakes to Do It': The Women's National Indian Association, 1879–1951" (B.A. thesis, Brown University, 1986), 56.

15. Frances E. Willard, "Address to the National Council of Women, 1888," in National Council of Women, *Transactions of the National Council of Women of the United States, Assembled in Washington, D.C., February 22 to 25, 1891*, ed. Rachel Foster Avery (Philadelphia: J. B. Lippincott, 1891), 39.

16. The primitive woman was therefore heralded as embodying the solution to the Indian problem and at the same time castigated for holding back the nation. "Let the women then give to the destitute tribes Christian homes and missions," exclaimed Amelia Quinton, member of the WNIA, in 1889, "for without these, no nation can rise, for as the women are so will the nation be." A. S. Quinton, "The Annual Address of the President, Mrs. A. S. Quinton," *Indian's Friend* 1 (January 1889): 3.

17. Alice C. Fletcher, "The Indian Woman and Her Problems," *Woman's Journal*, November 10, 1900, 354. According to Fletcher, this was a dominant view but not one she shared.

18. "Incidents of Indian Life at Hampton," *Southern Workman* 10 (January 1881): 7. Also see Laura Wexler, *Tender Violence: Domestic Visions in an Age of U.S. Imperialism* (Chapel Hill: University of North Carolina Press, 2000), 94–126.

19. Mark, *Stranger in Her Native Land*, 13, 18, 28–29.

20. Ibid., 39, 42, 45.

21. Alice C. Fletcher, "Among the Omahas," *Woman's Journal*, February 11, 1882, 46.

22. Alice C. Fletcher, *On the Lawlessness of the Indian Reservation System* (Boston: Frank Wood, 1884), 33. The same passage also appears in Alice C. Fletcher, "Land, Law, Education—The Three Things Needed by the Indian," *Southern Workman*, March 1885, 33.

23. Frederick E. Hoxie and Joan T. Mark, "Introduction," in E. Jane Gay, *With the Nez Perces: Alice Fletcher in the Field, 1889–1892*, ed. Frederick E. Hoxie and Joan T. Mark (Lincoln: University of Nebraska Press, 1981), xiv–xvi.

24. "The Cherokee Protest," *Independent* 30 (February 1878): 16.

25. Alice Fletcher, "The Crowning Act," *Morning Star* 7 (March 1887): 1.

26. Fletcher, "Indian Woman and Her Problems," 354.

27. Ibid.

28. For a discussion of Margaret Mead, see Newman, *White Women's Rights*, 158–80; and Louise Newman, "Coming of Age, But Not in Samoa: Reflections on Margaret Mead's Legacy for Western Liberal Feminism," *American Quarterly* 48 (June 1996): 223–72, reprinted with minor changes in *Reading Benedict/Reading Mead: Feminism, Race, and Imperial Visions*, ed. Lois W. Banner and Dolores Janiewski (Baltimore, Md.: Johns Hopkins University Press, 2005), 51–69.

29. See Newman, *White Women's Rights*, 132–57; and Bederman, *Manliness and Civilization*, 121–69.

30. Charlotte Perkins Stetson [Gilman], "Masculine, Feminine and Human," *Kate Field's Washington*, July 6, 1892, 7.

31. Sixteen to twenty thousand Filipino soldiers and 200,000 Filipino civilians also died in the conflict. Kristin L. Hoganson, *Fighting for American Manhood: How Gender Politics Provoked the Spanish-American and Philippine-American Wars* (New Haven, Conn.: Yale University Press, 1998), 133, 138.

32. Ibid., 141.

33. Ibid., 138.

34. Mrs. Jefferson Davis, "The White Man's Problem," *Arena* 23 (January 1900): 2 (emphasis in original).

35. Carl Schurz, *American Imperialism: The Convocation Address Delivered on the Occasion of the Twenty-Seventh Convocation of the University of Chicago, January 4, 1899* (Boston: Dana Estes, 1899), 4. Also see Carl Schurz, "Imperialism," *Independent*, July 14, 1898, 83–86. This debate lasted well into the twentieth century. See, for example, Albert Ernest Jenks, "Assimilation in the Philippines, as Interpreted in Terms of Assimilation in America," *American Journal of Sociology* 19 (May 1914): 773–91.

36. For a discussion of the race-gender theories of G. Stanley Hall, see Bederman, *Manliness and Civilization*, 89–110. For a discussion of Ward, Ross, and Veblen, see Newman, *White Women's Rights*, 143–47.

37. Lester Ward, "Our Better Halves," *Forum* 6 (November 1888): 275 (emphasis added).

38. Edward Ross coined the term "race suicide" in 1901, and it was later popularized by Theodore Roosevelt in 1903 through 1905. See Bederman, *Manliness and Civilization*, 200–206.

39. Gilman dedicated *The Man-Made World* to Lester Ward, stating that "nothing so important to humanity has been advanced since the Theory of Evolution, and nothing so important to women has ever been given to the world." Charlotte Perkins Gilman, preface to *The Man-Made World; or Our Androcentric Culture* (New York: Charlton, 1911), n.p.

40. Ibid., 31. For a fuller discussion, see Newman, *White Women's Rights*, 137.

41. Gilman, *Man-Made World*, 216.

42. Ibid.

43. Charlotte Perkins Gilman, "Men's Babies," manuscript in Charlotte Perkins Gilman Papers, Schlesinger Library, cited in Linda Gordon, *Woman's Body, Woman's Right: A Social History of Birth Control in America* (New York: Grossman, 1976), 145.

44. Charlotte Perkins Gilman, *The Home: Its Work and Influence* (New York: McClure Phillips, 1903; Urbana: University of Illinois Press, 1972), 89.

45. Since cooperative labor was also what led to altruism, Gilman disputed the notion that (white middle-class) women were more altruistic than men. See Newman, *White Women's Rights*, 151.

46. Woman's Occidental Board of Foreign Missions, *Annual Report* (1904), 53, cited in Peggy Pascoe, *Relations of Rescue: The Search for Female Authority in the American West, 1874–1939* (New York: Oxford University Press, 1990), 121.

47. "Address of Josephine St. P. Ruffin," *Woman's Era* 2 (August 1895): 15, 13 (emphasis in original).

48. Louise Newman, "Beyond the Accommodation/Resistance Divide: Race and Gender in the Discourse of Booker T. Washington," in *Booker T. Washington and Black Progress: Up from Slavery 100 Years Later*, ed. W. Fitzhugh Brundage (Gainesville: University Press of Florida, 2003), 183.

49. Glenda Elizabeth Gilmore, *Gender and Jim Crow: Women and the Politics of White Supremacy in North Carolina, 1896–1920* (Chapel Hill: University of North Carolina Press, 1996), 36.

50. Patricia Schechter, *Ida B. Wells-Barnett and American Reform, 1880–1930* (Chapel Hill: University of North Carolina Press, 2001), 25.

51. See Newman, *White Women's Rights*, 102–15, 152–57.

52. Laura Briggs, *Reproducing Empire: Race, Sex, Science, and U.S. Imperialism in Puerto Rico* (Berkeley: University of California Press, 2002), 42–43.

53. Ibid., 46.

54. Ibid., 67.

55. Ibid., 49.

Cain contra Abel

Courtship, Masculinities, and Citizenship in Southern California Farming Communities, 1942–1964

MATT GARCIA

The study of American empire requires attention to the unique movement of migrants back and forth across the U.S.-Mexican border. Although this migration has been traditionally interpreted as the result of push-pull factors, recently scholars have begun to complicate such interpretations by considering U.S. economic domination within Mexico and the often state-sponsored movement of Mexican people that has resulted from such conditions. More than simply victims of an underdeveloped economy in Mexico, Mexican immigrants have also been economic and political refugees of a binational system that favors U.S. domination. As this imbalance of power contributed to extreme rural poverty and unemployment in Mexico, the U.S. and Mexican governments have often sought to alleviate such social pressure by providing state-sponsored, temporary immigration from Mexico to the United States for labor reputed to be "work that Americans won't do." Such agreements have often, but not always, protected the hegemony of the ruling parties in each country and have protected U.S. corporate interests in maintaining a Mexican market for their products and the labor to produce those products.

Twentieth-century Mexican domestic rural unemployment had its origins in the land policies of the Mexican dictator Porfirio Díaz, who reigned from 1876 to 1910. Díaz favored the expansion of large haciendas over small farms and communally owned lands (*ejidos*), thereby displacing many *campesinos* (Mexican farmworkers) from their rural homes.[1] Díaz also encouraged the expansion of the railroad to the North by courting 80 percent of the investment from U.S. corporations.[2] These policies occurred simultaneously with the rise of corporate agriculture in the U.S. Southwest, which provided Mexican workers employment options north of the border. U.S. corporate investment and expropriation of capital from Mexico facilitated this "uneven development" between Mexico and the United States, while the U.S. government encouraged such trends through relatively lax immigration restrictions on the U.S.-Mexican border and incentives for U.S. corporate investment in Mexico.[3] These conditions gave rise to discontent in the Mexican countryside and famously contributed to the development of the Mexican Revolution, which lasted into the 1930s.

In the wake of the Great Depression and the beginning of World War II, the U.S. government went beyond facilitating Mexican migration north and U.S. corporate investment south by initiating formal, bilateral negotiations with Mexico to address Mexico's rural unemployment problem and U.S. agricultural and railroad companies' desires for low-cost Mexican labor. In 1942 Mexico and the United States signed an agreement that brought thousands of temporary Mexican contract workers ("*braceros*") to harvest crops and maintain rail lines throughout the West and Midwest.[4] This agreement had at least two precedents: a 1909 executive agreement between Presidents William Howard Taft and Porfirio Díaz that brought Mexican sugar beet workers to Colorado and Nebraska temporarily; and U.S. Congress's suspension of a U.S. prohibition against contract labor for approximately 73,000 Mexican workers during World War I.[5] The semipermanency and formality of the 1942 bracero program, however, distinguished it from previous incarnations of such arrangements. Although the U.S. government planned to terminate the program once potential workers returned from the war front, U.S. agribusiness acquired an addiction for the low-cost foreign laborers. The importation of railroad workers declined toward the end of the 1940s; however, through the passage of a series of public laws, agribusiness lobbyists extended the contract system through 1964. The agreement had a significant impact on agricultural labor in California, replacing many resident Mexican American men with temporary, male contract workers from Mexico. Although totals of contract workers varied according to the season and crop, California growers consistently attracted the highest number of braceros of all the states participating in the program. On California citrus farms, for example, industry spokespeople reported that Mexican nationals performed 60 percent of all picking in 1945. By 1946, braceros constituted around 13,000 members of the workforce in California citrus groves, or 80 percent of all pickers.[6]

The bracero program had a profound impact on U.S.-Mexican relations and U.S. farmworkers. Over time, the agreement demonstrated and reinforced the Mexican government's inability to maintain equal negotiating power in state-to-state relations with the United States. Domestically, the program undercut unions' abilities to organize farmworkers and, therefore, to bring about positive change in wages and conditions on U.S. farms. While these consequences are well documented, fewer scholars have explored the impact of the bracero program on the local Mexican American communities that frequently served as the informal "host" to bracero camp residents.[7] Conflicts among Mexican Americans and Mexican nationals during the heyday of the program expose the cleavages among ethnic Mexicans living and working "*afuera*" (north of the border) and demonstrate how differential citizenship status complicated the formation of a unified community and labor movement. As David Gutiérrez and Neil Foley have argued, we must appreciate how the "wall" of citizenship separated many Mexican Americans from Mexican immigrants whose common ethnicity, racialized experience, and place in the workforce often "mirrored" that of Mexican Americans.[8] Citizenship frequently created the illusion of equality for Mexican Americans in the United States, thereby mitigating the possibility of other potential affinities among co-ethnics from different generations and with different relationships to the state.

The importation of Mexican contract workers drew Mexican nationals into direct competition for jobs with Mexican American men, creating anxiety among Mexican American families who, not unlike families on the other side of the border, had become accustomed to thinking of male labor as their primary income. Additionally, mechanization and the gendering of packinghouse jobs as "female" during and after World War II contributed to further marginalization of Mexican American men in California's postwar agricultural economy. Seen as less organized and more vulnerable to labor exploitation (an idea I challenge in my book), women increased their presence within the agricultural workforce.[9] While employment brought wages and greater autonomy to young Mexican American women, some Mexican American men understood these changes as a threat to their role as breadwinners within the family and the community.

In this essay I focus on the intraethnic conflicts between Mexican American men and braceros within Mexican *colonias* throughout Southern California during the 1940s, 1950s, and 1960s. Incidents of violence and murder typified the social tensions influenced by transformations in the postwar economy; however, they also revealed Mexican American men's attitudes concerning the role of Mexican American women in matters of work and courtship. The employment choices of growers and the policies of both the U.S. and Mexican governments produced conditions that gave expression to a crisis of manhood within the *colonia* and workplaces of Southern California, bringing to the surface competing notions of what it meant to be a man among "brothers" from either side of the border.

My focus on Mexican masculinities complements the work of anthropologists who have attempted to get beyond the "machismo" stereotype of Mexican men to a more nuanced definition of Mexican manhood that takes into account the various ways and places in which Mexican men perform their male identities. Rejecting the biology-based and culture of poverty arguments of the past, recent scholars have sought to define male identities based "on what men say and do *to be men*, and not simply on what men say and do."[10] Such an approach takes into account the contingent nature of identities that are bound by historical, comparative, and as Mary Douglas argues, bodily concerns and constraints.[11] For example, José Limón, focusing on expressions of "*carnalismo*" (brotherhood) among a group of working-class and unemployed Tejanos in contemporary South Texas, argues that the masculine behavior among his "*carnales*" (brothers) constitutes "symbolic expressions of an essentially political and economic concern with social domination not from below . . . but from above—from the upper levels of the structure of power in both countries [United States and Mexico]."[12] This analysis of machismo situates "macho" behavior among the marginalized working and unemployed classes of men located within an emergent urbanizing, postmodern, border economy based increasingly on low-wage service industries and high-tech farming.

Yet, as Roger Lancaster and Matthew Gutmann illustrate, masculine behavior such as violence, bullying, alcoholism, abandonment of children, abuse of women, and gambling—to name some of the attributes commonly associated with machismo—cannot simply be reduced to an "effect" produced by material relations. To quote Lancaster, machismo is "its own economy," which has the capacity to produce effects independent of, and in concert with, material influences. Consequently, understanding masculine behavior requires an appreciation of not only the economic context but also the particular social relationships and history that give rise to such behavior.[13] In the case of postwar Southern California, questions of citizenship, the changing relationships among men and women, and the transformation of Mexican femininities also contributed to expressions of male violence that tore at the fabric of *colonia* life.

"A Gift to Women from God!"

Employers' decision to place the bracero camps next to preexisting Mexican immigrant settlements revealed the racialized landscape of Southern California that preceded the arrival of the Mexican contract workers. Mexican immigrants, who came as economic and political refugees in the wake of the Mexican Revolution between 1910 and 1930, settled into Mexican villages or *colonias* (colonies) at the margins of Southern California society. Such settlements came about in one of two ways: either growers built housing close to work sites on the outskirts of citrus suburbs, or Mexican people bought property in undesirable areas near railroad tracks, in the paths of washes, or in contaminated areas, where they avoided the daily insults from a hostile white society. Although "white by law," Mexicans experienced life in Southern California as nonwhite "foreigners," whose existence was often explained away as temporary and whose labor was defined as "casual."[14] George Pigeon Clements, a prominent spokesperson for agribusiness before World War II and the director of the Agricultural Department for the Los Angeles Chamber of Commerce, described Mexicans as "birds of passage" who appeared at harvest then went back to Mexico when their work was done. While such stories may have played well to a national audience, they did not convince local white residents, who saw in their midst the formation of Mexican *colonias*. Clements tried to allay their fears by drawing on culturalist arguments to explain away the perceived racial threat presented by Mexicans. In 1928 he told an audience in Claremont, California, "The cry that [Mexicans] are a biological menace is without foundation." "They are," he argued, "less a menace than our own negro, Filipino, the Japanese, or the Porto [*sic*] Rican negro." What made them so? Clements explained, "They are honest; they are generous to a fault; they are artistic; and as far as their light and knowledge will permit, seekers toward perfection; they have no idea of time or money or values as we know them; they are as primitive as we ourselves were 2,000 years ago; their hospitality knows no bounds." Although Mexicans represented a racial other, they remained less of a threat compared with other nonwhite workers because of their "years of servitude," which Clements argued produced in them a tendency to "always [look] upon his employer as his pardon [*sic*; padrone] and upon himself as a part of the establishment."[15]

The perception of Mexicans as racially unfit for cohabitation with white families justified the segregation of Mexican immigrants prior to the establishment of the bracero program. By sequestering Mexicans to the margins of society, citrus growers could have their "fully adapted" farm labor, while local white populations, theoretically, could live without the fear of contamination. Despite the best-laid plans, neither growers nor common white residents achieved their goals of containment. In the years leading up to the bracero program, Mexican workers challenged the authority of their employers and increasingly sought housing outside grower-owned labor camps and unincorporated territories. Although growers averted major strikes in the heart of the citrus-growing suburbs of the San Gabriel Valley, in nearby Orange County, Corona, and Santa Paula, Mexican workers walked off the job and formed unions in defiance of their employers.[16] Meanwhile, white citizens resorted to Ku Klux Klan "night rides" and the use of racial restrictive covenants in housing to check the ambitions of local Mexican residents who tried to buy property outside of their prescribed neighborhoods.[17] The Depression ultimately served as the justification for the ethnic cleansing of Mexicans from Southern California, when, between March 23, 1931, and April 5, 1934, relief agencies joined a national effort to rid the United States of Mexicans by repatriating approximately 18,824 Mexican immigrants and their U.S.-born children who were living in citrus-growing regions. Suddenly, jobs thought to be beneath white workers became valuable again, making Mexicans expendable. In all, approximately 500,000 Mexicans and Mexican Americans from across the country were repatriated to Mexico. Yet, while repatriation dealt a blow to Mexican *colonias*, most Mexican families in the citrus belt weathered the political storm and remained in their communities, where they had invested their labor, purchased property, and made their homes.

The persistence of these Mexican families—those who "became Mexican American"—to stay on the land and in the country demonstrates how, in the words of historian Mae Ngai, some immigrants could be "impossible subjects."[18] As time went by, however, many of these original immigrants and their children became citizens of the United States, adopting a political (if not racial) position that was, at times, closer to those who opposed their presence than to the new Mexican arrivals who continued to come during and after World War II. Growers ignored distinctions among Mexicans in their creation of bracero camps and assumed that all Mexicans, regardless of their legal status, belonged together. In the minds of growers who built the camps, the *colonias* and lands adjoining these settlements served two functions: to keep braceros out of the mainstream of white society and to place them alongside Mexican Americans with whom they had cultural and linguistic affinities. The tendencies of white growers and government officials to ignore the contributions and commitments of Mexican Americans as American citizens reveal the degree to which white society viewed all Mexicans as outsiders and expendable servants, who could be cast aside or sent to Mexico when they became defiant or their labor became redundant.

For citrus growers and the lawmakers they lobbied, the bracero program represented a chance at making the "birds of passage" theory of Mexican labor and migration a reality. The existence of Mexican spaces within the landscape served as landings for temporary contract workers, whose needs, desires, or problems would be absorbed by the preexisting Mexican American population and not by the discriminating white residents. Growers and politicians cared little about the impact of the bracero program on the wages and living conditions for Mexican Americans, whose main source of income continued to be work in local agriculture.

Wage differentials and unequal competition for jobs resulted in strong feelings of resentment toward braceros, particularly among Mexican American men. Interviewing local men from the Cucamonga barrio "Northtown" in 1957, researcher Daniel Martínez found that a majority "strongly opposed the bracero program and any additional program of [its] type." Martínez observed that Mexican American men "felt that the braceros took jobs away from them, as well as lowered wages in the area, or at least kept them at the same level year after year."[19] Former bracero Donato Bustos described the intraethnic tension, recalling that Mexican American men "didn't like us because we came to take the jobs away from them." Working alongside braceros in the La Verne orange groves, Frank Hernández recalled that Mexican Americans and Mexican nationals occasionally "tangled" over the best picking assignments and methods of picking. "Braceros were difficult," remembered Hernández, "because they picked it their way [and] they were not careful." He added, "Braceros would get a bike and start picking before the sun came up." Angry Mexican American pickers objected to such behavior since early-rising braceros got to the highest-yielding trees first and made the locals look lazy. Similarly, Julia Salazar commented that her husband, Roman, a foreman for the College Heights Lemon Association, routinely settled conflicts between Mexican Americans and braceros in the groves. "Once in awhile," Salazar recalled, "Roman would say that [a bracero] would get irritated because the one from here [Mexican American] would be telling him that he was [picking] wrong." Occasionally, fights erupted into violent confrontations. "Sometimes [braceros] would pull out knives!" Salazar recalled. She added, "My brother-in-law, Cuco, told Roman that one time [a bracero] even chased him with a knife because he was backing the one from here [a Mexican American]."[20]

Bustos objected to characterizations of Mexican contract workers as a burden on the Mexican American community. "We made the wages go up," Bustos asserted, "because when I started in Redlands picking oranges, they paid us 6 cents a box." Unable to pay their rent, Bustos and his fellow braceros initiated a strike to improve wages for all workers in the groves. Although such a strike made some employers question the use of potentially militant braceros, for the most part wage differentials between Mexican nationals and locals encouraged many growers to continue supporting the program.[21]

Bustos also claimed that Mexican Americans, not braceros, initiated most intraethnic conflict between the two groups. "[Mexican Americans] didn't like [braceros] because they were outsiders," he recalled. "Braceros usually went out in a group," Bustos added, "because otherwise . . . sometimes they beat us."[22] The doctor for the Cucamonga and San Antonio bracero camps, Walter W. Wood, reported that during the height of the program, he treated from eight to ten braceros weekly for injuries received in fights with locals. Work conditions informed much of the intraethnic conflict; however, contemporary observers also noted another source of tension: competition for Mexican American female companions in the local *colonias*. Citing the report of local judge William Hutton, Daniel Martínez summarized, "During the period from 1944 to 1946 eight to twelve men, braceros and locals, appeared before the Cucamonga District Court every Monday morning on knifing or shooting charges resulting from friction over local girls or employment."[23]

Conditions of life and labor in the *colonia*, as well as the structure of the bracero program, contributed to the tension. The fluidity of braceros' lives, traveling back and forth between Mexico and the United States, raised Mexican American suspicions about the intentions of Mexican nationals. For example, Alfonsa Bustos, Donato's wife, commented that initially her family did not like her dating Donato because, as she explained, "they thought he was going to take me to Mexico." Alfonsa put their fears to rest by informing Donato that she would not live in Mexico under any circumstances.[24] Others worried that Mexican nationals courted Mexican American women for sexual gratification and casual relationships that lasted only as long as their contracts. For example, the Mexican and U.S. governments inadvertently intervened in many relationships when the program temporarily withdrew Mexican nationals at the end of World War II. Although lacking a precise number, Martínez reported, "many of these local girls were left with children," a situation, he claimed, that outraged their families and confirmed Mexican American misgivings about braceros.[25]

Many Mexican American parents objected to marriages between Mexican nationals and their Mexican American daughters because they believed that braceros entered into such unions for the sole purpose of attaining U.S. citizen ship. Such marriages of convenience concerned Julia Salazar, who commented, "Some [Mexican American women] would not be so lucky. They would find out that [their bracero husbands] were married in Mexico and all [braceros] wanted was to get their visas."[26] Martínez found similar attitudes among seven Mexican American women who married or had lived with Mexican contract workers in Northtown. "All seven," he reported, "shared the opinion that the braceros were just opportunists seeking a way to remain in the United States and marriage was the easiest way for them to gain this end." One woman who failed to give her name reported that she had had three children with a bracero as his common-law wife. Despite having eventually married, the couple was separated when the U.S. government deported her husband once he had finished his contract. She then spent her life savings on lawyers to prove that they had, in fact, married and that he should be allowed to return to the United States. After two months of living with the family, her husband left them for a high-paying job in downtown Los Angeles. Although she attained a court order requiring him to pay child support, at the time of the interview the woman had not received any money from her estranged husband for over six months.[27]

Selling work clothes to braceros for the local retailer Miller's Outpost and hosting weekend dances at local ballrooms during the 1950s, Candelario Mendoza witnessed exchanges between Mexican contract workers and Mexican American women. He explained, "[Braceros] would talk to some of the *chavalas* [young women] that they used to see around the barrio here, and I think that was part of the animosity. The fact that they were wooing some of the available gals—perhaps already involved with somebody else or someone was looking at them—and these guys were pretty glib."[28]

According to Mendoza, Mexican American men resented Mexican nationals since braceros performed their "verbal love-making" in Spanish, an ability that many acculturated locals no longer possessed. Julia Salazar concurred, recalling that "at dances, [Mexican American men and braceros] used to fight." Many conflicts began when braceros approached wives and girlfriends of Mexican American men for a whirl on the dance floor. "Some of the men from here don't like just anyone to go get [their] wife and pull her out to dance," Salazar commented. She added, "[Braceros] thought anybody could dance, you know, with anybody here." For Salazar and other married local women, "braceros were too forward; they thought they were a gift to women from God!"[29]

In spite of the concerns of parents and local Mexican American men, the relative autonomy of a new generation of Mexican American women provided them the freedom to make their own decisions about whom they should and should not date. In particular, the employment of Mexican American women in citrus packinghouses contributed to greater freedom of activity and more assertiveness in the family. During the early 1940s, for example, Upland packinghouse worker Salud Pérez tested her father's will by playing the "American," "male" sport of baseball in order to socialize with girlfriends and meet boys outside her home. She remembered, "When I finished with my work . . . I went out to play ball. My father didn't know what I was doing playing ball . . . that I was also looking at the boys. My father didn't know that I had already met another boy friend. I had one before [my husband]. It was a shock to [my father] that I wanted to get married and settle down because in my home my father always had his favorites and I felt left out. So then, [when] I met my husband and I loved him. . . . I said I won't let him go."[30]

Other women packers remained conservative in their behavior but maintained autonomy when it came to decisions of courtship and marriage. "The Bañales sisters," Julia Salazar recalled, "were typical people from Mexico." She observed, "They used to go to work with sweaters even if it was warm. And if it got very hot, they would get a blouse that would go up to [the neck]. They wore a skirt and *medias* [knee-high stockings] . . . [and] never wore any socks or shoes like we used to. They had their hair combed back in a *chongito* [ponytail]." While their style of dress may not have attracted potential suitors, Carmen Bañales insisted that she and her sisters made a conscious decision never to marry: "We had no use to worry for a husband . . . or a son." As a young woman, Bañales remembered the anguish experienced by her mother when her brother would stay out late drinking at the pool hall after a hard day of work in the groves. "[Mother] used to bless the four corners of the house," she recalled, "and my father used to say, 'Why are you scratching the walls? Your son is alright.'" The argument often led to a fight that had a profound impact on the girls' attitudes about marriage and childrearing. Ultimately, all three women committed their lives to the packinghouse and the church and avoided men whom Carmen Bañales regarded as "drunks."[31]

Among the former packinghouse employees I interviewed, many noted that a significant number of full-time packers at the College Heights Packing House in Claremont, California, chose not to get married. Observing this phenomenon, Julia Salazar commented that "one of the Guerreros, the Bañaleses, Catie [Aguayo], Helen [Ruiz], and Trini Hernández never got married." The unusually high number of single women working in the packinghouse concerned foreman Glen Tompkins. "It always worried me," Tompkins reflected, "because they were nice girls who worked up there in that packinghouse, and they just never [found] anyone to marry them—about five or six of them." Tompkins blamed the situation on the "rowd[iness] of Mexican boys," while Julia Salazar attributed their marital status to personal preference. "They were attractive in their younger years," she explained, "[but] I guess they didn't care to get married."[32] The decision to remain single represented an alternative lifestyle for women of that generation, particularly among Mexican families who saw marriage and kinship as a source of survival. Wage labor, however, enabled packinghouse workers to make decisions not afforded to homemakers or daughters dependent on parental incomes. Having worked all her life in the packinghouse, Carmen Bañales never saw the need for a husband. "Why have one?" she stated rhetorically; "we worked all the time." For Carmen and her sisters, wage labor liberated them from the concerns and abuses some women experienced as wives and mothers.[33]

Conversely, these freedoms also availed women packers to date and marry braceros, whom they sometimes worked with in the packinghouses. Such intraethnic courtship, however, occasionally came at a high price. Daniel Martínez observed that, often, women who dated or married Mexican nationals "were ostracized by the community as well as by their families." Women with children who had been abandoned by braceros received particularly harsh treatment at the hands of local residents. In need of jobs to support their families, some of these women resorted to prostitution in bars designated for Mexican nationals. Bar owners took advantage of their situation, for as one proprietor explained, "since they have become outcasts in the community for associating with braceros, this is the only type of work they can find." The bar owner tried to justify his actions, explaining that "the braceros would look for [women] anyway so why not provide them with the companions in a place where they could not get into trouble with the locals and at the same time be protected from being 'rolled' [robbed and beaten while under the influence of alcohol]?" The proprietor saw his business as a service to "the nicer girls from the community" since braceros would not be as inclined to seek them out for dates when they had plenty of opportunities to meet "outcasts" at the bar. The prevalence of prostitution within these drinking establishments, however, influenced the attitudes of many locals who questioned the morality of any Mexican American woman seen publicly with a Mexican national.[34]

In spite of attempts to keep locals and Mexican nationals separate, conflicts often came to a head in the vice-ridden bar districts located in areas adjacent to bracero camps and Mexican American *colonias*. In Cucamonga's Northtown, for example, business from young, local men, some Mexican American women, and Mexican nationals supported six bars that provided a lively nightlife on the weekends.[35] Captain Mayer of the San Bernardino County Sheriff's Department and Cucamonga constable Oscar Raven reported a consistent escalation of crime and violence in the area since World War II, attributing most of the problems to unemployment, prostitution, and juvenile delinquency. Neither official, however, felt inclined to remedy the situation since both believed "there is very little that can be done until the residents themselves try to do something about it." Quite often, law enforcement authorities were slow to respond to conflicts due to their distance from these outlying areas and a pervasive attitude of apathy and neglect. Cucamonga judge William Hutton reflected the true feelings of many local officials when he explained, "[I] personally do not think that the residents of Northtown know the meaning of the word morals; otherwise they would try to clean up their own mess."[36]

"El México de Afuera" versus "El México de Adentro"

Intraethnic tension between Mexican Americans and Mexican nationals reached a boiling point on April 19, 1952, when four Mexican American youths murdered Ricardo Mancilla Gómez, a bracero employed in the Cucamonga area. The tragic death of the twenty-two-year-old Gómez typified a season of growing violence, in which one other Mexican national, Magdaleno Cornejo, had been killed and several others beaten. Reported as an "assassination" in the Pomona Valley newspaper *El Espectador*, the "cold blooded" killing disturbed Ignacio "Nacho" López, a local defender of Mexican American civil rights and co-owner of the Spanish-language weekly. Lamenting that Gómez's death had come "at the hands of brothers of the same race," López editorialized that if such murders continued, the "*México de Afuera*" (Mexico of the exterior) will exterminate the "*México de Adentro*" (Mexico of the interior). He blamed the mistreatment of braceros (whom he called "ambassadors in overalls") on the moral deprivation of young Mexican American "*valientes*" (bullies), corrupted by ignorance, vice, and the spiritual decay of a country living in the shadow of the atomic bomb attacks on Hiroshima and Nagasaki, Japan. According to López, a government capable of killing millions with a single bomb shared some of the responsibility for creating "a morbid psychosis in society at large."[37]

Reports that Gómez's underaged assailants—Manuel Fierro, Frank Mendoza, Felix Montoya, and Sabiel Mayo—had been smoking marijuana and drinking at the Cucamonga cantina "La Cita" reignited moral panic over juvenile delinquency among minority youth. Sharing the concerns of a generation of educated Mexican Americans who came of age just prior to World War II, López worried that many young Mexican men had forsaken education for a lifestyle of "hoodlumism." During the 1940s, López became an outspoken critic of zoot-suiters, whom he regarded as "*pachuco* miscreants" that inspired prejudicial attitudes among Anglos toward all Mexican Americans.[38] Yet, unlike the Los Angeles County Sheriff's Department, which attributed the problem of Mexican American juvenile delinquency to the "inherent vicious[ness]" of all Mexicans, López believed that the roots of "*El Pachuquismo*" were "deeply entrenched in the economic and social discrimination practices inflicted on minorities by the dominant groups of our nation." Consequently, although Mexican American critics like López blamed youth for the violence against braceros, they identified the larger societal problems of racism and warfare, rather than the biological proclivities of the Mexican race, as the origins of such delinquency.[39]

In response to the murder, Mexican consuls Salvador Duhart of Los Angeles and Roberto Urrea of San Bernardino immediately withdrew 178 Mexican contract workers from Cucamonga and announced the suspension of the bracero programs throughout the Pomona Valley. Acknowledging that the murder was not an isolated incident but rather part of a larger trend, Duhart expressed outrage at the "repeated abuses against our braceros that have been the motive [for the suspension]." Deliveries of workers, they concluded, would not resume until all possible measures had been taken to correct the problem of violence against Mexican nationals.[40] In all, Mexico recalled over 500 contract workers from the Southern California Farmers Association, the primary distributor of braceros in the Pomona Valley. Many braceros expressed their support of the consul's decision in a letter signed by 123 coworkers of Ricardo Gómez asking for the immediate termination of their contracts.[41]

The Mexican government's actions precipitated a community-wide conversation, held at the local elementary school, that revealed many of the social and economic tensions created by the bracero program. Not surprisingly, local ranchers expressed their disappointment over the loss of Mexican contract laborers and promised to exercise their political influence to bring about the reinstatement of the program for the Pomona Valley. Mexican Americans were less unified in their response to Mexico's actions since defining "the community interest" had become a complicated matter in the ten years leading up to the crisis. The Southern California Farmers Association encouraged the marginalization of Mexican nationals by placing work camps on the outskirts of towns near Mexican American *colonias*. Some Mexican American merchants and business owners took advantage of this arrangement by setting up shops and establishing bars that catered mainly to the Mexican contract workers. Although bracero patronage benefited a few middle-class Mexican *comerciantes*, the working-class majority of Mexican Americans opposed the program on the grounds that the presence of Mexican nationals created unfair competition in the workplace and inspired violence and vice in their community.[42]

Siding with the majority, López became the mouthpiece for aggrieved Cucamonga residents. Affixing blame to contracting agents, government officials, and local bar owners for the crisis, López also reported that the meeting produced a "plan of action" that prescribed a tentative solution to the intraethnic violence. A majority of the 150 participants expressed a desire for camp managers and law enforcement officials to enforce the separation of young Mexican American men and braceros upon the return of Mexican nationals. In spite of strong objections to the program, López conceded its eventual reinstatement given the significant political influence of ranchers. Instead, López saved his harshest criticism for profit-driven bar owners who, he explained, "have let loose a plague on the good citizens of Cucamonga." Alarmed by escalating violence in the bar districts of Northtown, López and other meeting participants called for a unified community movement to clean up Cucamonga by making it more difficult for irresponsible proprietors to acquire liquor licenses. López argued that only pressure from concerned citizens could alter the ethics of bar owners, whom he called "ostriches hiding their heads in the corrupt sand."[43]

By early August 1952, growers successfully petitioned for the return of the braceros to the Pomona Valley. Between April and August, López and local leaders joined together to produce a list of seven recommendations that encompassed the complete concerns of Northtown residents. In his weekly column "Marginal," López offered the following suggestions to returning Mexican nationals: they should dedicate themselves completely to their work; they should avoid, as much as possible, bar fights; they should respect the private property and dignity of locals; they should avoid personal friction that could lead to tragedy; they should establish cordial relations with local families and all their members; they should always demand employment conditions and salaries equal to that of domestic workers; and they should avoid displacing local workers in their jobs.

The list went beyond the blame game previously played by López and local leaders to confront the larger social and economic problems associated with the bracero program. In particular, the last two suggestions addressed the issue of job competition and the program's negative impact on wages and job security for local Mexican Americans. López, despite his middle-class background, shared the concerns of working-class Mexican Americans. He supported the American Federation of Labor's (AFL) and Congress of Industrial Organization's (CIO) opposition to the bilateral agreement and questioned why Mexico, with its rich agricultural lands, could not develop a program to sustain rural life in the Mexican countryside. Anticipating observations made by current scholars on the subject, López further argued that the bracero program prompted "illegal immigration" by creating an "obsession" among all Mexicans to "cross the Rio Bravo" for work.[44] In another editorial he likened the conflict of the "Mexican brothers" to the biblical story of Cain and Abel. Coming down squarely on the side of local laborers, López pointedly argued that "field workers of this country must have primacy over those other elements—even in the sad case when these elements are of our same race and language."[45]

Conclusion

Aimed at Mexican nationals, López's recommendations sought to curb bracero behavior while marking the domain of Mexican Americans, particularly the social spaces occupied by men. The language of López's editorials positioned Mexican nationals as eternal outsiders whose place in society could be accepted only after their acquiescence to rights and privileges that belonged first and foremost to Mexican Americans. Moreover, his characterization of braceros as potential threats to the "dignity, private property, and families" of Mexican Americans unfairly criminalized Mexican contract laborers. Given that most physical assaults had been perpetrated *against*, not *by*, braceros and that theft did not constitute a major source of tension between the two groups, such vague references left much room for interpretation. What could López have meant by these warnings?

Pregnant with multiple meanings, López's editorial conveys, both directly and indirectly, many of the fears Mexican Americans harbored about the bracero program. Although evidence suggests otherwise, the perception of bracero criminality and deviance—fortified by anecdotal information and biased media coverage—partially shaped the community's attitude toward Mexican contract workers in specific, and the bracero program in general. As the articles in *El Espectador* reveal, although newspapers reported incidents of murder and assault against braceros, reports tended to blame the victim, particularly the numerous opinions voiced by López in his editorial column.

Equally important, the competition for jobs in the fields and the difference in wages paid to contract and local workers contributed to the tension erupting in the dance halls, bars, and pool halls where the lives of Mexican American men, Mexican American women, and braceros frequently intersected. Although the bilateral agreement guaranteed Mexican nationals a wage at or above the standard wage in a given region, in practice braceros routinely earned less than what their contracts promised. For example, in the citrus orchards of Cucamonga, the prevailing wage during wartime had averaged seventy cents per hour. By 1958, the hourly wage for Mexican American workers had risen slightly to between eighty cents and one dollar depending on the season, but employers often paid braceros between ten and fifteen cents less than their local coworkers. In that year, local workers earned an average weekly gross income of $43.20, compared with $38.40 for braceros.[46]

Additionally, due to many of the provisions of the bilateral agreement, including free transportation and affordable lodging, braceros could support their families (immediate or extended) back in Mexico at a much lower cost than local Mexican American workers. During World War II, a Mexican national could support his entire family in Mexico with as little as ten dollars per month. Conversely, monthly expenditures for local Mexican Americans averaged twenty dollars for rent, thirteen dollars for utilities, ten dollars for transportation, ten dollars for clothing, ten dollars for leisure time, five dollars for medical care, and ten dollars for miscellaneous items. Moreover, increases in food prices during World War II pushed the monthly cost of maintaining a family of seven children from forty dollars at the beginning of the war to eighty dollars by its end. The exorbitant cost of living also provided added incentive for married Mexican women to break with tradition and enter the workforce. Furthermore, although employers sometimes did not honor all the provisions of the program, Mexican nationals enjoyed the security of a guaranteed full-time job during the life of their contracts, while Mexican American workers could be laid off at a moment's notice.[47] The economic imbalances between Mexico and the United States—produced, in part, by U.S. economic imperialism in Mexico—facilitated the exploitation of all ethnic Mexican workers during the bracero program. In his appearance before the House Subcommittee on

Equipment, Supplies, and Manpower in 1960, AFL-CIO representative Andrew Biemiller aptly labeled the program "imported colonialism."[48]

While convincing, these economic explanations cannot fully account for the levels of violence and animosity that existed between Mexican American men and braceros. Changing gender relations—albeit partly a result of economic transformations in the U.S. economy—also added to some of the tension. The hiring of Mexican American women in packinghouses not only broke with traditional notions of men serving as the sole breadwinner but also produced a new attitude of independence among young local women. Single and employed, these female packers achieved the freedom to choose (or not to choose) whom they would date and even marry, including braceros. These choices disrupted more traditional courtship patterns within the *colonia* that privileged local men, both fathers and suitors, in determining the course of social relationships among men and women. Wage labor and an American consumer culture transformed the attitudes and behavior of daughters of Mexican immigrant parents who expanded the space and freedom of their lives while at the same time respecting the bonds of community and family.[49] As my oral histories with packinghouse workers reveal, although relationships between Mexican women changed, they also strengthened homosocial relations among women workers and built bridges of understanding and respect across generations.

For men, on the other hand, these changes produced a crisis of manhood, as they found themselves not only competing for jobs but also for the favor of women, whose options for courtship had dramatically increased in the years during and after World War II. Youthful indiscretion may have accounted for some of the "rowdiness" that occurred among Mexican American men, but their attempts to keep Mexican contract workers away from Mexican American women through harsh warnings and physical threats and violence amounted to performances of masculinity that countered their loss of privilege and control within the *colonia*. Moreover, Mexican American men chose to contrast one form of Mexican manhood against another, stereotypical, and more deviant form supposedly practiced by braceros. Mexican American men assumed the classic role as protectors of women's virtue, while they cast braceros as opportunistic lovers and irresponsible husbands and fathers who threatened to bring disorder and even disease to the community.

Ignacio López reinforced Mexican American men's sense of ownership over "their" women and "their" jobs by merging a discourse of masculinity with one of citizenship. In spite of his condemnation of violence and "*pachuco* miscreants," López sanctioned Mexican American masculine behavior by validating their sense of privilege to women's bodies and jobs gained primarily by virtue of their gender *and* citizenship status. López's additional recommendation that braceros "dedicate themselves completely to their work" conveyed the hope that Mexican nationals would remain singularly focused on their jobs and that they would not seek diversions with local women in *colonia* bars, pool halls, and public dances. Perhaps naively, López remained committed to the belief that the presence of noncitizen Mexican workers was a temporary condition that would eventually pass over time.

The ideology and practice of citizenship pursued by labor and civil rights groups inadvertently laid the foundations for a post-bracero labor system that emphasized the hiring of undocumented immigrants and the further marginalization of Mexican American workers in particular and farmworkers in general. Leaders like Ignacio López and labor organizations like the AFL and CIO forged a unified front against the Mexican contract system by calling for rights and privileges for citizens of the United States. Although demands for citizenship rights helped end the bracero program, they also drew the line of membership around a national community that accentuated the differences between members and nonmembers, citizen and noncitizen. This line of inclusion/exclusion cut at right angles against potential class and ethnic solidarity and, ultimately, helped increase the vulnerability of those at the bottom of the community: initially braceros, and eventually undocumented workers.

The history of the bracero program provides important lessons for today's U.S. Latina/os, as questions of citizenship and the presence of women and "foreigners" in the U.S. workforce continue to shape relations among them. The intraethnic violence and the failure to address labor exploitation during the period of the bracero program demonstrate that exclusive, legalistic definitions of citizenship contribute to greater divisions among Latina/os and, therefore, to a more fragmented and vulnerable community. Perhaps the great labor leader Luisa Moreno said it best in 1940 when she encouraged Latina/os to disregard differences in nationality or formal citizenship status. Speaking of noncitizen, Mexican immigrants, she asserted, "These people are not aliens. They have contributed their endurance, sacrifices, youth, and labor to the Southwest. . . . A people who have lived twenty and thirty years in this country, tied up by family relations with the early settlers, with American-born children, cannot be uprooted without the complete destruction of the faintest semblance of democracy and human liberties for the whole population."[50] Moreno presaged the now popular concepts of "cultural citizenship" and/or "denizenship" in her remarks by placing greater emphasis on the historical presence of Spanish-speaking people in the continental United States, a history that in some cases predates the arrival of Anglo immigrants.[51] Although not considered by López and the Northtown community, such a redefinition of citizenship seems to be taking shape among the current generation of immigrants and their offspring, most importantly Latina/o immigrants who comprise the majority of the most recent arrivals to the United States. In an ever-expanding and uneven global economy that necessitates the constant migration of developing world workers to the United States, such a flexible definition of citizenship may be the only hope we have of achieving a true democracy among the many people who inhabit this nation.[52]

NOTES

1. George Sánchez, *Becoming Mexican American: Ethnicity, Culture, and Identity in Chicano Los Angeles, 1900–1945* (New York: Oxford University Press, 1993), 20–22.

2. Gilbert González and Raúl Fernandez, "Empire and the Origins of Twentieth-Century Migration from Mexico to the United States," *Pacific Historical Review* 71 (February 2002): 19–57.

3. Ibid.

4. The term *"bracero"* is derived from the Spanish word *"brazos"* (arms). Literally, the term refers to those who work with their arms; symbolically, it also demonstrates how employers and much of the U.S. public regarded these workers as disembodied ranch hands. See Barbara Driscoll, *The Tracks North: The Railroad Bracero Program of World War II* (Austin, Tex.: Center for Mexican American Studies, 1998); Manuel García y Griego, "The Importation of Mexican Contract Laborers to the United States, 1942–1964," in *Between Two Worlds: Mexican Immigrants in the United States*, ed. David Gutiérrez (Wilmington, Del.: Jaguar/SR Books, 1996), 45–85; Daniel Martínez Jr., "The Impact of the Bracero Program on a Southern California Mexican-American Community: A Field Study of Cucamonga, California" (M.A. thesis, Claremont Graduate School, 1958); Paul Garland Williamson, "Labor in the California Citrus Industry" (M.A. thesis, University of California, Berkeley, 1946); Ernesto Galarza, *Merchants of Labor: The Mexican Bracero Story.* (Charlotte, N.C.: McNally and Loftin, 1964); and Stephen Pitti, *The Devil in Silicon Valley: Northern California, Race, and Mexican Americans* (Princeton, N.J.: Princeton University Press, 2003).

5. García y Griego, "Importation of Mexican Contract Laborers."

6. Williamson, "Labor in the California Citrus Industry"; "Mexican National Program to Continue," *California Citrograph*, February 1946.

7. Matt Garcia, *A World of Its Own: Race, Labor, and Citrus in the Making of Greater Los Angeles, 1900–1970* (Chapel Hill: University of North Carolina Press, 2001); Pitti, *Devil in Silicon Valley*; and Mae N. Ngai, *Impossible Subjects: Illegal Aliens and the Making of Modern America* (Princeton, N.J.: Princeton University Press, 2004). The impact on sending families and communities in Mexico is yet another angle waiting to be researched. University of Southern California graduate student Anna Rosas has begun such investigations.

8. David Gutiérrez, *Walls and Mirrors: Mexican Americans, Mexican Immigrants, and*

the Politics of Ethnicity (Berkeley: University of California Press, 1995); Neil Foley, "Becoming Hispanic: Mexican Americans and the Faustian Pact with Whiteness," in *Reflexiones 1997: New Directions in Mexican American Studies*, ed. Neil Foley (Austin, Tex.: Center for Mexican American Studies, 1998), 53–70.

9. Garcia, *World of Its Own*.

10. Matthew C. Gutmann, *The Meanings of Macho: Being a Man in Mexico City* (Berkeley: University of California Press, 1996), 17.

11. Mary Douglas, *Purity and Danger: An Analysis of Concepts of Pollution and Taboo* (London: Routledge and Kegan Paul, 1978).

12. José E. Limón, *Dancing with the Devil: Society and Cultural Poetics in Mexican-American South Texas* (Madison: University of Wisconsin Press, 1994), 12.

13. Roger N. Lancaster, *Life Is Hard: Machismo, Danger, and the Intimacy of Power in Nicaragua* (Berkeley: University of California Press, 1992), 236; Gutmann, *Meanings of Macho*.

14. Ian F. Haney-López, *White by Law: The Legal Construction of Race* (New York: New York University Press, 1996).

15. George P. Clements, "Mexican Immigration and Its Bearing on California Agriculture," *California Citrograph*, November 1929, n.p. I explain the full range of attitudes regarding Mexican racial identity in *World of Its Own*.

16. Douglas Cazaux Sackman, *Orange Empire: California and the Fruits of Eden* (Berkeley: University of California Press, 2005); Margo McBane, "The Role of Gender in Citrus Employment: A Case Study of Recruitment, Labor, and Housing Patterns at the Limoneira Company, 1893–1940," *California History* 74 (Spring 1995): 69–81; José Alamillo, *Making Lemonade out of Lemons: Mexican American Labor and Leisure in a California Town, 1880–1960* (Urbana: University of Illinois Press, 2006); Gilbert González, *Labor and Community: Mexican Citrus Worker Villages in a Southern California County, 1900–1950* (Urbana: University of Illinois Press, 1994).

17. Garcia, *World of Its Own*.

18. Sánchez, *Becoming Mexican American*; Ngai, *Impossible Subjects*.

19. Martínez, "Impact of the Bracero Program," 44.

20. Donato and Alfonsa Bustos, interviewed by Margo McBane, 1994; Julia Salazar, interviewed by the author, 1998; Frank Hernández, interviewed by Margo McBane, December 18, 1994. The Bustos and Hernández interviews are archived in the La Verne Mutual Orange Distributors Citrus Packinghouse Oral History Project, City of La Verne, Calif.

21. Donato and Alfonsa Bustos interview. Most bracero strikes were over work camp conditions, especially the poor quality of food, not wages. Mario T. García, *Mexican Americans: Leadership, Ideology, and Identity, 1930–1960* (New Haven, Conn.: Yale University Press, 1989); Martínez, "Impact of the Bracero Program"; Robert J. Thomas, *Citizenship, Gender, and Work: Social Organization of Industrial Agriculture* (Berkeley: University of California Press, 1985).

22. Donato and Alfonsa Bustos interview. See also Julia Salazar interview.

23. Martínez, "Impact of the Bracero Program," 55, 67.

24. Donato and Alfonsa Bustos interview; Julia Salazar interview.

25. Martínez, "Impact of the Bracero Program," 55.

26. Julia Salazar interview.

27. Martínez, "Impact of the Bracero Program," 55. Although braceros had camps, they were permitted to live outside these prescribed areas if they could find a host or provide for themselves. Donato and Alfonsa Bustos interview; Julia Salazar interview.

28. Candelario José Mendoza, interviewed by the author, 1994.

29. Ibid.; Julia Salazar interview.

30. Salud (Sally) Pérez, interviewed by Betty Maxie, 1975, Upland Public Library, Upland, Calif.

31. Julia Salazar interview; Carmen Bañales, interviewed by the author, 1998. After retiring from the packinghouse, Carmen, Amparo, and Maria Bañales worked as volunteers at the local Catholic church, Our Lady of Assumption. Amparo and Carmen live in a house two blocks from the old College Heights Packing House and across the street from their church. They have willed the house to the church.

32. Julia Salazar interview; Glen Tompkins, interviewed by the author, 1998.

33. Carmen Bañales interview. See also Robert Alvarez Jr., *Familia: Migration and Adaptation in Baja and Alta California, 1800–1975* (Berkeley: University of California Press, 1987).

34. Martínez, "Impact of the Bracero Program," 56–57.

35. Candelario José Mendoza interview.

36. Martínez, "Impact of the Bracero Program," 60–61.

37. *El Espectador*, April 25, 1952.

38. *El Espectador,* June 11, 1943; Ignacio Lópcz, FBI file, File no. 100-200298, Part 1, copy in author's possession.

39. *El Espectador*, June 11, 1943. For an example of another Mexican American critic of juvenile delinquency, see Ruiz Papers, Stanford University Special Collections, Stanford, Calif. The career of Manuel Ruiz Jr. is discussed in Eduardo Obregon Pagan, "Sleepy Lagoon: The Politics of Youth and Race in Wartime Los Angeles, 1940–1945" (Ph.D. diss., Princeton University, 1996).

40. *El Espectador*, April 25, 1952.

41. *El Espectador*, May 2, 1952.

42. *El Espectador*, May 9, 1952; Martínez, "Impact of the Bracero Program." Martínez reported, "The 200 residents of Northtown interviewed, with the exception of the businessmen, all believe that their problems have been aggravated by the presence of the Braceros." He concluded, "They feel very strongly against the Bracero Programs and if a solution is not found soon, additional complications will result."

43. *El Espectador*, May 9, 1952. López said of local growers: "All these men, will use their political prestige and force for the general benefit of the entire community."

44. *El Espectador*, June 22, 1951; García y Griego, "Importation of Mexican Contract Laborers"; Gutiérrez, *Walls and Mirrors*; Testimony of Elizabeth Sasuly, in U.S. Senate, Committee on Agriculture and Forestry, *Hearings on Farm-Labor Supply Program*, 80th Cong., 1st sess., 1947. Although López only mentioned the AFL, the CIO also opposed the bracero program.

45. *El Espectador*, October 6, 1950.

46. Martínez, "Impact of the Bracero Program."

47. Ibid.

48. Ngai, *Impossible Subjects*, 48.

49. Vicki Ruiz, " 'Star Struck': Acculturation, Adolescence, and the Mexican American Woman, 1920–1940," in *Building with Our Hands: New Directions in Chicana Studies*, ed. Adela de la Torre and Beatríz Pesquera (Berkeley: University of California Press, 1993), 109–29; Douglas Monroy, "An Essay on Understanding the Work Experiences of Mexicans in Southern California, 1900–1939," *Aztlán* 12 (Spring 1981): 59–74; Mary E. Odem, "Teenage Girls, Sexuality, and Working-Class Parents in Early Twentieth-Century California," in *Generations of Youth: Youth Cultures and History in Twentieth-Century America*, ed. Joe Austin and Michael Nevin Willard (New York: New York University Press, 1998), 50–64; Garcia, *World of Its Own*. As packinghouse employees, and therefore "industrial" workers, Mexican women had collective bargaining rights under the provisions of the National Labor Relations Act (Wagner Act), whereas Mexican American men, who performed mostly agricultural labor, were not guaranteed these same rights. Although women in the citrus industry rarely used these rights, these unequal conditions of labor demonstrate important differences between the rights of Mexican American men and women in the U.S. workforce during the postwar period. For a fuller treatment of women's work within packinghouses, see Garcia, *World of Its Own*.

50. Luisa Moreno, "Caravan of Sorrows," in *Between Two Worlds*, ed. Gutiérrez, 122.

51. William V. Flores and Rina Benmayor, eds., *Latino Cultural Citizenship: Claiming Identity, Space, and Rights* (Boston: Beacon Press, 1997); Rachel Buff, *Immigration and the Political Economy of Home: West Indian Brooklyn and American Indian Minneapolis, 1945–1992* (Berkeley: University of California Press, 2001).

52. I am inspired here by the Oregon Students of Color Coalition, who in 2003, fought for the passage of Oregon Senate Bill 10, which would expand in-state tuition rates to include all students, regardless of immigration status. Students would have to fulfill the following minimum criteria: graduate from an Oregon high school; attend an Oregon high school for at least three consecutive years; show they are working toward residency; or be accepted to an Oregon public university. Similarly, Brown University student and daughter of Dominican immigrants Evelyn Duran has organized a statewide campaign to make higher education accessible and affordable to undocumented students in Rhode Island.

Private Suffering and Public Strife
Delia Alvarez's War with the Nixon Administration's POW Publicity Campaign, 1968–1973

NATASHA ZARETSKY

In the frantic moments after his fighter plane was shot down, and he ejected from his aircraft and hit the waters off the Gulf of Tonkin, twenty-six-year-old naval lieutenant Everett Alvarez Jr. tore off his wedding ring and let it sink to the ocean floor. He believed that ridding himself of the ring would prove essential to his survival should he be captured by the North Vietnamese. "Survivor school instructors had warned us not to wear them in combat," he recalled in his 1989 memoir, *Chained Eagle*, "because communists would inflict further mental torture on a captured married pilot by fabricating stories about the aviator's wife abandoning him for another man."[1] As Alvarez's wedding band sank to the bottom of the ocean, the current carried the pilot toward dry land, and soon he was discovered by the North Vietnamese coastal militia. On the afternoon of August 5, 1964, Everett Alvarez Jr. became the first U.S. fighter pilot to be taken prisoner in the North, where he remained in captivity for eight and a half years. By the time he returned home to the United States in February 1973, he had become the longest-held American prisoner of war (POW) in North Vietnam.[2]

There are several ways readers of Alvarez's memoir might interpret this account of his capture. At one level, the discarding of the wedding ring signals Alvarez's departure from the world of marriage and his entry into the solitary world of the prison camp. At another level, as readers later learn, it is a moment of foreshadowing, since Alvarez's wife eventually fell in love with another man and divorced him while he remained imprisoned in Hanoi.[3] This early scene in the memoir is also notable for its selective treatment of violence. Predictably, given the patriotic genre of the POW memoir, the violence unleashed by the U.S. bombing raids over North Vietnam is far from view. In its place are images of the shoot-down itself: Alvarez's fighter plane coming apart in midair, the sensation of his body hitting the water, and Alvarez feverishly tearing off his face mask and helmet as he struggles for orientation. But Alvarez's fear about the violence that awaits him should he be taken prisoner is even greater than his fear of crashing. Immersed in the waters off the Gulf of Tonkin, Alvarez thinks first about what he had been told during his military training: that for the communists, even the most intimate spaces are violable. By dropping his wedding ring into the ocean, Alvarez attempts to shed his personal identity, believing that the North Vietnamese will trade on domestic secrets (either contrived or real) in order to inflict psychological injury, and that this strategy could prove devastatingly effective as an instrument of torture.

When Everett Alvarez made the fateful decision to pursue a career as a naval pilot in the early 1960s, the threats of captivity and torture in a foreign war seemed remote. Born and reared in northern California, Alvarez was a young Mexican American man from a working-class family who hoped that by entering an elite corps of the military, he would be able to secure a viable economic and professional future for himself. In choosing this path, he was also participating in a long tradition of minority men affirming their patriotism and vying for their citizenship rights through military service. Only dimly aware of the war in Southeast Asia when he joined the navy, he could hardly have imagined that he would find himself at its center.

But between 1964 and 1973, Everett Alvarez and his family were in fact at the center of several local, domestic, and global transformations: the bloody and protracted conflict in Vietnam, rising international opposition to the war, heightened generational tensions within the Mexican American community, the advent of women's liberation, and the explosion of the Chicano movement. The story of the Alvarez family touched on all of these transformations, while also revealing a constitutive feature of the POW controversy—the fear, expressed by Alvarez in his memoir, that the private realm of the family would be incorporated into the public world of war and politics. This fear had surfaced first in 1968, when the Nixon administration launched a publicity campaign to call attention to Hanoi's alleged refusal to comply with the rules for prisoners of war laid out in the 1949 Geneva conventions. At the heart of the campaign was the specter of an innocent family drawn into a war over which it had no control. Between 1968 and 1973, a range of sentimental images designed to elicit both rage at the North Vietnamese and sympathy for the relatives of POWs bombarded the American public: bewildered children growing up without fathers, frightened wives living in a state of quasi widowhood, mothers and fathers desperate for any information about their captured sons. With little available information about the condition of the captives, prisoners themselves were conspicuously absent from the campaign. Instead, the campaign focused almost entirely on the prisoners' families, precipitating a host of questions: When and how could the stories of POW families be "made public"? What was the connection between the private suffering of individual families and the

Nixon administration? Above all, what was the relationship between the POW's familial identity as a husband, brother, father, or son and his military status as a fighter pilot and, in the eyes of the North Vietnamese, a war criminal?

This history of the POW publicity campaign between 1968 and 1973 adds a new layer to the cultural history of the Vietnam War. Scholars have shown that as the war ended and in the years that followed, the POW became an object of intense emotional and cultural investment. Historian George Herring has argued that when the POWs returned to the United States in early 1973, they received the "only heroes' welcome" from a war nearly devoid of heroism.[4] Noting the ubiquity of the POW in post-Vietnam literature, film, and television, Elliott Gruner and Susan Jeffords have suggested that the POW embodied the rebirth of heroism out of defeat, a rebirth tied to the project of national re-militarization in the 1980s. What defined the POW, they argue, was his hyper-masculinity: the complete and successful exclusion of any traits traditionally identified with the feminine, including weakness, passivity, vulnerability, or loss. According to Gruner, the POW evoked a nation "whose most recent heroes are overmuscled male bodies bristling with an array of lethal weaponry."[5] The POW narratives, according to Jeffords, conform to the larger picture of American war narratives. Their defining feature is that they are "a 'man's story' from which women are generally excluded." The story of the POWs, like that of American war in general, Jeffords concludes, was shaped precisely by what it repressed—the feminine realm.[6]

This essay takes issue with this contention. Regardless of the hypermasculinity associated with the POW in post-Vietnam film and literature, the "go public" POW campaign proceeded from a radically different logic. Between 1968 and 1973, it consistently identified the captured soldier with those realms traditionally linked to femininity and womanhood: domesticity, sentimentality, privacy, and the affective ties of the family. By linking captured men to their families and transforming the POW story into a domestic drama, the campaign simultaneously vilified the North Vietnamese as transgressors of the boundaries between the public and the private and figured the American nation as the war's victim rather than aggressor.

By placing the family at the center of the drama, the POW publicity campaign drew on a second literary tradition—not traditional war stories but the captivity narratives that were so popular in the colonial landscape of the late seventeenth century.[7] Often featuring a white female captured by Indian savages and torn away from her community, these first-person accounts—not unlike Alvarez's memoir—typically opened with violent scenes of family disruption, dissolution, and death. While these accounts declined in popularity over the course of the eighteenth century, scholars have shown that they exerted a lasting influence on both American literary and political culture. The captivity narrative's tropes of bondage and family disruption have reappeared at moments of national upheaval, ranging from the American Revolutionary War to the Iranian hostage crisis of 1979.[8] In such moments, captivity narratives work by analogizing the nation to the family in ways that idealize both institutions simultaneously. Within these narratives, the entire nation is transformed into a family under siege, the private sphere of the family becomes a locus of unjust injury inflicted from the outside, and the enemy's violent act of separating captive from kin constitutes incontrovertible proof of national righteousness and unity.

The POW publicity campaign between 1968 and 1973 constitutes a significant moment in this longer history. In contrast to many of the first-person accounts that emerged from Puritan New England, the campaign did not feature female captives. But it did not have to in order to make its case. The power of the campaign hinged not on whether the prisoner was a man or woman but rather on the successful identification of the prisoner of war with the affective bonds of family life. As Melani McAlister has pointed out, the classic move of the captivity narrative is to identify the captive "with the feminized space of the family and sexuality" as a way of conferring innocence on the nation.[9] In contrast to the images of hypermasculine POWs that pervaded the popular culture in subsequent decades, this move underwrote the POW publicity campaign of the late 1960s and early 1970s.

But if the publicity campaign's cultural power resided in domestic images of imperiled families, the relatives of American prisoners were not passive participants in this process. Its very emphasis on the private sphere made it possible to challenge the captivity narrative from within. Because Alvarez was the longest-held prisoner in the North, he was one of the most visible prisoners of war, and the plight of his family was the subject of considerable media attention. During the early years of the campaign, the women in Alvarez's family were portrayed as the innocent victims of Vietnamese aggression, drawn into the conflict through no fault of their own and left in an unnerving state of suspense as they awaited word about Alvarez's fate. But by 1971, Alvarez's sister Delia began speaking out publicly against the war and the Nixon administration. In the process of publicly condemning the war, she challenged many of the campaign's defining features: its unrelenting emphasis on family suffering; its insistence that the wives, sisters, and children of American prisoners were the war's true victims; and its implicit claim that the American nation was a casualty rather than itself bearing some of the responsibility for the violence.

Like Everett Alvarez's decision to join the military, Delia Alvarez's condemnation of the war was linked to a struggle over racial identity. As historian

Lorena Oropeza has shown, the opposing choices made by a brother and sister—to fight in a war and to fight against it—captured two distinct moments in the history of race after 1945.[10] Everett Alvarez's choice was dictated by a postwar definition of racial pride that equated masculinity, militarism, and patriotism. But by the early 1970s, when Delia Alvarez began speaking out against the war, the racial landscape had changed dramatically, and nowhere more so than in her native northern California. There, Chicanos were analyzing their racial subordination in ways that challenged earlier definitions of patriotism; they were positing theories of nationalism that undermined traditional conceptions of the nation-state; they were developing new understandings of manhood, womanhood, and family life; and they were questioning the authority of their elders. Ultimately, it was Delia Alvarez's growing affiliation with this movement that enabled her to break with the Nixon administration and challenge the POW publicity campaign. Drawing on a radicalized notion of Chicano racial identity, Delia Alvarez was able to develop a powerful critique of the official POW story that circulated throughout the public sphere during the Vietnam War.

At the time that Everett Alvarez became the first American prisoner of war in North Vietnam, his shoot-down and capture received relatively little attention in the press. Still, on August 6, 1964, the front page of the *San Francisco Chronicle* featured a photograph of the fresh-faced, youthful pilot in naval uniform.[11] The photograph's caption described him as "an introspective man," and the accompanying story reported that he was one of two naval lieutenants from the USS *Constellation* whose plane had been shot down by North Vietnamese antiaircraft fire. One of the two pilots was dead. Unconfirmed reports suggested that the other pilot had been captured. No one knew which pilot had lived and which had died.

The next day, the *Chronicle* published a second story confirming that it was Everett Alvarez who had survived his shoot-down and been taken prisoner. His portrait appeared again, but this time, it was featured within a second photograph of Alvarez's wife, Hortencia (who went by Tangee), and his young goddaughter Denise Sanchez. In the photograph the little girl looks small and vulnerable as she clings to her godmother with one arm and to Alvarez's portrait with the other. The godmother protectively holds the little girl close to her, as she stares down at the picture of her husband. A quiet smile on her face suggests that she is relieved to have learned that her husband is alive, yet she is still apprehensive.[12]

Although this story appeared four years before the launching of the formal POW publicity campaign, it anticipated several of the campaign's defining features. Importantly, the photographic image of Alvarez in uniform was not displaced entirely but was subsumed within a domestic portrait of an innocent woman and child newly imperiled by the conflict in Vietnam. The setting for the article was not Southeast Asia but rather the Alvarez family's "sunny ranch style home" in Santa Clara, California, where readers were introduced to a cast of family characters: Alvarez's mother Soledad and father Everett Sr.; his twelve-year-old sister Madeleine; his "slim and graceful" wife Tangee; and his twenty-three-year-old sister Delia, who, when the family was asked to speculate about her brother's capture, eloquently told reporters that "it is enough right now to know that he is alive."[13]

Given the significance accorded to the POWs after the war, the fact that Alvarez's capture received little press coverage in 1964 may be surprising. But it is important to realize that, although U.S. personnel were captured and taken prisoner in Southeast Asia as early as 1961, the dramatic story of the POWs and their families did not begin to receive public attention until 1966.[14] Prior to that time, the government had pursued what it called a policy of "quiet diplomacy," later dubbed the "keep quiet policy" by one disillusioned POW wife.[15] Premised on the assumption that publicizing information about the POWs might jeopardize their safety and derail ongoing negotiations with the North Vietnamese, this policy advised the families of captured and missing men to stay out of the public eye, refrain from contacting the press, and keep their private concerns about their men precisely that: private.

In the beginning, the Alvarez family complied with the policy of quiet diplomacy, a compliance that reflected their faith in the government and support of the war effort at the time of Alvarez's capture. "We all used to have great respect for the flag and the uniform," Delia Alvarez recalled about her family in a 1973 interview. "I believed in the domino theory, fighting communism and killing the enemy."[16] According to Everett Alvarez's memoir, Delia had "cursed her gender for disqualifying her from a combat role" when she learned of her brother's capture.[17] Yet by the time that Everett Alvarez returned to the United States in 1973, his family had publicly denounced the Nixon administration, and his sister Delia had emerged as a highly visible and outspoken critic of the war. What had changed during the eight and a half years of Alvarez's captivity?

Part of the change had to do with the gradual collapse of the official policy of quiet diplomacy. This collapse was due to pressures both within and outside of the government. Within the government, officials began to receive reports of prisoner mistreatment, and the Johnson administration established a Committee on Prisoner Matters within the State Department in April 1966. Around the same time, both the Central Intelligence Agency and the Defense Intelligence Agency became heavily involved in POW information-gathering. Two months later, the theme assumed greater public urgency when the North Vietnamese (in what U.S. intelligence forces interpreted as a misguided attempt to garner international sympathy) released film footage showing manacled American prisoners, among them Everett Alvarez, being marched at gunpoint through the streets of Hanoi, surrounded by hostile crowds.[18] Less than a year later, in April 1967, *Life* magazine featured a full-page photograph of captured naval officer Richard Stratton at a Hanoi press conference, apparently bowing in submission. It was, according to one sympathetic POW chronicler, an arresting image of "a big, husky pilot" now looking "like an automaton, like someone who had been made into a puppet." A haunting reminder of the speculations about brainwashing and collaboration that had surrounded the experience of Korean War POWs, Stratton's "Pavlovian performance" alarmed his family, government officials, and the American public.[19]

However disturbing these images, what the press would later dub the "go public" campaign did not take off in earnest until late 1968. By the late 1960s, many of the relatives of POWs had grown angry and frustrated, not only by the dearth of information coming out of Vietnam, but also by the policy of quiet diplomacy, which they had come to see as an excuse for government inaction. Sybil Stockdale, a mother of four whose husband, naval commander James Stockdale, had been captured in 1965, had met on numerous occasions with officials in the Naval and State Departments and had come to the disheartening conclusion that "official silence and secrecy can cover up incompetence and just plain inertia."[20] On October 27, 1968, she defied the government's policy and went public with her husband's story in the *San Diego Union Tribune*. Stockdale was not acting alone but rather was part of an informal network of POW wives, parents, and siblings who were taking matters into their own hands and engaging in grassroots organizing, many for the first time in their lives. Launching letter-writing campaigns to members of Congress and the White House, they appealed to the press, attempted to establish direct contact with Hanoi in the hope of gathering information, and sent POW wives to Washington, D.C., and to the Paris peace talks to demand North Vietnamese compliance with the terms of the Geneva conventions. In 1970 this informal network of family lobbyists became the National League of Families of American Prisoners and Missing in Southeast Asia. The league is still in operation today.[21]

By 1969 the Nixon administration had its own reasons for wanting to publicize the POW issue. With opposition to the war growing, the new president believed that Hanoi's refusal to disclose information about missing and captive men could become a public relations boon, one that would deflect attention away from disturbing reports coming out of Vietnam: reports of the My Lai massacre, the indiscriminate killing of Vietnamese civilians, the free-fire zones, napalm, and defoliation. Indeed, within a context of widening scrutiny of

American war conduct, the interests of POW families, the Nixon White House, and Congress converged, however provisionally. On May 19, 1969, Defense Secretary Melvin Laird formally ended the policy of quiet diplomacy, publicly charging Hanoi with prisoner mistreatment and demanding that if the Vietnamese did not release the prisoners, they at least had a humanitarian obligation to disclose information about their condition.[22]

As an aggressive POW publicity campaign replaced the policy of quiet diplomacy, the Alvarez family also underwent a transformation. In truth, their lives had begun to change from the moment they learned about Everett Alvarez's shoot-down. In his memoir, Alvarez recalled that as soon as he was taken prisoner, his parents attempted to steep themselves in Vietnamese history. Despite their lack of formal education, they scoured public libraries and seized on any book or article about Vietnam that they could find. Gradually, this process of self-education convinced Alvarez's mother Soledad (known as Chole) that the war was misguided. "As she read about the millennium of subjugation by the Chinese, followed by a century of colonial rule," Alvarez recalled, "she began to doubt the wisdom of the American presence in Vietnam."[23]

Significantly, Chole's political education led her to a deepening sense of racial affiliation with the Vietnamese people. As Alvarez later recalled, Chole's passion for history was rooted in an attempt to understand her own Mexican American identity. As a girl, she had played among the ruins of a mission in Lompoc, California, and the landscape had provoked questions: "Where did [my ancestors] come from? Why were some in [my] family light-complected and blue-eyed while others resembled burnished, copper-colored Aztecs?" By the time her son became the first American POW in North Vietnam, Chole had visited twenty Christian missions throughout the state of California in an attempt to make sense of her own racial and national past. As her son remained imprisoned, she became convinced that there "was something comparable . . . between the poorly armed Mexicans who fought for their sovereignty against a much better equipped army, and the out-gunned Vietnamese who appeared night after night on her television screen."[24]

Everett Alvarez's father (who went by Lalo) came to a different set of conclusions about the conflict that had embroiled his son. While Lalo speculated about the possible motivations for U.S. military involvement in Vietnam, he felt strongly that any doubts about the war should be voiced only in private. Lalo was a sheet-metal welder and pattern maker in a missile plant, whose identity as a male breadwinner was tied to the military economy. He felt he had a duty "to support the government and respect the president's decision."[25] "What a man said in the confines of his own home was his own business,"

Everett Alvarez later wrote of his father's position, "but he'd better watch his tongue in public."[26]

As Alvarez later realized, the power struggle within his family hinged not on the morality of the war but rather on identifying the appropriate line of demarcation between the public and the private spheres. Initially, his father was successful at policing that line. His mother asked deeply troubling questions about the war, but only "in the privacy of her own home." What Alvarez later called the family's "free-for-alls" about the war were hidden from "the watchful and critical eye of the public." As Alvarez's captivity approached the extraordinary five-year mark, his family continued to abide by the policy of quiet diplomacy, remaining, in Alvarez's words, "forever conscious of the boundaries between private license and public constraints."[27]

It was Delia, Everett Alvarez's sister, who ultimately insisted that her family break their silence about the war and "go public." Shortly after Alvarez's capture, his father had appointed Delia the spokesperson for the family. It was a choice that made sense, particularly in light of the cultural authority sometimes ascribed to the younger generation within Mexican American families.[28] Delia was charismatic, beautiful, and educated, and she "articulated with ease what her parents struggled to express."[29] By 1969, however, father and daughter were on divergent paths. At a moment when many youths both within and outside of the Mexican American community were questioning the authority of an older generation, Delia insisted that the family publicly condemn the war despite her father's objections. Lalo lamented the decision as one that undermined his own authority and revealed that he was no longer "the final arbiter in his own home."[30]

Delia's political evolution from cold warrior to dissenter was shaped by local, national, and international forces. Like many relatives of POWs, Delia found herself frustrated by Defense Department officials who provided virtually no information about captured and missing men. Like her mother, the more she read about Vietnam's history, the more convinced she became that the United States was on an errant mission. But Delia's growing critique of the war also emerged from what she was witnessing at home and overseas. After college, she had worked for the Santa Clara County Welfare Department, where she observed young Mexican American men who should have been enrolled in college being sent to Vietnam in disproportionate numbers. In 1967 she quit her job and traveled for twenty months in Europe, where she palpably felt "the depth of rage against the American role in Vietnam." Winding her way through thirteen countries, she saw protests everywhere she went and watched as the American flag was "torn, trampled on, and burned."[31]

But it was ultimately the burgeoning Chicano movement within the United

States that compelled Delia Alvarez to turn against the war. As she explained in a 1973 interview in *La Raza*, a Chicano activist newspaper, "My involvement with the Chicano movement has done more than anything to open my eyes to things as they really are."[32] In the fall of 1965, as Everett Alvarez began his second year in captivity, the movement exploded in the California town of Salinas, where brother and sister had come of age. As Everett Alvarez remembered postwar Salinas, it was "a town divided . . . by the tracks of the Southern Pacific Railroad."[33] To the east lay the camps where Mexican migrant workers lived, and to the west stood the affluent homes of the Anglo businessmen and farm owners, who controlled and profited from the Central Valley's rich agricultural resources. In 1965 Mexican farmworkers, under the leadership of César Chávez and Dolores Huerta, fought back against these stark economic and geographic inequalities by going on strike against the large agribusiness companies that dominated the region.[34]

After 1965, the Chicano movement gained momentum, particularly in the West and Southwest, where Mexican Americans fought for labor, land, and educational reform. As Chávez and Huerta organized laborers in California, Reies López Tijerina spearheaded a land grant movement in New Mexico. In 1966 Rodolfo "Corky" Gonzales founded the Crusade for Justice, an organization that sought to reach out to urban Mexican youth. By 1969, Chicano activists were drawing connections between racial oppression at home and the war abroad, in which working-class men of color bore the brunt of the fighting. In 1970 antiwar activists formed the Chicano Moratorium Committee, and in August of that year, they organized a rally against the war in East Los Angeles that drew 20,000 demonstrators.[35]

This was the world that Delia Alvarez came home to when she returned to northern California in 1969. Meanwhile, she had left Europe with a new determination to do more to secure her brother's release from captivity.[36] At a family gathering on Labor Day in 1969, she joined with other members of the extended family in drafting a petition demanding that "more forceful, positive action" be taken toward the release of Alvarez and the other American prisoners of war. Throughout the fall, family members went door to door, stood on street corners, and approached strangers at churches, banks, and businesses.[37] By December they had gathered over 70,000 signatures, and the petition had received national media coverage. But while the petition drive was a courageous step for the Alvarez family, it was one that remained consistent with the larger aim of the "go public" campaign—to keep the plight of POWs and their families in the public eye. The navy even voiced its approval of the petition, although one official revealingly felt the need to remind the Alvarez family to "place the blame where it most properly belongs, namely the North Vietnamese government."[38]

In May 1971, however, Delia Alvarez went further. Along with several other relatives of POWs who had originally been involved in the National League of Families, she formed a splinter group called POW-MIA Families for Immediate Release. The group urged the families of POWs to adopt an overtly antiwar position. "We are advocating complete withdrawal," Delia Alvarez explained in the *Los Angeles Times* on May 18; "The only way the prisoners are going home is by the cessation of hostilities." By July 1971, approximately 300 relatives had joined the group, claiming that the Nixon administration was using the prisoners as a justification for prolonging the war; they demanded that Nixon negotiate the prisoners' release without regard to the political fate of South Vietnam. As one member of the new group exclaimed, "They cannot use my husband to spread the blood of 45 young men a week on Viet Nam." Rejecting the ostensible political neutrality of the National League of Families, these relatives insisted that their missing men were now being held hostage by both Hanoi and the Nixon administration.[39] While some of them aligned themselves with the antiwar movement for pragmatic reasons (believing that ending the war would be the quickest way to get the prisoners home), others had come to believe that American military involvement in Vietnam was morally wrong, above and beyond the POW issue.

After the formation of POW-MIA Families for Immediate Release, Delia Alvarez emerged as one of a handful of POW relatives who openly condemned the war. Between May 1971 and her brother's repatriation in February 1973, she spoke at protest rallies, appeared with high-profile antiwar activists like Jane Fonda, participated in press conferences, and traveled to Paris to meet with a peace delegation from Indochina.[40] Turning against the National League of Families, she dismissed the women involved in the organization as "Pentagon Princesses."[41] These actions entailed personal risk and violent confrontation. POW wives appeared at meetings where Alvarez was a featured speaker to publicly scorn and ridicule her. She received hate mail and anonymous phone calls accusing her of being a communist traitor.[42] Once a staunch supporter of the war, she now blamed her brother's lengthy captivity on the failure of political leadership within the United States. As she explained it at the May 1971 press conference announcing the formation of the splinter group, "I remind people that my brother was first sent to Vietnam under the Kennedy administration, he was captured under the Johnson administration, and he has been used by the Nixon administration, and I don't want to stay around here any longer to wait for another administration to do something."[43]

In the process of condemning the war and breaking with the National League of Families, Delia Alvarez subverted the logic of the "go public" campaign in complex ways. In order to understand how she did this, it is necessary to take a closer look at the campaign itself. Initially, the explicit aim of the campaign had been relatively narrow: to bring international pressure to bear on the North Vietnamese by calling attention to Hanoi's alleged refusal to comply with the rules for prisoners of war that had been laid out in the 1949 Geneva conventions. The conventions, which the North Vietnamese had signed in 1957, required that the names of all captured prisoners of war be released, that all prisoners receive adequate medical care and food, that camps be inspected by a neutral third party, and that captives and their families be allowed to exchange mail. While the United States accused North Vietnam of flagrantly violating these requirements, the North Vietnamese countered that, because the United States had never formally declared war against North Vietnam, the requirements did not apply. In their estimation, the men being held captive were not prisoners of war at all but were, in fact, war criminals.

When viewed historically, however, it is clear that the "go public" campaign hinged on much more than the correct interpretation of the Geneva conventions. In truth, the campaign advanced a vision of American victimization that would shape Vietnam War discourse for years to come. Whatever physical wounds the U.S. military had inflicted on Vietnam, the psychological wounds inflicted by the Vietnamese on the United States were ultimately direr. The claim that, through defying the Geneva conventions, communism had extended its vile reach into the most intimate sphere of the family became a constitutive part of the process of recasting the United States as a victim rather than an aggressor. By repudiating the role that the state had scripted for her as a loyal, domestic victim of Vietnamese violence, Delia Alvarez refused to be implicated in this narrative, one that cited family suffering as proof of American virtue.

Delia Alvarez's refusal was no simple matter. Rather, it required that she thwart several of the campaign's defining discursive strategies. At the most basic level, Alvarez challenged the campaign by insisting that the POW issue could not be divorced from the larger politics of the war. Throughout the campaign, government officials and other POW family members insisted that Hanoi's silence regarding the POWs constituted a humanitarian crime rather than a political or military one. Despite its informal ties to the Republican Party, the National League of Families positioned itself as "politically neutral," and military officials advised POW relatives to adopt an explicitly humanitarian approach when talking to the press, one that shied away from partisan politics and emphasized the anxieties they were forced to endure as a result of Hanoi's refusal to release information about their loved ones' welfare.[44]

The North Vietnamese, by contrast, insisted that the prisoner of war issue was deeply political, in that it spoke to the illegality of U.S. military intervention in

Southeast Asia. But American government officials countered that compliance with the Geneva conventions was a "basic, simple humanitarian question."[45] This claim was a central feature of the National Ad Council's 1971–72 campaign, which, using photographs of POW wives and children, called on Hanoi to allow neutral official observers into the prison camps in order to assure the world that they were treating the prisoners "according to humane standards long practiced by civilized nations." "That's the issue," the advertisement declared; "It's that simple. It's that non-political. It's that human." Through developing radio spots and print advertisements that appeared in nationally syndicated newspapers and magazines, the campaign attempted to delineate the terms of the debate for the public. Through complying with the Geneva conventions, Hanoi would not only "earn the gratitude of millions of Americans," the campaign promised, but it would also "find new stature in the eyes of the world."[46] As the international community expressed mounting horror at the war's deadly toll among Vietnamese civilians, the "go public" campaign attempted to shift the humanitarian burden to the North Vietnamese, contending that the central humanitarian question of the war revolved not around the U.S. military's war conduct but rather around the treatment of captured American soldiers: would Hanoi act in compliance with the universally accepted norms laid out in the Geneva conventions, or would it continue to violate them?

By using her position as a POW relative as a platform for condemning the war, Delia Alvarez undercut the campaign's central premise. By breaking with the Nixon administration and insisting that the fate of the POWs depended on the withdrawal of U.S. forces from Vietnam, Delia Alvarez challenged the campaign's efforts to separate the POW issue from the legality and morality of the war. In transgressing the circumscribed role that the Nixon administration had envisioned for the wives, sisters, and mothers of POWs, family members whom they hoped would provide a "human face" for the POW story, but nothing more, Delia Alvarez forced the suppressed political content of the POW issue to the fore.

A second, related strategy of the campaign was its erasure of the POW's military identity and the foregrounding instead of his civilian, and specifically his familial, identity.[47] In contrast to the working-class and minority men who were disproportionately represented on the frontlines in Vietnam, the vast majority of captured men were elite and overwhelmingly white, a fact that reflected the stratified character of the military. On the whole, they were "glamorous aviators" and commissioned officers whose planes had been shot down during Operation Rolling Thunder, the planned bombing raids over North Vietnam between 1965 and 1968.[48] But as the publicity campaign took off, the military role that these men had played slipped from view as the public was instructed to consider the POW problem through the eyes of a child. "Pretend you're 12 years old and your father's a Prisoner of War in Southeast Asia," instructed the National Ad Council's 1971–72 POW advertising campaign. A twelve-year-old child would not understand the "maneuvers of the bargaining table," the advertisement conjectured, but would only want someone believable to tell him that his father was safe. Calling on Hanoi to allow neutral observers into the prison camps, the advertisement claimed to speak for "all the boys and girls, wives and parents whose fathers, husbands, and sons are being held in secret captivity."[49]

Because she was Everett Alvarez's sister, Delia Alvarez served as a reminder of her brother's identity as a member of a family. But Alvarez also refused to elide her brother's military role. "When he was captured he was a lieutenant jg [junior grade]," she explained to an ABC News reporter in a television news story that aired on October 12, 1972, "and he is now a lieutenant commander." Gesturing toward her mother, she continued, "she [Chole] doesn't want him to remain in prison to become an admiral."[50] By informing viewers of her brother's changing military rank, Alvarez's ostensible aim was to illustrate the long duration of her brother's captivity. Moreover, her reference to her mother's desire to have her son return home certainly conveyed the family's suffering, an objective that was at the heart of the publicity campaign. But Delia Alvarez's reference to her brother's military rank was also jarring in light of the news story's intimate domestic setting: mother and daughter were filmed sitting on their couch in the Alvarez family living room, watching television. If news stories like these served to convey the sense that this could be any American family, then Delia Alvarez's invocation of her brother's changing military rank reminded viewers that he was a war combatant, not a civilian.

News stories like these reflected the most significant feature of the POW campaign—its focus on family suffering, rather than on the trials of the POWs themselves. Indeed, the campaign was obsessed with the impact of a father's absence on those families left behind. Editorials in both the military and the mainstream press blamed the North Vietnamese for transforming the home front into a "fatherless world," one of sons and daughters who, according to one editorial in the *Armed Forces Journal*, had "a right to know if their fathers [were] dead or alive."[51] In December 1970 *Life* and *Look* magazines featured photo-essays documenting POW children growing up without fathers, contrasting early photographs of cheerful, intact families with more recent, somber photographs in which the father was absent.[52] Meanwhile, the POW wife was left with the painful task of explaining her husband's disappearance to children with no understanding of war. As Frank Sieverts, the State Department's top official on POW/MIA matters, reported, "The telephone rings all the time. In the holiday season, it is especially bad. Wives call up asking me what to say to their children, how to explain that they don't know where their husbands are, whether they are dead or alive, when all the other kids have their fathers."[53] Through its policy of silence and secrecy, according to these accounts, Hanoi had placed innocent women and children in a cruel state of suspension, alienating them from the rest of society and generating enormous confusion and uncertainty within the family. "It's a very lonely existence," explained one POW wife whose husband had been shot down in 1967; "You're married but you're not married. You're not single. You're not divorced or widowed. Where does that put you in society? That puts you in your own world."[54]

These portraits of family suffering emphasized women's traditional roles as wives, sisters, mothers, and daughters. By asserting herself as a moral and political actor in the public realm, Delia Alvarez challenged this exclusive association of women with familial obligation and attachment, a challenge that resonated powerfully with the women's liberation movement of the era. By the early 1970s, Alvarez was not alone in countering the highly traditional gender constructions that shaped the early "go public" campaign. On the contrary, by that time, many women associated with the campaign were beginning to question its narrow conceptions of female identity through both political action and personal life choices, suggesting that the rise of feminism shaped the campaign's history in significant ways.

In order to understand the relevance of feminism to the Alvarez story, it is important to recall the women who spearheaded the campaign in the late 1960s. Initially, the women who formed the National League of Families insisted that their cause was apolitical. While they condemned the government's policy of "quiet diplomacy," they repeatedly expressed their discomfort at having to take an antagonistic stance vis-à-vis the state.[55] Many of these women had spent their entire lives in military communities, strongly supported the war in Southeast Asia, and insistently distanced themselves from protest movements. To be sure, they were engaging in women's grassroots organizing, but they were worlds apart from the feminist activists of the period, not least in their divergent approaches to the family. In contrast to feminists, who identified motherhood and marriage as primary sites of women's oppression, the military wives were mobilizing a maternalist discourse that appealed to essentialist ideals of motherhood in order to make demands on the state. But while maternalism had historically been aligned with pacifism, these women were unapologetic hawks, foregrounding their roles as wives and mothers in order to demand more American military intervention, not less.[56] Thus, the political profile of the woman-turned-activist was complex: loyal to the government but also increasingly antagonistic and distrustful of it; maternalist in her rhetoric but in the service of militarism; longing for her loved one's safe return while simultaneously wanting him to wage and win the war. What was not ambiguous, however, was that the POW wife, mother, and sister believed that she was acting in the prisoner's interest and doing what he would have wanted her to do. During the early years of the publicity campaign, she emerged as his loyal advocate, the champion of his cause, and a heroine who worked tirelessly to remind the nation of its "forgotten men."

But by the early 1970s, as more and more women like Delia Alvarez became active in the antiwar movement, this portrait began to change. In contrast to the original founders of the National League of Families, the later recruits insisted that they were moral, intellectual, and political arbiters who could draw their own conclusions about the war regardless of their private suffering. Their growing activism challenged the earlier image of the ever-loyal wife, sister, and mother. By 1970, reports of the burgeoning antiwar movement in the United States had penetrated the prison camps, and POWs recalled feeling demoralized by the news.[57] Their memoirs suggest the extent to which prisoners not only felt uniquely wounded by women's opposition to the war, but also how much they identified antiwar activism with women, regardless of the movement's actual gender composition. Highly visible antiwar figures like Joan Baez and Jane Fonda were angrily labeled "traitorous bitches," women's antiwar organizations like Women Strike for Peace were singled out for condemnation, and POWs expressed a sense of shock that American women could turn on them through wartime opposition.[58] One POW recalled his captors forcing him and other prisoners to listen to an audiotape of women demonstrating outside an army base at Fort Dix, New Jersey, singing a song entitled "Fuck the Army!": "We sat there in shock, trying to adjust to the harsh realization that these were our own American women! We couldn't believe that they would involve themselves in such filth to show their dissension and encourage our soldiers to desert!"[59]

Adding to the POW's sense of political betrayal was the fear that women might abandon their marriages and families while men remained imprisoned. Indeed, political mobilization turned out to be a transformative experience for many women. Despite the sentimental images of marriage that dominated the campaign, a significant percentage of POW marriages collapsed between 1964 and 1973, and several highly publicized divorce proceedings were initiated by POW wives who chose not to wait for their husbands' return.[60] Even within marriages that survived, things changed irrevocably. During their husbands' captivity, many POW wives managed household economies, reared children by themselves, and pursued paid employment for the first time in their lives. By 1973, news accounts noted the irony, pointing out that many wives who had become active in the National League of Families in their husband's behalf were unwilling to "return to the role of a docile homebody whose highest achievement is a casserole," "to change back into major's sweet wife," or to "revert to their passive 'yes, dear' roles."[61] For their part, many women described themselves in similar terms. One POW wife remarked that she had "become pretty aggressive" in her husband's absence, while another stated simply, "I'm not a honey anymore."[62] By the early 1970s, many POW wives wondered what would happen to their newfound independence once their husbands returned to the family fold. If the early years of the "go public" campaign had showcased an ideal of the traditional nuclear family, by 1973, the year that the POWs returned to the United States, the campaign evoked themes that were at the heart of the contemporary women's movement: the diminishing role of male authority in the family, the political and moral agency of women in the public realm, and the impact of women's growing economic, emotional, and intellectual autonomy in heterosexual love and marriage.

Thus, the women's liberation movement, like the Chicano movement, provided a crucial backdrop for Delia Alvarez's break with the Nixon administration. Between 1971 and 1973, the years that Alvarez was most visible as an antiwar activist, the "go public" campaign continued to mobilize the image of an imperiled but united family. But at the same time, the politics of feminism was subtly but unmistakably transforming the campaign, pushing to the surface the private conflicts and public constraints that the idealized image of an imperiled family had concealed. When Delia Alvarez rejected her sentimentalized, sisterly role as the only legitimate justification for her political activism, she did so within this context. At the same time, her activism departed from mainstream feminism in two revealing ways. First, Delia Alvarez consistently emphasized her race rather than her gender, telling the press that when her brother returned to the United States, she hoped to convince him that "Chicanos are the Vietnamese of this country."[63] Perhaps this decision reflected the constraints confronting Chicanas during this period, who often felt forced to choose publicly between their allegiance to feminism and their loyalty to the Chicano movement, even as they engaged in their own passionate debates about gender and family life within the Mexican American community.[64] But this was also a strategic choice when considered in relationship to the "go public" campaign. By emphasizing her racial identity, Alvarez posited an alternative model of kinship, one in which the biological family model so central to the campaign was replaced by a kinship model based on racial affiliation among people of color across national borders. The campaign had proceeded from the premise that blood ties to captive family members gave POW relatives their moral authority. Alvarez, in contrast, suggested that it was her racial identification with the Vietnamese people rather than her identity as a POW sister that ultimately determined her political loyalties.

The second way that Alvarez's activism deviated from mainstream feminism concerned the status of the private realm throughout the "go public" campaign. In the early 1970s the women's liberation movement insisted on the inherently political character of private life, an insistence captured in the famous slogan, "the personal is political." This meant that feminists challenged the historical division between the public and private spheres in order to reveal the political content of ostensibly private activities, including housework, childrearing, and sex.[65] But privacy took on a very different hue throughout the campaign. Because the Nixon administration was attempting to appropriate the private suffering of POW families for political ends, Alvarez found herself in the position of defending and safeguarding her family's right to privacy, even as she insisted that they publicly condemn the war. Because the campaign encouraged family members to enact and express their pain on the public stage, at crucial moments Delia Alvarez strategically insisted on a clear line of demarcation between the public and the private in order to undermine the efforts of the Nixon administration and the National League of Families.

Delia Alvarez policed this line between public and private in several ways. By focusing on private family suffering, the campaign aimed to elicit public sympathy for POWs and their relatives. Alvarez dismissed this aim as a dangerous diversion from the real business of ending the military conflict. "Sympathy is not enough for any of us," she declared in an interview about her brother in *La Raza* magazine in February 1973. There was no shortfall of public sympathy for prisoners and their families, she insisted. Rather, the problem was that Americans had been too apathetic for too long in the face of an unjust and immoral war.[66] Delia Alvarez's earlier belief in a foreign communist enemy had given way to perceptions of a different kind of danger. "Now the enemy to me is the apathy of the American people," she explained in the same interview; "That is the enemy we have to fight. Nixon is the opponent, instead of the Vietnamese."[67] By foregrounding apathy rather than sympathy, Alvarez sought to bring the POW story back from the realm of sentimentality and into the realm of political action. By rejecting her prescribed role as an object of pity, Alvarez sought to remind the public that, ultimately, the POW issue was not about wounded families and grieving women within the United States but rather about the violence unleashed by the United States in Southeast Asia.

Alvarez's eschewal of domestic sentimentality was evident in an ABC report that aired on December 22, 1971.[68] A news story broke that was rife with the potential to make audiences teary: Shortly before Christmas, the North Vietnamese released 1,001 letters from captured men, including eighteen letters from South Vietnam, that provided the first confirmation to families that their loved ones were still alive. The ABC news story portrayed the very different responses of two POW relatives (one of whom was Alvarez) to the arrival of the letters. The report focused first on Mrs. Peyton Mecleary, the mother of a navy pilot who had been captured five years earlier. Visibly overjoyed, Mrs. Mecleary shared her son's letter in its entirety at a press conference, smiling broadly and beginning by reading its reassuring generic opening lines: "Hi Mom! I'm okay and in good health." Understandably relieved to have received her son's letter, Mrs. Mecleary provided reporters with an uncomplicated and instantly recognizable family image—that of a grateful and jubilant mother who has received an invaluable gift just in time for Christmas.

Delia Alvarez provided a marked study in contrast. She appeared somber, wary, and fatigued before the camera, as the reporter relayed in a voice-over, "Delia Alvarez . . . wanted more than a letter." "This is the eighth Christmas mailing we have received from my brother. There are four letters and three cards," she stated simply and without even the hint of a smile. "But we would have appreciated and wanted my brother home instead of the letters." Appearing over six months after Delia Alvarez had formed POW-MIA Families for Immediate Release, the story suggested that her disappointment and frustration were directed not at the North Vietnamese but at the Nixon administration for its refusal to name a withdrawal date for U.S. troops. In contrast to Mrs. Peyton Mecleary's very public moment of private disclosure, Alvarez refused to divulge either the content of the letter or her family's emotions upon receiving it. In this instance, she became a powerful guardian of family privacy. By refusing to disclose her brother's personal letters, she subverted her scripted role of domestic sentiment and condemned American foreign policy instead.

Press conferences like these advanced the U.S. government's thesis that Hanoi had drawn innocent women and children into the fold of war. Significantly, this accusation was also premised on a racial discourse that assigned Asian captors a unique capacity for psychological cruelty. Here, too, Delia Alvarez deviated from the logic of the administration's campaign. The stereotype of the sadistic Vietnamese captor hinged on the claim that, for American prisoners of war, the experience of Asian captivity was demonstrably worse than the experience of captivity in the West. With little information at their disposal, military psychologists drew on historical examples in order to speculate about what might be occurring in Southeast Asian prison camps. Contrasting the repatriation of POWs from Germany to those from Japan and Korea, they concluded that being captured by "Oriental forces" entailed a higher degree of stress and that prisoners returning from "Oriental captivity" were more prone to auto accidents, mental breakdowns, divorces, and suicides.[69] In an argument that attempted to offer a historical explanation for this purported difference, Dr. Charles Stenger, a clinical psychologist for the Veterans Administration POW program, attributed this pattern of "Asian cruelty" to the excesses of Western imperialism, speculating that Asian captors seized the opportunity to direct their rage at Western arrogance toward their captives. Referring specifically to the Japanese treatment of American prisoners during World War II, Stenger recalled, "They had to humiliate them and show them that they weren't king. So there was a purposeful humiliation and degradation in Oriental POW situations."[70]

Both throughout the "go public" campaign and in the years after repatriation, condemnations of Hanoi's silence surrounding the POWs appealed to this notion that Asian captors possessed a unique propensity for psychological cruelty and were inherently more secretive than their Western counterparts.[71] This racial profile combined with the Cold War contention that communists refused to honor the sanctity of the private sphere. According to one congressman speaking at a Committee on Armed Services hearing in 1970, North Vietnam had adopted a "barbaric policy," one that was using the prisoners as "pawns" in an attempt to "wage psychological warfare against the United States."[72] The communists of both Hanoi and Korea were "master psychologists," a representative speaking on the House floor proclaimed.[73] Taken together, such accusations formed a damning portrait of the prototypical Vietnamese captor, one that POWs would revive in their memoirs after the war.[74]

While the campaign was preoccupied with the distinct racial character of Asian captors, Delia Alvarez chose a path of racial identification with the North Vietnamese people. "The mentality that calls Vietnamese 'gooks' is the same mentality that calls brown people 'spics,'" Alvarez explained to a *New York Times* reporter in February 1973. "It's the same battle," she added.[75] In light of her affiliation with the Chicano movement, it is not surprising that Alvarez drew analogies between domestic racial politics and the war in Southeast Asia. By the early 1970s, many race-based social movements (including the Chicano movement) were contending that persistent racial oppression within the nation and U.S. foreign policy in places like Asia, Africa, and Latin America were, in fact, cut from the same colonialist, white-supremacist cloth.[76] Alvarez's claim that anti-Vietnamese racism abroad and antibrown racism at home were part of the "same mentality" reflected the deep influence of this mode of analysis within the Chicano movement.

The statement is more remarkable, however, when viewed within the context of the POW publicity campaign. Delia Alvarez's assertions appeared in the *New York Times* on February 8, 1973, only four days before the first POWs (including Everett Alvarez) were repatriated to the United States via Clark Air Force Base in the Philippines. A month earlier, American and North Vietnamese officials had signed a ceasefire agreement in Paris that included a provision for the repatriation of American prisoners of war. As the long-awaited return of the prisoners approached, POW relatives and government officials wondered about their condition. How had these men fared psychologically, emotionally, and physically? How would they be reintegrated into their families and communities? Would they confirm earlier reports of indoctrination, malnutrition, and torture within the camps? What had they endured?

All of these questions proceeded from a premise that would prove crucial to the POW's symbolic valence in the decades after the war: the premise that returnees were simultaneously victims and heroes. They were victims because they had endured incalculable suffering at the hands of Vietnamese aggressors, and they were heroes for having survived and adhered to the military's code of conduct. At a moment when many were exonerating the POWs and hailing their return as an opportunity for national reconciliation, Delia Alvarez offered a more complicated picture, reminding readers that it was the Vietnamese, not the POWs and their families, who had been the war's primary victims.

Ultimately, this attempt to remind the public of the actual relationship between the war's victims and its perpetrators was Alvarez's fiercest challenge to the campaign. The campaign identified the relatives of POWs as the innocent victims of North Vietnamese aggression, even though they remained within the territorial boundaries of the United States. According to one 1969 editorial, POW wives, no less than their husbands, were "captives of fear as the Communists play cat and mouse with their emotions."[77] This was the linchpin of the "go public" campaign: through extending its reach into the sanctified sphere of the family, Hanoi was violating not only the rules of war but also the norms of Western liberal humanitarianism. At the moment when a burgeoning antiwar movement was accusing the American military of indiscriminately bombing Vietnamese schools, hospitals, and homes, the "go public" campaign deftly redirected the accusation: it was communist Hanoi, through its conspiracy of silence, that had drawn innocent civilians into the hellish world of war.

With her family's emotional suffering the source of widespread speculation and curiosity, Delia Alvarez refused to play the role assigned to her. Ten months before her brother's repatriation, she reflected on the prerequisite for his safe return in the pages of La Raza: "Everett will return when Vietnamese children will be able to look at the sky and clouds and not fear that a bomb will drop that will burn and tear their bodies. Everett will return because the Vietnamese will live! Because the Vietnamese will win!"[78] While the National League of Families and the Nixon administration urged the public to direct its sympathies to the children of American POWs, Delia Alvarez insisted that Vietnamese children deserved not only sympathy but also justice.

When Everett Alvarez did return to the United States in February 1973, the reunion between brother and sister was not seamless. In a press conference shortly after his return, Alvarez diminished the significance of his sister's opposition to the war, telling reporters who were curious about the family rift that "I'm convinced to a large degree, her activities were based on emotion. We were there for a long time and she wanted us home."[79] His conviction is ironic given Delia Alvarez's efforts to purge the POW story of its excessive emotionalism. Like most returnees with relatives who turned against the war, Everett Alvarez eventually reconciled with his sister. Relieved that the ordeal of captivity was over, they agreed to disagree about the morality of the war. But it was clear that the political differences engendered by the war within his family had been deeply unsettling for Everett Alvarez. As late as 1991, Alvarez lamented his sister's "defection from the cause I'd nearly died for and suffered a long time for."[80] The breach between brother and sister reflected divisions in the United States that have persisted to our own time.

In the early 1980s, former secretary of state Henry Kissinger would remember the Vietnam War as a conflict between two aggressors who had wielded very different kinds of weapons, writing that "Hanoi and Washington had inflicted grievous wounds on each other; theirs were physical, ours psychological and thus perhaps harder to heal."[81] The notion of the war "coming home," as suggested by Kissinger, remains a standard feature of both scholarly and popular treatments of the Vietnam War, and it is usually used to connote the profound domestic political divisions engendered by it. But to those who were championing the cause of the POWs between 1968 and 1973, the war had come home in a more literal sense. According to the administration and its supporters, Hanoi had wreaked emotional havoc on the private sphere by creating a world robbed of fathers, husbands, brothers, and sons, one in which loyal women did not know whether they were wives or widows and innocent children did not know whether their fathers were dead or alive. Tender images of women and children generated a resilient narrative, one that identified the United States as the war's primary casualty.

The image of an endangered family helps explain the persistence of this narrative. The prisoner of war story was never solely about the martial virtue or imperiled masculinity of captured men. The story was also always about the interior feminized space of the family, a space that was constructed as the site of the war's most grievous wounds and injuries. But the history of the "go public" campaign does more than shed light on the war's cultural afterlife. It also provides a crucial prehistory to contemporary debates about terrorism. Today, policy experts and scholars define terrorism as a form of political violence that deliberately targets civilians; what differentiates terrorists from other actors is their refusal to honor the distinction between civilians and combatants. Without denying the vital need to differentiate terrorism from other forms of political violence, I would argue that the POW publicity campaign reminds us that these contemporary accusations are not wholly new, but rather they resonate with earlier Cold War constructions of the enemy. The story of Delia Alvarez reminds us that these constructions always require consent.

NOTES

1. Everett Alvarez Jr. and Anthony S. Pitch, *Chained Eagle: The True Heroic Story of Eight and One Half Years as a POW by the First American Shot Down over North Vietnam* (New York: Donald Fine, 1989), 20–25.

2. Jim Thompson, imprisoned in South Vietnam from March 1964 until February 1973, was the longest-held American prisoner of war.

3. While this essay does not focus on the collapse of Alvarez's marriage, it is an interesting story in its own right. Public revelations that Tangee Alvarez was involved with another man and filed for divorce during her husband's imprisonment were part of a larger wartime discourse about women's betrayal at home. See Elliott Gruner, *Prisoners of Culture: Representing the Vietnam POW* (New Brunswick, N.J.: Rutgers University Press, 1993), 89–108. For examples of news coverage about the divorce, see "Wife of Longest Imprisoned U.S. POW Seeking Divorce," *Los Angeles Times*, October 12, 1972, 1; and "POW Wife's Story: Mrs. Alvarez Tells of New Marriage," *San Francisco Chronicle*, October 13, 1972, 1.

4. George Herring, *America's Longest War: The United States and Vietnam, 1950–1975* (New York: Knopf, 1986), 257.

5. Gruner, *Prisoners of Culture*, 171.

6. Susan Jeffords, *The Remasculinization of American Culture: Gender and the Vietnam War* (Bloomington: Indiana University Press, 1989), 49.

7. On the cultural history of the captivity narrative, see Richard Slotkin, *Regeneration through Violence: The Mythology of the American Frontier, 1600–1860* (Middletown, Conn.: Wesleyan University Press, 1973), 94–145. Useful literary histories include Roy Harvey Pearce, "The Significances of the Captivity Narrative," *American Literature* 19 (March 1947): 1–20; and Tara Fitzpatrick, "The Figure of Captivity: The Cultural Work of the Puritan Captivity Narrative," *American Literary History* 3 (Spring 1991): 1–26. For a study that traces the endurance of captivity narratives into the twentieth century, see Christopher Castiglia, *Bound and Determined: Captivity, Culture Crossing, and White Womanhood from Mary Rowlandson to Patty Hearst* (Chicago: University of Chicago Press, 1996).

8. See, for example, Greg Sieminski, "The Puritan Captivity Narrative and the Politics of the American Revolution," *American Quarterly* 42 (March 1990): 35–56. On the Iranian hostage crisis, see Melani McAlister, *Epic Encounters: Culture, Media, and U.S. Interests in the Middle East, 1945–2000* (Berkeley: University of California Press, 2001), 198–234.

9. McAlister, *Epic Encounters*, 209.

10. Lorena Oropeza, *Raza Si! Guerra No! Chicano Protest and Patriotism during the Vietnam War Era* (Berkeley: University of California Press, 2005).

11. "2 California Pilots Down in the Raid," *San Francisco Chronicle*, August 6, 1964, 1.

12. "Downed Pilot's Joyful Family," *San Francisco Chronicle*, August 7, 1964, 1.

13. Ibid., 16.

14. Stuart Rochester and Frederick Kiley, *Honor Bound: American Prisoners of War in Southeast Asia, 1961–1973* (Annapolis, Md.: Naval Institute Press, 1999), 600.

15. On this policy of "quiet diplomacy," see George Veith, *Code-Name Bright Light: The Untold Story of U.S. POW Rescue Efforts during the Vietnam War* (New York: Free Press, 1998), 243; Rochester and Kiley, *Honor Bound*, 201; and Jim and Sybil Stockdale, *In Love and War: The Story of a Family's Ordeal and Sacrifice during the Vietnam War* (New York: Harper and Row, 1984), 307.

16. "Interview with Delia Alvarez, POW Sister," *La Raza: News and Political Thought of the Chicano Struggle* 1 (February 1973): n.p.

17. Alvarez and Pitch, *Chained Eagle*, 155.

18. On the Hanoi March, see Rochester and Kiley, *Honor Bound*, 188–207.

19. On Richard Stratton, see John G. Hubbell, *P.O.W.: A Definitive History of the American Prisoner-of-War Experience, 1964–1973* (New York: Reader's Digest Press, 1976), 264; and Hay Parks, John Thornton, Paul Galanti, Richard Stratton, and James Stockdale, *The Code of Conduct* (Annapolis, Md.: U.S. Naval Institute Press, 1987). On the ways in which the experience of POWs in Korea informed the Vietnam POW discourse, see Gruner, *Prisoners of Culture*, 10; and "A Celebration of Man Redeemed," *Time*, February 19, 1973, 17.

20. "At Least I Know Jim's Alive," *Good Housekeeping*, February 1970, 78–79, 215–22.

21. On the history of the National League of Families of American Prisoners and Missing in Southeast Asia (hereinafter referred to as the National League of Families), see T. Christopher Jespersen, "The Politics and Culture of Nonrecognition: The Carter Administration and Vietnam," *Journal of American–East Asian Relations* 4 (Winter 1995): 397–413. For the perspective of its founders, see Stockdale and Stockdale, *In Love and War*.

22. On the history of the "go public" campaign, see H. Bruce Franklin, *M.I.A. or Mythmaking in America* (New York: Lawrence Hill Books, 1982), 49–60; and T. Christopher Jespersen, "The Bitter End and the Lost Chance in Vietnam: Congress, the Ford Administration, and the Battle over Vietnam, 1975–1976," *Diplomatic History* 24 (Spring 2000): 265–93. On the connection between the "go public" campaign and revelations about American war atrocities, see Gruner, *Prisoners of Culture*, 19; and "Dear President Nixon . . . ," *New York Times Magazine*, October 3, 1971, 56–59.

23. Alvarez and Pitch, *Chained Eagle*, 153.

24. Ibid., 154.

25. Ibid.

26. Ibid.

27. Ibid., 153.

28. On generational divisions within Mexican American families, see George Sánchez, *Becoming Mexican American: Ethnicity, Culture, and Identity in Chicano Los Angeles, 1900–1945* (New York: Oxford University Press, 1993), 173, 263–65.

29. Alvarez and Pitch, *Chained Eagle*, 154.

30. Ibid., 209. The record is confused about Lalo's stance on the war. Although Everett Alvarez insisted throughout his memoirs that his father never wavered in his support of the war effort, some media sources suggest that Lalo, like his wife and older daughter, became a vocal opponent of the war by the early 1970s. See, for example, "Parents of POW Call Nixon 'Liar,'" *San Francisco Chronicle*, December 21, 1972, 16.

31. Alvarez and Pitch, *Chained Eagle*, 155, 207–8.

32. "Interview with Delia Alvarez, POW Sister," 36–37.

33. Everett Alvarez with Samuel Schreiner Jr., *Code of Conduct: An Inspirational Story of Self-Healing by the Famed Ex-POW and War Hero* (New York: Donald Fine, 1991), 58.

34. On the relationship between the Chicano movement and the movement against the Vietnam War, see Oropeza, *Raza Si! Guerra No!*; Ian F. Haney-López, *Racism on Trial: The Chicano Fight for Justice* (Cambridge, Mass.: Harvard University Press, 2003); Carlos Muñoz, *The Chicano Movement: Youth, Identity, Power* (2d ed.; London: Verso, 2003); and Ernesto Chávez, *"Mi Raza Primero!": Nationalism, Identity, and Insurgency in the Chicano Movement in Los Angeles, 1966–1978* (Berkeley: University of California Press, 2002). On the Chicano experience in Vietnam, see George Mariscal, ed., *Aztlán and Vietnam: Chicano and Chicana Experiences of War* (Berkeley: University of California Press, 1999); and Charley Trujillo, ed., *Soldados: Narratives of the Vietnam War* (San Jose, Calif.: Chusma House, 1990).

35. On the Chicano moratorium, see Haney-López, *Racism on Trial*, 193.

36. Alvarez and Pitch, *Chained Eagle*, 208.

37. Ibid., 211.

38. Ibid. On the petition, see "Bay Wife's Vigil for POW Pilot," *San Francisco Chronicle*, December 19, 1969, 8; and "70,000 Petition Nixon for Action in Flyer Release," *San Francisco Chronicle*, December 10, 1969, 22.

39. The *Los Angeles Times* article was reproduced in *Regeneración*, another Chicano movement publication. See "Sister of Longest-Held POW Starts Protest," *Regeneración* 1, no. 10 (1971): 19. On the formation of POW-MIA Families for Immediate Release, see "POWs: Speaking Out," *Time*, October 11, 1971, 21; "The Families Are Frantic," *Time*, July 26, 1971, 17–18; "Politics and POWs," *New Republic*, June 3, 1972, 17–19; "Prisoners of War: They Also Serve," *Newsweek*, December 27, 1971, 17–18; "POW Wife," *Life*, September 29, 1972, 32–42; and "POW Politics," *New York Times Magazine*, October 3, 1971, 56.

40. On Alvarez's antiwar activism during this period, see Raul Ruiz, "The POW," *La Raza* 1 (April 1972): 30; "Overseas Call Set for Peace Rally," *San Francisco Chronicle*, April 21, 1972, 16; and "Jane Fonda, Kin of POW Plan Protest," *Los Angeles Times*, August 19, 1972, 19.

41. "Sister of POW Thinks He Will Face a Shock," *New York Times*, February 8, 1973, 16.

42. Alvarez and Pitch, *Chained Eagle*, 273.

43. Press conference announcing formation of group, CBS Evening News, May 28, 1971, Vanderbilt University Television News Archive, Nashville, Tenn.

44. On the connections between the National League of Families and the Republican Party, see "Politics and POWs," *New Republic*, June 3, 1972, 17–19. Although many members of the league were members of the Republican Party, they insisted that their work in behalf of POWs was nonpartisan. On the ways in which POW relatives were advised to handle the media, see "The P.O.W. Families," *New York Times Magazine*, October 3, 1971, 56.

45. U.S. House, Committee on Armed Services, *Hearing on Problems of Prisoners of War and Their Families*, 91st Cong., 2d sess. (Washington, D.C.: Government Printing Office, 1970), March 6, 1970, 5994.

46. Advertising Council Collection, Box 6, File: National League of Families of American Prisoners and Missing in Southeast Asia, 1971–1972, John W. Hartman Center for Sales, Advertising, and Marketing Collection, Duke University Rare Book, Manuscript, and Special Collections Library, Durham, N.C. The Ad Council POW-MIA campaign was initiated on behalf of the American Red Cross and the National League of Families in 1971.

47. On the similar ways in which hostages were identified with their families during the Iranian hostage crisis, again see McAlister, *Epic Encounters*, 198–234.

48. On who was likely to be a POW, see "Healthier Adjustment for Vietnam POWs," *Science News*, September 17, 1977, 182. Rochester and Kiley describe the POWs as "glamorous aviators" in *Honor Bound*, ix–x.

49. Advertising Council Collection, Box 6, File: National League of Families of American Prisoners and Missing in Southeast Asia, 1971–72.

50. ABC News, October 12, 1972, Vanderbilt University Television News Archive.

51. "A National Disgrace," *Armed Forces Journal*, September 27, 1969, reprinted in appendix A of the House Committee on Armed Services, *Hearing on Problems of Prisoners of War and Their Families*, 6048.

52. "Memories of Divided Families," *Life*, December 4, 1970, 36–40+; "What Is Christmas to the P.O.W. Wives?" *Look*, December 15, 1970, 36–40.

53. "Families Who Wait Back Home," *Time*, December 7, 1970, 20.

54. Ibid., 19.

55. See, for example, letter from Ann Griffiths to General Richard Lawson, November 15, 1974, Theodore C. Marrs File, Box 16, File: Missing in Action/National League of Families, Gerald R. Ford Library, Ann Arbor, Mich.

56. On the connection between maternalism and pacifism, see Margaret Randolph Higonnet, Jane Jenson, Sonya Michel, and Margaret Collins Weitz, eds., *Behind the Lines: Gender and the Two World Wars* (New Haven, Conn.: Yale University Press, 1987); and Jean Bethke Elshtain, *Women and War* (New York: Basic Books, 1987).

57. See Rochester and Kiley, *Honor Bound*, 412; and John McCain with Mark Salter, *Faith of My Fathers* (New York: Random House, 1999), 217.

58. On the role of women in the antiwar movement, see Rhodri Jeffreys-Jones, *Peace Now! American Society and the Ending of the Vietnam War* (New Haven, Conn.: Yale

University Press, 1999), 142–77. For examples of POW anger toward highly visible women and women's organizations, see Hubbell, *P.O.W.*, 336–37; and Larry Guarino, *A P.O.W.'s Story: 2,801 Days in Hanoi* (New York: Ivy Books, 1990), 157.

59. Guarino, *P.O.W.'s Story*, 322.

60. POW divorce rates were about 30 percent, a rate that, while in line with divorce rates within the general population, was significantly higher than rates of divorce within military communities. See Edna J. Hunter, "Combat Casualties Who Remain at Home," *Military Review* 60 (January 1980): 29–36.

61. "They Are Different Men Now," *New York Times*, February 11, 1973; "When Johnny Comes Marching Home Again—or Doesn't," *Life*, November 10, 1972, 32–39; "P.O.W. Wives Await Peace with Joy and Dread," *New York Times*, December 6, 1972, 1.

62. "When Johnny Comes Marching Home Again—or Doesn't," 32–39; "An Emotional, Exuberant Welcome Home," *Time*, February 26, 1973, <http:www.time.com/time/magazine/article/0,9171,910550,00.html> (March 3, 2007).

63. "Ex-POW: Re-Entering a New World," *Washington Post*, February 18, 1973, 1.

64. On the relationship of women's liberation and the Chicano movement, see Alma M. García, "The Development of a Chicana Feminist Discourse, 1970–1980," in *Unequal Sisters: A Multicultural Reader in U.S. Women's History*, ed. Vicki L. Ruiz and Ellen Carol DuBois (New York: Routledge, 1994), 418–31; Alma M. García, ed., *Chicana Feminist Thought: The Basic Historical Writings* (New York: Routledge, 1997); and Norma Alarcón et al., *Chicana Critical Issues* (Berkeley, Calif.: Third Woman Press, 1993).

65. On the centrality of privacy and personal life to the women's liberation movement, see Sara Evans, *Personal Politics: The Roots of Women's Liberation in the Civil Rights Movement and the New Left* (New York: Random House, 1979); Alice Echols, *Daring to Be Bad: Radical Feminism in America, 1968–1975* (Minneapolis: University of Minnesota Press, 1988); and Ruth Rosen, *The World Split Open: How the Modern Women's Movement Changed America* (New York: Penguin Books, 2000).

66. "Interview with Delia Alvarez, POW Sister," 36–37.

67. Ibid.

68. ABC News, December 22, 1971, Vanderbilt University Television News Archive.

69. "Therapeutic Considerations in Planning the Return of American POWs to Continental United States," *Military Medicine* 138 (February 1973): 73–77; "Psychological Hangups of Returning Prisoners of War," *Science Digest* 81 (October 1973): 10–15; "Re-entry Problems," *Newsweek*, July 31, 1972, 23.

70. "Psychological Hangups of Returning Prisoners of War," 12.

71. On the history of these stereotypes within American popular culture, see Robert Lee, *Orientals: Asian Americans in Popular Culture* (Philadelphia: Temple University Press, 1999).

72. House Committee on Armed Services, *Hearing on Problems of Prisoners of War and their Families,*, 6000–6001.

73. "Treatment of American Prisoners by the North Vietnamese," *Congressional Record*, September 17, 1969, 8024. Copy in Edward R. Hutchinson Papers, 1959–1976, Box 110, File: House Congressional Resolution 360 (19), Gerald R. Ford Library.

74. See, for example, Guarino, *P.O.W.'s Story*. These images also abound in Hubbell, *P.O.W.*

75. "Sister of POW Thinks He Will Face a Shock," *New York Times*, February 8, 1973, 16.

76. See Robert Blauner, *Racial Oppression in America* (New York: Harper Collins, 1972).

77. "Fighting Women," *San Diego Union*, November 29, 1969, reprinted in appendix 1 of House Committee on Armed Forces, *Hearing on Problems of Prisoners of War and Their Families*, 6034.

78. Ruiz, "The POW," 30–32.

79. Alvarez and Pitch, *Chained Eagle*, 282.

80. Alvarez and Schreiner, *Code of Conduct*, 15.

81. Henry Kissinger, *Years of Upheaval* (Boston: Little, Brown, 1982), 42.

PART IV

Crossings

Desengaño
A Confederate Exile in Cuba

MATTHEW PRATT GUTERL

So I rode away from Arlington, leaving the sugar-house crowded to its utmost capacity with the entire crop of sugar and molasses of the previous year for which we had been unable to find a market within "our lines," leaving cattle grazing in the fields, sheep wandering over the levee, doors and windows flung wide open, furniture in the rooms, clothes too fine for me to wear now hanging in the armoires, *china in the closets, pictures on the walls, beds unmade, table spread. It was late in the afternoon of that bright, clear, bracing day, December 18, 1862, that I bade Arlington adieu forever!*
—Eliza [McHatton] Ripley, From Flag to Flag: A Woman's Adventures and Experiences in the South during the War, in Mexico, and in Cuba (1888)

For many slaveholders in the Deep South, the early optimism of the American Civil War gave way to the dreariness of a longer conflict, and then, eventually, to the prospect of defeat and prostration before the North. Border-crossing was a certain topic of conversation, especially flight to Cuba and other similarly welcoming locations. For some, the urge to flee came in the wake of the Emancipation Proclamation, as Union armies swept into southern states and upended the slave economy. For others, it came with the onset of Radical Reconstruction, when the racial status quo ante bellum was dramatically, if incompletely, over-turned. In 1863 the port cities of Galveston, New Orleans, and Mobile were not yet the overexcited sites of Confederate exodus, as they would be in the later 1860s, but they were buzzing with rumors, and, as the logical points of departure for Brazil, British Honduras, Cuba, and Mexico, they witnessed a slow trickle of the most disenchanted. Whenever it happened, small communities of true believers gathered in river cities along the Gulf coast and then fled the forcibly reuniting states, clinging to antebellum dreams of yeoman republics built on a foundation of hard work, docile labor, and racial entitlement.[1] This essay is about one such true believer who left for Cuba hoping to rebuild this lost world and who explored, in the process, the dynamic relationship between her white-ness, her womanhood, her Americanness, and her status as a New World slaveholder.

Of all of these exiles, the few who went to Cuba are the most interesting—if only because they seem to have been wealthier than their comrades who went elsewhere and because there seem to have been far fewer of them. Of course, for the southern master class, Cuba had long been a singularly special place. If British and American abolitionists saw Cuba as the most grotesquely abusive slave system in the Atlantic world, southerners believed that the island had a certain mystique about it, an intoxicating aroma of decadence and profit, decay and slavery. With a long history of cross-national connections and shared experiences—what Louis Pérez has called a set of "binding familiarities"—the island colony of Spain was a very familiar location to most travelers from the United States; indeed, as the growing split between North and South threatened to halve the republic, conspiratorial defenders of slavery and ardent celebrants of the "manifest destiny" of the United States urged the purchase, or even the outright annexation, of Cuba from Spain.[2] On the eve of civil war, the children of the Cuban elite were being educated in the United States, the island's sugar estates were populated with American mechanics, and a number of stateside southerners were absentee landlords or property owners in Cuba. Goods and people regularly crossed from Mobile or New Orleans to Havana. It seemed only logical in this context that the "manifest destiny" of southern planters should lead not just to the filibuster movement or to the illegal intervention into Central America and the Caribbean—an extension of the process through which Texas had become a state in the republic—but also to formal negotiations between nations, and that such efforts should focus most closely of all on Cuba.[3] So when the North and South went to war, well-off southerners who desired a mature slave economy with tremendous short-term upside escaped to Cuba, and not to Brazil or British Honduras, for their immediate salvation.

Eliza McHatton was one such person. Born in 1832 in Lexington, Kentucky, and raised in New Orleans, Eliza was a child of the American border surging westward during the nineteenth century. At the time of her arrival in Cuba, she was a young mother, thirty-two years old, with brown hair and brown eyes, a "fair" complexion and "Aquiline" nose.[4] She was married to James McHatton, a Deep South planter with deep roots in Kentucky politics, whose forebears included a distinguished military man of the Revolution and a member of the House of Representatives, and who could list as onetime family friends the generals Lafayette and Jackson. James and Eliza were members of the elite planter class in the frontier South, a fact not lost on their children; when writing of his mother's side of the family, young Henry would proudly note his great-grandfather's limitless wealth and his grandfather's frontier friendship with Henry Clay.[5] Eliza's marriage to James was, therefore, a union of dynasties, and they soon settled at the handsome sugar plantation named Arlington, where their two-story mansion with fluted columns and alluring verandas was nestled up against the curving banks of the lower Mississippi, just south of Baton Rouge. Leaving the Confederacy for Texas and Mexico in the early 1860s, she eventually went to Cuba and stayed there for about a decade, at which point she returned to the United States.

The story of Eliza's border-crossing and relocation to Cuba is illustrative of the long nineteenth century, when national boundary lines were impossibly blurry, when citizens of one nation or colony were very often landowners or occasional residents in another, and when the United States was just one of many white settler colonies or republics struggling to survive. And yet, this same century was also the great era of nation building, when borders and cultures and destinies were being defined and then more closely redefined. Postslavery debates about labor, land, race, and citizenship took shape from this context and were as much transnational as national, as much about the fate of the "master class" everywhere as they were about a particular set of circumstances in one specific place. On the one hand, Eliza's own racial pride and national chauvinism reflected the growing self-aggrandizement of the United States, which increasingly styled itself as the North Star of the hemisphere, bringing progress by example or expansion to the continent; on the other hand, her enthusiasm for slavery and bondage as the foundations of good agriculture, civilization, and industry was of a piece with the self-imaginings of the planter class throughout the West Indies and the Caribbean. When, over the course of this narrative span, Eliza grappled with the widening gaps between her interests as an American, her interests as a "white" person, and her interests as a slaveholder, it illuminates those postemancipation debates. In following her from the Mississippi River to just south of Matanzas, we can note the dissonance between the island of Cuba, the imperial South, and the imperial United States.

As the Confederacy slowly collapsed, the Trans-Mississippi became, as another exile put it, a "City of Refuge from which it is hoped a door of escape may be found to Mexico or Cuba."[6] Eliza thought along those same lines. "We have been annoyed and harassed by the Yankees," she wrote, "until we begin to think the time may not be far distant when we will have to flee for our lives—We turn our thoughts to Texas—as a kind of 'Land of Canaan' to which we may have to journey, without a Moses to guide us."[7] Arlington had been a profitable plantation in 1860, but the years that followed had been disastrous. Union occupation meant brutish savagery and forced emancipation, and so the McHattons attempted to send their slaves to the Texas plantation of Eliza's "loving brother," Richard. Along the way to Texas, those same slaves elected, instead, to present themselves to the Union army and escape their bondage. Such a situation was hardly unique, as the *New York Herald* reported that "the rebels" had been running caravans of slaves to Texas and Mexico in the hopes, perhaps, of getting them to Cuba, and one such group, captured by Union general Godfrey Weitzel, was 400 wagons large.[8] Concerned about freed slaves, Union armies, and social disorder, a pregnant Eliza found herself, in 1862, following James first to Texas, and then on to Mexico, in a slapdash escape from their old home.[9] The American memsahib thus came to Mexico, though she arrived dirty and sweaty from her inglorious escape from the marauding Union army.

Still, Mexico, where slavery was already illegal, was hardly a safe haven. High-ranking southern army officers shared a martial affinity with the emperor Maxmilian, and, in the aftermath of the war, agricultural settlements like Carlota—a wartime Confederate oasis in Mexico—would spring up overnight. But it was clear to some that only the royalists in Mexico welcomed Confederate exiles, and that these smallish expatriate communities could flourish only if protected by royalist troops. Tellingly, Eliza's brother, Richard, dined with one of Maxmilian's adjutants in Matamoros, before leaving for Cuba in 1864.[10] Maxmilian, of course, was executed in 1867; Carlota was burned to the ground soon afterward.[11] Mexico, in short, was unstable and dangerous. Eliza could not have anticipated the execution of the emperor, but she had plenty of cause to worry about her future in Mexico anyway, chiefly because of the long-standing prohibition against the ownership of slaves. Upon her arrival in Matamoros, Humphrey (the oldest of the three remaining McHatton slaves) had raced straight to the Mexican authorities, and fourteen-year-old Martha had already been too closely questioned by the *alcalde*, or chief administrator, who had also tried to separate her from the family.[12] Eliza could not stay in Mexico and keep her slaves.

Eliza's one other slave was Zell, a teenaged Louisiana creole boy, whom she derisively described as "black as ebony . . . with a big mouth, full of dazzling ivories."[13] In Mexico (and later in Cuba) Zell handled the horses, acted as a driver for Eliza and guests, and was a surrogate protector for her in the absence of her husband. He also shepherded young Henry to school and served as a critical financial agent, trading and bartering for much-needed supplies and quickly learning Spanish. Eliza clucked dismissively about his corner bodega schools, where he provided English instruction for meager profit in his spare time. And she fussed over his supposedly deteriorating work habits. "We really had very little for Zell to do," she worriedly wrote to her sister-in-law, Anna. "If he had liked to cook & had been less dirty about it—it would have suited me to have made a cook of him—but Martha does better in the kitchen." To keep Zell busy, and to quite literally *keep* him as a possession, James and Eliza sent him to Havana. They would eventually join him in Cuba and would, she believed, then be "*nigger sure*," an ominous phrase that reveals a deep desire for slaves.[14]

Once in Havana, the McHattons joined a heterogeneous ruling class of white planters, composed of native-born criollos, American entrepreneurs, and plucky escapees from other former slave societies, most notably rebellious Haiti or prostrate Jamaica. Like other unwilling American exiles, then, Eliza soon found herself in Havana and at the Hotel Cubano, where she and her husband were guests of the talented "Mrs. Brewer," dining and gossiping with the finer class of southern expatriates, most notably former Confederate secretary of state Judah P. Benjamin, former vice president and U.S. senator John C. Breckinridge, and Confederate generals Robert Toombs and Jubal Early.[15] Brewer, herself an expatriate American with considerable Confederate sympathies, ran the hotel on "American lines," where those who "chafed at Cuban cooking" and who were "sick of garlic and crude oil diet" could happily consume batter cakes and mince pies while proclaiming the virtues of the slave power.[16] There was a regular buzz about which famous (or infamous) Confederate had shown up, including a supposed sighting of Jefferson Davis in May 1865, who, the rumor went, had been shuttled to Matanzas from Galveston on an old Confederate blockade-runner.[17] "How prosperous and rich Cuba was in those days!" Eliza remembered later; "How animated and gay! We arrived when it was at the very acme of its opulence, when fairly drunk with the excess of wealth and abundance."[18]

By 1866, James had purchased from "a Cuban named Royo" an impressive home—a former *cafetal* (coffee plantation) that had been converted by a Spanish slave trader into a sugar plantation.[19] Gathering up their "possessions" (including Zell), Eliza and her husband left for the aptly named Desengaño—the word means "disillusionment"—in Los Palos near Matanzas, on the northern coast of the island, some sixty miles east of Havana. The broad single-story home was whitewashed in the Spanish style, with Romanesque arches opening up on a large veranda that, in turn, looked down a main entrance nearly one-third of a mile long and lined with mature palm trees, their smooth gray trunks reaching skyward in excess of 100 feet. The house stood upon an area roughly the size of a baseball diamond. In the bright sun, surrounded by the impossibly verdant green of the Cuban countryside, the McHattons' new home was a singularly impressive structure, "the most pretentious and substantial in the Matanzas district."[20] The property itself included more than 1,000 acres, which, in turn, demanded considerable brawn to produce profit. Within two years of the arrival of James and Eliza, there were sixty-five slaves at Desengaño (forty men and twenty-five women) and nineteen Chinese workers (all male) on temporary contracts. Those numbers would grow slowly over the decade or so that Eliza was in residence.

When visitors arrived at Desengaño on horseback or by *volante* (an ornate carriage), after having taken the train from Havana to Matanzas, they passed first through a road lined on both sides with a short stone wall and then on through that grand avenue of palms. They would have seen impenetrably thick and impossibly long fields of cane growing up behind the stone wall and on the other side of the palm trees. Sugarcane is a profitable, but unruly and labor-intensive crop. The base of the plant—a kind of tall grass—can tilt and bend, sending each jumble of shafts shooting off randomly in every direction. Fibrous and sap-filled, it is tough to cut by hand. Leaning back in the seat and looking down the avenue toward the dark heart of the plantation, visitors would certainly have seen the mansion gleaming in the distance, a bright white against a rich green backdrop. Off to the left was the tall, broad chimney and long roofline of the sugarmill itself. And there would have been slaves and coolies all around, bending and lifting, sweating and cutting that wild, hard cane with long knives. If one came by *volante*, Zell would have been seated right there handling the lead horse.

Settling in, Eliza decorated her new Cuban plantation with those few remaining things brought from their old southern home, and she marveled at the thickness of the walls, designed to stand up to the terrible weather of the hurricane season.[21] But if conjuring up furniture, tapestries, and silverware for the inside of their new home was relatively easy, populating their *ingenio*, or sugar estate, with the "right" sort of laborers proved much more difficult. Domestic labor, she believed, was different than work in the cane fields. Remembering the "horrors of the early days," Eliza was most especially disturbed by the memory of "the black woman, in a dirty, low-necked, sleeveless, trailing dress, a cigar in her mouth, and whining child on one arm, [who] went about spreading the table, scrupulously wiping . . . plates with an exceedingly suspicious-looking ghost of a towel."[22] "Until a tidy Chinaman was installed in the kitchen," she remembered later, "I was very dainty."[23] And as for the many laborious tasks waiting in the cane fields, there simply were not enough African slaves to go cheaply around. A trusted overseer soon departed for Havana to "secure the only kind of labor available—Chinese coolies."[24]

Eliza's choice between African slaves and Chinese coolies reflected the changing economy of work in the nineteenth-century Caribbean. Before the so-called sugar revolution came to Cuba, the island had possessed only a smallish population of about 200,000, some 20 percent of whom were slaves. The lure of profits from sugar cultivation soon encouraged greater attention to this cash crop, and by 1828, Cuba was the largest producer of sugar in the West Indies—this despite having "only" 286,942 slaves, "a figure deemed highly inadequate for the successful pursuit of sugar cane growing."[25] By the 1850s, there were roughly half a million slaves on the island. To complicate matters, slave traders invariably brought mostly male Africans to Cuba, many of whom would be worked to death, leaving the island with a seemingly insatiable and counterproductive appetite for male slaves. "Natural increase is disregarded," the abolitionist Joseph John Gurney noted in 1840, in a letter to Henry Clay; "The Cubans import the stronger animals, like bullocks, work them up, and then seek a fresh supply."[26] Long before the arrival of James and Eliza, then, Cuban planters had been worried about the production of sugar in the age of "the labor problem."[27] In the case of Cuba, it was the end of the supply of slaves that posed the problem (rather than the end of slavery), but many of the pressures were the same. Unlike the British, planters and investors in Cuba could not boast of colonial ties to a land such as India, where poverty, famine, and "imperialist disruptions" drove thousands from the Raj to other British colonies suffering after emancipation, most notably Natal, Jamaica, and British Guiana. In this context, Cuban planters invested in two readily available "reforms": new technologies of production and Chinese "coolies."

From the vantage point of the 1860s, it must have been astounding to survey the transformation of the Cuban socioeconomic fabric. By then, Cuba had already been changed by newer, more efficient technologies of sugar production and the massive construction of railroads to speed and cheapen the connections between coastal ports and inland plantations.[28] All this progress, Eliza did not see. It was all right in front of her, of course, but her life—her past in the South, her disdain for those racially distinct from herself, her veneration of America—made it impossible for her to properly understand and appreciate the changes all around her. "The native Cubans," she wrote dismissively, "are a century behind the age in agriculture, as well as everything else." They were "a race that could not economize time, labor, or anything else." Visiting a neighboring plantation, she noted that "nobody seemed to be working, every living thing had a lazy, idle air." "Cuba," she summed, "is a paradise for those who are too lazy to do anything but exist."[29] Here, then, were her American gifts to the island: a proper sense of time management, an acute awareness of how to better maximize profits, and the supposedly generous bestowal of technology and knowledge. In short, Eliza proposed a cold-hearted scientific management of bound labor and land in Cuba, and she offered it as if she alone (and certainly no Cuban) could see its virtues. In doing so, she echoed and, in some cases, anticipated the great body of Victorian literature on white women outsiders in untidy, racially complicated places.[30] Members of the Cuban planter class who visited Desengaño, she wrote with great self-satisfaction, would gaze in spellbound adoration at the McHatton family library, as if the rows and rows of books brought from Arlington were ironbound chests washed up on a beach and as if the information within were pirate treasure. Such was her life as plantation mistress in supposedly backward Cuba, where she had only enlightenment to impart and nothing at all to learn herself.[31]

Despite the various "modern" improvements to the island, Eliza—like many other American visitors—wondered at the whiteness of an upper crust suspended somewhere between the questionable achievements of Spain and the more troubling world of racial amalgamation in Cuba. Noting that the features of "whites" in Cuba were outwardly "opaque" and "beautiful," one unnamed author wondered whether there was any inner beauty: "I wonder," he or she asked, "where the Cuban people keep their souls?"[32] "The more we see of the Cuban character," Eliza confided to her sister, "the more we are convinced that a military government is what they need. They are totally unfit for freedom & the pusillanimous puppies will never have it unless some strong nation fights for it, for them."[33] The average Cuban, she argued elsewhere, lacked a refined awareness of social boundaries, choosing to mingle dangerously with all sorts of undesirables "at every street corner and every cross roads grocery."[34] She was hardly alone in thinking this way. Indeed, many of her contemporaries saw the future of democracy in Cuba as one of American outsiders gently and slowly leading the childish *mestizaje* toward "civilization." As early as 1873, popular penny plays staged on the eastern seaboard of the United States urged either direct American intervention or individualist participation in Cuba's wars for independence. Perhaps the most telling of these was *Little Cuba*, an unflattering fictional story of how one young white woman, in "male disguise" and aided by the timely arrival of U.S. forces, "led" and inspired the dusky masses of that "Western Eden" to victory.[35] Even small and dainty white women, the lesson went, were better able to fight for freedom than Cuban men, whether Spanish or African or Chinese. This protracted commentary about the abilities of Cubans—white, black, yellow, and everything else—to properly govern themselves socially and politically would eventually inspire the turn-of-the-century generation to satisfy its long-standing fantasies about white American stewardship of the island.[36] And, to a certain extent, the United States continues to do so today, in the age of the embargo.

The emergence of the Cuban "coolie trade" was the fitting complement to the island's technological innovation of the mid-nineteenth century. In 1847, much like the rest of the Caribbean, the West Indies, and Latin America (most everyone except for Brazil, in fact), Cuban planters turned to the human abundance of Asia, and more specifically to Chinese laborers tricked or coerced into boarding coffin ships, as the solution to the perennial problems of scarcity and cost. The first group of Chinese coolies arrived in June of that year, and they were subsequently doled out to "the island's most prominent planters and a railroad company."[37] There was, perhaps not surprisingly, some debate about the comparative virtues of Africans and Asians. Champions of "Asiatic colonization" stressed the economy and efficiency of their new field hands, railroad builders, and factory workers and urged planters to consider the "in-born" intelligence of the Chinese when deciding on certain punishments. Those seeking greater numbers of Africans blamed the failures of the former slaves in Jamaica on abolitionist permissiveness, also hinting that the Chinese were pitifully weak and brought with them numerous epidemics. Strict rules and uncompromising authority, and not wages, were what the emancipated slave needed. Despite the disagreements, the combined influx of these two unhappy peoples, the U.S. consul reported, had at least lowered the price of slaves considerably.[38]

For transplanted Confederates in Cuba like Eliza and her husband, the need for labor came down to a hard choice between two very dissimilar peoples ("stupid negroes and dazed Chinese," she called them), one familiar and the other inexpensive, one "tidy" and the other not.[39] The appearance of the Chinese sharpened racial sensibilities by forcing some slaves away from work requiring technological skills and limiting them to work primarily as field hands and manual laborers, further solidifying a connection between blackness and backwardness.[40] Here, Eliza McHatton's disdain for her African housewoman and her eager appreciation of the Chinese cook were part of a broader racial division of labor. When Eliza advised the readers of the *New Orleans Times* (who were then thinking about getting coolies of their own to replace newly emancipated slaves in the United States), she described her erstwhile Asian cook as entirely ignorant of English or Spanish, or the virtues of the Victorian home; however, "it was astonishing," she wrote, "the rapidity with which he learned. At first, by dint of soap, and ashes, and rags, and signs, he was given to understand that 'cleanliness was next to godliness.' So he rapidly got 'order out of chaos' in our Cuban kitchen, over which a Creole darkie had ruled supreme." He had, she claimed, learned everything about the culinary arts and the keeping of a Caribbean kitchen in less than a week. Indeed, within just a few busy years of her arrival at Desengaño, Eliza had even come to believe that the Chinese were better in the home than the Irish—"As a house servant, John is preferable to Bridget," she wrote.[41] Gender was an interesting dynamic in all of this, for Eliza, much like other Americans in and outside of the United States, often gendered Chinese labor in confusing and contradictory ways: their labors were fine, relying on precision and nimble fingers; they were less well suited, she thought, to working outdoors; they made ideal house servants, at least when compared with the stereotypical Irish woman, "Bridget," who was herself usually described as impossibly mannish.[42]

Cuban planters and visitors from the United States and Europe were "learning" (or inventing the idea) that Chinese laborers were best suited to "household service" or "lighter work in the new and modern sugar mills."[43] Contemporary observer Ramón de la Sagra suggested that the "initial disappointment" in Chinese coolies stemmed from a deeper ignorance about how "to use or manage a more intelligent labor force."[44] Some came to believe that the Chinese were strikingly different, and that "practical" grimoires written to advise sugar planters on "breaking in" new slaves were useless when it came to "the celestials."[45] U.S. consul William H. Robertson even suggested that the African slaves were themselves almost immediately aware of this distinction and had "great confidence" in the natural wisdom of the Chinese. "Negroes," he offered, "have already been heard to remark, 'Los Chinos saben mucho' . . . and on being questioned why they say so, the reply is again, 'The Chinese know much; they know everything.' "[46] Samuel Hazard, an aging Civil War veteran, noted that Chinese workers in a local cigarette factory were "scrupulously neat and clean," a contrast to "colored human nature," which he sketched as pure, unadulterated laziness. His drawings of "the negro" in Cuba are grotesquely comical, featuring cartoonishly large breasts, the barest rudiments of technological intelligence, open mouths, doltish expressions, and a striking absence of gender differences between African men and women. The presumption, then as now, was that the qualities of the Chinese as a "model minority" stood in stark contrast to the supposed lack of such qualities in African slaves. "The Chinese," Eliza herself summed comparatively, "were intelligent."[47]

On this exact comparison, Eliza McHatton soon gained a certain amount of well-noted expertise, publishing short essays solicited from her by popular newspapers in the United States, where a postwar southern readership was wondering about whether it could claim coolies of its own.[48] "Buying a chino," she reminded her readers, was tricky business. It began with an ethnological process of "selection," wherein a coolie with "a good face" was chosen from the lot as they left the boat after their "long hard ocaen [sic] voyage" from China, as if their physical strength and mental character could be more clearly divined when they were at their weakest.[49] After a brief period of seasoning during the first year, a carefully chosen coolie would work as "regular as an automaton."[50] The machinelike result was perfect, she believed, when paired with the tropic brute strength of the bestial African slave. "The Chinese," she advised, "when once acclimated and accustomed to the routine, were docile and industrious; they could not stand the same amount of exposure as an African, but they were intelligent and ingenious; within-doors, in the sugar factory, in the carpenter-shop, in the cooper-shop, in driving teams, they were superior to the negro."[51] Cuban "negroes," Eliza thought, were perfect for the dreary, mindless, bloody work of cane harvesting—"[they] were," she summed, "more or less stupid and stolid, like 'dumb-driven' cattle."[52]

If Eliza sought the most efficient means to exploit coolies and slaves, the relationship between Zell and the labor force at Desengaño was not nearly so easy to summarize. Several times (to Eliza's chagrin) he served as a gentle mediator of sorts between the concerns of the Asian contract laborers and those of Eliza. At other moments, Zell's liminal position worked to Eliza's advantage. In the mind of the planters, the "natural" intelligence of the Chinese for more sophisticated work could pose other problems, and it seemed often to lead to collective legal action. "These indentured laborers," historian Rebecca Scott writes, "were aware of a distinction between slave labor and free, one which they felt was not being observed."[53] One morning, Eliza remembered:

> Our ears were assailed by a low, rumbling noise in the distance, which rose rapidly to shouts and unearthly yells. . . . The Chinese were in full rebellion: stripped to the middle, their swarthy bodies glistening in the hot sun, they rushed with savage impetuosity up the road, leaped the low stone fence that surrounded the cluster of plantation-buildings, of which the massive dwelling-house formed the center, brandishing their hoes in a most threatening manner, and yelling like demons, as with hastily grasped rocks from the fences they pelted the retreating overseer.[54]

After invoking the grand leitmotif of southern race relations—the threatened rape of a white woman by a person of color—Eliza's memoir only casually mentions the ultimate cause of the uprising: a "demand for an unlimited supply of food."[55] Perhaps her own tightfistedness was to blame, as she was perennially in search of less expensive fare for her coolies and prone to test the tender limits of their hunger.[56] But, on this particular day, the truculence of the Chinese at Desengaño ended quickly once Zell fired a gun into the air. And to ensure that such wanton displays of technological mastery would not be needed in the future, Eliza had their queues, their "long pig-tail," removed. "How quickly they wilted!" she squealed, "how cowed they looked!"[57]

Zell's broader role at Desengaño was understandably unique. His arrival with the McHattons set him apart from the plantation slaves and coolies. He was American; he was southern; he was Creole from Louisiana. He had control of a dangerous weapon, an ancient blunderbuss, as well as a pocket watch with which to mark his duties and those of others. In public, he acted as Eliza's ceremonial *calisero*, the driver of the trace horse of the *volante*, though she also described him as a simple *mandadero*, or messenger. As the *calisero*, he would have been gaudily dressed, wearing gold-plated buckles and bracelets, a formal uniform of some sort, and a feather-plumed hat of spectacular scale. Given his young age and the range of horrible possibilities in Cuba, that position would have indicated to all that he was a favorite of some kind (whether he wanted the reputation or not). I can find no reference to him cutting a single piece of cane or working a single hour in the sugar-house. Still, he acted as a critical liaison between Eliza and her laboring force, teaching them English, learning their many languages even as they learned his. He appears, therefore, to have mastered the art of shuttle diplomacy, keeping the diverse and conflicting interests of the McHattons, the various African peoples, and the Chinese in reasonable focus—no easy task considering that he was the only trustworthy line of communication between any two of these groups. His developing skill with numbers would have been as important to the Chinese, who were concerned about being cheated, as it was to Eliza, who was equally concerned with cheating them.

Zell's efforts to mitigate the effects of indenture and to ease the lives of the Chinese were, of course, unsuccessful. Trapped in the barracoons at night, stuck on a hot, lonely island in the Caribbean, the Chinese toiled in burned-out fields of sugarcane, and they were beaten ruthlessly until they worked "like slaves." Sadly, many chose to take their own lives. "I have seen some 20 men commit suicide," Lin A-pang remarked sadly, "by hanging themselves and by jumping into wells and sugar cauldrons."[58] Hoping that in death they would return to their faraway homeland, Chinese contract laborers committed half of all suicides in Cuba in 1862 (173 out of 346).[59] American interpretations of the suicides of the Chinese were often ghoulishly clinical, revealing an abiding concern for rich profit margin and little else. Visitor Julia Woodruff, for one, only noticed with disdain that the Chinese seemed stuck in "a state of chronic sullenness," and she took "comfort" in that "their propensity to suicide operates as some check upon the worst forms of cruelty."[60] Eliza's brother, for one, believed that a few clever Chinese coolies had faked their deaths by suicide to escape bondage.[61] Eliza herself blithely suggested that the "nostalgia" and "melancholia" behind the self-destructive urges of the coolie in Cuba were limited to the "the lower classes" and should be understood as evidence of mental defect.[62]

The spectacle of abuse and the regularity of suicide soon led China to end "the coolie trade" to Cuba. With that, the perilous fault lines of the labor problem in Cuba were revealed. Where once African slaves had been inexcusably expensive and there were too many Chinese coolies, now there were too few of either. At the first sign that China's agreement with Spain would soon end, Richard Chinn, Eliza's brother and junior partner in Cuba, rushed out to inspect six coolies, newly contracted to a dissatisfied planter outside of Havana. He happily paid $700 in gold for them—roughly the cost of one very good male slave—and bragged to Eliza that it was quite a bargain, as they were already seasoned to the Caribbean climate and had "gotten through their change of blood."[63] So desperate was the labor situation that Chinn went so far as to "spoil" the Chinese, providing them with too generous quantities of food.[64] In

1875, on the eve of losing some of these priceless coolies, Chinn and Henry McHatton raced to Matanzas and begged for the intervention of a Spanish official to force these unhappy sojourners to re-sign with the transnational planter family from Desengaño. "It was," Henry wrote to his mother, "just the closest shave that I ever saw."[65] By the mid 1870s, the McHattons unhappily concluded that the era of human bondage would soon pass. "During the latter years of our residence," Eliza wrote bitterly, "the gradual emancipation of slaves was enforced, the importation of coolies prohibited, and, as an inevitable sequence, an untold number of valuable estates were abandoned by their impoverished owners, thereby revolutionizing the entire financial and domestic status of the island." "A few years later," she remembered, "we left the island forever."[66]

There were, I suspect, other reasons for her departure. As the idealism of Reconstruction collapsed under the weight of political compromise and then quickly faded from memory, the American South and Cuba seemed to be on different paths—the former rebuilding its regional commitments to white supremacy but dependent on the North in disturbing ways; the latter engaged in a remarkable series of anticolonial struggles against the aging Spanish empire and profiting from nearly half a century of technological investment and modernization. In 1868 an unbalanced coalition of Cuban dissenters—ranging from planters who witnessed the collapse of the American South with horror and who favored very gradual emancipation, to free people of color hoping for an immediate abolition of slavery—found common ground in their distrust of Spain and launched an armed rebellion that would last ten years. While antiracism was only occasionally (and usually rhetorically) at the forefront of this so-called Ten Years' War, the revolutionary Liberation Army was a sizable force composed of every conceivable group of peoples in Cuba, including former slaves and coolies. The contrast between these two places, then, was as great as it had ever been, for the trend in the southern United States was toward separate development and racial hierarchy. "The escalation of racial violence," writes historian Ada Ferrer, "the spread of spatial segregation by race, and the dismantling of political gains made during Reconstruction in the South occurred in the United States precisely as black and mulatto leaders gained increasing popularity and power in Cuba."[67] This world turned upside down likely made balmy Cuba seem much more immediately threatening than the United States.

For southern expatriates, the same revolutionary forces that had driven them abroad into the Caribbean and Latin America now encouraged another exodus back to the United States. "When my family went to Cuba," Eliza explained in 1912, "it was to escape from war troubles at home. We sought for rest and peace, but it was not long before we felt we may have 'jumped from the frying pan into the fire.' "[68] The advent of the Ten Years' War witnessed the devolution of Cuba into an unwelcome state of "lawlessness," and the now aggressive attitude of men of "diminutive size and questionable appearance" posed serious racial threats to the safety of Eliza, herself the flower of white southern womanhood.[69] Soon, she and her daughter were unable to "promenade" anywhere other than on the carefully groomed, tree-lined avenue that led to their plantation home. The specter of rape and murder at the hands of smallish, swarthy brigands of "inferior" type was everywhere. But in America, regional rapprochement and the emerging architecture of Jim Crow would provide precisely the sort of "quiet" for which she and her husband had so eagerly hoped. Having escaped a war to free the slaves once before, the powerful antiracist rhetoric of the Liberation Army, with its well-armed men of many colors, seemed even more dangerous to Eliza. No wonder, then, that she and her new husband (James had died unexpectedly in March 1872) soon chose to leave Cuba altogether, entrusting the care of Desengaño to Zell.[70]

She would never again find what had been lost at Arlington and Desengaño. Remarried to a lawyer and living Brooklyn, she had a new baby and a young daughter from her marriage to James to worry about. The newborn occupied most of her time. "The library," she wrote with tired contentedness, "is littered with blocks and toy books." Still, she could not let Cuba go. Before the baby had been born, she had regularly taken a steamer to Havana and then caught the train out to Matanzas, where Zell or some other slave would be waiting in the *volante*. When at home in Brooklyn, she kept a series of "Chinese knives" taken back from Cuba on a display table in the library. She was hard at work (in her spare time) on her memoirs of a peripatetic life in the Caribbean, as well as on a series of semifictional stories about Zell, about coolies, and about sugarcane. She was biting her nails, again. And she was dreaming of the "Ever Faithful Isle." "I fell asleep last night thinking of you," she wrote to Henry. "I dreamed that I went to Havana with four trunks. . . . and the vessel was ordered to land her passengers in California and go by stage to Havana and I was in great stress about my baggage."[71] Eliza missed her old life, and could not get it back.

For his part, Zell stayed on in Cuba, married an Afro-Cuban woman named Maud, and started a family. When Eliza sold Desengaño in the mid-1870s, she arranged for him to receive U.S. citizenship and, by her recollection, deposited a small amount of money in a bank account for him. She also bound him by contract to the new owners of the estate, much like the Chinese coolies he had chased away with the blunderbuss that morning. In the concluding passages of her memoirs, as her thoughts turned to those left behind in Cuba, Eliza recalled the many letters she had received from Zell. She commented on the signature line he attached to each missive: "*Serviente*," she wrote, "was the conventional phrase used from equal to equal, and may not have appeared expressive enough to suit Zell, so it was *esclavo*."[72] Perhaps this was so. But Eliza preserved every possible shred of paper relating to her sojourn in Cuba—every passport, hundreds of letters, countless Spanish and American documents—but not a single letter from Zell. And against the grain of her intentions, he emerges from her memoirs as a clear-eyed, politically savvy, and otherwise intelligent person, who could hardly have been unaware of the contradictory drifts of Cuban and American politics. He was still young and now multilingual and binational in ways that Eliza (always the self-styled expatriate) could never have been. And by the late 1870s, it would already have been clear that, for a former slave, an antiracist republic jointly led by people of color must have seemed far more promising than a return to the United States. The same forces that lured Eliza back and drove her from Cuba encouraged him to stay.

The pan-American "crossings" of Eliza McHatton reveal, to a certain extent, the passage of the old "southern dream of a Caribbean empire" into the dustbin of history.[73] Cut off from the everyday connections to the hemisphere by the federal government and the Union armies and navies, the Old South struggled to keep alive its liminal sense of self and place. But there is no romance to this story—no "transnational love story" of the sort so wonderfully described by historian Martha Hodes.[74] There is only the brutal search for the best possible combination of cash-crop agriculture, cheap labor (slave, immigrant, or coolie), and racial authority (white over yellow and brown and off-white) outside of the South, where the war brought economic hardship and racial uncertainty. Thus, in addition to illuminating the dissonance between two systems of thought and meaning through the narrative plotline involving the acquisition of outsider status, the location of new vantage points from which to survey the homeland, and the inevitable act of self-discovery and reinvention, border-crossings can also reveal corridors of power—used, in this case, by a transnational slaveholding class—that are supernational, hemispheric, or global. Such a story tells us, I think, a great deal about the future of the United States, for Eliza's life in Cuba tells us much about the sense of civilizational advantage that the republic was thought to enjoy in the Americas, and even more about the profit-hungry, globe-trotting entrepreneurial capitalism that serves as the elemental culture of *el coloso del norte*. When the rules of southern labor were transformed by the Civil War, and former slaveholders seemed at a disadvantage to the future-oriented Midwest and its growing immigrant populations, Eliza and her husband did just what any twenty-first century corporate capitalist would do: they packed up their tents and shifted their operations to some other hemispherically disadvantaged location where their profit margin would be greater and their social position would be unassailable.

1. Rollin G. Osterweis, *The Myth of the Lost Cause, 1865–1900* (New York: Anchor Books, 1973), 8; Robert E. May, *The Southern Dream of a Caribbean Empire, 1854–1861* (Baton Rouge: Louisiana State University Press, 1973), 46–76. Also see Clement Eaton, *The Waning of the Old South Civilization, 1860–1880s* (Athens: University of Georgia Press, 1968); Cyrus B. Dawsey and James M. Dawsey, eds., *The Confederados: Old South Immigrants in Brazil* (Tuscaloosa: University of Alabama Press, 1995); Eugene C. Harter, *The Lost Colony of the Confederacy* (Jackson: University Press of Mississippi, 1985); William Clark Griggs, *The Elusive Eden: Frank McMullan's Confederate Colony in Brazil* (Austin: University of Texas Press, 1987); Donald C. Simmons Jr., *Confederate Settlements in British Honduras* (Jefferson, N.C.: McFarland and Co., 2001).

2. Louis A. Pérez Jr., *On Becoming Cuban: Identity, Nationality, and Culture* (Chapel Hill: University of North Carolina Press, 1999), 16.

3. Samuel L. Walker, *Cuba and the South* (n.p., 1854), 3; *The Commercial Guide or Manual, Comprising All the Most Important Information Required by Merchants, Shipowners, and Others, Transacting Business with the Island of Cuba* (Havana: n.p., 1861); Louis A. Pérez, *Cuba: Between Reform and Revolution* (New York: Oxford University Press, 1995); Basil Rauch, *American Interest in Cuba: 1848–1855* (New York: Columbia University Press, 1948).

4. Physical description given on Eliza's travel visa, dated November 2, 1870, in the McHatton Family Papers, Hargrett Rare Book and Manuscript Library, University of Georgia, Athens, Ga.

5. Diary of Henry McHatton, dated 1870, which contains a family genealogy; and the affidavit of James McHatton, February 15, 1872; both in McHatton Family Papers.

6. Eliza Frances Andrews, from her diary of May 1865, in Spencer B. King Jr., ed., *The War-Time Journal of a Georgia Girl, 1864–1865* (New York: Appleton Press, 1908), 198.

7. Eliza McHatton to Mrs. R. H. Chinn, August 28, 1862, McHatton Family Papers.

8. "Four Hundred Wagonloads of Negroes," *New York Herald*, November 20, 1862.

9. Balance sheet for the Arlington plantation, 1861; affidavit of James McHatton, February 15, 1872; both in McHatton Family Papers. Also see Andrew Rolle, *The Lost Cause: The Confederate Exodus to Mexico* (Norman: University of Oklahoma Press, 1992).

10. "Dictation of Richard Chinn, Solano County, 1888," Bancroft Library, University of California, Berkeley.

11. Rolle, *Lost Cause*, 31.

12. Eliza [McHatton] Ripley, *From Flag to Flag: A Woman's Adventures and Experiences in the South during the War, in Mexico, and in Cuba* (1888; reprint, New York: D. Appleton and Co., 1896), 123.

13. Ibid., 119, 150. Zell's age is impossible to verify, though it is clear that sometime during their stay in Cuba, he turned twenty years old. See ibid., 291.

14. Eliza McHatton to Anna Chinn, October 31, 1864, February 21, 1865 (emphasis in original); James Hewett and J. H. P. Aldersbery to Eliza McHatton, April 8, 1865; R. Atkinson to Eliza McHatton, April 21, 1865—all in McHatton Family Papers.

15. Ripley, *From Flag to Flag*, 132.

16. Eliza [McHatton] Ripley, *Social Life in Old New Orleans: Being Recollections of My Girlhood* (New York: D. Appleton, 1912), 287–92.

17. "The Situation," *New York Herald*, May 18, 1865.

18. Ripley, *From Flag to Flag*, 126.

19. Draft version of "From Flag to Flag" and diary of Henry McHatton, 1870, both in McHatton Family Papers.

20. Ripley, *From Flag to Flag*, 150.

21. Eliza McHatton to ?, October 15, 1870, McHatton Family Papers.

22. Ripley, *From Flag to Flag*, 151.

23. Ibid., 152.

24. Ibid., 149–50, 155, 163–66.

25. Franklin Knight, *Slave Society in Cuba during the Nineteenth Century* (Madison: University of Wisconsin Press, 1970), 29. On the specific demographic and economic transformations engendered in Cuba by this "sugar revolution," see Knight, *Slave Society in Cuba*, 25–84; and Pérez, *Cuba*, 70–103.

26. Joseph John Gurney, *A Winter in the West Indies, Described in Familiar Letters to Henry Clay, of Kentucky* (London: John Murray, 1840), 209.

27. William Green, *British Slave Emancipation: The Sugar Colonies and the Great Experiment, 1830–1865* (Oxford, U.K.: Clarendon Press, 1976), 261–93; Alan H. Adamson, *Sugar without Slaves: The Political Economy of British Guiana, 1838–1904* (New Haven, Conn.: Yale University Press, 1972), 41–56; Thomas C. Holt, *The Problem of Freedom: Race, Labor, and Politics in Jamaica and Britain, 1832–1938* (Baltimore, Md.: Johns Hopkins University Press, 1992).

28. On these advances and transformations, see especially Manuel Moreno Fraginals, *El ingenio. Complejo económico social cubano del azúcar,* 3 vols. (Havana: Editorial de Ciencias Sociales, 1978), condensed and translated as Manuel Moreno Fraginals, *The Sugarmill: The Socioeconomic Complex of Sugar in Cuba* (New York: Monthly Review Press, 1971); Laird W. Bergad, *Cuban Rural Society in the Nineteenth Century: The Social and Economic History of Monoculture in Matanzas* (Princeton, N.J.: Princeton University Press, 1999), 107–14; Rebecca Scott, *Slave Emancipation in Cuba, 1860–1899* (Princeton, N.J.: Princeton University Press, 1985), 20–41; Louis A. Pérez Jr., *Winds of Change: Hurricanes and the Transformation of Nineteenth-Century Cuba* (Chapel Hill: University of North Carolina Press, 2001).

29. "Planting in Cuba," *Home and Hearth*, August 20, 1870.

30. Margaret Strobel, *European Women and the Second British Empire* (Bloomington: Indiana University Press, 1991); Nuper Chaudhuri and Margaret Strobel, eds., *Western Women and Imperialism: Complicity and Resistance* (Bloomington: Indiana University Press, 1992).

31. Ripley, *From Flag to Flag*, 233, 254, 162.

32. Anonymous, *Rambles in Cuba* (New York: Carleton, 1870), 9.

33. Eliza McHatton to Robert and Anna, August 26, 1866, McHatton Family Papers.

34. "Chinese Servants," *New Orleans Times*, February 11, 1871.

35. George Barclay, *Little Cuba; or, Circumstantial Evidence: Being a True Story of Love, War, and Startling Adventures.* (Philadelphia: Barclay and Co., 1873).

36. Michael H. Hunt, *Ideology and U.S. Foreign Policy* (New Haven, Conn.: Yale University Press, 1987); Kristin L. Hoganson, *Fighting for Manhood: How Gender Politics Provoked the Spanish-American and Philippine-American Wars* (New Haven, Conn.: Yale University Press, 1998).

37. Evelyn Hu-Dehart, "Race Construction and Race Relations: Chinese and Blacks in Nineteenth-Century Cuba," unpublished manuscript in author's possession.

38. William H. Robertson to William L. Marcy, August 6, 1855, in *Report of the Secretary of State, in Compliance with a Resolution of the Senate of April 24, Calling for Information Relative to the Coolie Trade*, Senate Documents, 34th Cong., 1st and 2d sess., 1855–56 (Washington, D.C.: A. O. P. Nicholson, 1856), 15.3:828.

39. Ripley, *From Flag to Flag*, 155.

40. Mary Turner, "Chinese Contract Labour in Cuba, 1847–1874," *Caribbean Studies* 14 (July 1974): 66–81. "Once the quest for agricultural laborers for the Cuban planters had shifted from Europe," historian Franklin Knight writes, "the words 'white' and 'free' underwent an interesting semantic change." Knight, *Slave Society in Cuba*, 116.

41. "Chinese Servants."

42. For these representations of the Chinese and others, see Robert G. Lee, *Orientals: Asian Americans in Popular Culture* (Philadelphia: Temple University Press, 1999), 15–105. Lee's notion of the Chinese as a "Third Sex" is especially important here; more recently, Najia Aarim-Heriot has compared the plight of African Americans and Chinese immigrants in her brilliant work, *Chinese Immigrants, African Americans, and Racial Anxiety in the United States, 1848–82* (Urbana: University of Illinois Press, 2003).

43. "Slaves on efficient modern plantations with steam-driven mills," one historian has remarked, "were treated more inhumanely than those on the old oxen-driven mills: they were confined to menial and manual labour; and they were regarded and treated as economic rather than human units." Arthur Corwin, *Spain and the Abolition of Slavery in Cuba, 1817–1886* (Austin: University of Texas Press, 1967), 109–10.

44. Ramón de la Sagra, *Cuba en 1860, o sea cuadro de sus adelantos en la población, la agricultura, el comercio y las rentas públicas, suplemento a la primera parte de la historia política y natural de la isla de Cuba* (Paris: L. Hachette y Cia, 1863), 43–44.

45. The classic example is *Practical Rules for the Management and Medical Treatment of Negro Slaves in the Sugar Colonies, by a Professional Planter* (London: J. Barfield, 1811).

46. William H. Robertson to William L. Marcy, September 3, 1855, in *Report of the Secretary of State*, 15:4 (emphasis in original). See also Hu-Dehart, "Race Construction and Race Relations."

47. Ripley, *From Flag to Flag*, 175.

48. "Chinese Servants"; "Planting in Cuba.". See also Moon-Ho Jung, "Outlawing 'Coolies': Race, Nation, and Empire in the Age of Emancipation," *American Quarterly* 57 (September 2005): 677–701.

49. Autobiographical draft, "Chinese Murder," in McHatton Family Papers.

50. "Chinese Servants."

51. Ripley, *From Flag to Flag*, 177.

52. Ibid., 180.

53. Scott, *Slave Emancipation in Cuba*, 33–34.

54. Ripley, *From Flag to Flag*, 172.

55. Ibid., 173.

56. Charles Jackson to Eliza McHatton, September 22, 1873, McHatton Family Papers.

57. Ripley, *From Flag to Flag*, 174.

58. Denise Helly, ed., *The Cuba Commission Report: A Hidden History of the Chinese in Cuba* (Baltimore, Md.: Johns Hopkins University Press, 1993), 101. .

59. Hugh Thomas, *Cuba: The Pursuit of Freedom* (New York: Harper and Row, 1971), 188.

60. W. M. L. Jay, *My Winter in Cuba* (New York: E. P. Dutton and Co., 1871), 222. See also Hu-Dehart, "Race Construction and Race Relations." By 1860, all Chinese coolies were forced to re-sign contracts at the conclusion of their original eight-year labor term, or leave the island. Knight, *Slave Society in Cuba*, 116–18. As Knight notes, traveler Antonio Gallenga had noted during his visit to Cuba that it was often heard that one was off to "buy a chino." See Antonio Gallenga, *Pearl of the Antilles* (London: Chapman and Hall, 1873), 88.

61. R. H. Chinn to Eliza McHatton, September 17, 1874, McHatton Family Papers.

62. Ripley, *From Flag to Flag*, 178.

63. R. H. Chinn to Eliza McHatton, July 23, 1874, McHatton Family Papers.

64. R. H. Chinn to Eliza McHatton, July 9, 1874, McHatton Family Papers.

65. Henry McHatton to Eliza McHatton, June 10, 1875, McHatton Family Papers.

66. Ripley, *From Flag to Flag*, 293.

67. Ada Ferrer, *Insurgent Cuba: Race, Nation, and Revolution, 1868–1898* (Chapel Hill: University of North Carolina Press, 1999), 4, 15–89.

68. Ripley, *Social Life in Old New Orleans*, 292.

69. Ripley, *From Flag to Flag*, 210.

70. Eliza mentions this detail about Zell in *From Flag to Flag*, 295; however, letters from him do not appear to have been preserved in the McHatton Family Papers.

71. Eliza McHatton to Henry McHatton, September 17, 1876; Eliza McHatton to Henry McHatton, February 16, 1876; "Chinese Murder"—all in McHatton Family Papers.

72. Ripley, *From Flag to Flag*, 295.

73. A phrase taken from the title of Robert May's 1973 publication, *The Southern Dream of a Caribbean Empire*.

74. Martha Hodes, "The Mercurial Nature and Abiding Power of Race: A Transnational Family Story," *American Historical Review* 108 (February 2003): 84–118.

Pauli Murray in Ghana

The Congo Crisis and an
African American Woman's Dilemma

KEVIN K. GAINES

In a United States riven during the late 1950s by organized white southern resistance to desegregation, Pauli Murray, an African American attorney and writer, was an impassioned fighter for the cause of civil rights. While her brief stay in Ghana did not alter her fundamental support for civil rights, it worked a profound if fleeting metamorphosis on her politics. Her presence in Africa at a perilous juncture in that continent's struggle against colonialism landed her at the heart of debates over the vexed matter of African American consciousness and citizenship. Murray hoped that living in Ghana would help her resolve what she termed the question of identity for the American Negro. Her singular reflections on African American identity came during her three-year appointment to teach constitutional law at the University of Ghana beginning in February 1960. She relished the task of training the young nation's lawyers and helping construct its judicial system. But overtaken by political turmoil during what was widely hailed in the Western press as the Year of Africa, Murray left Ghana after only eighteen months. She defended her country against the Ghanaian government's criticisms of segregation and U.S. foreign policy during the Congo Crisis. Finding herself caught up in the bitter struggle between Kwame Nkrumah and his opposition, Murray incurred the Ghanaian government's suspicion by advocating the universality of what she understood as American values of democracy and individual rights, values whose application back in the United States was at best inconsistent. Unlike Ghanaian officials, Murray was reluctant to consider the contingent nature of American ideals and was even less willing to regard the United States as implicated in destabilizing policies that opposed the democratic and nationalist aspirations of African peoples.

Murray's faith in American constitutionalism and color-blind citizenship placed her at odds with the Ghanaian government and its left-wing expatriate sympathizers of all backgrounds. Murray's adherence to color-blind ideals, while typical of civil rights attorneys of her era, was also informed by her personal and professional dilemmas stemming from her outsider status as a black woman. That said, Murray's political choices in Ghana are best understood in the context of the struggle over the legitimacy of an expansive, transnational African American citizenship. Murray's politics in Ghana took a profoundly different turn than would have been the case had she remained in the United States. In Ghana, Murray insisted on the Negro's fundamental Americanism and denied the validity of transnational black solidarities. Above all, Murray saw herself as defending the American image in Ghana. The perspective Murray voiced in Ghana raises challenging questions about the specific content of the patriotism she espoused and the policies of the American nation she defended. In retrospect, the pro-American ideology Murray articulated from Ghana coincided with a recasting of liberal understandings of race, citizenship, and nationhood at an unsettling moment in the United States. Although Murray asserted her patriotism in response to events in Ghana and Africa and racial turmoil back in the United States, the form that patriotism took also suggests the pervasive influence of an American liberal ideology that was not race-neutral in the disembodied, platonic sense she had envisioned. Rather, dominant understandings of American identity and national belonging were being reformulated directly in response to the activism of black people in the United States and in Africa.

Murray's many talents and varied career have made her a fascinating subject for historians of the civil rights and women's movements.[1] Yet her sojourn in Ghana, part of a postwar phenomenon of black women's civic participation as U.S. representatives abroad, has gone largely unexplored.

Born Anna Pauline Murray in Baltimore but reared in segregated Durham, North Carolina, Murray was among the cadre of lawyers trained at Howard University Law School under Charles Houston during the 1930s. Murray's pursuit of education was in itself a struggle, as she was barred from the graduate school of University of North Carolina and Harvard Law School on grounds of race and sex, respectively. Murray had been active in New York City's left-wing culture during the 1930s. She graduated from Hunter College and participated in the city's vibrant radical politics. During this time, she and National Association for the Advancement of Colored People (NAACP) organizer Ella Baker became lifelong friends.[2] Joining such prominent African American leaders as Mary McLeod Bethune and A. Philip Randolph, Murray worked on the unsuccessful campaign to save the life of Odell Waller, a Virginia sharecropper condemned to death for killing his employer. Another friend, trade unionist Maida Springer, first met Murray in connection with the Waller defense campaign. Springer recalled her initial glimpse of Murray, a small woman with close-cropped hair speaking atop a table, on fire with indignation at racial injustice.[3] During the 1940s, Murray was arrested in Virginia for her direct-action protest against segregated bus facilities. Murray was also a literary celebrity, author of the widely anthologized poem "Dark Testament" and the book *Proud Shoes* (1956). Through her wartime civil rights activism, Murray met Eleanor Roosevelt and caught her attention with the publication of an angry poem denouncing President Franklin Roosevelt's inaction on civil rights. Later, Murray was active in New York City Democratic politics, working in both of Adlai Stevenson's unsuccessful presidential campaigns. Her civil rights activism and her prior associations with radicals led to a federal investigation in 1953. As a result of this investigation, Murray's application for a visa to serve as a legal consultant in Liberia was denied. Murray fought back, writing the family memoir *Proud Shoes* as a tribute to her grandparents, whose struggles and perseverance during the late nineteenth century represented what Murray saw as a more authentic Americanism than that espoused by the House Un-American Activities Committee (HUAC) and the loyalty boards.[4]

Having earned law degrees from Howard and the University of California, Murray pioneered in the study of race in U.S. law.[5] Her prospects were limited by racism, as well as the systemic barriers imposed on women in the legal profession. Murray watched from the sidelines as her African American male peers entered government service as part of New Deal and Fair Employment Practices Commission reforms or joined the NAACP's legal struggle against segregation. During the mid-1950s, Lloyd K. Garrison, a senior partner with Adlai Stevenson's New York corporate law firm and a descendant of abolitionist William Lloyd Garrison, hired Murray. True to his heritage, Garrison was a staunch supporter of civil rights; he also served as Langston Hughes's counsel when the poet testified before HUAC. At Garrison's firm, professional fulfillment remained elusive for Murray, as she encountered clients and coworkers uncomfortable with a black woman attorney. Murray remained active within civil rights circles, serving on the defense team of radical NAACP leader Robert Williams. In 1959 the association suspended Williams, a brash advocate of armed self-defense from Monroe, North Carolina, after he urged blacks to employ retaliatory violence in the wake of the acquittal of a white man charged with assaulting a black woman. Before the NAACP board, Murray argued that Williams had spoken out of understandable frustration at the level of antiblack violence tolerated not only by southern courts but also by President Dwight Eisenhower.[6]

Murray's young adulthood was defined by rebellion against dominant sexual mores, as well as struggle against racial and gender barriers. Readers of Nancy Cunard's leftist *Negro Anthology: 1931–1934* would have been surprised to find a short story by a youthful Murray, not listed in the table of contents, based on her experience of riding the rails with a female companion as both women masqueraded as men. On this occasion, Murray adopted the more androgynous name "Pauli." After a brief marriage was annulled by mutual agreement, Murray engaged in same-sex relationships, though not without considerable ambivalence. Murray's rebelliousness was tempered by her wish to maintain leadership status within a black public culture that required a decorous silence on homosexuality. Noting the evident pride Murray exhibited in transgressing gender boundaries in her body language and clothes while posing for photographs during her young adulthood, Doreen Drury has written of Murray's struggle to reconcile "her desire for certain kinds of freedom—to travel, to write, to play, to love women, to pursue a masculine persona—with her responsibility for fulfilling her family's and community's dreams of her respectable achievements as a Black woman." After years of painful struggles over her sexuality, Murray settled into a public persona of spinsterhood and the stability of a long-term partnership.[7] In the face of personal and professional adversity, she achieved an astonishingly active and productive career. She cherished friendships with professional women like herself who battled sexism. Murray was determined, within the bounds of propriety, to seek her own path against societal or group norms. She entertained a platonic notion of a sexless self in the public sphere, a demeanor appropriate to her status as a woman in a male-dominated profession.

In Ghana, Murray emphasized a raceless ideal in defiance of local expectations of racial and political solidarity. Against those expectations, Murray espoused a dominant color-blind American individualism that mirrored the ideology promoted overseas by U.S. officialdom. As a civil rights lawyer, Murray was powerfully drawn to color-blind principles. It is likely, too, that her previous encounter with leftist political circles that prioritized class struggle fostered a skepticism toward racial affiliations.

The question of identity weighed heavily on Murray on the eve of her voyage. How would she respond to Africa? How would Africans respond to her? She sensed that the answers to those questions would be deeply revelatory at a personal level. Work also held mysteries, though she imagined that the position with the Ghanaian government promised an international horizon of public service. Springer had given Murray a sense of what to expect, having introduced Murray to visiting African nationalists in New York City. George Padmore had recruited Springer to the cause of pan-Africanism in London during the 1940s. An official in the International Ladies Garment Workers Union, Springer provided educational and material assistance to African trade unionists. She frequently hosted and gained the confidence of African nationalist leaders and had pulled strings with Nkrumah in Murray's behalf. Soon, with Garrison's blessing, Geoffrey Bing, Ghana's British expatriate attorney general, recruited Murray to help train the new nation's lawyers. Bing hired a staff that included exiles from South Africa and elsewhere who, like Murray, faced social constraints in their countries of origin.[8]

Murray's reflections on her identity as an American of African descent were shaped by the turbulent politics of Ghana and Africa, which led her to view herself as fundamentally American. Her initial task of building a legal infrastructure in Ghana evolved into a mission to defend U.S. constitutional values and America's image. Springer may well have been a model for Murray's political engagement. At the time, Springer was a frequent observer at pan-African conclaves, representing the international division of the American Federation of Labor and Congress of Industrial Organizations (AFL-CIO), which sought to promote a noncommunist African trade union movement.[9]

Murray's arrival in Ghana coincided with the ratification of Ghana's new republican constitution and the government's advocacy of socialism as the path to economic development, events that politicized her task of teaching U.S. constitutional law. The transition to republic status completed Ghana's independence from British authority, but the new constitution was also the mechanism by which Nkrumah, as president of Ghana, sought to neutralize his vocal and sometimes violent opposition. Murray's reservations regarding the new constitution's emphasis on executive power at the expense of Parliament and the courts and the curbs on civil liberties she witnessed put her on a collision course with Nkrumah's desire to strengthen his hand against his opponents.

In the classroom Murray argued for the universality of U.S. constitutional ideals, separation of powers, civil liberties, and the rule of law. The difficulty for Murray went beyond the emergency powers the Ghanaian government claimed were necessary for its security. Her case was weakened by the racial turmoil in the U.S. South and the upheaval in the Congo, crises that led to sharp criticism of U.S. domestic and foreign policy in Ghana's state-controlled press.[10] Murray defended the United States in the face of such criticism, but she was hard-pressed to convince Nkrumah, who had studied in the United States during the 1930s and 1940s, that her idealized vision of U.S. democracy bore any resemblance to an American society ripped apart by racial conflict.

Along with Nkrumah's political opponents, Murray clashed with the Ghanaian government over the 1958 Preventive Detention Act, which jailed without trial for up to five years those deemed threats to national security. Defenders of the act claimed that in cases of subversion, the courts were often hampered when witnesses in criminal trials refused to testify, fearing retribution. Defenders thus viewed preventive detention as a necessary expedient against threats to state security, including assassination plots against Nkrumah. To members of the opposition and Ghana's critics in the Western press, preventive detention confirmed reports of Nkrumah's autocratic leadership. To be sure, critics of the policy also included such longtime allies as African American pacifist Bill Sutherland, an expatriate employee of the Ghanaian government who strongly objected to the policy and told Nkrumah so.[11]

Recruited as a presumed sympathizer of the Ghanaian government, Murray broke with her employers in criticizing the concentration of presidential power in the new constitution and the government's repression of its opposition. Murray had ample occasion to discuss with Bing and others the rationale for strong executive power in Ghana's constitution. She grasped the need for emergency powers and preventive detention to counter threats to stability, including political violence. Murray well understood the risks of speaking against Ghanaian governmental policies and struggled to remain impartial in her teaching. But her law classes were attended by opposition members of Parliament and monitored by government intelligence agents. Undaunted, Murray brought her criticisms to the attention of the Ghanaian government. Dismayed by the surveillance, Murray eventually provided clandestine assistance to opposition legal challenges to preventive detention. That affiliation joined her principled commitment to the rule of law with the opposition's legal defense of its civil liberties. Indeed, Murray shared the values of her profession with such lawyers as J. B. Danquah and Joseph Appiah, both of whom were prominent members of the opposition. Alienated by the government's anti-Americanism and with her attempts at dialogue rejected by Nkrumah, Murray joined forces with an opposition that at the time still enjoyed a measure of legitimacy within Ghanaian politics.

The political crisis in the Congo heightened tensions on all sides. In late September, Nkrumah addressed the United Nations General Assembly, condemning Belgium's neocolonial attack on the sovereignty of the independent Congo, urging the United Nations (UN) to uphold that sovereignty, and denouncing the Union of South Africa, France, and Portugal for their colonial policies.[12] This, along with the advocacy of socialism by Ghana's ruling Convention People's Party, was the background for a testy exchange of letters between Murray and Labor Minister John Tettegah. Murray defended the American press and capitalism against Tettegah's criticisms, which were prompted by negative coverage of Nkrumah in *Time* magazine.[13] In mid-October Nkrumah angrily refuted "pernicious" reports that Ghana planned to nationalize foreign enterprises; Murray may have come under suspicion for spreading these rumors.[14] In November Murray broached her concerns to Nkrumah, who curtly dismissed her charges of dictatorship. Through his private secretary, Nkrumah refused Murray's request to meet with him. That official rebuff solidified Murray's opposition to the Ghanaian government.[15]

Stung by criticism of the United States in Ghana's press, Murray's self-appointed role as defender of the image of American democracy against criticism by Cold War adversaries framed her discussions of race, identity, and U.S. citizenship. The Americanism Murray espoused was a raceless, unhyphenated ideal with little place for ethnic identification. The appeal of color blindness for Murray went beyond U.S. Supreme Court justice John Marshall Harlan's formulation of the principle in his dissent from the majority opinion in *Plessy v. Ferguson* (1896). Insofar as color became shorthand for an array of discriminatory practices under Jim Crow, Murray and other blacks of the wartime generation saw race and color as a badge of servitude and the basis for the Jim Crow South's legal and extralegal deprivation of the full citizenship rights of African Americans. Murray and others saw color-blind constitutional rights as the remedy for all-too-common judicial atrocities such as the Odell Waller execution. In Murray's eyes, color-blind jurisprudence meant due process, equal protection, and fairness in criminal trial procedures such as jury selection. No wonder, then, that on U.S. terrain this color-blind construction of American citizenship epitomized freedom and equality for Murray and many others at a hopeful if uncertain moment of change. Largely unexamined within this mindset was the assumption that a "color-blind" state ideology obliged African Americans to renounce a black or African identification, an assumption that restricted claims for citizenship to national criteria inflected by the Cold War and white supremacy; it also illustrated the assimilationism among black leadership that E. Franklin Frazier and Lorraine Hansberry, to name two prominent examples, found so troubling. Unlike Frazier, Hansberry, and others, however, Murray seemed unable to distinguish the negative ascription of racism from a positive affirmation of blackness. In retrospect, Murray's ideal of color-blind citizenship overlooked the racialized character of a U.S. citizenship that, as David Roediger has put it, has historically been colored white. Indeed, much of the broad-based appeal of the color-blind ideal resulted from the fact that it left unquestioned structural, economic manifestations of white privilege and power.[16]

Murray's ideological sparring with the Ghanaian government was informed by a dominant, ostensibly color-blind American liberalism that in effect banished an independent black political identity to a Siberia-like realm of otherness, its racialized logic accusing African American dissenters of "thinking like blacks" instead of "like Americans." (Afro-American writer and Ghanaian expatriate Julian Mayfield debunked this dominant logic as late as 1984, when it was invoked during Jesse Jackson's presidential campaign by those hostile to the candidate's progressive politics and criticism of U.S. foreign policy.)[17] While quite valid reasons existed for Murray's belief in color-blind Americanism, the coercive Cold War climate and the traumatic experience of her federal investigation may also have shaped her views, affecting her embrace of the same injunctions of national loyalty wielded by HUAC to bring dissenters and liberals like herself to heel. Transnational black solidarities were widely viewed as subversive during the 1950s. Moreover, criticism of U.S. foreign policy was decidedly off-limits for prominent African Americans. Well into the next decade, both black leaders and white officials censured Martin Luther King Jr. when he opposed the war in Vietnam. That unspoken but widely understood restriction of black leadership to the purview of domestic civil rights epitomized the subordinated citizenship of African Americans under the regime of Cold War liberalism. In other words, U.S. officialdom routinely subordinated the rights of blacks to regional, national, international, and corporate interests. In large part, for their attacks on this logic and their advocacy of African liberation, the State Department seized the passports of Paul Robeson and W. E. B. Du Bois during the 1950s. And they were not the only ones disciplined by the Jim Crow state. Liberals with prior radical associations, including Ralph Bunche and Murray, were investigated.[18] Herself a target of such harassment, Murray would not have actively supported this ideological regime of Cold War suspicion of black internationalism and solidarity. At the same time, that regime's potential wrath led many black spokespersons to seek legitimation by disassociating themselves from dissident internationalists. In this fashion, Murray took sides in internal ideological struggles between black liberals and leftists.

Murray's views on the responsibilities of being an American Negro in Africa were in part influenced by the State Department's selection throughout the 1950s of prominent African Americans, including women, as international spokespersons. To counter Soviet and neutralist criticisms of American racism, U.S. officials sent African American intellectuals and public figures abroad, hoping that they could persuade emerging nonwhite nations in Africa, Asia, and the Middle East that the United States was committed to racial equality. Another friend of Murray's, Chicago attorney Edith Sampson, probably influenced Murray's approach to representing the United States abroad. Sampson became a lightning rod for African Americans who objected to her defenses of American democracy to overseas audiences amid the antiblack violence and upheavals of the 1950s. In 1952, as Murray awaited the conclusion of her loyalty investigation, she defended Sampson after radical African American journalist William Worthy disputed the rosy assessment of improving U.S. race relations offered by Sampson in a speech she delivered in Copenhagen. Murray shared Sampson's concern for presenting the United States to overseas audiences in the best possible light. Murray later emulated Sampson's willingness to defend American democracy from attacks from the leftist Ghanaian government.[19]

Before her trip, Murray's friend Harold Isaacs urged her to write up her impressions of the encounter between American Negroes and Africans on the continent. Isaacs, a journalist and scholar of international affairs, was researching the impact of emergent African nationhood on black Americans' identity. Through Isaacs, Murray inadvertently helped craft a new journalistic image of alienation between African Americans and Africans that debunked notions of pan-African solidarity as illusory and inauthentic.

In Ghana, Murray viewed herself as fundamentally American. Her experiences led her to view this identification as normative for American Negroes in Africa. As she saw it, American Negroes and Africans could not have been more different in outlook. This premise functioned for Murray as a political litmus test where Ghana was concerned. She was disconcerted by African Americans (or anyone, really) who supported Nkrumah or criticized the United States and its domestic and foreign policy. Springer recalled that she and Murray had quarreled bitterly over Springer's support of Nkrumah.[20]

In letters home, Murray adopted an upbeat tone as she described coping with unwieldy mosquito nets and the myriad challenges of life in Ghana and related her halting initiation into the ways of indigenous cultures in West Africa. In a spirit of self-examination, however, she confided to her journal a profound loneliness, self-doubt, and sense of isolation from Ghanaians and other African American expatriates and her intense disapproval of the political situation in Ghana. She was further taxed by the chronic malaria she stoically kept from correspondents until her impending departure. Murray felt estranged from Ghana's sympathizers, black and white. In one anguished diary entry, in which she reflected on the source of her personal and political estrangement, Murray attributed her unhappiness to "self," a formulation that was both circumspect and telling.[21]

The Congo Crisis and the Struggle over America's Image

Murray's difficulties in Ghana were exacerbated by the worldwide repercussions of the outbreak of civil strife in the Congo on July 5, 1960, almost one week after the ceremony marking its independence from Belgian rule. Congolese troops revolted against continued Belgian control over the military. In response, Prime Minister Patrice Lumumba dismissed Belgian officers, but he was unable to halt the looting, rioting, and violent harassment of Belgians. Lumumba approved the intervention of Belgian paratroopers to restore order, but they worsened the situation with violent attacks against the Congolese. On July 11, Belgian officials engineered the secession of the mineral-rich province of Katanga. Demanding an end to the secession and the withdrawal of Belgian troops, Lumumba appealed for international assistance. On July 14 a United Nations military force with a substantial Ghanaian contingent arrived to act as peacekeepers. Thus began what became known as the Congo Crisis, a defining event in Africa's struggle for independence. The Congo became a proxy Cold War battleground for the United States and the Soviet Union and a test for Nkrumah's positive neutralism, which held that African diplomatic and military initiative in concert with the UN should play a leading role in resolving the conflict.

Despite assumptions in the Western press that he had fallen under communist influence, the democratically elected Lumumba was a moderate radicalized by the nationalism of the Congolese people and his attendance at the 1958 All African People's Conference in Ghana. The secession of Katanga, the country's wealthiest region, was a bold attempt by Belgium to maintain neocolonial control over the nation's economy. For several years, the secession, led by pro-Western Congolese politician Moise Tshombe, was subsidized by the Union Minière du Haut Katanga, a Belgian mining company that had historically dominated politics in that region. Backed by Belgian advisers and Union Minière personnel, Tshombe became the poster child for neocolonialism from the perspective of sympathizers of the global anticolonial movement. Under Tshombe's titular leadership, Katanga's military included Belgian troops, as well as mercenaries from white-dominated South Africa and Rhodesia, and even some former Nazi SS soldiers and Italian Fascists. Belgium fomented other secessions, succeeding in the South Kasai region. As Belgium came under fierce criticism from African and Asian nations and the Soviet Union, the Eisenhower administration quietly supported the Katanga secession and the Central Intelligence Agency (CIA) funneled French military planes to Katanga.[22]

In late July Lumumba traveled to New York and Washington, vainly seeking support from the United Nations and the Eisenhower administration. American officials were convinced that Lumumba was irrational, unstable, and a communist. Lumumba found few allies at the UN, which was effectively financed and controlled by the United States.[23] To Lumumba's consternation, UN troops made no effort to end Katanga's secession. In late August Lumumba accepted a Soviet military airlift, playing into American fears of a Moscow takeover of the Congo. At the urging of U.S. officials, Congolese president Joseph Kasavubu dismissed Lumumba as prime minister. Lumumba easily outmaneuvered Kasavubu's coup. Appealing directly to the Parliament, Lumumba persuaded the body to honor his mandate.[24]

Lumumba's resourcefulness and popular support led to concerted efforts by the Belgian and U.S. governments to eliminate him by any means. According to historian Madeline Kalb, the CIA, along with Western embassies in Leopoldville, had financed the Congolese army with infusions of cash to Joseph Désiré Mobutu, an ambitious young officer and former journalist.[25] Finally, after intense international criticism, the UN assisted Lumumba and condemned Belgium's presence in Katanga. UN troops formed a cordon around Lumumba's residence, protecting him from arrest by Congolese officials in league with Belgium. On November 27, while Lumumba was attempting an escape to Stanleyville to rally his supporters, Congolese troops captured him near Thysville. Belgian officers, working in tandem with their Congolese factotums, assassinated Lumumba and two of his aides on January 17, 1961. With Lumumba's death, Belgium and the United States had achieved their objectives in the Congo.[26] The West's role in the assassination of Lumumba was roundly condemned worldwide when Belgium released the news of Lumumba's fate a month after his execution. From Ghana, Nkrumah observed that Lumumba's murder was "the first time in history that the legal ruler of a country has been done to death with the open connivance of a world organization on whom that ruler put his trust."[27]

Well before Lumumba's disappearance and death, the turmoil in the Congo overshadowed all events, including the First Conference on Women of Africa and African Descent held in Accra in July 1960. Murray attended that conference, which, like similar international gatherings, became an ideological battleground over the worldwide image of American democracy. Another conference participant and an acquaintance of Murray's dating back to the Waller campaign was civil rights activist Anna Arnold Hedgeman, who had held a federal appointment in the Health, Education, and Welfare Department during the Truman administration. She was later appointed to the cabinet of New York City mayor Robert Wagner. As with Murray, Hedgeman's involvement in international affairs provided a refuge from racism and sexism in American public life. After a well-publicized swearing-in at City Hall, Wagner showed no intention of employing her in any capacity. Hedgeman mobilized allies in the black press to prevent Wagner from reneging on her appointment. Shunted to a basement office, Hedgeman, who had previously traveled to India on a goodwill mission for the State Department, hosted visiting African diplomats and their wives, a courtesy repaid by the invitation to deliver a keynote address at the conference.

Hedgeman recalled her visit to Ghana in a 1964 memoir, which contained a bitter indictment of a northern liberalism defined by a white ethnic chauvinism resistant to sharing power in New York City with African Americans and Puerto Ricans. Hedgeman, who also encountered sexism within the civil rights establishment as the only woman on the executive committee of the March on

Washington, described a nation at a crossroads and symbolized by an organized Christian church torn asunder by racism.[28]

Hedgeman recalled that "the shadow of the Congo hung over the convention," and she sympathetically portrayed Nkrumah. In her address Hedgeman balanced candor about the realities of racism at home with a reminder that many whites supported desegregation, stressing "the continuous struggle for freedom in which Americans of African descent have always engaged." She believed it important to remind her audience that African Americans "have had cooperation from like-minded people of many races and creeds." To ringing applause, Hedgeman encouraged women of new African states to join the new United Nations Commission on the Status of Women.[29]

While the conference sessions were devoted to the social concerns of African women (legal status, problems of vocational and professional training, the expansion of educational opportunities, maternal and child health, and nutrition and disease control), the Committee on Resolutions focused on the political controversies affecting the continent. Two resolutions sparked heated debate. First, the conferees called for the UN Security Council to uphold the Congo's sovereignty against secessionist challenges. The second, proposed by an African delegate, was "a resolution on discrimination linking the United States with [colonial repression in] Algeria, the Congo and the Union of South Africa." Hedgeman protested the linkage of the United States with South Africa, but other U.S. delegates (including Shirley Graham Du Bois) supported the resolution. In the ensuing discussion, delegates from the United States clarified distinctions between apartheid in South Africa and racial discrimination in America. In her memoir Hedgeman praised Murray for explaining the history of the Constitution and its amendments and the Supreme Court "as basic to our struggle for freedom." Although twenty of the delegates, mindful of the frequent reprisals against blacks in the South, equated white supremacy in the South with the apartheid regime, the position advocated by Hedgeman, Murray, and others prevailed.[30]

In her diary Murray wrote glowingly of Hedgeman's role in this U.S. diplomatic victory. Murray praised the teamwork of members of the American community, which included personnel from the U.S. embassies in Ghana and Nigeria.[31] Perhaps with this experience in mind, Murray castigated Attorney General Robert Kennedy in a letter for his demand that activists from the Congress of Racial Equality call a halt to the Freedom Rides. Murray told Kennedy that his reluctance to enforce federal desegregation law undermined American credibility on race relations, confirming many Africans' perceptions of the United States and South Africa as partners in white supremacy. What effect this missive had on Kennedy, if any, is difficult to determine.[32] While Murray, Hedgeman, and other African Americans effectively countered anti-American rhetoric in Ghana, they appeared unable to dislodge the Kennedy administration's Cold War mind-set, which could not seem to view racial justice as an end in itself.

A Question of Identity: African American "Strangers in Africa"

Murray set herself the task of writing an essay on the American Negro in Africa for publication back in the United States. Her motivation to do so was kindled by a visit from her friend Isaacs, who stayed at her house while attending the Accra women's conference as an observer. Adelaide Cromwell, an Africanist sociologist and member of the U.S. delegation, recalled that some members of the Committee on Resolutions, which met at Murray's house, were miffed to find Isaacs intent on hearing the deliberations, totally unfazed at being the lone white male in a gathering of black women.[33] Murray later sent Isaacs a draft of her essay, "A Question of Identity," crediting her friend as a major influence on its contents. Based on her encounters with other American blacks and her experiences in Ghana, Murray's essay reflected a dominant liberal construct of a normative black identity. Adopting the prescriptive and gendered tone then common in writing about race and identity, Murray argued that the "American Negro" visiting Africa discovers there that "his peculiar history and unending search for unqualified acceptance . . . have made him uniquely American." From Africa, she continued, African Americans are able to see "the American dream of freedom and equality" as they are unable to see it in America, "in shining perspective." At the same time, Murray acknowledged that Africans had serious concerns about African Americans' loyalties. Educated Africans, she observed, vacillated between viewing American blacks as "our brothers" and as "agents of imperialism." Murray regarded such suspicions not as political differences but instead as emblematic of Africans' psychological and cultural differences from African Americans. Educated Africans seemed unable to view America through any lens other than segregation and neocolonialism. Convinced of this mistrust, Murray disagreed with members of the American Society for African Culture and others who argued for a strategic interest in increasing African American representation in foreign service posts in Africa. Interestingly, given her argument to Kennedy that the Cold War should not outweigh black demands for equality, Murray invoked the Cold War in support of her view that African Americans should not be placed in such sensitive diplomatic positions. Murray argued for a normative black identity aligned with the American nation and its national security imperatives.[34]

Murray hoped that Isaacs, now back in the United States, would assist her in placing her essay with a major magazine. Why this never happened is an interesting question. *Harper's* claimed to like the piece but refused it, citing a backlog of material on race and Africa. By late November, Murray had gotten several rejections and had apparently laid the essay aside.[35]

Murray's unpublished essay anticipated a shift in the liberal preoccupation with containing black political expression and limiting the ideological boundaries of citizenship. To the usual Cold War suspicion of black and African movements as instigated by communists was added a new argument, less driven by the terms of Cold War anticommunism and instead involving the question of racial authenticity—or, rather, inauthenticity. Against considerable evidence of African American identification with African peoples and their struggles, this new argument posited a fundamental alienation between African Americans and Africans, debunking linkages between the two groups' freedom struggles.

To appreciate the significance of this new argument, it is instructive to consider the relationship between the Cold War and the black freedom movement. As Penny Von Eschen has shown, the political repression of black leftist supporters of African anticolonialism during the early 1950s led African American civil rights leaders to craft a Cold War rationale for desegregation. Seeking political leverage and distancing themselves from proscribed anticolonial alliances, civil rights leaders shifted the framework of claims for citizenship and civil rights away from Africa and toward the American nation. They insisted that racial justice was essential to U.S. national security and containment of the Soviet threat.[36] That attempt to turn the Cold War into a justification for desegregation was double-edged. Although the Supreme Court embraced this logic as part of the rationale for the 1954 *Brown v. Board of Education* decision, segregationists and ultraconservatives just as often demonized the cause of racial justice by accusing black activists, leaders, and organizations of communist affiliations. Moreover, as Mary L. Dudziak has argued, it was commonplace for liberals, including President John F. Kennedy and his brother Robert, the attorney general, to prioritize the national security imperatives of the Cold War over African American demands for equality. By this logic, civil rights protesters played into the hands of Soviet adversaries. Some viewed civil rights demonstrators as disloyal to America's national security.[37] The gatekeepers of American liberalism subjected even African American assertions of cultural equality—specifically, the claim that ancient African kingdoms had contributed to Western civilization—to red-baiting and ridicule. For example, *Newsweek* published without attribution reproductions of Afrocentric paintings by African American expatriate Earl Sweeting that it had obtained in Accra. The works challenged the racist erasure of Africa from Western modernity by portraying Africans sharing their knowledge with the Greeks. "If you have no history, invent one," *Newsweek* sneered, adding that "Ghana, apparently, has taken that bit of Russian advice." Sweeting unsuccessfully sued the magazine for the unauthorized use of his work.[38]

As *Newsweek*'s contempt for the idea of an African contribution to Western civilization suggested, this version of red-baiting spoke explicitly to those subscribing to Western white supremacy. This was also an example of a generic, Manichaean anticommunism that led many Americans to view the Soviets as incapable of an accurate or truthful assessment of global affairs. These Americans (including, of course, many of African descent) remained highly susceptible to their government's ideological biases and propaganda. For many, the truth—if not God's favor—resided with the "Free World," a belief reinforced by pervasive anxieties at the threat of nuclear annihilation. Thus, within government circles, which included powerful segregationist senators, insurgent African Americans were synonymous with subversion. This synthesis of Cold War anticommunism and white supremacy influenced U.S. opinion on the Congo Crisis. At the height of the turmoil there, many U.S. politicians and opinion leaders believed that the Soviet Union had orchestrated the international criticism of U.S., Belgian, and UN policies. Despite worldwide protests in the wake of Lumumba's death and the validity (as hindsight has shown) of criticisms of Belgian neocolonialism by African and Asian nonaligned nations, Soviet officials, and African American radicals and nationalists, many liberal officials and commentators, apparently including Pauli Murray, dismissed those criticisms out of hand as mere communist propaganda.[39]

September 1960 found Murray on the defensive about the Congo situation as well as heightened Cold War tensions as a result of U.S. secretary of state Christian Herter's assertion of Nkrumah's communist sympathies, which provoked more anti-American rhetoric from the Ghanaian press. Murray balked at Dorothy Padmore's assertion that UN secretary general Dag Hammarskjöld was the instrument of Belgian interests in the Congo. The radio broadcast network Voice of America became Murray's balm against criticisms of U.S. policy as well as homesickness. On one occasion she hosted a luncheon for four African American couples, the men employed by the U.S. government or engaged in business in Ghana. Murray savored the lengthy discussion of their favorite topics, the American Negro in Africa and the Congo. One of her male guests predicted war between the United States and the Soviet Union within six months.[40]

The war itself, with thousands of military and civilian casualties, would occur over the next several years as Congolese forces loyal to Lumumba's legacy and Antoine Gizenga's Stanleyville government would continue their fight for control over the country. Their revolt was suppressed in late 1964 as Belgian forces, with U.S. air support, invaded Stanleyville and engaged in the mass slaughter of an estimated 3,000 Congolese civilians. War in the Congo, if not the suffering of the Congolese, ended only after Mobutu instituted a corrupt and brutal dictatorship that lasted until his overthrow and exile in 1997.[41]

For its part, the American and Western press, preoccupied with the spread of communism and the specter of Congolese violence against Belgians, scarcely felt the need to justify Lumumba's removal to its audience.[42] Indeed, Lumumba's whereabouts remained unknown for several weeks after his execution by firing squad and the grisly destruction of his dismembered remains in sulfuric acid by Belgian troops. Before his death was announced, Belgian authorities reported that Lumumba and his aides had escaped from Mobutu's troops, a patently false account that provoked immediate suspicion among Belgium's critics. This fabrication was the prelude to the official Belgian cover-up of Lumumba's murder: the Congolese prime minister was reported to have been killed by vengeful members of a rival tribe. While laying the cornerstone for a new institute for the training of socialist cadres, Nkrumah denounced the official story of the death of Lumumba and his aides as "the most absurd fabrication, that could emanate only from the diseased brains of Belgian colonialists and their puppet agents."[43]

As tacit U.S. support for Belgium and apartheid South Africa came under attack by Ghana and other African nations, Afro-Americans already angered by racial oppression at home had further cause to doubt their government's goodwill. Such opposition erupted in February 1961 when several African Americans, outraged by Lumumba's death, interrupted a speech by U.S. ambassador to the United Nations Adlai Stevenson with a demonstration in the gallery of the Security Council. Screams and shouts of "Murderers!" rang through the hall, and the demonstrators, men and women alike, physically resisted UN guards. After calm had been restored, Stevenson apologized for what he called an obviously "organized" disturbance. Predictably, contemporary press accounts (including editorials, opinion pieces, and newsreels) proclaimed that the demonstrators, like the slain Lumumba, were the willing dupes of communists.[44]

Closer to the truth was that the demonstrators reflected the appeal of African nationalism rather than communism among blacks in New York City. In a rebuttal to the widespread charges of communist influence, James Baldwin warned that this view exposed white liberals' "dangerous" penchant for self-delusion. When blacks mobilized against southern segregation, their opponents claimed that they were activated by "outside agitators." When northern blacks protested, Baldwin observed, the Kremlin was to blame. For Baldwin, who claimed that he had intended to join the protesters, the belief that the demonstration was orchestrated by communists insulted the intelligence of the many blacks who needed no prodding to sensitize them to the discriminatory conditions of northern ghettoes, including poverty, unemployment, police harassment, and slum conditions.[45]

Of course, Baldwin's analysis did not put an end to such crude red-baiting. Soon thereafter, U.S. periodicals published two widely discussed articles that appeared to steal Murray's thunder in contending that African Americans and Africans were strangers to each other, their relationship defined by vast, insurmountable differences. This argument echoed not only Murray's unpublished essay but also, ironically, Baldwin's prior claim, in his report on the First World Congress of Negro Writers in Paris, that an unbridgeable gulf separated African Americans and Africans.[46] Baldwin and Murray were not the only commentators to voice such sentiments. Like Richard Wright, African American journalist Era Bell Thompson had written candidly of her feelings of estrangement from African peoples and their cultures. Unlike Wright, she affirmed her American identity and loyalties in response to her pilgrimage to Africa.[47] Thompson's pro-American stance, mediated in part by the gender tensions she experienced in Africa, may well have served as a precedent for Murray's reflections.

As these earlier statements suggest, the position taken in these two new articles—one penned by Murray's friend Harold Isaacs and published in the *New Yorker*, and the other by Russell Howe, a British-born journalist—was hardly unprecedented. However, the timing of their appearance and perhaps the circumstances of their authorship struck African American supporters of African national independence movements as a none-too-subtle attempt to discourage African American activism on African affairs. Isaacs wrote of misunderstanding, hostility, and "mutual prejudice between Africans and American Negroes." According to historian Carol Polsgrove, Isaacs had scooped Murray. Accused of plagiarism by another friend of Murray's, Isaacs insisted that his article, while based in part on conversations with Murray, reflected his findings. Polsgrove also notes that Isaacs told Murray in a letter that his *New Yorker* article was prompted by the UN demonstration. Although the provenance of Howe's article is less clear, like Isaacs, Howe argued in the liberal periodical *Reporter* that the relationship between African Americans and Africans was one of mutual alienation rather than solidarity. Howe claimed that African Americans would do more damage than good in diplomatic and other nation-building tasks. For some African American critics, it was hardly coincidental that the journalistic debunking of pan-African solidarity came so soon after the explosive African American and global outrage over UN and Western complicity in Lumumba's death.[48]

Members of the American Society for African Culture and that segment of the African American intelligentsia with direct ties to Ghana and a commitment to the cause of African freedom strongly objected to Howe's and Isaacs's claims and hastened to refute them. But African American critics had a difficult time gaining a hearing in mainstream periodicals. Horace Mann Bond, former president of Lincoln University, which had for many years educated future African nationalist leaders, eventually published his rebuttal in the *Negro History Bulletin*.[49] In his keynote address at the American Society for African Culture conference in June, St. Clair Drake faulted Isaacs for failing to differentiate by political status and national distinctions within the category "African." Noting the preponderance of members of the "non-Communist, socialist left" in Ghana, Drake may have been referring to Murray when he observed that Ghanaians rejected African Americans' propagandizing for capitalism.[50] Even Murray's erstwhile ally Anna Hedgeman, who had by then returned to New York black leadership circles eager to join forces with African nationalists active at the UN, later wrote that "some so-called experts on Africa and the American Negro present distortions which further confuse the picture for the white American public and even for some Negroes and some Africans." She quoted a prominent African diplomat at the UN who objected to an article that presumed to tell how Africans and African Americans should feel about one another: the author was "merely trying to [drive] a wedge between you and us." For Hedgeman, who added that a major New York newspaper refused to publish her favorable account of Nkrumah, the African diplomat's words rang with truth. She had talked with Isaacs in Ghana, perhaps at Murray's bungalow. Hedgeman and others present shared with him views contrary to the thesis of his article, only to have them disregarded.[51]

In her memoir Hedgeman quoted Bond's rebuttal at length. Bond saw an insidious pattern behind the two prominent articles appearing at roughly the same time, "with remarkably parallel themes. . . . American Negroes were misfits in Africa, and Africans did not identify themselves with American Negroes." Against this view, Bond recounted the detailed history since the nineteenth century of New World blacks' concern for the welfare of African peoples. He emphasized the prescriptive intent of this new line on black identity: "It is not difficult to see that there must be a powerful public feeling, that it *is* dangerous to send Negroes to Africa; and that, whether true or not, American Negroes *ought* to dislike Africans, and vice versa. This is one of the oldest of racial stereotypes." Both Hedgeman and Bond believed that the crux of the matter lay in the hypocrisy of those who presumed to speak for black Americans. Summing up her experiences in Africa, Hedgeman recast the problem of racism in world affairs in terms of Christian morality: "If America, which presents herself as a great Christian nation with a belief in the equality of mankind, does not respect her own citizens of color, what can Africa expect of her?" Although Hedgeman and Murray had banded together to defend America against critics of its racial inequality, the two clearly differed on the question of African American identification with Africans. The different positions they took may well be explained by the different political realms they inhabited. Perhaps Hedgeman's immersion in New York City politics, with its long traditions of bruising ethnic conflict and black nationalism, impressed on her the necessity of group consciousness and solidarity with African peoples. Unlike Hedgeman, Murray's belief in color-blind individualism resonated with her interventions in national and international politics, where articulations of black particularity were suspect.[52]

As the turmoil in the Congo heightened the level of political intrigue in Ghana, Murray risked expulsion by criticizing the Ghanaian government's lack of adherence to Western liberal conceptions of multiparty parliamentary democracy, civil liberties, free market capitalism, and the rule of law. Fearing that Ghana was in danger of "going communist," Murray corresponded with Ghanaian officials and communicated her experiences to politically connected friends in the United States. Keenly attuned to racial integration's importance to overseas audiences, Murray lobbied the incoming Kennedy administration to appoint her law school mentor, William Hastie, as the first African American member of the Supreme Court.

Murray's political activities were driven in large part by her search for community. In March 1960 Murray joined the American Women's Association of Accra, an unofficial group that sought to foster understanding between its members and Ghanaians. The group amassed news clippings and similar documentation to counter hostile propaganda and refute anti-American statements disseminated by the state-controlled press. A year later, Murray recommended that the group seek a more formal relationship with the embassy and other U.S. foreign service missions abroad.[53] Murray found a sympathetic ear for her criticisms of Nkrumah in her friend Lloyd K. Garrison Jr., a *New York Times* correspondent covering West Africa and the son of her mentor in the legal profession. Like the younger Garrison, Murray viewed Ghanaian criticisms of biased Western press accounts as evidence of a creeping authoritarianism.

The new Kennedy administration sparked a flurry of correspondence on behalf of Murray by the elder Garrison. Missives to members of the foreign policy establishment, including G. Mennen Williams, assistant secretary of state for African affairs, and recent Kennedy appointees George Ball and Chester Bowles, apprised them that Murray had valuable insights into the political situation in Ghana gained from her struggles against the left-wing attorney general over curbs on civil liberties and an independent judiciary. Murray had felt keenly the rigors of a police state. Garrison further confided that an African American on the embassy staff in Accra whom he believed to be a CIA informant was in constant touch with Murray. Garrison quoted from Murray's letters describing her precarious situation in Ghana. He seemed to be angling for a suitable exit strategy for her.

Not much came of Garrison's efforts. Williams, who had met Murray during a visit to Ghana, probably found little new in the information Murray had to offer. In any case, official criticism of Ghana potentially undermined congressional support for the Volta River project, a joint venture of the U.S. government and the U.S.-based Kaiser Corporation. Murray's political views and associations with members of Nkrumah's opposition made it increasingly difficult for her to function in Ghana. She and her colleagues at the law school encountered a climate hostile to academic freedom. The precise nature of Murray's cooperation with the CIA agent (a member of Murray's social circle of African American U.S. government personnel) is difficult to determine. If she confided to Garrison that she was in contact with an African American CIA agent (as Garrison reported to State Department officials), she could have been something more than an unwitting asset.[54] At the very least, Murray championed American influence in Ghana with a steadfastness that made her serviceable to those engaged in gathering intelligence.[55]

Murray's efforts in Ghana and her departure just ahead of what would certainly have been her expulsion are best understood within a broader context of political intrigue. Among Accra's conspicuous community of American expatriates and visitors were personnel from the U.S. embassy seeking intelligence on Ghanaian politics and leadership. The U.S. government and its covert representatives actively sought such cooperation, not only from well-placed African Americans, but also from members of the Ghanaian government. Murray's opposition to Nkrumah and her tendency to privilege an identification with America over solidarity with Ghana and African nationalism made her the subject of attention from U.S. government personnel. Springer reintroduced Murray to an old acquaintance from the 1930s, Jay Lovestone, an ex-communist cold warrior, director of the AFL-CIO's international free trade union initiative, and CIA operative.[56]

The vicissitudes and intrigues of the Ghanaian postcolonial situation seemed to turn Murray's politics and principles upside down. In Ghana, her commitment to due process and civil liberties, which were transformative in the United States, informed her alliance with opposition lawyers, including John B. Danquah, in their legal challenge to the government's Preventive Detention Act. From the Ghanaian government's standpoint, this stance placed her squarely in the camp of a reactionary colonial iteration of jurisprudence that shielded subversive activities. Her criticism of threats to civil liberties in Ghana expressed a principled faith in American judicial values. Indeed, Murray rendered a crucial service to Ghanaian political culture at a moment when the country's government was turning away from the rule of law. Her efforts did not go unappreciated in government circles. One official was sufficiently impressed to recommend to the State Department that Murray receive an American specialist grant to another English-speaking African country, cautioning, however, that she would not consent to being sent as a Negro, as "she considers herself just an American."[57] There would be no such return engagements to Africa. By the end of 1961, Murray returned to the United States to begin doctoral study at Yale Law School in the hope that law schools would eventually begin hiring women faculty in greater numbers.

While her response to the volatile political situation in Ghana during the Congo Crisis was singular, Pauli Murray's dilemma was far from unique. Her plight resembled that of Anna Hedgeman, Maida Springer, and other African American women for whom social constraints in the United States made the international arena a vital outlet for activism. At the Conference on Women of Africa and of African Descent, Murray and Hedgeman found common cause, defending the United States against critics of its racial strife and in the process laying claim to the leadership denied to them in the male-controlled domains of American politics and the civil rights movement.

Yet if their plights were similar, Murray and Hedgeman responded quite differently as domestic and international racial crises prompted liberal officials and opinion makers to circumscribe African American citizenship within the narrow dictates of the Cold War, prioritizing so-called national security over the cause of African American and African freedom. The optimism of the Year of Africa had within months unraveled with the Sharpeville Massacre, the prolonged civil strife in the Congo, and the UN disturbance over Lumumba's death. As the Kennedy administration faulted civil rights demonstrators for playing into the hands of America's Soviet adversaries, the transnational vision of African American citizenship in solidarity with the struggles of African peoples envisioned by such African Americans as Hedgeman, Bond, and Drake, as well as the nationalists and radicals who revolted at the United Nations, became the target of quasi-official liberal propaganda. So it seemed to Hedgeman and other African American advocates of African freedom. For her part, Murray was too preoccupied with Ghana to note anything amiss in a construction of American Negro identity that corresponded with her views.[58]

Murray's thoughts on the question of identity that resulted from her brief, unhappy sojourn in Ghana marked a critical moment in the ongoing confrontation over the terms and conditions by which American citizenship would be extended to Americans of African descent. Assertions of estrangement between the African and the American Negro unquestionably differed qualitatively from the outright seizure of the passports of such black internationalists as Robeson and Du Bois or the widespread declarations, uttered by those both in and out of government, that civil rights demonstrators and radical African nationalist leaders were communists. Yet the denial of legitimacy to American blacks' ties to African peoples and their liberation struggles did more than presume to tell African Americans, in effect, who they were or ought to be. It also dictated for blacks a conditional American citizenship with the implicit injunction that they eschew pan-African solidarities and an independent critique of U.S. foreign policy.

Murray's sojourn in Ghana coincided with that nation's embrace of socialism and, after the Congo Crisis, a gradual recasting of its nonaligned stance through increased trade and assistance from the Eastern bloc and China, positions that convinced her, as well as hawkish U.S. officials, of Ghana's drift toward communism. From that time on, Ghana's African American expatriate community would take on a strongly leftist orientation, far more supportive than Murray of Ghana's anti-imperialist agenda and far more critical of U.S. policies at home and abroad. Working within the Ghanaian government and activated by the political culture of the U.S.-based black left, these newcomers deplored claims of alienation between African Americans and Africans as an utter falsehood refuted by the African Americans' presence in Ghana. Proponents of this view regarded such propaganda as part and parcel of the U.S. government's repression of black dissenters since the mid-1950s, a phenomenon that some observers, including Julian Mayfield, Shirley Graham Du Bois, Victoria Garvin, and Preston King, knew firsthand.

Murray returned to the United States, graduated from Yale Law School, and later received a tenured position in American studies at Brandeis University. She remained active in civil rights and women's rights causes. Years later, Murray wrote in her autobiography of her time in Ghana. Her account consists largely of direct quotations from her letters home, describing her opposition to the policies of preventive detention, the surveillance of her classroom by Convention People's Party officials, and the mundane details and impressions of her daily existence. While she acknowledged the tumultuous impact of the Congo Crisis on Ghanaian politics (though Lumumba's death and the worldwide condemnation of it remained unmentioned) and discussed her clandestine work for opposition members who brought legal challenges to preventive detention laws, Murray disclosed little about her staunch pro-American interventions. As she wrote not long after her arrival in Ghana, "The human spirit is nationless, raceless, sexless. It is, and it will continue to be—whether we have cold wars, hot wars, positive neutrality, Nkrumahism, McCarthyism."[59] This wish to transcend race and sex did not transcend but in fact defined an idealized American nationhood whose virtues were confirmed by her direct experience with Ghana's curbs on civil liberties.

Murray's desire for public influence and recognition through her efforts in Ghana responded to her need to overcome the liabilities she associated with her status as a black woman. Writing years later with considerable evidence that U.S. policies had not lived up to the lofty moral standard she championed in Ghana, Murray was less than candid about her pro-American activities. Murray was hardly unique in engaging in the self-protective filtering of memory, a silencing universally practiced by authors of life-writing regardless of political persuasion. Her silences resemble those of Carl Rowan, an African American journalist and director of the U.S. Information Service during the Belgian-U.S. military campaign against Congolese rebels in 1964, which black leaders across the ideological spectrum roundly condemned. Rowan's memoir of a distinguished career in journalism and public service omits any mention of that indefensible policy.[60] Murray may have determined that her staunch defense of Americanism, in retrospect inseparable from the repressive forces of empire and neocolonialism, was untenably anachronistic, incompatible with the progressive image she wished to create for posterity. Such a disclosure would only be a disturbing reminder of her voicelessness and marginalization and the measures she took to overcome them.

NOTES

1. The republication of Murray's autobiography was a catalyst for renewed scholarly interest in various aspects of her life and career. See Pauli Murray, *Pauli Murray: The Autobiography of a Black Activist, Feminist, Lawyer, Priest, and Poet* (Knoxville: University of Tennessee Press, 1989), originally published as Pauli Murray, *Song in a Weary Throat: An American Pilgrimage* (New York: Harper and Row, 1987); and roundtable in *Journal of Women's History* 14 (June 2002): Patricia Bell-Scott, "'To Write Like Never Before': Pauli Murray's Enduring Yearning," 58–62; Susan Ware, "Pauli Murray's Notable Connections," 54; Glenda E. Gilmore, "Admitting Pauli Murray," 62; Rosalind Rosenberg, "The Conjunction of Race and Gender," 68.

2. Barbara Ransby, *Ella Baker and the Black Freedom Movement: A Radical Democratic Vision* (Chapel Hill: University of North Carolina Press, 2002), 72.

3. Yevette Richards, *Maida Springer: Pan-Africanist and International Labor Leader* (Pittsburgh, Pa.: University of Pittsburgh Press, 2000), 75–76.

4. Pauli Murray, *Proud Shoes: The Story of an American Family* (New York: Harper, 1956).

5. Pauli Murray, *States' Laws on Race and Color* (Athens, Ga.: Woman's Division of Christian Service, 1951).

6. On Williams and Murray's association with his defense, see Timothy B. Tyson, *Radio Free Dixie: Robert F. Williams and the Roots of Black Power* (Chapel Hill: University of North Carolina Press, 1999), 159–60.

7. Doreen Drury, " 'Experimentation on the Male Side': Race, Class, Gender, and Sexuality in Pauli Murray's Quest for Love and Identity, 1910–1960" (Ph.D. diss., Boston College, 2000), 69, 79–80; Rosenberg, "Conjunction of Race and Gender."

8. Geoffrey Bing, *Reap the Whirlwind: An Account of Kwame Nkrumah's Ghana from 1950 to 1966* (London: MacGibbon and Kee, 1968), 321; Richards, *Maida Springer*, 206–7.

9. Richards, *Maida Springer*, 204.

10. See, for example, "Ghanaian Embassy Distributes Anti-American Propaganda," Department of State Instruction, CW-1136, August 7, 1961, Bureau of African Affairs, Records of G. Mennen Williams, Subject File, 1961–66, Box 15, U.S. State Department Records, Record Group 59, National Archives, College Park, Md. This document discusses attacks on U.S. Congolese policy that appeared in the Ghanaian publication *Voice of Africa*.

11. Bill Sutherland with Matt Meyer, *Guns and Gandhi in Africa: Pan-African Insights on Nonviolence, Armed Struggle, and Liberation in Africa* (Trenton, N.J.: Africa World, 2000), 45.

12. Kwame Nkrumah, *I Speak of Freedom: A Statement of African Ideology* (New York: Praeger, 1962), 262–81.

13. Pauli Murray to John Tettegah, October 25, November 1, 1960, Tettegah to Murray, October 27, 1960, Box 41, Folder 714, Pauli Murray Papers, Radcliffe College Archives, Schlesinger Library, Harvard University, Cambridge, Mass.

14. "Dr. Nkrumah Re-States His Policy," *West Africa*, October 15, 1960, 1179; Dorothy Padmore to Richard Wright, October 17, 1960, Box 103, Folder 1521, Richard Wright Papers, Beinecke Rare Book and Manuscript Library, Yale University, New Haven, Conn.

15. Personal Secretary to Pauli Murray, November 28, 1960, Box 41, Folder 714, Murray Papers.

16. David Roediger, *Colored White: Transcending the Racial Past* (Berkeley: University of California Press, 2002).

17. Julian Mayfield, "Black First or American First?: Sorting Us Out," *Washington Post*, April 20, 1984, 32.

18. Penny M. Von Eschen, *Race against Empire: Black Americans and Anticolonialism, 1937–1957* (Ithaca, N.Y.: Cornell University Press, 1997); Anthony Platt, *E. Franklin Frazier Reconsidered* (New Brunswick, N.J.: Rutgers University Press, 1991).

19. See Pauli Murray to Edith Sampson, April 26, 1952, Sampson to Murray, April 28, 1952, Box 100, Folder 1787, Murray Papers. Murray protested the publication of Worthy's attack in the *Crisis* to its editor, James Ivy; see Pauli Murray to James Ivy, May 5, 1952, Box 100, Folder 1787, Murray Papers. For another attack on Sampson's Denmark speech, see Eslanda G. Robeson, "Mrs. Edith Sampson Tells Europeans Negroes Are Happy, Almost Free," *Freedom*, June 1952, 2.

20. Richards, *Maida Springer*, 207; Pauli Murray to Immanuel Wallerstein, February 4, 1961, Wallerstein to Murray, February 16, 1961, Box 41, Folder 714, Murray Papers.

21. See Pauli Murray diary, June 5, 1960, Box 41, Folder 710, Murray Papers.

22. David N. Gibbs, *The Political Economy of Third World Intervention: Mines, Money, and U.S. Policy in the Congo Crisis* (Chicago: University of Chicago Press, 1991), 77–86.

23. Thomas Borstelmann, *The Cold War and the Color Line: American Race Relations in the Global Arena* (Cambridge, Mass.: Harvard University Press, 2002), 129–31.

24. Gibbs, *Political Economy of Third World Intervention*, 94–95.

25. Madeline Kalb, *The Congo Cables: The Cold War in Africa from Eisenhower to Kennedy* (New York: Macmillan, 1982).

26. Gibbs, *Political Economy of Third World Intervention*, 98–99.

27. "Death of Patrice Lumumba," Accra, February 14, 1961, in *Selected Speeches of Kwame Nkrumah*, comp. Samuel Obeng (Accra: Afram, 1997), 15.

28. Anna Arnold Hedgeman, *The Trumpet Sounds: A Memoir of Negro Leadership* (New York: Holt, Rinehart, and Winston, 1964).

29. Ibid., 137.

30. Ibid., 138–39.

31. Pauli Murray diary (typescript), July 22, 1960, Box 41, Folder 723, Murray Papers.

32. Pauli Murray to Robert F. Kennedy, May 25, 1961, Box 103, Folder 1866, Murray Papers.

33. Adelaide Cromwell, interview by author, September 21, 1998.

34. Pauli Murray, "A Question of Identity," unpublished manuscript, Box 85, Folder 1478, Murray Papers.

35. Carol Polsgrove, *Divided Minds: Intellectuals and the Civil Rights Movement* (New York: W. W. Norton, 2001), 137; Murray, "Question of Identity."

36. Von Eschen, *Race against Empire*.

37. Mary L. Dudziak, *Cold War Civil Rights: Race and the Image of American Democracy* (Princeton, N.J.: Princeton University Press, 2000), 152–202.

38. "Surprise," *Newsweek*, October 31, 1960, 45; "Artist Sues Newsweek," *Mr. Muhammed Speaks* (special ed.), n.d., 23.

39. Brenda Gayle Plummer, *Rising Wind: Black Americans and U.S. Foreign Affairs, 1935–1960* (Chapel Hill: University of North Carolina Press, 1996), 303–4.

40. Pauli Murray diary, September 18, 1960, Box 41, Folder 710, Murray Papers.

41. Ludo de Witte, *The Assassination of Lumumba* (London: Verso, 2001), 163–64.

42. For example, see "Lumumba's Legacy: Troubles All Over," *Life*, February 24, 1961, 18. On the prosecession, anti-Lumumba bias at the United Nations and in the Belgian and Western press, see de Witte, *Assassination*, 9–26.

43. Obeng, *Selected Speeches*, 24. De Witte, *Assassination*, 97–124, 140–43, provides details regarding Lumumba's execution by Belgian officials and military personnel and the destruction of his remains.

44. A visual record of the demonstration in the UN gallery, with footage of Lumumba and his aides in custody of Congolese troops and scenes from other demonstrations

around the world, appears in a 1961 Pathé Studios newsreel in possession of author. I am indebted to Ron Gregg for this extraordinary footage.

45. James Baldwin, "A Negro Assays the Negro Mood," *New York Times Sunday Magazine*, March 12, 1961, 25, 103–4.

46. James Baldwin, "Princes and Powers," in *Nobody Knows My Name* (New York: Dell, 1962), 13–55.

47. Era Bell Thompson, "Africa, Land of My Fathers," in *Apropos of Africa: Sentiments of American Negro Leaders on Africa from the 1880s to the 1950s*, ed. Adelaide Cromwell Hill and Martin Kilson (London: Cass, 1969), 272–77.

48. Harold Isaacs, "A Reporter at Large—Back to Africa," *New Yorker*, May 13, 1961, 105–42; Russell Howe, "Strangers in Africa," *Reporter*, June 22, 1961, 34–35; Polsgrove, *Divided Minds*, 141–42. For perspectives linking the articles to the UN demonstration, see St. Clair Drake, "The Negro's Stake in Africa," *Negro Digest*, June 1964, 42–43; and Julian Mayfield, "Ghanaian Sketches," in *Young Americans Abroad*, ed. Roger H. Klein (New York: Harper and Row, 1962), 185.

49. Horace Mann Bond, "Howe and Isaacs in the Bush: The Ram in the Thicket," *Negro History Bulletin* (1962), reprinted in *Apropos of Africa*, ed. Hill and Kilson, 278–88.

50. Drake believed the articles were "inevitable," recalling that soon after the UN demonstration, he received a call from an editor for *Reporter* who solicited an article from him, showing "the American Negroes once and for all that these Africans don't care . . . about them and that there is really no kind of tie between them." According to Drake, the editor claimed to be acting on the suggestion of a couple of African American leaders who wished to emphasize that the American Negro identified with America rather than with Africa. Drake begged off and claimed that his "paranoic suspicions" had been sparked by Isaacs's article. Drake, "Negro's Stake," 43–45.

51. Hedgeman, *Trumpet Sounds*, 145; Horace Mann Bond, "Howe and Isaacs in the Bush": The Ram in the Thicket," *Negro History Bulletin* 25 (December 1961): 67–70. On the difficulty of publishing rebuttals to the new discourse on African Americans and Africans, see Adelaide Cromwell to St. Clair Drake, February 7, 1962, Box 5, Folder 50, St. Claire Drake Papers, Schomburg Center for Research in Black Culture, New York Public Library, New York, N.Y. For African American objections to Howe's article, see Claude Barnett to Drake, July 22, 1961, Box 6, Folder 12, Drake Papers.

52. Hedgeman, *Trumpet Sounds*, 149.

53. See Murray's memorandum to the American Women's Association of Accra, "Pilot Project—What Can We Do for Our Country?," Box 41, Folder 712, Murray Papers.

54. Archie Lang, political affairs officer at the U.S. embassy in Accra from 1957 to 1959, confirms that Murray's acquaintance in the U.S. embassy, Earl Link (deceased), was a CIA agent (Lang to author, August 2001, in possession of author). Garrison informed Williams that Murray was in constant touch with Link, "an American Negro on the staff of the Embassy in Accra (and who I think reports to the CIA)." Lloyd K. Garrison to G. Mennen Williams, January 23, 1961, Box 96, Folder 1686, Murray Papers.

55. Murray kept in touch with U.S. government personnel after her departure from

Ghana as part of her effort to raise funds for a Ghanaian student's travel for study in the United States. The opposition activities of this student as a courier for Murray's legal briefs written for opposition leader J. B. Danquah had placed the student at risk of detention. One U.S. Information Agency official wrote to Murray of "the hushed conferences we had on your correspondence with Nkrumah and Tettegah." David J. Du Bois to Pauli Murray, July 30, 1962, Box 93, Folder 1615, Murray Papers.

56. Under Lovestone's guidance, Springer assisted African nationalist trade unions and attended pan-African conferences as an observer, sending her reports to Lovestone. Ted Morgan ambiguously refers to Springer as one of Lovestone's "agents." Yevette Richards disputes such allegations of Springer's involvement with covert attempts to influence African trade unions. See Ted Morgan, *A Covert Life: Jay Lovestone: Communist, Anti-Communist, Spymaster* (New York: Random House, 1999), 304–9; Richards, *Maida Springer*; Jay Lovestone to Pauli Murray, September 26, 1960, Box 41, Folder 714, Murray Papers.

57. A report to the State Department Bureau of African Affairs on American specialists stationed in Ghana under U.S. auspices had high praise for Murray, referring to her as "a continual embarrassment to the Government party. She is good. . . . After she quits . . . she would be excellent for other English-speaking countries in Africa. She has never taught before but is obviously a brain. . . . Her line [on race] is that it doesn't exist, or rather, that you pay no attention to it." "Report by Frederick A. Colwell, American Specialist Branch, Accra—March 4–7," Bureau of African Affairs Records, Box 1, Folder 17.0, State Department Records.

58. Murray was undoubtedly aware of the controversy among blacks regarding Isaacs's article. A manuscript copy of Bond's rebuttal, "Howe and Isaacs in the Bush: The Ram in the Thicket," is contained in Box 97, Folder 1708, Murray Papers.

59. Pauli Murray, "American in Ghana," March 20, 1960, Box 41, Folder 722, Murray Papers.

60. Carl Rowan, *Breaking Barriers: A Memoir* (New York: HarperCollins, 1991). On Rowan's dismay at U.S. military participation along with Belgian forces and white South African mercenaries in their campaign against Congolese rebels, see his memorandum to President Lyndon Baines Johnson, "Propaganda Problems Relating to the Congo," August 14, 1964, White House Central Files, Confidential File, Box 8, Folder "CO 52 Congo," Lyndon Baines Johnson Presidential Library, Austin, Tex.

Nina Simone's Border Crossings

Black Cultural Nationalism and
Gender on a Global Stage

RUTH FELDSTEIN

On September 15, 1963, Nina Simone learned that four young African American girls had been killed in the bombing of the Sixteenth Street Baptist Church in Birmingham, Alabama. Immediately thereafter, she wrote the song "Mississippi Goddam." It came to her in a "rush of fury, hatred and determination" as she "suddenly realized what it was to be black in America in 1963." It was, she said, "my first civil rights song."[1]

Up to that point, Simone, an African American singer, pianist, and songwriter, had an eclectic repertoire that blended jazz with blues, gospel, and classical music. In contrast to her earlier work (one critic had dubbed her a "supper club songstress for the elite"), "Mississippi Goddam" was a political anthem.[2] The lyrics were filled with both anger and despair, and they stood in stark contrast to the fast-paced and rollicking rhythm. Over the course of several verses, Simone vehemently rejected the notions that race relations could change gradually, that the South was unique in terms of discrimination, and that African Americans could or would patiently seek political rights. "Me and my people are just about due," she declared. Simone also challenged principles that are still strongly associated with liberal civil rights activism in that period: religion as a source of solace and protest for African Americans, and the viability of a beloved community of whites and blacks. As she sang toward the end of "Mississippi Goddam":

> All I want is equality
> For my sister, my brother, my people, and me.
> Yes, you lied to me all these years
> You told me to wash and clean my ears
> And talk real fine, just like a lady
> And you'd stop calling me Sister Sadie.
> But this whole country is full of lies
> You're all gonna die and die like flies
> I don't trust you anymore
> You keep on saying, "Go slow."

While "Mississippi Goddam" expressed pain and rage on a cultural terrain, it also offered one of a range of political perspectives that people in and out of movements were developing in the early 1960s, well beyond the emphasis on interracial activism that predominated among liberal supporters of civil rights.[3] It suggests themes this essay engages at greater length: the multiple ways in which cultural production mattered to black activism—far more than as merely the background soundtrack to the movement, and not simply as a reflection of the preexisting aspirations of political activists; the ways that culture was a site at which racial politics circulated across national boundaries; and the significance of gender to these dynamics.

Despite the swirling range of ways African Americans envisioned freedom in the early 1960s, activism that had little to do with integration or federal legislation has, until recently, been marginal to civil rights scholarship. What the historian Robin D. G. Kelley refers to as a "neat typology" chronologically and analytically separates liberal interracial activism—associated with a unified national success story—from more radical black activism and calls for black power—associated with the end of a beloved community and with failure.[4] This prevailing narrative has led to significant, and symptomatic, absences in public memories of the 1960s. Simone's political activism and fiery denunciations of the well-mannered politics of "going slow" were well noted at the time. In the decade that followed, she supported the struggle for black freedom in the United States earlier, more directly, and in a more outspoken manner around the world than many other African American entertainers. In these same years, she recorded nearly twenty albums and received critical and commercial acclaim in and out of the United States; by the late 1960s, Simone had a global audience for recordings ranging from Beatles songs to those about the assassination of Martin Luther King Jr. There was a near-consensus internationally that the controversial Simone was "the best singer of jazz" in years.[5] Nevertheless, beyond brief references to "Mississippi Goddam," Nina Simone has largely fallen through the cracks of scholarship—on civil rights, on women's activism, and on music.[6] The relative silence about her is not simply a problem of categorization (a song is not the same as a speech) or of recovery (women's historians and others have not appreciated Simone as an activist). Rather, Simone's absence emerges from the ways that certain kinds of cultural productions and particular expressions of female sexuality have often been placed beyond the parameters of African American political history.

Building on the work of scholars who complicate this "neat typology," this essay explores the nature and implications of Nina Simone's activism in the 1960s and the sources for the subsequent invisibility of that activism. I argue that gender and sexuality were central to Simone's reception and to her racial politics in the late 1950s and early 1960s—well before she recorded "Four Women" in 1966, a song about color consciousness that addressed gender and racial discrimination in relation to each other and brought her additional notoriety.[7] More specifically, Simone drew on Africa to offer a vision of black cultural nationalism, in and out of the United States, that was free of misogyny and insisted on female power.[8] She did so well before the apparent ascendance of black power or second-wave feminism in the late 1960s and 1970s. Simone's interventions demonstrate that events and issues from the 1960s that are often treated as separate were in fact deeply intertwined. These are the development of black cultural nationalism, the role of women in black activism more generally, and the emergence of second-wave feminism. These were connected and widespread before the "official" rise of black power or second-wave feminism.

Moreover, Simone was not alone—in her assessments of liberal activism, in her rage, or in her gendered racial politics. Musically, socially, and politically, she came of age in the late 1950s and early 1960s as part of an interracial avant-garde in Greenwich Village, which included Langston Hughes, Lorraine Hansberry, Leroi Jones (later Amiri Baraka), Abbey Lincoln, Harry Belafonte, Miriam Makeba, and James Baldwin, among others.[9] Her political education began as a result of her friendship with the playwright Lorraine Hansberry; Simone chose to write explicitly political songs shortly after influential jazz critics censured vocalist Abbey Lincoln for making a similar move. Certainly, Nina Simone's music and politics stood out in 1963 when she wrote "Mississippi Goddam"; coming just one month after the record-setting March on Washington for Jobs and Freedom and Martin Luther King's famous "I have a dream" speech, she provocatively departed from conventional wisdom and posed a challenge in a moment often remembered as the heyday of liberal interracial activism. Yet she was emphatically not a solitary figure or a voice out of nowhere. Rather, Simone is a window into a world beyond dominant liberal civil rights organizations and leaders and into networks of activist cultural producers in particular. She matters not necessarily because she explicitly caused a specific number of fans around the world to change their behavior, but because the perspectives on black freedom and gender that she, among others, articulated circulated as widely as they did in the early 1960s.

"A Triple Threat Artist": Simone and the Politics of Showing Up

Nina Simone, whose birth name was Eunice Waymon, was born in 1933 in the small town of Tryon, North Carolina. Her mother was a housekeeper by day and a Methodist minister at night; her father worked mostly as a handyman.

Simone started tapping piano keys when she was three years old and was soon playing hymns and gospel music at her mother's church. By the time she was five, and as the result of local fund-raising efforts on the part of whites and blacks in her town, she was studying classical music with a white teacher. After high school, Simone continued her classical studies at Juilliard in New York City. She planned to go from Juilliard to the Curtis Institute of Music in Philadelphia and hoped to be the first African American classical pianist. She was dismayed when the Curtis Institute rejected her in 1951.[10]

Several years later, tired of giving piano lessons and in need of money (in part so that she could continue her own classical training), Simone started to play popular music at an Atlantic City nightclub. Under pressure from her boss, she began singing, and then writing her own music and lyrics. Simone's first popular hit came in 1958—with a ballad-like recording of the George Gershwin song, "I Loves You Porgy," which received considerable airtime on the radio.[11] The song reached the Top Twenty in the summer of 1959 and number two on the R&B charts.[12] Soon thereafter, Simone moved to Manhattan, performing widely and recording regularly. In 1959 one critic suggested that she might be "the greatest singer to evolve in the last decade and perhaps the greatest singer today. . . . The greatest compliments could only be understatements of her talent." Within the world of jazz vocalists, a critically acclaimed star was born. Or, as Simone later put it, "I was a sensation. An overnight success, like in the movies. . . . Suddenly I was the hot new thing."[13]

Press coverage of the "hot new thing" accelerated rapidly. Simone was the subject of discussion in publications that crossed racial, political, and cultural divides—from the premier jazz journal of the day, *Down Beat*, to black newspapers and magazines like the *Amsterdam News* and *Ebony*, to mainstream media like the *New York Times* and *Time*. Even before her first performances in Europe in 1965, jazz magazines abroad had praised her extensively. In discussions of Simone from around the world, fans and critics gave up on efforts to define the type of music she played. "She is, of course, not exactly a jazz performer—or possibly one should say that she is a lot more than just a jazz performer," wrote a reviewer for *Down Beat* after Simone performed at the Newport Jazz Festival for the first time in 1960.[14]

In the critical discourse about Simone, she emerged as a performer who straddled the worlds of high art and mass culture, of so-called authentic blackness and a universal genius that transcended race and gender. She was a "at least a triple threat artist," according to the *Nashville Tennessean*, because she had studied classical piano at Juilliard and combined "musical range with her dramatic way . . . and composes, sometimes on the spot." It was no coincidence that when a seventeen-year-old in England formed a club devoted to Simone's career in 1965, he intentionally named it the "Nina Simone Appreciation Society," rather than the more common "Fan Club," which peers had formed for African American R&B musicians who had "cult followings" in England. "Because of the kind of music she was doing . . . because of her history in music . . . I felt it was just appropriate to call it an Appreciation Society and not a fan club. It just didn't sound right to me to say Nina Simone Fan Club."[15] Europeans and Americans alike tended to depict Simone in terms of both musical virtuosity and racial authenticity, but for Europeans, this meant that Simone was quintessentially African American at the same time that she was a cosmopolitan figure whose affiliations were not tethered to any one nation. Her performances of songs in French (three songs on her 1965 album *I Put a Spell on You*) and her French-derived professional name led some people initially to assume that she was a "French chanteuse." Yet European fans also raved about her unique ability to evoke "the shame" of American segregation and racial violence with her "burning political discourse."[16] According to one enthusiastic British reviewer, Simone could "take a predominantly white and initially indifferent audience and by sheer artistry, strength of character and magical judgment, drive them into a mood of ecstatic acclamation."[17]

In other words, as her recording and performing career took off, Simone departed—in her own self-representations and as the object of representation—from then-dominant depictions of African entertainers as "natural" entertainers and from entrenched associations between African American women entertainers, commercial culture, and sexualized vice especially. Her background as a classically trained musician who bridged cultural hierarchies enabled her to bridge other seemingly contradictory positions: critics and fans represented her as nationally and racially specific on the one hand and as international and cosmopolitan on the other.[18]

By 1963, Simone was maintaining the relentless schedule of recording and performing that had characterized her career for several years, but she was also accelerating her involvement in black freedom struggles. Well before she wrote "Mississippi Goddam," she supported national civil rights organizations like the Student Nonviolent Coordinating Committee (SNCC), the Congress of Racial Equality (CORE), and the National Association for the Advancement of Colored People (NAACP) and local organizations like the Harlem Young Men's Christian Association (YMCA) by offering her name as a "sponsor" and performing at numerous benefit concerts.[19] At that point, she did not think of herself as "involved" because she was only "spurring them [activists] on" "as best I could from where I sat—on stage, an artist, separate somehow." That feeling of detachment did not last, however, as Simone became "driven by civil rights and the hope of black revolution."[20] In 1964 she headlined for SNCC several times in just a few months, including an event at Carnegie Hall that added to her reputation as a musician worthy of that location and as committed to the movement. The following year, Simone's husband and manager, Andrew Stroud, volunteered her "services" to CORE, agreeing to a deal in which Simone would perform at CORE-sponsored fund-raisers around the country at a minimal cost. These benefit concerts were very important to the treasuries of civil rights organizations. According to one estimate, CORE planned to raise close to $2,000 per Simone concert, considerably more than many other musicians and entertainers raised in benefit performances.[21]

Simone also traveled south to the sites of many civil rights battles. The "ever-arresting Simone," as a journalist for the *New York Amsterdam News* described her, was on the roster of stars scheduled to perform at an "unprecedented show" in Birmingham, Alabama, in the summer of 1963. In Birmingham the American Guild of Variety Artists, together with SNCC, the Southern Christian Leadership Conference (SCLC), CORE, the NAACP, the Urban League, and the Negro American Labor Council, sponsored a "Salute to Freedom '63" concert. Designed in part to raise money for the upcoming March on Washington, the concert was originally planned for an integrated audience at Birmingham's city auditorium. When organizers faced opposition from local whites, they moved the show to a local all-black college. According to one estimate, the controversial concert raised $9,000. Simone also performed in Atlanta and for marchers during the Selma to Montgomery march in 1965.[22]

Historian Brian Ward has argued that this kind of visible political engagement on the part of African American popular musicians—those with mass appeal among African American and white audiences—was relatively rare in the early to mid-1960s, and that going to the South as Simone did was especially noteworthy. Entertainers risked alienating white fans, as well as the deejays who chose what music got airtime. Not surprisingly, then, when SNCC organizers compiled lists of musicians and entertainers who were potential sponsors in these years, they often targeted a cultural avant-garde oriented around Greenwich Village and the political left. They focused on jazz musicians more than on those with more popular mass appeal.[23] Simone was recording with Philips, a label associated with sophisticated, elite, and educated consumers of jazz across lines of race. She was performing and socializing at the Village Gate, a place where, as she put it, "politics was mixed in with so much of what went on . . . that I remember it now as two sides of the same coin, politics and jazz."[24]

Nevertheless, it would be a mistake to conclude that because of Simone's presumed respectable audience and her associations with elite high culture, it was "safe" for her to make the political choices that she did. Performers took significant risks when they supported African American activism. To cite just one example, in November 1961 the jazz journal *Down Beat* published a scathing review of *Straight Ahead*, a jazz album that featured Abbey Lincoln as vocalist and music by the drummer Max Roach and the saxophonist Coleman Hawkins, among others. *Down Beat* critic Ira Gitler accused Lincoln of being a "'professional negro,'" who was "wearing," repetitive, and "banal" as a singer and who was "sincere" but "misguided and naïve" with her "African nationalism." The controversy over this album effectively, if temporarily, helped to silence Lincoln as a singer. Although she continued to perform in film and to write, she did not release another album under her own name until 1973.[25]

Organization activists knew that they could not necessarily count on performers who, like Lincoln among many others, faced threats of critical censure or even censorship. SNCC personnel courted stars to get them engaged with the movement, flattered them after the fact, and hoped that African American entertainers would attract even more popular white entertainers to their cause. "I would like to express our deep appreciation to you for your assistance," wrote one SNCC staff assistant to Simone after a benefit performance; "It is not often that we are incapable of expressing the beauty of a performance or the extent of our gratitude, but such was the case this time."[26]

While showing up was clearly a risky political choice that Simone made, she did more than perform her standard "supper club" music at political events. Rather, the lyrics to the songs she wrote changed, becoming more explicitly political. As one reviewer noted approvingly, "Her music comes from a particular point of view." The album that marked this transition was *In Concert* (1964). Because it was relatively rare for musicians outside of the world of folk music to bring culture and politics together so directly in this period in their lyrics, it is worth considering how Simone made this move.[27] *In Concert* offers a framework for understanding the intersections of gender and music, art and activism, in Simone's career both before and after this album's release.

Gender and Racial Politics on *In Concert*

In Concert, like other albums by Simone, blended moods, styles, and genres. Over the course of seven songs, recorded from a live performance in New York, Simone moved from tender love songs to more classic blues to folk songs. Simone's expressive strategies, her skillful transitions between styles, and her engagement with the live audience all added to the album's power and confirmed the challenge she posed to conventional cultural categories. Three songs on the album indicate with particular clarity how gendered strategies of protest were consistent parts of Simone's repertoire. Indeed, rejecting any singular definition of African American womanhood was part of the album's racial politics, and remained central to Simone's participation in black activism beyond *In Concert*.

In the song "Pirate Jenny," Simone transformed a song about class relations in London from Kurt Weill and Bertolt Brecht's *The Threepenny Opera* into a song about race, class, and gender relations in the American South. By maintaining ties to the original version, Simone associated her own antiracism with Brecht's antifascism and evoked a historical alliance between African American musicians and a political left—one that, according to Michael Denning, "permanently altered the shape of American music."[28] But there were unique aspects to Simone's version of a song about a poor and abused woman's fantasies of revenge. After the ominous beating drum, in the opening bars the lyrics introduced a black woman scrubbing a floor:

> You people can watch while I'm scrubbing these floors
> And I'm scrubbing the floors while you're gawking.
> Maybe once you'll tip me and it makes you feel swell
> In this crummy southern town in this crummy old hotel.
> But you'll never guess to who you're talking.

In the verses that followed, the woman envisioned violence and her own empowerment. She witnessed a "ship, the black freighter," come into the town "shooting guns from her bow" and leaving every building in the town but the hotel "flattened." The woman then determined the fate of the abusive town members—deciding whether they should be killed "now or later." In a powerful whisper, devoid of any musical accompaniment, Simone offered her protagonist's answer: "right now."

From the opening bars until the final drum, the rhythm, instrumentals, and Simone's rich contralto voice—together with the lyrics—conveyed this woman's rage. Significantly, African American women and their labor were Simone's point of entry in "Pirate Jenny." They were the means through which she exposed the socioeconomic and gendered dimensions of racism and expressed a fantasy about vengeance. In singing about this fictional woman in a Brecht-Weill song, which had classical undertones and links to the Old Left, in an era known for "We Shall Overcome," Simone also rejected expectations of what protest music should and should not be. "Perhaps it is a masterpiece; certainly it is a warning," suggested the liner notes.[29]

Like "Pirate Jenny," the song "Go Limp" also featured an African American woman protagonist, but here, the similarities ended. In terms of genre, "Go Limp" was a parody of folk songs—this as folk music was enjoying a celebrated revival.[30] During the live recorded performance, Simone repeatedly invited the audience to sing along during "hootenanny time," only to mock the participatory ethos of the genre. ("And if I have a great concert, maybe I won't have to sing those folk songs again," she sang in one verse.)

Quite aside from genre, the lyrics of "Go Limp" foregrounded Simone's alternatively amusing and ironic interweaving of sexual and racial politics. The song focused on a young woman civil rights activist who must defend to her mother the choice she has made to join the civil rights marchers. In response to her mother's warnings, the daughter promised self-restraint: she would remain nonviolent, she assured her worried mother, *and* she would remain a virgin. Simone used humor to suggest that it would not be easy for the young woman to meet these dual goals. As Simone sang:

> Oh mother, dear mother, no I'm not afraid
> For I'll go on that march
> And return a virgin maid
> With a brick in my handbag
> And a smile on my face,
> And barbed wire in my underwear to shed off disgrace.

The high point of this song—the moment when the live audience was most involved—occurred when Simone teased the crowd with the fate of this young woman. Sang Simone, as the narrator:

> One day they were marching, a young man came by;
> With a beard on his chin and a gleam in his eye.
> And before she had time to remember her brick . . .

At this point, Simone stopped singing. Over the course of the long indefinite pause that followed, the laughter and applause from the audience increased, crescendoing as the audience came to its own conclusions about the implied rhyme with "brick." It was only after this long pause—only after a laughing Simone encouraged her audience to draw these conclusions—that she repeated the verse and concluded, "and before she had time to remember her brick / they were holding a sit down on a neighboring hay rig." With these performance strategies and lyrics, Simone played with gender roles and invited the audience in—making them complicit in this bawdy acceptance of premarital sex and the spoof of folk music. Yet, she did not cast off her extratextual reputation as a classically trained musician either. Simone evoked a tradition of black female musicians who sang about sex, but she did so in a masterful *performance* of bawdiness.

In subsequent verses Simone explained what had happened to the woman and why the brick and barbed wire had not been more useful. This young woman, sang Simone, agreed to have sex not in spite of her desire for self-restraint (the brick in the bag and the barbed wire). Rather, the sex took place precisely because of the nonviolent civil rights training that the young woman had received. Activists had taught the young woman two things: to "go perfectly limp" *and* to be "carried away" if anyone approached her. Consequently, sang Simone slyly, again amid considerable laughter from her audience, "when this young man suggested it was time she was kissed, she remembered her briefing and did not resist."

The song thus invoked the unanticipated consequences of "nonresistance" and of being "carried away." In the song's final verse, Simone sang that the young woman had a baby, and the bearded young man had vanished—hardly a desirable outcome. Nevertheless, as the upbeat young woman, Simone declared in the final line of the song that because of the choices "she" and the young man had made, the child would not have to march like his parents did. Thus, in "Go Limp," Simone mocked, but did not quite reject, the value of passive nonresistance as a means to improve race relations. By contrast, in the album's most famous song, "Mississippi Goddam," Simone aggressively questioned non-violence as a strategy. Like "Pirate Jenny," the song was musically, lyrically, and politically ferocious. Here as in "Pirate Jenny," Simone's public rage was intentionally incendiary and emphatically unladylike, as far from the respectability of a classically trained female performer as one could imagine.

Beyond *In Concert*:
Gender, Liberalism, and Black Cultural Nationalism

Overall, *In Concert* questioned patient nonviolence, Christianity, the interracial folk revival and the related celebration of freedom songs, and white-defined images of blacks, while it celebrated a more racially politicized black culture. In these three songs especially, Simone's focus on sexuality allowed her to put women at the center of multiple struggles for civil rights. In "Go Limp," by inserting a playful sexual narrative into a song about marching and nonviolence, she turned an ironic gaze on "self-restraint" and nonviolence, hallmarks of liberal civil rights activism. So, too, in "Mississippi Goddam," when Simone rejected the impulse to "talk like a lady," she effectively claimed that doing so would not halt discriminatory practices like calling black women "Sister Sadie." Simone was effectively undermining a historically potent gendered politics of respectability that had persisted in African American activism of the late 1950s and early 1960s.[31] In a critique of both whites and blacks, she challenged the notion that certain kinds of gender roles were a route toward improved race relations. Her lyrics in these songs unleashed a liberation of another sort—the liberation from doing the right thing in the hopes of being recognized as deserving. In her performance of rage—and "Mississippi Goddam" and "Pirate Jenny" were just two early examples—Simone defied the very expectations of respectable black womanhood with which she herself had frequently been associated earlier in her career. In addition to the specific if brief reference to "Sister Sadie," Simone's delivery and performance of "Mississippi Goddam" was nothing short of a declaration of independence for "Sadies" everywhere—including in the civil rights movement.

The challenges to liberalism that Simone posed in her songs about race relations led many fans to associate her with militant racial politics and black cultural nationalism. Associations between Simone and a racial militancy that most white Americans only acknowledged (and worried about) in the late 1960s heightened her notoriety in these years, but they obscured the fact that Simone's militancy predated the end of the decade and differed significantly from that of many African American men with whom this militancy was equated.

Black power and black cultural nationalism were fluid and broad phenomena with long histories and multiple manifestations. Both found expression in diverse arenas—ranging from Maulana Karenga's US organization, which stressed the importance of African traditions among African Americans, to the Deacons for Self-Defense and Justice, a Louisiana-based armed organization for self-defense formed in 1964, and to the Black Arts Movement, with its belief that politicized black cultural producers and cultural products were essential preconditions to black liberation.[32] James Brown popularized (and commodified) these very different impulses when he sang "Say it loud, I'm black and proud," in 1968. Political histories of the civil rights movement tend to associate the phrase "black power" with Stokely Carmichael, the SNCC activist who issued a formal call for black power in 1966, months after organizing a third party in Alabama (the Lowndes County Freedom Organization) with a black panther as its symbol.[33] Despite this diversity, black power and black cultural nationalism were often conflated—with each other and with the Black Panther Party, formed in Oakland, California, under the leadership of Bobby Seale and Huey Newton in 1966—and associated with the late 1960s.

African American women participated significantly in movements and expressions of black cultural nationalism and black power. A growing body of scholarship and memoirs suggests that women were leaders, grassroots activists, and cultural producers.[34] Yet many organizations remained, for the most part, male-dominated; further, in the late 1960s, assertions of black *male* pride remained at the center of calls for black power, which were implicitly and explicitly gendered male.[35]

Not surprisingly, then, few Americans, white or black, were likely to associate

African American women with the perceived shift from nonviolent civil rights activism to black power. In 1967 one critic suggested that part of what made songs like "Mississippi Goddam" so powerful was that they sounded as if they should have been written by "some black power disciple of the caliber of Leroi Jones or Stokely Carmichael," while in fact, they were the words of a "woman who has become one of the show world's most popular and controversial entertainers."[36] A journalist at the *New York Post* cemented the link between Simone and a male racial militancy that became notorious in the late 1960s: alluding to Black Panther Eldridge Cleaver's prison memoir, *Soul on Ice*, which in 1967 had shocked readers with its visions of black violence, the *Post* headlined its profile, "Nina Simone: Soul on Voice." From the time of its initial release, rumors had circulated widely that "Mississippi Goddam," known for its "bold lyrics and profane title," was banned from radio stations in the South. At least one observer suggested, however, that it "was banned by radio stations because a woman dared put her feelings into song. . . . The principal objection raised by most critics to the Mississippi song was apparently not so much its militant lyrics, but the fact that an entertainer, and a woman entertainer at that, had dared to put them to music."[37]

But Simone had dared to do so well before this observation was made in 1967. She wrote "Mississippi Goddam" and "Go Limp" at a time when black male activists were just beginning to articulate meanings of African American sexuality and civil rights under the rubric of black cultural nationalism. Simone regarded Carmichael and other black male leaders as friends and teachers. Still, her vision exposed sexual aggression on the part of many male activists as potentially problematic. "Go Limp" was a frank satire of masculinist impulses in black activism, in which authentic blackness and black power could only be signified through male toughness and sexual potency.[38] With its ambiguity and tongue-in-cheek nature, and with its consistent lack of clarity, Simone spoofed the sexual politics of civil rights activists. It was unclear whether the woman "did not resist" or was "carried away" by her own sexual desire; it was unclear as to the circumstances under which the brick should stay in her handbag (and against whom it should be used); and, not the least, it was unclear who, or what, was going to "go limp." What was clear was that, in her *performance* of this song and others, Simone claimed the power of sexuality from a black woman's point of view and that this power was central to her vision of black political liberation.[39]

"Mississippi Goddam" and the genealogy of that song also suggest that Simone was among those who helped to create a version of black cultural nationalism as early as 1963 in ways that did not devalue women. According to Simone, "Mississippi Goddam" "erupted out of me" right after she heard about the church bombing. As she explained it, she had first used materials that her husband, an ex–police officer, had around the house to try to build a gun. Then she realized, "I knew nothing about killing, and I did know about music. I sat down at my piano. An hour later I came out of my apartment with the sheet music for 'Mississippi Goddam' in my hand."[40] The song thus anticipated the arguments that Amiri Baraka would make about the political purposes of culture when he organized the Black Arts Movement in 1965. His poem "Black Art" envisioned African American poetry as a necessary form of black activism and political resistance. But Baraka and others forged links between black culture and revolutionary politics with associations between militant poems, militant men, violence, and sex: "Poems that shoot guns," for example, were those "that come at you, love what you are, breathe like wrestlers, or shudder strangely after pissing."[41] Simone's creative contributions to black cultural nationalism are important because they indicate that this type of misogyny was not a given or inherent to black cultural nationalism and black power.[42] She undercut masculinist assumptions about how and why African American culture had political meaning and challenged models of black womanhood that were widespread, though never hegemonic, in and out of the civil rights movement.

Simone was not alone in this regard. As scholars have shown, black women writers such as Alice Childress, Claudia Jones, and Lorraine Hansberry were among those who "developed a model of feminism" in the late 1950s, in the words of Mary Helen Washington. Beyond the realm of performance, in the mid-1960s women in SNCC directly and indirectly addressed the intersections of racism and sexism—within and beyond the civil rights movement. By 1968, members of the Third World Women's Alliance were just some of the women who criticized black men for defining "the role of black women in the movement. They stated that our role was a supportive one; others stated that we must become breeders and provide an army; still others stated that we had kotex power or pussy power." The publication of *The Black Woman: An Anthology* in 1970 was a landmark not because the ideas were brand-new, but because editor and activist Toni Cade Bambara captured competing strands of black feminism that had been developing for years in this single-volume collective manifesto.[43] Simone contributed to this discourse early in the decade and on the cultural front, where she was literally center stage.

"I'd Arrived Somewhere Important": Africa and Black Cultural Nationalism in the United States and Europe

While Simone had many influences, Africa, as she both imagined and experienced it, was a crucial resource for her articulation of a black cultural nationalism that emphasized female power and that found clear expression on the album *In Concert*. In December 1961, just days after her second marriage (to Stroud), Simone joined a group of thirty-three black artists, musicians, and intellectuals for her first trip to Africa; the group was going to Lagos, Nigeria, on behalf of the American Society for African Culture (AMSAC). AMSAC, an organization founded in the late 1950s by the activist John A. Davis, was committed to promoting African culture as "high" culture in the United States and to encouraging collaboration between African and African American artists and intellectuals in particular. The trip to Lagos in 1961 marked the opening of an AMSAC West African Cultural Center in Lagos and the beginning of an exchange program between African and African American performers. Simone was part of a group notable for its diversity, in terms of performance styles and gender; participants included Langston Hughes, opera singer Martha Flowers, dancers Al Minns and Leon James, jazz musician Lionel Hampton, and a range of educators and academics.[44] What they shared—with each other and with other African American entertainers who traveled to Africa in this period—was some commitment to an international vision of racial politics and culture as these informed each other. Simone later described her arrival this way: "All around us were black faces, and I felt for the first time the spiritual relaxation any Afro-American feels on reaching Africa. I didn't feel like I'd come home when I arrived in Lagos, but I knew I'd arrived somewhere important and that Africa mattered to me, and would always matter . . . . It wasn't Nigeria I arrived in—it was AFRICA."[45] This perspective, romanticized as it was, emphatically rejected then-dominant conceptions of Africa as backward or undeveloped.

Simone continued thereafter to emphasize the importance of Africa to African Americans. She embraced physical markers of black cultural nationalism in ways that joined the struggle of African Americans to a more transnational vision African freedom, making both visible through her female body. She dressed more frequently in what critics called African garb and performed African music at the Dinizulu African Festival. In promotional photos from 1961, she appeared with her hair "natural"—in an Afro.[46] These styles persisted, if inconsistently, into the late 1960s. In a performance at New York's Philharmonic Hall in 1966, Simone "stirred up excitement in her audience," according to one critic, "by walking on stage in a stunning African motif hat and gown ensemble."[47]

Simone's appearance—the ways in which she drew on Africa to perform black womanhood and comment on racial politics—was particularly significant in Europe. "Why am I so roused by different music, different folklore of Africa," she asked a French reporter before performing in Algiers. "Now, the 'gut bucket blues' . . . and the religious music of our people are obviously attached to our African tradition." As she elaborated, "that which we are (but that we never ceased to be in reality despite appearances), more and more is something that is very close to Africa."[48] In England and France especially, such statements, together with her music and overall presentation, offered Europeans an unfamiliar perspective on African American women entertainers. Scholars have shown that while performers like Josephine Baker and Billie Holiday had appeal and success in Europe, Baker especially was subject to a primitivist discourse. By contrast, even though both fans and critics, white and black, may have regarded Simone as exotic, her well-known reputation for political activism, coupled with the ways in which she aggressively claimed certain styles for herself, made it harder for her to be the object of a primitivist discourse. One critical review described Simone as "looking almost tribal with her cone-shaped hairdo and an African-type habit," but also acknowledged both her power and the "vociferous" reception the crowd gave her.[49]

Simone's proactive self-fashioning added to her stature as a critic of American race relations. With her appearance and with her performances—especially of "Mississippi Goddam" and her version of the song Billie Holiday made famous, "Strange Fruit"—Simone spotlighted American race relations for European audiences. In doing so, she often reached a receptive audience. "'Mississippi' is one of the most emotional pieces that it has ever befallen me to hear," wrote one French reviewer; others appreciated how she "attack[ed] 'Strange Fruit'" or raised the hope for "a perfect world, one in which White is worth the same as Black." When she performed these and other civil rights songs, she generated enthusiasm among both jazz lovers and the "general public." She was, according to one fan, the "darling" of France.[50] A British teenager completed a school assignment on American race relations by playing Simone's version of "Strange Fruit" to his high school class because "she was my introduction to civil rights." While he had "read newspapers like everyone else," Simone's songs "totally opened my eyes to a reality that I didn't know."[51]

Simone was direct about her desire both to educate and entertain in Europe. As she put it to French journalists toward the end of her first European tour, she considered herself an ambassador of sorts for her race: "because of the lack of respect that has lasted for hundreds of years, each time I go to a new country, I feel obliged to include in my repertoire songs which proudly affirm my race."[52] In this context, as a female entertainer who produced and performed certain kinds of music—and who was an object of consumption herself—Simone helped to export American civil rights activism in general, and black nationalism in particular. Her politics and her performances were deeply and self-consciously intertwined.

Yet Simone was not simply one in a long line of African American entertainers who achieved greater success among audiences in Europe than in the

United States; nor did she merely compare non-American race relations favorably with those in the United States and position Europe as an oasis.[53] Instead, as her international fame grew, she conceived of racism as an international and not simply a domestic American problem. As she observed to European journalists, she had "found prejudice in Britain, in Holland, and even Morocco. . . . Now I love being in London—it has its own personality and character and I love the way the people talk; but I don't really feel any more welcome in London than I do at home."[54] Simone was able to infuse her eclectic repertoire—including African chants—with meanings that were not solely national. Farah Jasmine Griffin has argued that when Billie Holiday sang "Strange Fruit" in Europe, audiences could indict violent abuses like lynching without having to consider histories of colonialism and race relations in their own countries. By contrast, Simone was popular and performing at a time of rising student and anti-colonialist activism in Europe; that temporal overlap, combined with her own outspokenness and appearance, helped make such distancing more difficult. For example, at one concert in England, she declared that the performance was "for all the black people in the audience." Whites were shocked, including ardent fans, and were well aware that at this British club Simone was talking to, naming as black—and identifying with—those of West Indian and African descent and not African Americans. Or, as she told one British reporter, "The Negro revolution is only one aspect of increasing violence and unrest in the world." In 1969 she questioned assumptions that the civil rights movement had improved the lives of African Americans, but she also suggested that her recording of the song "Revolution" was significant because it was about far more than "the racial problem."[55]

Here, too—when she located American race relations in an international context in ways that drew attention to gender as well as race—Simone was part of a larger cohort of black women who evoked international as well as specifically American issues in their discussions of race. In the United States, South African singer Miriam Makeba forged links between anti-apartheid activism and civil rights activism during her years of fame—as she performed on television, at civil rights benefit concerts, and even at John F. Kennedy's Madison Square Garden birthday celebration in 1962. In Ghana, African American expatriate women articulated political agendas in which gender equity was central.[56] It was in this broader context that Simone used her body, her music, and her words to forge links between Africa and African Americans and disseminated ideas about black freedom that were not specifically about the United States.

Black Activism and Feminism, or Movements in Motion

It is worth emphasizing that Nina Simone was making these interventions and claiming these styles early in the 1960s. She was part of a larger group that historian Robin Kelley has identified in the late 1950s and early 1960s as "black poets, writers, musicians . . . for whom the emancipation of their own artistic form coincided with the African freedom movement."[57] As has become clear, women cultural producers, and their fictional female heroines, played a significant part in this turn-of-the-decade subculture: the jazz singer Abbey Lincoln, the folk singer Odetta, the actress Cicely Tyson, and the fictional Beneatha, heroine of Lorraine Hansberry's landmark play *A Raisin in the Sun*, were just some of the other women who wore their hair in Afros in the late 1950s and early 1960s.[58] Simone's shift from a glamorous performer to a singer with a militant physical presentation associated with black power and Africa became more pronounced after 1965, but it was not new to that period. What was relatively new was that the Afro and other styles became widespread among black male militants—sufficiently so as to make it seem that anyone who had done so prior to that point was "early."[59] Individually, each woman might seem to have been "ahead of the times." Taken together, we can begin to see a male-centered periodization at work, revealing how much our sense of "the times" and the ways in which we narrate black activism and black cultural nationalism have tended not to include women.

This point has historical and historiographical implications. Scholars have become more aware that black cultural nationalism was ascendant well before the late 1960s—that the liberal political activism and the beloved community of the early 1960s did not simply "give way" to a more radical cultural nationalism of the late 1960s, and that Africa did not suddenly become important to African Americans after 1966. Simone highlights the centrality of African American women to these reconceptualizations and the relevance of black feminism to transnational circulations of black activism more generally. Songs from *In Concert* and Simone's subsequent performance strategies suggest how women forged black cultural nationalism through the prism of gender and did not just critique the assumptions about masculinity in black power and black cultural nationalism after the fact, important as those later critiques were.[60]

The ways in which Simone played with gender roles and crossed borders as well as cultural categories indicate, too, that a concern with gender politics did not necessarily develop out of or after concerns with civil rights and racial politics.[61] In other words, black women's role in black activism has implications for analyses of second-wave feminism. In her autobiography Simone located "sisterhood" as the central catalyst to her politicization around race. It was her friend Lorraine Hansberry, she wrote, who launched her "political education" in 1961 and "first took me out of myself and allowed me to see the bigger picture." As a result of Hansberry's influence, "I started to think about myself as a black person in a country run by white people and a woman in a world run by men."[62] In the 1960s and subsequently, Simone emphasized how constitutive gender solidarity was to her "political education." When she introduced "To Be Young, Gifted, and Black," a song that became an anthem of black pride and reached the Top Ten on the R&B charts in 1969, Simone repeatedly paid tribute to Hansberry, who had died in 1965. At a concert in Berkeley, California, for example, she exhorted her audience to sing the chorus of the upcoming song with her and then explained, "This song is dedicated to the memory of my dear, dear friend whom I miss very much, and if I don't control myself, I could talk about all night. Lorraine Hansberry, who wrote *Raisin in the Sun* and died before her time." Here and elsewhere, Simone made relationships between women central to the very idea of black pride. She later noted that in the early 1960s, she and her more politically informed friend had "never talked about men or clothes or other such inconsequential things when we got together. It was always Marx, Lenin, and revolution—real girls' talk."[63] This account certainly turned upside down assumptions about what "girls' talk" was. Here as in her songs, Simone also playfully reversed the usual model in which women first joined civil rights organizations only to have issues of gender inequities dawn on them.

It would be anachronistic to impose second-wave feminism on Nina Simone in 1963 and 1964. As has been suggested, in the titillating "Go Limp" Simone played with a tradition of African American female singers who sang about sex in the 1910s and 1920s as much as she anticipated a tradition of second-wave feminists who would write about sex in the late 1960s and 1970s. Nevertheless, in considering how protest and politics converged in Simone's music, it is important to see that gender and sexuality informed her denunciation of racial discrimination. Elements of what we now call feminism were prefigured in this music and were integrally linked to her black activism generally. Finally, it is important to recall the relevance of Simone's experiences in and attitudes toward places beyond the United States. Historian Kevin Gaines has shown that there was, in the early 1960s, an "affinity" between an "articulation of black feminism and the rhetoric of internationalism."[64] This "affinity" was evident in Simone's career even though she was not a political leader, a traditional intellectual, or a diplomat. Instead, through her position as an African American female entertainer she absorbed and disseminated a gendered vision of black freedom and culture, one that was not based only on national specificity, in ways that were eminently consumable by her many fans.

Culture and Civil Rights Scholarship

Over the course of the 1960s, Nina Simone stood out in several respects. Her music defied categorization, blurring the lines between jazz, classical, folk, blues, and soul music; representations of her as a performer with classical training who blended many styles made it impossible to "fit" her into any one musical genre. At the same time, with her explicitly political lyrics as early as 1963, Simone defied a liberal civil rights ethos. Finally, by making gender central to her radical racial politics in the context of her international fame, she unlinked what some men had linked: racial progress, power, and heterosexual masculine aggression.

These same qualities have made it hard to incorporate Simone into historical analyses of the 1960s, whether the subject is music, gender, racial politics, or the areas of considerable overlap between them. Assumptions about what kind of culture mattered at different points in the 1960s have contributed to Simone's relative invisibility. For instance, Simone, never a traditional jazz singer, clearly departed from the "freedom songs" we associate with the early to mid-1960s—such as the ubiquitous "We Shall Overcome," "This Little Light of Mine," and "Go Tell It on the Mountain," to name only a few.

While these songs did (and do) have power and appeal, it took work and time to produce this "freedom song" canon. It took shape in 1963–64 in songbooks and albums that SNCC used for fund-raising, for instance, and in tours that the Freedom Singers and others gave.[65] According to editors of the anthology *We Shall Overcome: Songs of the Freedom Movement*, first published in 1963, freedom songs were "sung to bolster spirits, to gain new courage and to increase the sense of unity."[66] This canon-in-the-making tended to include songs that were easy for large numbers of people to sing (with relatively few lyrics, in other words); songs that were adapted from "church music" ("spiritual after spiritual began to appear with new words and changes," according to one activist); and songs that were "unrehearsed" or "improvisational."[67] Many songs came out of the Highlander Folk School, where black and white activists had spent time, evoking associations with interracialism and with an ethos of folk music as pure, authentic, and noncommercial.[68]

The process of canon formation that took place in the mid-1960s reinforced a myth that still persists: that "authentic" civil rights music in the period before 1965 meant rural, "grassroots," church-inspired freedom songs that were the soundtrack to the nonviolent movement.[69] The iconic power of "freedom songs" has made it difficult to incorporate cultural expressions from this same period that had opposing qualities—more urban-based and complicated compositions with themes of sex or violence, for instance—into analyses of culture and black activism before 1965. Songs with overt sexual content, like "Go Limp," songs that considered the "whole country" implicated in racism, or songs that did not necessarily embrace nonviolence, like "Mississippi Goddam," became something other than "authentic" freedom songs. These are not the melodies worthy of recuperation and celebration in public schools eager to commemorate Martin Luther King Day every January. In other words, the political, commercial, and ideological choices activists made in the 1960s as they produced the canon of freedom songs have continued to reverberate and, in some instances, have been reinscribed. One result is that the politics of sex and gender has been segregated from the politics of race—far more so, in fact, than they were at the time.

In the 1970s Nina Simone suffered a series of setbacks. Her second marriage ended, she had numerous financial difficulties and legal conflicts with the Internal Revenue Service, and, with the repression of black radicalism by the U.S. government and the decline in African American activism, she grew increasingly pessimistic, if not despairing. In the face of personal, legal, and political difficulties, she performed and recorded infrequently. Simone led a peripatetic life, living in Liberia, France, Barbados, and Switzerland over the course of the 1970s and 1980s, returning to the United States only briefly.[70] When Simone died in April 2003, obituary writers from around the world discussed her relationships to civil rights activism, and some referred to her internationalism. At the funeral service in France, Miriam Makeba offered the "condolences of the whole South Africa," and according to some accounts, Simone's cremated body was to be scattered across several African countries. Many of these reports, however, depicted Simone as a historical relic from a bygone era, or as an entertainer who had supplied background music for the civil rights movement rather than as an activist in her own right. Even in acknowledging her contributions, then, these discussions of Simone implicitly reinforced a dichotomy between culture and politics.[71]

Today, it is all too easy to document the ways in which politics is shaped, if not supplanted, by entertainment and popular culture. One might forget that creative and productive meshings of progressive political movements and diverse cultural commodities seemed possible in the 1960s; further, many people concluded that doing so would invigorate and transform both arenas. As Simone explained in 1969, "When I'm on that stage . . . I don't think I'm just out there to entertain." The journalist from *Time* then elaborated: "Nina is a Negro and proud of it: she is out there to share with audience what Soul Singer Ray Charles calls her 'message things.' "[72]

It is worthwhile for historians of politics, as well as historians of culture, to take these assertions seriously. Simone—on- and offstage and in and out of the

United States—was a political subject. She points to the importance of getting past cultural and political hierarchies that took shape in the 1960s and subdisciplinary divides that have persisted subsequently. Nina Simone's stardom over the course of the 1960s—her music, her activism, her reception and self-presentation, and the intersection of all of these in her highly visible public persona—help us to render black activism in all of its richness.

NOTES

1. Nina Simone, "Mississippi Goddam," performed by Nina Simone, *In Concert—I Put a Spell on You* (Philips, 1964; reissued on compact disk, Polygram Recorders, 1990); Nina Simone, with Stephen Cleary, *I Put a Spell on You: The Autobiography of Nina Simone* (New York: Pantheon, 1992), 89–90.

2. Phyl Garland, *The Sound of Soul* (Chicago: Henry Regnery Co., 1969), 176.

3. A rich body of scholarship that takes up these various perspectives includes, for example, Martha Biondi, *To Stand and Fight: The Struggle for Civil Rights in Postwar New York City* (Cambridge, Mass.: Harvard University Press, 2003); Nikhil Pal Singh, *Black Is a Country: Race and the Unfinished Struggle for Democracy* (Cambridge, Mass.: Harvard University Press, 2004); Jeanne F. Theoharis and Komozi Woodard, eds., *Freedom North: Black Freedom Struggles Outside the South, 1940–1980* (New York: Palgrave, 2003); and Timothy B. Tyson, *Radio Free Dixie: Robert W. Williams and the Roots of Black Power* (Chapel Hill: University of North Carolina Press, 1999).

4. For "neat typology," see Robin D. G. Kelley, *Freedom Dreams: The Black Radical Imagination* (Boston: Beacon Press, 2002), 60. For a "master narrative" in civil rights movement scholarship, see Brian Ward, "Introduction: Forgotten Wails and Master Narratives: Media, Culture, and Memories of the Modern African American Freedom Struggle," in *Media, Culture, and the Modern African American Freedom Struggle*, ed. Brian Ward (Gainesville: University Press of Florida, 2001), 3.

5. For "the best singer," see Maurice Cullaz, "Une Divine Nina," *Jazz Hot*, May 1969, 7. Quotations from French sources were translated into English by Eren Murat Tasar.

6. Scholarly references to Simone include Reebee Garofalo, "The Impact of the Civil Rights Movement on Popular Music," *Radical America* 21 (1987): 14–22; and Brian Ward, *Just My Soul Responding: Rhythm and Blues, Black Consciousness, and Race Relations* (Berkeley: University of California Press, 1998), 289–93. For the gendered dimensions of jazz, see, especially, Ingrid Monson, "The Problem with White Hipness: Race, Gender, and Cultural Conceptions in Jazz Historical Discourse," *Journal of American Musicological Society* 48 (Fall 1995): 396–422.

7. For discussions of Simone as controversial, see Earl Calwell, "Nina Simone's Lyrics Stir Storm of Protest," *New York Post*, September 2, 1966, 10, Nina Simone Clipping File, Schomburg Center on Black Culture Clipping File, 1925–1974 (hereinafter cited as SCBCCF), Widener Library, Harvard University, Cambridge, Mass.

8. For domestic civil rights in an international perspective, see, for example, Mary L.

Dudziak, *Cold War Civil Rights: Race and the Image of American Democracy* (Princeton, N.J.: Princeton University Press, 2000); and Kevin Gaines, "E. Franklin Frazier's Revenge: Anticolonialism, Nonalignment, and Black Intellectuals' Critiques of Western Culture," *American Literary History* 17 (Fall 2005): 506–29. For gender, culture, and the transnational dimensions of civil rights in relation to each other, see Mary L. Dudziak, "Josephine Baker, Racial Protest, and the Cold War," *Journal of American History* 81 (September 1994): 543–70; Kevin Gaines, "From Center to Margin: Internationalism and the Origins of Black Feminism," in *Materializing Democracy: Toward a Revitalized Cultural Politics*, ed. Russ Castronovo and Dana Nelson (Durham, N.C.: Duke University Press, 2002), 294–313; Ingrid Monson, *Freedom Sounds: Jazz, Civil Rights, and Africa, 1950–1967* (New York: Oxford University Press, forthcoming); and Penny Von Eschen, *Satchmo Blows Up the World: Jazz Ambassadors Play the Cold War* (Cambridge, Mass.: Harvard University Press, 2004). The impact of Paul Gilroy, *The Black Atlantic: Modernity and Double Consciousness* (Cambridge, Mass.: Harvard University Press, 1993), cannot be underestimated.

9. For this village subculture and an interracial left, see, especially, Robin D. G. Kelley, "Nap Time: Historicizing the Afro," *Fashion Theory* 1 (December 1997): 330–51; Simone, *I Put a Spell on You*, 66–72; and Judith Smith, *Visions of Belonging: Ordinary Families, Popular Culture, and Postwar Democracy, 1940–1960* (New York: Columbia University Press, 2004).

10. Simone, *I Put a Spell on You*, 42. Biographical information throughout is based on consistent accounts in memoirs, secondary sources, and sources from the 1960s.

11. This was one of several songs associated with Billie Holiday that Simone recorded. For Holiday's legacy, see especially, Farah Jasmine Griffin, *If You Can't Be Free, Be a Mystery: In Search of Billie Holiday* (New York: Free Press, 2001).

12. Joel Whitburn, *Top R&B Singles, 1942–1995* (Menomonee Falls, Wis.: Record Research Inc., 1996), 402; David Nathan, liner notes, *The Very Best of Nina Simone, 1967–1972: Sugar in My Bowl* (compact disk, RCA 67635, 1998).

13. "The greatest singer," quoted in Garland, *Sound of Soul*, 175; Simone, *I Put a Spell on You*, 67.

14. John S. Wilson, "Newport, the Music," *Down Beat*, August 18, 1960, 18.

15. Joan Crosby, "As the Lyrics Go, So Go the Songs," *Nashville Tennessean*, February 15, 1965, Simone file, SCBCCF; David Nathan, telephone interview with the author, November 2001.

16. "French chanteuse," in Nathan interview; "the shame," in Jean-Pierre Binchet, "Antibes 65: Soirees des 24 et 25 juillet (Nina Simone)," *Jazz Magazine*, September 1965, 22; "burning political discourse," in F. Hofstein, "Nina: Back to Black," *Jazz Magazine*, 1969, 13.

17. Michael Smith, "The Other (More Serious) Side of Nina . . . ," *Melody Maker*, December 7, 1968, 7.

18. This tradition has been ably explored. See especially, Hazel Carby, " 'It Jus Be's Dat Way Sometime': The Sexual Politics of Women's Blues" (1986), in *Unequal Sisters: A Multicultural Reader in U.S. Women's History*, ed. Vicki L. Ruiz and Ellen Carol DuBois

(New York: Routledge, 1994), 330–42. For a more comprehensive discussion of Simone's biographical narrative and her enduring reputation as difficult, see Ruth Feldstein " 'I Don't Trust You Anymore': Nina Simone, African American Activism, and Culture in the 1960s," *Journal of American History* 91 (March 2005): 1349–79.

19. For SNCC, see "SNCC Backers," *New York Amsterdam News*, July 6, 1963, 5; "Sponsors of Carnegie Hall, February 1st [1963] Benefit for SNCC," n.d., *SNCC Papers, 1959–1963* (microfilm; Sanford, N.C.: Microfilming Corporation of America, 1982), Reel 45: B-I-13, #1094. For CORE, see Jesse H. Walker, "Theatricals," *New York Amsterdam News*, July 20, 1963, 15. For the NAACP, see advertisement, "Mammoth Benefit to Fight Segregation and Brutality, New York State Conference of NAACP Presents the Amazing Nina Simone," *New York Amsterdam News*, May 25, 1963, 14. For the YMCA, see "Nina Sings for YMCA on Sunday," *New York Amsterdam News*, February 27, 1965, 16.

20. Simone, *I Put a Spell on You*, 90–91.

21. For Carnegie Hall, see letter from Julia Prettyman to Nina Simone, May 5, 1964, *SNCC Papers*, Reel 45: B-I-12, #1053; letter from Julia Prettyman to Andrew Stroud, June 17, 1964, *SNCC Papers*, Reel 45: B-I-12, #1058. For CORE, see letter from Andrew Stroud to Jim McDonald, April 26, 1965, *The Papers of the Congress on Racial Equality—Addendum, 1944–1968* (hereinafter *Core-ADD*) (microfilm; Sanford, N.C.: Microfilming Corporation of America, 1982), Reel 12: E-II-44, #0892; letter from Alan Gartner to Andrew Stroud, *Core-ADD*, Reel 12: E-II-44, #0892; and telegram from Jesse Smallwood to Allen Gardner [*sic*], *Core-ADD*, Reel 12: E-II-44, #0895. For $2,000, see "Fund Raising Department Report," October 1965, *Core-ADD*, Reel 8: B-I-13, #0735; and Simone, *I Put a Spell on You*, 108.

22. *New York Amsterdam News*, August 10, 1963, 42; "Fund Raisers for Freedom: Celebrities Rally to Civil Rights Call by Helping to Raise Thousands in Cash," *Ebony* 18 (October 1963): 120–26; $9,000 estimate in Ward, *Just My Soul Responding*, 302; Simone, *I Put a Spell on You*, 101–3; Bob Hunter, "Singer Gloria Lynne in Her Glory," *Chicago Defender*, February 16–22, 1963, 22.

23. Ward, *Just My Soul Responding*, 289–93; for the willingness of deejays to boycott controversial songs, see *Variety*, October 3, 1965, 63; for the efforts SNCC organizers made, see, for example, "Sponsors of Carnegie Hall, February 1st [1963] Benefit for SNCC"; letter from Charles McDew to Mr. Max Roach and Miss Abby Lincoln [*sic*], December 22, 1962, *SNCC Papers, 1959–1972*, Reel 27: #40–0816.

24. Simone, *I Put a Spell on You*, 67.

25. Abbey Lincoln, *Straight Ahead*, performed by Abbey Lincoln (compact disk; Candid, 1989 [1961]); Ira Gitler, "Review: Abbey Lincoln, *Straight Ahead*," *Down Beat*, November 9, 1961, 35–36. See also Gitler et al., "Racial Prejudice in Jazz, Part I," *Down Beat*, March 20, 1962, 20–26, and "Racial Prejudice in Jazz, Part II," *Down Beat*, March 29, 1962, 22–25; and Ingrid Monson, "Abbey Lincoln's *Straight Ahead*: Jazz in the Era of the Civil Rights Movement," in *Between Resistance and Revolution: Cultural Politics and Social Protest*, ed. Richard G. Fox and Orin Starn (New Brunswick, N.J.: Rutgers University Press, 1997), 171–94.

26. Letter from Julia Prettyman to Nina Simone, May 5, 1964, *SNCC Papers*, Reel 45:

B-I-12, #1053. For another example of such courtship and flattery, see letter from Charles McDew to Mr. Max Roach and Miss Abby Lincoln [*sic*], December 22, 1962, *SNCC Papers*, Reel 27: #40-0816.

27. Bill McLarney, "Caught in the Act," *Down Beat*, January 23, 1969, 34. For the reluctance of other musicians to bring politics into their music, see Ward, *Just My Soul Responding*. For a rich intellectual and cultural history of African American jazz musicians, see Eric Porter, *What Is This Thing Called Jazz?: African American Musicians as Artists, Critics, and Activists* (Berkeley: University of California Press, 2002).

28. Kurt Weill and Bertolt Brecht, "Pirate Jenny," performed by Nina Simone, *In Concert—I Put a Spell on You*; Michael Denning, *The Cultural Front: The Laboring of American Culture in the Twentieth Century* (New York: Verso, 1996), 324.

29. Nat Shapiro, liner notes, *In Concert: I Put a Spell on You*.

30. Alex Comfort and Nina Simone, "Go Limp," performed by Nina Simone, *In Concert—I Put a Spell on You*. On folk songs, see, for example, Robert Cantwell, *When We Were Good: The Folk Revival* (Cambridge, Mass.: Harvard University Press, 1996).

31. For gender and the politics of respectability, see Evelyn Brooks Higginbotham, *Righteous Discontent: The Women's Movement in the Black Baptist Church, 1880–1920* (Cambridge, Mass.: Harvard University Press, 1993). For respectability and the civil rights movement, see William Chafe, *Civilities and Civil Rights: Greensboro, North Carolina, and the Black Struggle for Freedom* (New York: Oxford University Press, 1980).

32. For the diverse arenas in which black cultural nationalism and calls for black power took shape, see, for example, Scott Brown, *Fighting for Us: Maulana Karenga, the US Organization, and Black Cultural Nationalism* (New York: New York University Press, 2003); Nikhil Pal Singh, "The Black Panthers and the 'Undeveloped Country' of the Left," in *The Black Panther Party Reconsidered*, ed. Charles Jones (Baltimore, Md.: Black Classic Press, 1998), 57–108; James Smethurst, *The Black Arts Movement: Literary Nationalism in the 1960s and 1970s* (Chapel Hill: University of North Carolina Press, 2005); Tyson, *Radio Free Dixie*; and, for primary sources, see Leroi Jones and Larry Neal, eds., *Black Fire: An Anthology of Afro-American Writing* (1966; New York: William and Morrow, 1968), 303.

33. Henry Hampton and Steve Fayer, *Voices of Freedom: An Oral History of the Civil Rights Movement from the 1950s through the 1980s* (New York: Bantam, 1990), 276, 291; Robert Weisbrot, *Freedom Bound: A History of America's Civil Rights Movement* (New York: Penguin, 1999), 195.

34. A short sampling of memoirs, poetry, and scholarship includes Elaine Brown, *A Taste of Power: A Black Woman's Story* (New York: Pantheon, 1992); Nikki Giovanni, *The Selected Poems of Nikki Giovanni* (New York: William and Morrow, 1995); and Cheryl Clarke, *After Mecca: Women Poets and the Black Arts Movement* (New Brunswick, N.J.: Rutgers University Press, 2005).

35. For how masculinity constituted expressions of black power and black cultural nationalism, see, for example, Kelley, *Freedom Dreams*.

36. "Nina Simone: Angry Woman of Jazz," *Sepia* 16 (March 1967): 60.

37. Lee Dembart, "Nina Simone: Soul on Voice," *New York Post*, March 15, 1969,

Simone file, SCBCCF; Eldridge Cleaver, *Soul on Ice* (New York: Dell Publishing, 1968); "Nina Simone: Angry Woman of Jazz," 61–2l; for Simone and censorship, see Cordell Thompson, " 'Young, Gifted and Black' Tune May Have Nixed Nina's TV Showing," *Jet*, May 14, 1970, 60–61.

38. Simone, *I Put a Spell on You*, 87, 98. For an early expression of black male sexual aggression as related to liberatory black politics, see Leroi Jones, "Dutchman" (1964), in *The Leroi Jones/Amiri Baraka Reader*, ed. William J. Harris (New York: Thunder's Mouth Press, 1991), 76–99.

39. Clearly, "Go Limp" could be interpreted in various ways, at the time and subsequently. I am not suggesting that there is or was one singular meaning or message in the song; rather, the multiplicity of meanings is itself significant.

40. Simone, *I Put a Spell on You*, 89–90.

41. Baraka, "Black Art," (1969), in *Leroi Jones/Amiri Baraka Reader*, ed. Harris, 219.

42. For black feminism and black power, see also Gaines, "From Center to Margin."

43. Mary Helen Washington, "Alice Childress, Lorraine Hansberry, and Claudia Jones: Black Women Write the Popular Front," in *Left of the Color Line: Race, Radicalism, and Twentieth-Century Literature of the United States*, ed. Bill V. Mullen and James Smethurst (Chapel Hill: University of North Carolina Press, 2003), 185; for women in SNCC and the Third World Women's Alliance, see Frances Beale, "Double Jeopardy: To Be Black and Female" (1970), in *The Black Woman: An Anthology*, ed. Toni Cade (New York: New American Library, 1970), 95–98; Third World Women's Alliance, "Statement" (1968), reprinted in *Dear Sisters: Dispatches from the Women's Liberation Movement*, ed. Rosalyn Baxandall and Linda Gordon (New York: Basic Books, 2000), 65.

44. "33 Americans Going to Negro Art Fete," *New York Times*, December 3, 1961, AMSAC file, SCBCCF; Morris Kaplan, "U.S. Negro Artists Go to Africa to Join in Cultural Exchange," *New York Times*, December 14, 1961, AMSAC file, SCBCCF. A growing body of scholarship on Africa and African Americans includes Thomas Borstelmann, *The Cold War and the Color Line: American Race Relations in a Global Arena* (Cambridge, Mass.: Harvard University Press, 2001); James Meriwether, *Proudly We Can Be Africans: Black Americans and Africa, 1935–1961* (Chapel Hill: University of North Carolina Press, 2002); and Francis Njubi Nesbitt, *Race for Sanctions: African Americans against Apartheid, 1946–1994* (Bloomington: Indiana University Press, 2004). For a longer tradition of African American internationalism on the left, see Penny Von Eschen, *Race against Empire: Black Americans and Anticolonialism, 1937–1957* (Ithaca, N.Y.: Cornell University Press, 1997).

45. Simone, *I Put a Spell on You*, 80–81.

46. See advertisement for "Mammoth Benefit to Fight Segregation and Brutality"; "The Rareness of Nina Simone," *Metronome*, June 1960, 30.

47. Raymond Robinson, "Nina Simone Thrills, Oscar Brown Chills," *New York Amsterdam News*, December 3, 1966, 10.

48. "Why Am I," in Maurice Cullaz, "Antibes," *Jazz Hot*, September 1965, 41.

49. For Josephine Baker, see, for example, Sieglinde Lemke, *Primitivist Modernism: Black Culture and the Origins of Transatlantic Modernism* (New York: Oxford University Press, 1998); for Holiday, see Griffin, *If You Can't Be Free*, 99–103. For "looking almost

tribal," see Alan Walsh and Jack Hutton, "Antibes Jazz Festival Report: Miller, Peterson, and Nina on Form," *Melody Maker*, August 2, 1969, 6.

50. For " 'Mississippi is," see Maurice Cullaz and Michel Dellorme, "Nina Simone: Affirmer orgueilleusement ma race," *Jazz Hot*, September 1965, 28; for " 'Strange Fruit,' " see Jacques Creuzevault, "Antibes," *Jazz Hot*, September 1965, 16–27, esp. 18; for "a perfect world," see Binchet, "Antibes 65," 22; for "general public, see Cullaz, "Une Divine Nina"; for "darling" see Nathan interview.

51. Nathan interview; David Nathan, *Soulful Divas: Personal Portraits of Over a Dozen Divas from Nina Simone, Aretha Franklin, and Diana Ross to Patti Labelle, Whitney Houston, and Janet Jackson* (New York: Billboard Books, 1999), 53.

52. Cullaz and Dellorme, "Nina Simone," 7.

53. See, for example, "Americans in Europe, a Discussion," *Down Beat*, July 2, 1964, 64–73.

54. Smith, "Other (More Serious) Side of Nina," 7.

55. Griffin, *If You Can't Be Free*, 106; for "all the black people," see Nathan interview; for "the Negro revolution," see Smith, "Other (More Serious) Side of Nina," 7; for "Revolution" and the "racial problem" see Royston Eldridge, "Nina's the Medium for the Message," *Melody Maker*, April 19, 1969, 5.

56. Miriam Makeba with James Hall, *Makeba: My Story* (New York: New American Library, 1987); Gaines, "From Center to Margin," 305; Becky Thompson, "Multiracial Feminism: Recasting the Chronology of Second-Wave Feminism," *Feminist Studies* 28 (Summer 2002): 337–55.

57. Kelley, "Nap Time," 344.

58. For others, and for the role of the fashion industry in this process, see Kelley, "Nap Time."

59. For a scholarly emphasis on the late 1960s and 1970s, see, for example, William Van Deburg, *New Day in Babylon: The Black Power Movement and American Culture, 1965–1975* (Chicago: University of Chicago Press, 1992), esp. 192–204.

60. See "Combahee River Collective, A Black Feminist Statement"(1977), reprinted in *The Black Feminist Reader*, ed. Joy James (Malden, Mass.: Blackwell, 2000), 261–70.

61. For a now-classic analysis of feminism developing out of and after a commitment to civil rights, see Sara Evans, *Personal Politics: The Roots of Women's Liberation in the Civil Rights Movement and the New Left* (New York: Knopf, 1979).

62. Simone, *I Put a Spell on You*, 86–87.

63. Nina Simone, "To Be Young, Gifted, and Black" (1968), *Platinum Series Nina Simone* (D3 Entertainment, 2000); Nathan, liner notes, *Very Best of Nina Simone*; Simone, *I Put a Spell on You*, 86–87.

64. Gaines, "From Center to Margin," 20.

65. See, for example, the brochure "Freedom Gifts: Posters, Books, Holiday Seals, Calendar," n.d., SNCC Papers, 1959–1972, Reel 27, #39: 0748–50; letter from Dinky Romilly to Irwin Silver, February 25, 1964, SNCC Papers, 1959–1972, Reel 27, #34: -0122; Guy and Candie Carawan, eds., *Sing for Freedom: The Story of the Civil Rights Movement Through Its Songs* (Bethlehem, Pa.: Sing Out Corp., 1990).

66. Carawan and Carawan, *Sing for Freedom*, 12.

67. Ibid., 4, 5, 12.

68. See Benjamin Filene, *Romancing the Folk: Public Memory and American Roots Music* (Chapel Hill: University of North Carolina Press, 2000), 3.

69. For freedom songs in contrast to "entertainment," see R. Serge Denisoff, "Protest Songs: Those on the Top Forty and Those of the Streets," *American Quarterly* 22 (Winter 1970): 807–23.

70. Nathan, *Soulful Divas*, 60–63; "Nina Simone Ends Voluntary Exile from U.S.," *Jet*, April 22, 1985, 54–55.

71. See, for example, Ann Powers, "Jazz Festival Reviews: A Diva Who Holds Fans in the Palm of Her Hand," *New York Times*, July 2, 2001, E5; Somini Sengupta, "The Voice of Misfit Girls Like Me," *New York Times*, June 24, 2001, II-28; John Fordham, "Nina Simone: Soul-Jazz Diva Whose Music Spoke of Love, Respect, and Their Opposites—Particularly in Relation to Race," *Guardian Leader*, April 22, 2003, 23; Richard Harrington, "Nina Simone, a Voice to Be Reckoned With," *Washington Post*, April 22, 2003, C1; "condolences" from Susan Bell, "Friends and Family Pay Their Tributes to Jazz Legend's Political Courage at Packed Funeral," *The Scotsman*, April 26, 2003, 17. For exceptions, see, for example, Craig Seymour, "An Appreciation: Nina Simone's Voice Fused Art, Politics," *Atlanta Journal and Constitution*, April 23, 2003, 1E.

72. "Singers: More Than an Entertainer," *Time*, February 21, 1969, Simone file, SCBCCF.

PART V

End Times

Redefining Americanness by Reformulating Hinduism
Indian Americans Challenge American Academia

PREMA KURIEN

Contemporary immigrants are likely to bring about dramatic shifts in American culture and identity. While their very presence calls into question traditional conceptions of Americanness as white, Christian, and Anglocentric,[1] many immigrant groups are also challenging these conceptions directly by confronting American institutions, practices, and norms that they consider to be hostile to their cultures. This chapter looks at one such example: Indian Americans who have been mobilizing on the basis of a pan-Hindu, or an "Indic," identity to protest the Eurocentric bias of many American institutions. Such groups have focused their attention on a variety of targets, such as the misrepresentations or the negative portrayals of Hinduism and of India within the American media and the wider society, the commercialization and the misuse of Hindu deities, icons, and texts by the music, entertainment, and advertising industries, and the lack of attention to Hinduism and Hindu American issues by the American administration.[2]

However, in this essay, I focus specifically on what has become an increasingly important and emotional issue for Hindu American groups: the portrayal of Hindu and Indian culture within American academia. Hindu American spokespersons charge that the Eurocentrism of the academy and of the scholars (including those of Indian origin) specializing in Hindu and Indian studies has resulted in a deeply biased and negative academic representation of Hinduism and India. This mobilization against the academy also includes questioning fundamental notions regarding Western culture and civilization that often tend to be at the heart of beliefs about American national identity. These challenges are mounted by arguing that many of these ideas about Western cultural and scientific superiority are Eurocentric, colonial, or neocolonial fabrications that have no basis in historical reality, and that they are maintained to deny the contributions of non-Western groups like Indians. The leaders of this movement emphasize revisionist versions of Hinduism, Indian history, and world civilization as a corrective to the dominant Eurocentric perspective. In the process, Hindu American leaders are redefining both the United States and India.

This Hindu American critique is particularly hard-hitting since the academy imagines itself to be the bastion of multiculturalism in society. Hindu American leaders, however, argue that while multicultural education now positively includes several non-European groups, India and Hinduism continue to be marginalized. Such Hindu American leaders position their denunciation of the academy within a dynamic, multicultural model of national identity, arguing that the United States needs to redefine itself to take account of the large and growing group of non-European, non-Christian citizens who now comprise part of the nation. This conception of nationhood is very different from that of scholars like Samuel P. Huntington, who view the essence of American identity as being defined by its Protestant, Anglocentric origins.[3] Although Hindu American groups advocate a multicultural model of nationhood for the United States, their challenge to Eurocentrism is grounded in a valorized, unicultural model of Indianness that is in many respects the mirror image of what they seek to critique, since they disseminate interpretations of Hinduism and of Indian history that glorify "Indic" traditions as the original source for much of world civilization. By falling into the mirror-image trap, they end up, I argue, undermining many of their own arguments for the importance of pluralism.

In the next section I present the theoretical framework for the essay, where I argue that conventional paradigms of immigrant incorporation have overlooked immigrant agency, and I make the case that we need a new model to understand the transformative effects that post-1965 immigrants have been having on the United States. I then turn to providing some background on Hindu Indians and Hindu Indian American organizations. The second part of the essay focuses on the issues within the academy that have been of particular concern to Hindu Americans. Hindu American leaders have mounted four major critiques against the academy. First and most broadly, Hindu American leaders charge that American academia is dominated by a Eurocentric perspective that views Western culture as being the font of world civilization and refuses to acknowledge the contributions of non-Western societies such as India to European culture and technology. Second, they maintain that the academic study of religion in the United States has been based on the model of the "Abrahamic" (Judaism, Christianity, and Islam) traditions and that this model is not applicable to religions such as Hinduism. Related to this critique of Abrahamic religions is the condemnation of the ways in which Hinduism has been studied and presented by American scholars. Hindu Americans leaders maintain that unlike the academic study of Abrahamic religions, Western scholars of Hinduism like to focus on the sensationalist, negative attributes of the religion and present it in a demeaning way that shows an utter lack of respect for the sentiments of the practitioners of the religion. Finally, Hindu

American leaders denounce South Asian studies programs in the United States for creating a false identity and unity between India and the other Muslim countries in the South Asian region, like Pakistan and Bangladesh, and for undermining India by focusing on its internal cleavages and problems. In each of these four areas, Hindu American leaders are working to introduce and popularize a Hindu (or Indic) perspective as a corrective to the biases they perceive as being entrenched in the academy. For a variety of reasons, the events of September 11, 2001, provided an added impetus to these critiques, and thus we will also look at how the arguments and strategies of the Hindu American groups were impacted by 9/11. In conclusion, I turn to an examination of the lessons Hindu American activism has for the academy, for American society, and more broadly, for understanding immigrant activism and its impact on host and home countries.

A characteristic of most of the studies of post-1965 immigration has been a focus on the reception and the integration of immigrants.[4] This orientation has a long tradition in American sociology and is a legacy of the assimilationist lens through which early American sociologists examined the impact of the large-scale European immigration on the United States. This assimilationist approach in turn was a product of a static model of identity that viewed national culture as given or already accomplished, usually at origin. In other words, according to this view, the cultural essence of a nation is defined at its birth and then needs to be maintained and safeguarded throughout its history. While immigrants' adaptation to the host society and their incorporation within it are undoubtedly important issues, the almost exclusive adoption of the assimilationist paradigm has meant that immigrant agency, particularly the ways in which immigrants have been able to have an impact on the United States, has been overlooked.[5]

However, contemporary international migration takes place under very different circumstances than the earlier European immigration, "ones that are likely to affect the capacity of immigrants and ethnics to reshape American institutions."[6] First, the fact that immigrants today hail from well-defined nation-states, and usually arrive in search of better economic opportunities, means that assimilation or "becoming American" is often not the goal of the migrants. New transportation and communication technologies facilitate the maintenance of ethnicity by permitting immigrants to return to their home countries frequently and to stay in close contact with friends and relatives. The Internet and satellite television enhance the ability of immigrants to learn about events taking place in their homelands and to research their identity, culture, and religion. Finally, norms of multiculturalism that are in place today often work to encourage the maintenance and cultivation of ethnicity.

These norms of multiculturalism, unlike those of assimilation, are based on a dynamic model of identity that views national culture as constantly in the making, shaped by significant national and international events and, most important, by the backgrounds and actions of the people who make up the nation. Consequently, multiculturalism views immigrants to the country as agents who can and should recraft national identity. This paradigm therefore provides immigrant groups with the means to seek and receive national membership as valued contributors to the pluralist fabric. At the same time, it also provides the rationale for such groups to demand an end to demeaning portrayals and a lack of positive acknowledgment by arguing that such treatment is discriminatory and harmful.

According to the 2000 census, Asian Indians in the United States numbered close to 1.7 million. By 2005, the community had increased to 2.3 million, making it the fastest-growing group in the country.[7] Most adults of Indian origin in the United States today are immigrants who arrived after the passage of the 1965 Immigration and Naturalization Act. Although relatively small in terms of numbers, Indian Americans often wield a disproportionate influence since they are among the wealthiest and most educated foreign-born groups in the country.[8] In the past decade, Indians have become prominent in the field of information technology and are now important players within the American computer industry. There are no official figures on the religious distribution of Indians in the United States. According to census figures, Hindus constitute more than 80 percent of the population in India.[9] However, it is likely that they constitute a much smaller proportion of Indian Americans since Indian religious minorities, particularly Sikhs and Christians, are present in much larger numbers in the United States. Estimates of the proportion of Indian Americans from a Hindu background range from 45 to 76 percent.[10]

Hindu American depictions of the academy as a neocolonizing force draw on ideas first articulated as part of the Hindutva movement, so I turn to a brief background to this movement. While the term "Hindutva" literally means "Hinduness," it has now come to stand for the Hindu nationalist movement. Hindu nationalism emerged in India in the early twentieth century as a reaction to Western colonialism, and it resurged again in the late 1980s around the issue of the building of a Ram temple in Ayodhya, in northern India, on a site occupied by a sixteenth-century mosque. Besides specific issues such as the Ram temple, the Hindutva platform is characterized by a worldview that embraces several distinct but interrelated issues, outlined below.[11] First, the Vedic period—when the central Hindu texts, the Vedas, were composed in northwestern India by the Aryan people—is viewed as representing the essence of Indian culture. This period, conventionally dated between 1500 and 1000 BCE, is believed to have been several thousand years more ancient than conventional historical accounts have acknowledged (Hindutva supporters date it at least as early as 3000 BCE), making it the oldest culture known to mankind. Vedic India is characterized as being a highly sophisticated civilization with knowledge of advanced mathematical and scientific concepts and a highly developed understanding of the human mind and consciousness. *Hindutva-vadis* (supporters of Hindutva) also argue that India was the original homeland of the Aryans, the group from which Europeans are believed to have descended. For these reasons, Vedic India is described as being the "Cradle of Civilization."[12] Hindutva proponents view Indian culture and civilization as Hindu, whose true nature and glory were sullied by the invasions of Muslims and the British and by the postcolonial domination of "pseudo-secular" Indians. According to the Hindu nationalist perspective, these historical wrongs can only be righted by a state that is openly and unashamedly Hindu.

Not surprisingly, a central concern of the Hindutva movement has been the reexamining and revising of Indian history from a Hinducentric perspective. The concept of "indigenousness" is central to this revisionist history, with "Hindus" being defined as those whose religions are indigenous to India. Thus, this definition includes groups like the Buddhists, Jains, and Sikhs but excludes Indian Muslims and Christians, who are often described as "foreigners," despite the fact that both groups are composed almost entirely of indigenous members and both Islam and Christianity have existed in India for well over 1,200 years. The Hindutva movement is characterized by a marked hostility toward these two groups, who (particularly Muslims) have been the target of mobilization and violence in India on several occasions in the contemporary period. Hindu nationalist organizations also stress the greatness of Hinduism and Hindu culture, the importance of Hindu unity, and the need to defend Hinduism and Hindus against discrimination and defamation.

Several scholars have argued that the "Hinduism under siege" Hindutva message, with its emphasis on the need for Hindu pride and assertiveness, is particularly attractive to Hindus in the United States, who become members of a racial, religious, and cultural minority upon immigration and have to deal with the largely negative perceptions of Hinduism in the wider society. Coalescing to defend a beleaguered Hindu identity has become an important way for Indians from a Hindu background to counter their relative invisibility within American society and to obtain recognition and resources as American ethnics.[13] The campaign against the biased presentation of Hinduism and of India in school and college textbooks and within the academy more broadly has been an important part of this strategy.[14]

As children grow up in the United States, immigrant parents find to their dismay that many of them absorb the negative messages about Hinduism and India from the wider society and turn away from their culture and traditions. Indian American Internet groups feature frequent discussions about insensitive, ignorant, Eurocentric teachers and classmates and the pain they cause Indian American students. A letter from a fourteen-year-old Indian American schoolgirl from Houston, Texas, that appeared in many Indian American newspapers, websites, and Internet groups, poignantly describes the way that "every day, young *desi* [Indian] children and teenagers are unreasonably tormented [in American schools] because of our perceived background." The writer continues, "The school textbooks are half the cause. The average American doesn't know squat about India, and with the help of poorly researched textbooks, they learn nonsense."[15] Since second-generation Indian Americans have been entering American high schools and colleges in large numbers over the past few years, it is not surprising that the surveillance and shaping of the presentation of Hinduism and of Indian history in American school textbooks and within academia have become such central and emotional issues for some sectors of the Hindu American community. Scholars who are viewed as being critical of any aspect of Hinduism or India, or of Hindutva conceptions of history, have come under attack. It is important to point out here that these attacks have not just been directed against Euro-American scholars. In fact, the leaders of the movement, such as Rajiv Malhotra, founder-president of the Infinity Foundation, make clear that the "insider-outsider" distinction that they make is not based on skin color or ethnicity but on "practice": in other words, between individuals whom they define as Hindu practitioners and those (including scholars from Hindu backgrounds) whom they define as non-Hindus or "pseudo" Hindus.[16] Thus some of the harshest criticisms of the movement have been leveled at Indian American scholars who have been characterized as being stooges of the Western academy.

While not all of the Indian American leaders who are at the forefront of the mobilization against the American academy can be described as being Hindutva-vadis (for instance, Rajiv Malhotra explicitly criticizes and distances himself from the movement), as we will see, most share some of the central assumptions of the movement, and thus, the Hindutva mobilization and the campaign to have Hinduism and India positively represented in the academy are closely linked. Leaders like Rajiv Malhotra are harnessing the passions roused by the Hindutva mobilization to obtain support for their cause, and their presentation of the disrespectful treatment accorded to Hinduism by teachers in schools and colleges further feeds into the grievances of those already galvanized by the Hindutva movement. Hindu American leaders like Rajiv Malhotra also draw on the ideas of Swami Vivekananda, a Western-educated Indian *sannyasin* (Hindu ascetic).

Swami Vivekananda was one of the foremost exponents of the neo-Hinduism, or the intellectual, syncretic, reformist Hinduism, that developed in India in the late colonial period and uplifted the morale of Hindus, paving the way for the subsequent nationalist movement. In the United States Swami Vivekananda is best known for his powerful oratory at the World Parliament of Religions, held in Chicago in 1893. Since he developed his ideas through an engagement with the West, it is not surprising that many of them have become pivotal to the contemporary Hindu mobilization of Indian Americans.

Many Hindu groups that are interested in challenging the academic portrayal of their religion and culture are increasingly identifying and mobilizing under an "Indic" identity. The term "Indic" refers to religious groups, cultures, and traditions that are "indigenous" to India—and thus theoretically includes groups such as Jains, Buddhists, and Sikhs, but in practice usually refers to Hindus. The term was originally used in linguistics and Indology to refer to the linguistic group from which Sanskrit and several other Indian languages originated, as well as to early Indian texts, but recently "Indic" has been reappropriated and redefined by Hindus in the United States and United Kingdom as an academic term to denote the philosophy, science, culture, and spirituality of Vedic India. Even more broadly, it is employed to signify a cultural—some would even argue a civilizational—identity with "deep roots" in India.[17] The first major Indic studies organization to be established in the United States was the Dharam Hinduja Indic Research Center (DHIRC) at Columbia University, formed in 1995 along with a similar institute at Cambridge University in England. The DHIRC came under a great deal of criticism from those charging that the term "Indic" was manufactured to disguise a Hindutva agenda under the garb of academic respectability.[18] These attacks and disagreements between DHIRC faculty and the Hinduja Foundation led to the center finally closing down in 2000 (the Cambridge University center closed in 2004). The next Indic studies organization established in the United States was the Educational Council of Indic Traditions (ECIT), which was founded in 2000 under the auspices of the Infinity Foundation. The Infinity Foundation has since come to be the most prominent and active Indic studies organization in the United States. Several other Indic organizations followed, such as the Center for Indic Studies at the University of Massachusetts at Dartmouth, the Foundation for Indic Philosophy and Culture at the Claremont Colleges in California, and the Indic Culture and Traditions Seminars in Houston, all of which focused on the study and promotion of "Indic traditions," primarily the religious, philosophical, and scientific traditions of ancient India.

The Infinity Foundation was founded in Princeton, New Jersey, in 1994 by wealthy Indian American entrepreneur Rajiv Malhotra, who, after a career in the software, computer, and telecom industries, had taken an early retirement to pursue philanthropic and educational activities. In 2000 Malhotra founded ECIT, and since then, Indic studies has become the central focus of the organization.[19] Except for the year 2000–2001, when a religious studies Ph.D. from Columbia University, David Gray, was appointed as the executive director of the ECIT, the foundation has functioned without any full-time workers, with the exception of Rajiv Malhotra himself. All of the members of the volunteer advisory board are described as being "Indian American entrepreneurs."[20] Most work in the software industry, and none are academics. When the ECIT was founded, its mission was described in the following way: "This Council . . . will be involved in the process of conducting independent research to (a) document the contributions by India to world civilization and to (b) ascertain the degree to which the Indic traditions and their contributions are accurately and adequately portrayed in contemporary American society. Preliminary findings indicate that Indic traditions, which include Hinduism, Buddhism, Sikhism and Jainism, have been and continue to be misrepresented, stereotyped, or pigeon-holed both in academic institutions and by the mass media."[21]

The mission statement made clear that the term "Indic" excluded religions that were "imported" into India, such as Islam and Christianity, and in practice the focus of the foundation has been largely on Hindu traditions and culture. Although not an academic himself, Rajiv Malhotra has been an influential figure within Indic studies in the United States. He was a prominent speaker at an international conference held at the Center for Indic Studies at the University of Massachusetts at Dartmouth in July 2002, and he is a board member of the Foundation for Indic Philosophy and Culture at the Claremont Colleges in California. Since 2000, Malhotra has succeeded in building up a large constituency of support from sections of the Hindu American community, primarily through his writings on Hindu and Indian American Internet discussion groups and e-zines like Sulekha.com, Rediff.com and Outlookindia.com.

Many of the Hindu activists in the United States are computer scientists, and like them, Rajiv Malhotra approaches his critique of American academia with a firm belief in the superiority of the natural sciences and a contempt for the humanities, its methods, and its scholars (who are frequently described as being individuals who turned to the humanities when they could not get into a science field).[22] He also uses his background in the business sector (a background which is also common to many Hindu American activists) to argue for the need for a "business model of religion," specifically that Hinduism needs to adopt the model of other religions, like Christianity, which are run like businesses. Thus, he argues that Hinduism should assess its market position and strategic direction, while engaging in better advertising and brand management practices to sell its assets, maintain and increase market share, and deal with competitors.[23]

Through his indefatigable effort and dedication, shrewd use of resources, and the mobilization of Hindu American supporters, Malhotra has able to become an influential although often controversial voice within the academy (in the United States, and also in the United Kingdom and India) in a very short period of time. The Infinity Foundation has provided small grants to many of the major universities in the country to support a variety of programs, such as a visiting professorship in Indic studies (Harvard University), yoga and Hindi classes (Rutgers University), the research and teaching of nondualist philosophies (University of Hawaii), a Global Renaissance Institute and a Center for Buddhist Studies (Columbia University), a program in religion and science (University of California, Santa Barbara), an endowment for the Center for Advanced Study of India (University of Pennsylvania), and lectures at the Center for Consciousness Studies (at the University of Arizona). The foundation also provided some funding to the Association for Asian Studies for a special journal issue of *Education about Asia*, on the topic of "Teaching Indic Traditions." Besides this, the foundation is also sponsoring several book projects on ancient Indian contributions to science, mathematics, technology, psychology, and music, a multivolume *Encyclopedia of Indian Philosophy*, research projects on topics such as the U.S. media bias in reporting on India, American attitudes toward Indic traditions, and Indian women, as well as several seminars and conferences in India and the United States on Vedanta, yoga, India's contributions to the world, and India's traditional knowledge systems.[24]

We will now examine the four major critiques against the American academy mounted by Hindu American leaders. The first criticism has to do with the domination of Eurocentric perspectives within academia. Rajiv Malhotra has been at the forefront at the Hindu American movement to challenge the Eurocentrism of the academy. In an article coauthored with David Gray, then the executive director of the Infinity Foundation, Malhotra writes that traditional accounts of the development of Western thought tend to emphasize its continuity. Modern philosophy and science, we are told, go back in an unbroken lineage to the ancient Greeks. This narrative, like all myths, is remarkably resilient. It also has what we might call a dark subtext; as a product of cultural chauvinism, it has served to downplay or gloss over the very real contributions of non-European civilizations to European thought and technology. The authors go on to argue that many of the foundational concepts of Western mathematics, such as the "Arabic" numerals and the decimal system, were borrowed from India by Arabs and then picked up by Greeks and Romans. They also point out that many leading Western intellectuals—thinkers such as Ralph

Waldo Emerson and Henry David Thoreau, philosophers like Arthur Schopenhauer, psychologists Carl Jung and Ken Wilber, poets like Goethe, Walt Whitman, W. B. Yeats, and T. S. Eliot, and physicists like Erwin Schrödinger—were all influenced by Indian writing and literature, but that these Indic contributions to Western thought have been obscured by the Eurocentrism of the academy.[25]

In July 2002 Rajiv Malhotra and Robert Thurman, a professor in the Religious Studies Department at Columbia University who specializes in the study of Tibetan Buddhism, organized a colloquium on "Completing the Global Renaissance: The Indic Contributions," which brought together prominent scholars of Hinduism and Buddhism. This conference was a follow-up to a Global Renaissance Institute that they had established at Columbia University in 2000. In the mission statement for the conference, Malhotra and Thurman argue that the Renaissance was European and incomplete since it was based primarily on knowledge from the physical, or "outer," sciences, where the contributions of non-Western sources have been denied. Insisting that knowledge based on the "spiritual or inner sciences" (philosophy, psychology, epistemology, linguistics) is equally important, they go on to write, "We believe that the mother lode of these inner sciences is to be found within the matrix of Indian civilization, loosely associated with the numerous Hindu, Buddhist, and Jain subcultures that thrived throughout that most populous and wealthy subcontinental part of Eurasia for thousands of years, until foreign conquerors impoverished it almost beyond recognition."[26] Thus, they contend that what the world needs is a "second renaissance," this time a "more holistic and truly global" one, which can be achieved by incorporating the "Indic traditions," both those of the outer and the inner sciences.[27]

Rajiv Malhotra has frequently criticized Indian American scholars writing in the postcolonial and subaltern traditions as being "neocolonized." He writes, "None of these movements ever tried to use the native categories, so even their criticism of Eurocentrism was in Eurocentric frames of reference. These scholars were so neocolonized that even their criticisms of colonialism [were] sanctioned and approved by colonial sponsors and [these scholars] had no knowledge or grounding in the native cultures that they claimed to speak for."[28] Central to this argument about neocolonized scholars is Rajiv Malhotra's "U-turn" theory, which he discusses repeatedly in his writings and which has been picked up by many of his supporters. According to Malhotra, the West has repeatedly appropriated and then denied Indic contributions and has been able to mobilize Indian American "*sepoys*" (Indian police who served the British in colonial India) and *becharis* (whom he describes as "women who overdo the 'I have been abused' roles . . . in exchange for a benefit") to focus on the negative aspects of the tradition.[29]

Malhotra also argues that for a variety of reasons, most of the scholarship on Indic traditions has to date been conducted by "outsiders" and that "no other major world religion has such a low percentage of insiders as does Hinduism, in its academic study today."[30] He is a fierce critic of anthropologists and their methods, arguing that they set themselves up as the authority to interpret non-Western cultures and traditions and do not allow the "natives" to challenge them or to talk back. The domination of Indic studies by Westerners, he maintains, has led to Western academic and media biases against the tradition, and the many contributions the tradition can and should make in the areas of psychology, linguistics, postmodernism, political and social theory, eco-vegetarianism, feminism, religious studies, and philosophy have been neglected or overlooked. He therefore calls for a "Satyagraha [Gandhi's term for nonviolent protest or agitation] against the establishment, a review of the ethics of the academic treatment of India's civilization," and the need to have more "insider" or practitioner, scholars.[31] All this is necessary, he argues, to revise history to focus on India's achievements and the "true historical causes of India's problems" today, to reveal India's role in world history, and to learn from Indic traditions.[32] He feels that such revisionism is important to promote multiculturalism in the United States, to prepare American children for globalization, and to address the needs of Indian Americans.[33]

Not surprisingly, Malhotra's academic targets, both those of Indian and non-Indian ancestry, have strongly denied his charges. While many of these scholars concede that he raises some valid issues, they argue that most of his critique against the academy is based on a lack of understanding of humanities and social science scholarship. According to them, the aim of such disciplines is not to create a brand name or to market the traditions that they study; rather, it is to analyze and understand these traditions using established canons of inquiry and of verifiability. Again, they point out that the lack of Hindus in religious studies is primarily because Indian parents prefer that their children enter into more lucrative careers.

The resurgence of the Hindutva movement has provided further ammunition for Hindus to attack Eurocentrism. As I have mentioned, one of the important tenets of the Hindutva movement is that civilization developed on the banks of the river Saraswati in northwestern India around 5,000 years ago, and from there spread to the rest of the world. This assertion, however, is disputed by most academics around the world in a wide range of disciplines (historians, Indologists, linguists, archaeologists) whose research has a bearing on the issue, and who instead support some version of an Aryan migration theory (AMT) into India.[34] The issue of whether the movement was into or out of India has become an emotional one for many contemporary Hindu leaders since it is perceived to cut to the heart of Indian national and cultural identity. Specifically, the Aryan migration theory would seem to imply that Sanskrit and some of Hindu culture had non-Indian and even European origins, challenging the indigenousness argument that has become so central to Hindu nationalism. The "out of India" (OIT) argument, on the other hand, reverses this claim and instead attributes the source of European civilization to India.

The theory of a movement of Aryans into India was first propounded by Max Müller, a nineteenth-century German Indologist, based on linguistic evidence of the similarity between Sanskrit and many European languages, the then-prevalent belief (in accordance with biblical ideas) that the human race originated somewhere in the Middle East region, and descriptions in the Vedas of numerous battles between Aryans and the apparently darker-skinned non-Aryans. Subsequent archaeological, linguistic, and textual evidence (from the Vedas, but also the Iranian text, the Avesta) refined many of these propositions.[35] However, the evidence for this Aryan migration theory is sketchy and far from conclusive, a weakness that has been seized on by Hindu scholars who argue that the AMT scholars have merely taken over the missionary and Eurocentric biases of the colonial scholars.

The resurgence of the Hindutva movement in the contemporary period led to a virtual publishing industry devoted to disputing the Aryan migration theory, with the alternative "out of India" theory. The OIT theorists argue that the Aryans were autochthonous to India and that a branch of this group subsequently migrated from the Punjab in northern India to Iran and to Europe. The first Vedic text, the Rig Veda, which is dated between 1200 to 1500 BCE by the AMT scholars, is dated to 2500 BCE, or even to 4000–5000 BCE, by members of the OIT group.[36] While there are some non-Hindu academics, mostly archaeologists, who support some versions of the OIT, by and large the best-known contemporary exponents of this school today are self-styled Hindu scholars in India and the United States and Hindu Indian American computer scientists who claim that they have been able to use their Western scientific training and access to modern technology to uncover this evidence. Many of these scholars also maintain that the Vedas enshrine knowledge of advanced scientific, mathematical, and astronomical concepts, encrypted in code form, such as the speed of light, the Pythagoras theorem,[37] quark confinement, bosons and fermions, gamma-ray bursts,[38] airplanes, atomic energy, and even the atom bomb.[39] The Infinity Foundation has recently taken a leadership role in the sponsorship of some of these and other kinds of Hinducentric revisionist scholarship to examine ancient Indian contributions to mathematics, science, technology, philosophy, and psychology and to document the destructive effects of the Muslim invasions on India.[40]

The second important argument made by Hindu American leaders is that the categories that are imposed on Indic traditions are a product of specifically European histories and are therefore inapplicable to Hinduism. For instance, American Internet groups and websites often feature discussions to make the case that the term "religion" does not apply to Hinduism, since Hinduism is a "way of life" (that is, that it is difficult to make the distinction between sacred and secular aspects of life). Support for this position is provided by the fact that Hindus do not even have an indigenous term that is equivalent to "religion." The closest equivalent is the term *dharma*, which means righteousness, duty, a moral and social obligation. So some Hindus prefer to use the term *Sanatana Dharma* (eternal, universal dharma), or Hindu dharma, to refer to the panoply of their beliefs and practices. Hindu American leaders have mapped the distinction between Indian and European traditions onto a distinction between Indic and Abrahamic traditions; as a result, much of the recent efforts of these leaders has focused on pointing to the distinction between the two traditions and defining the distinctiveness and superiority of Indic cultures. These arguments hark back to those made in the colonial period by Hindus and their supporters, synthesized and articulated by Swami Vivekananda. Thus, Hindu Americans frequently compare and contrast Hinduism, or Dharma, with the Abrahamic traditions (particularly Islam and Christianity), arguing that unlike these religions, which make exclusive claims to the truth and are therefore intolerant, Hinduism is tolerant and pluralistic. The Rig Veda verse (1.164.46), "truth is one, sages call it by different names," is frequently reiterated to support this claim.

Some Hindu Indian scholars based in the West, like S. N. Balagangadhara at Ghent University in Belgium and Arvind Sharma at McGill University in Canada, have elaborated on the distinction between Indic and Abrahamic traditions. In a book published in 1994, Balagangadhara argues, following Wilfred Cantwell Smith, that the concept of religion as a "belief" system that is accepted as "true" and is validated by textual tradition is derived from Christianity and was subsequently adopted by Jews and Muslims.[41] Thus it is a concept that "cuts across the three Semitic religions."[42] However, Balagangadhara maintains that Hinduism is not a religion in that sense since it does not provide a single authoritative belief system, scripture, or adjudicatory body. Arvind Sharma has made similar arguments in his own work.[43] Both Balagangadhara and Sharma go on to point out that such a definition of the concept of religion has wider implications. Balagangadhara argues that it can shape the nature of science since it constrains the types of questions and theories that can be formulated, while Sharma focuses on its implications for defining the nature of secularism and religious freedom.[44] Both scholars have become well known to Hindu Americans through their participation in Internet discussions, and their arguments have generated considerable interest and enthusiasm in these discussion groups.

The terrorist attacks on the United States on September 11, 2001, brought about a change in the religious configuration of the country and led to a shift in the discourse about Abrahamic traditions in the United States. In the days following 9/11, a number of interfaith services were organized in different parts of the country. These services, typically conducted by Protestant ministers, Catholic priests, and Jewish rabbis, also for the first time included Muslim clerics. Muslim spokespersons traveled around the country emphasizing that they were part of the same tradition as Christians and Jews and proclaimed that "we worship the same God as you do." It appeared as though their lobbying yielded immediate results, most visibly in the attempt to enlarge the American "Judeo-Christian" sacred canopy into an "Abrahamic" one that included Muslims.

This reconfiguration of American religion was viewed with alarm by Hindu American leaders, who feared that it would further marginalize non-Abrahamic religions like Hinduism. Thus, September 11 resulted in a shift in the patterns of activism of Hindu American groups, with Hindus mobilizing to stress the differences between Hinduism and Islam. There has been a lot of literature on the impact of September 11 on Muslims in the United States and around the world but little recognition that 9/11 also affected the religious framing of other religious groups, particularly those non-Judeo-Christian groups like Hindus, who, before and after the attacks, were often lumped together with Muslims. In the wake of September 11, several Hindu American individuals and groups mobilized on a public anti-Islamic platform, bombarding their politicians and the media with anti-Pakistani and anti-Islamic propaganda, filled with quotations from the Koran, and also calling into radio and televisions shows to criticize Islam. Others spoke up at town meetings to condemn the treatment of minorities in Muslim countries and to challenge the positive portrayals of Islam by Muslim speakers.[45]

Anti-Abrahamism also resulted in a growing anti-monotheistic mood within Hindu American Internet groups after September 11, with the Indic versus Abrahamic difference being transmuted to a distinction between polytheistic and monotheistic traditions. Earlier, many Hindus had taken offense to Hinduism being described as "polytheistic"; they argued that although the Hindu pantheon consisted of an array of deities, these were but different forms manifested by one Supreme Being. However, increasingly in the post-9/11 period,

Hindus were beginning to take pride in not being monotheistic by arguing that monotheism led to triumphalism, proselytization, and violence against other faith communities.

This mood was very much in evidence at the Dharma conference, organized by second-generation Hindu Americans with the support of Hindu American organizations like the Vishnu Hindu Parishad of America (VHPA) and held in Edison, New Jersey, in July 2003 with around 2,000 attendees. Kanchan Banerjee, chief organizer, drew on Swami Vivekananda's contrast between Hinduism and other major world religions to explain that goal of the conference was to make a distinction between Dharma, defined as the "natural law of Truth and its universal and eternal principles," and "religion," or belief-oriented traditions such as Christianity and Islam that rely on a savior or a prophet to "reveal" the truth.[46] Hinduism was portrayed as a positive, scientific, and rational complete system (including "religion, yoga, and mysticism, philosophy, arts, science and culture as part of a single reality"), as opposed to the above religions, which were criticized implicitly and sometimes explicitly for being simplistic and dogmatic, and for instigating violence.[47]

Many of the Hindu arguments against Abrahamic traditions enumerated in this section were brought together by Rajiv Malhotra in an article on Sulekha .com, which he circulated to several religious studies scholars and which also formed the basis for several of his presentations at academic venues.[48] Entitled "Problematizing God's Interventions in History," the article is a restatement of an argument made by Swami Vivekananda and a critique of Abrahamic traditions "on scientific and ethical grounds."[49] Malhotra argues that Abrahamic traditions and Indic traditions are based on "two different, and often competing ways of arriving at spiritual truth," with the Abrahamic traditions relying on historical narratives (about "holy" events) and the Indic traditions relying on *adhyatma-vidhya* (inner "science" or esoteric processes). He concludes that the Abrahamic traditions are less scientific since they are based on unique historical events, which adherents believe in not because there is any compelling empirical evidence to substantiate the beliefs, but because the historical narrative was passed down through the generations by the faith community. In contrast, the Indic traditions are not dependent on the histories of the saints who contributed to them, just like the laws of nature are not contingent upon the validity of the histories of the scientists who discovered them; therefore, "no fracture of natural law is necessary for Brahman to act in Indic systems."[50]

On ethical grounds, Malhotra argues that "non-negotiable Grand Narratives of History" lead to conflicts since they promote triumphalism and the belief "that there is only One True History. Monotheism turns into My-theism, the belief that only one's own conception of theism is valid, and that all others must be falsified and demonized." However, since Indic traditions are "not hand-cuffed to history" and also accept multiple manifestations of the Supreme Being, they are inherently pluralistic. Through these arguments Malhotra and other leaders are turning conventionally accepted ideas of the superiority and scientific nature of Western traditions on their head.[51]

The hot-button issue in the controversy regarding the Eurocentric bias within American academia has undoubtedly been the portrayal of Hinduism and Hindu deities by American religious studies scholars. This is the third major critique offered by Hindu American leaders. Western scholars of Hinduism and of Hindu nationalism had come under attack from Hindu American leaders from at least the 1990s with the rise in the Hindutva movement. However, the year 2000 was a watershed in terms of Hindu American activism targeted at academia. Over the course of that year, several dozen Hindu and Indian American Internet discussion groups were formed, some of which had the explicit goal of providing Hindu- or Indic-centered critiques of Western scholarship on Hinduism and ancient Indian history. Some Hindu activists, including Rajiv Malhotra, also attended the annual meeting of the American Academy of Religion (AAR) that year. In an article, "A Hindu View of the American Academy of Religion's Convention, 2000," which was widely circulated on Indian American Internet groups, Malhotra criticized the presentation of Hinduism at the meeting, describing it as "Hindu-bashing."[52] The December 2000 issue of the *Journal of the American Academy of Religion* (*JAAR*), which carried a special feature on "Who Speaks for Hinduism," was also severely criticized by Rajiv Malhotra in a follow-up article.[53] Malhotra's critique came to the attention of the editors of the international Hindu magazine *Hinduism Today*, and subsequently they, too, published a critique of the *JAAR* issue in their magazine.[54]

Particularly since the year 2000, the monitoring and shaping of the presentation of Hinduism and Indian history in American school textbooks and within academia have become important goals of many Hindu American groups. One of the first of such mobilizations was against the book *Kali's Child*, by Jeffrey Kripal, published by the University of Chicago Press in 1995, which won a book award from the American Academy of Religion the same year. Using a psycho-analytical approach, Kripal argues that the mystical and visionary experiences of Ramakrishna, a revered nineteenth-century Bengali Hindu saint, were driven by his conflicted, latent, homoerotic impulses. Many Hindus who came to know about this book were angry and upset. However, the major fallout in the United States began primarily after 2000 when Swami Tyagananda, a member of the Ramakrishna order and the Hindu chaplain at Harvard, produced a long, meticulously argued tract entitled, "Kali's Child Revisited; or, Didn't Anyone Check the Documentation?" (now archived at the website of the Infinity Foundation), which was distributed at the annual meeting of the AAR that year. He argued that many of Kripal's interpretations were based on his lack of understanding of the nuances of Bengali language and culture. In 2001 a group of Hindu activists wrote to the Religion Department at the University of Chicago (where Kripal had written his dissertation on Ramakrishna) to protest the book and the role of the department in its production.[55] In the spring of 2002, other Hindu groups also contacted the administration at Rice University (where Kripal was a candidate for a position) in an attempt to prevent him from being hired. Between the years 2001 and 2003, *Kali's Child* was critiqued in two issues of the *Harvard Divinity Bulletin* (Winter and Spring 2001), the first issue of the Indian journal *Evam* (2002), and in several articles on Sulekha.com. While Kripal responded to his critics in each of these venues, his responses failed to satisfy Hindu American activists.

Hindu American activists have been very critical of the Religions in South Asia (RISA) subsection of the American Academy of Religion. These criticisms became particularly pronounced after the events of September 11. Soon after, members of an Internet discussion group shot off letters to the then president of the AAR, Vasudha Narayanan, demanding that the organization sponsor panels on Islamic fascism and on "Jihad: God as Weapon of Mass Destruction" in the upcoming annual meetings to counterbalance what they claimed was the organization's excessive focus on Hindu fascism. Another member of the group compiled a list from the Internet archives of Religions in South Asia and from the Internet archives of the Society for Hindu-Christian Studies to document the alleged contempt for Hinduism and Hindus by Hinduism scholars and sent it to the president of the AAR and several Internet discussion groups. At a presentation at the American Academy of Religion meeting in November 2001 (where he had been invited as a representative of "practicing Hindus"), Malhotra criticized what he characterized as the "five asymmetries in the dialog of civilizations" and accused American scholars of Hinduism of "denying agency and rights to non westerners," of "academic arson" or the "age old 'plunder while you denigrate the source' process," and of "intimidating name-calling to affect censorship." He concluded with the demand that Hindus in the diaspora be included as "dialog representatives" in a joint study of the tradition.[56]

The "tipping point" in the relationship between "the academic and faith community," according to religious studies scholar Arvind Sharma, came in September 2002, when an article by Rajiv Malhotra, entitled "RISA Lila—1: Wendy's Child Syndrome" (the term "Lila" in Hinduism conventionally refers to divine play or the sport of the gods), was published on Sulekha.com and was widely read (it received over 20,000 hits).[57] In the article, Malhotra launches a blistering attack against religious studies scholars such as Wendy Doniger of the

University of Chicago (whom he refers to as the "Queen of Hinduism") and others like Sarah Caldwell, Jeffrey Kripal, and Paul Courtright, who adopt a psychoanalytical approach to the study of Hindu deities and saints. With quotations from the most sensational of such passages in each of their works to illustrate his argument, Malhotra argues that the Freudian psychoanalytical approach has been discredited even among Western psychologists, that religious studies scholars have no training in psychoanalysis, and furthermore that the approach is not valid when it is applied to non-Western subjects. Claiming that Hinduism scholars want to "demonize it [Hinduism], in order to create Hindu shame amongst the youth," he goes on to argue, "History shows that genocides have been preceded by the denigration of the victims. . . . The time has come to ask: Are certain 'objective' scholars consciously conspiring, or unconsciously driven by their Eurocentric essences, to pave the way for a future genocide of a billion or more Hindus . . . ?"[58] The article also included a brief discussion of the treatment of the elephant-headed deity Ganesha by Paul Courtright, which became the basis of a series of subsequent events, discussed below.

Another article on Sulekha.com later that month examined the article on Hinduism in Microsoft Corporation's Encarta encyclopedia, 2002, which was written by Wendy Doniger. The author of the article, Sankrant Sanu, one of the advisers of the Infinity Foundation, argued, with excerpts from the respective articles that Doniger's article on Hinduism was unsympathetic and negative, in contrast to the articles on Islam and Christianity in the encyclopedia, which were respectful and positive in tone. Subsequently, in 2003 the Hindu American community was successful in getting Encarta to replace Doniger's article with an article on Hinduism by Arvind Sharma, a professor of religion and a practicing Hindu.[59]

On October 6, 2003, a petition against the book *Ganesha: Lord of Obstacles, Lord of Beginnings*, by Paul Courtright of Emory University in Atlanta, launched by a Hindu group in Louisiana, started circulating on the Internet. Ganesha is a popular elephant-headed Hindu deity, regarded with much affection by his devotees. The first edition of *Ganesha* was published in 1985 by Oxford University Press, but in 2001, an Indian edition was published with a picture of a nude baby Ganesha on the cover (Courtright maintains that he was not involved in the selection of the picture). The Internet petition objected to the cover of the book and to passages that applied a Freudian framework to analyze the stories about Ganesha found in Hindu texts. Excerpting a few of the passages that the authors of the petition considered to be the most offensive (such as the description of Lord Ganesha's trunk as a "displaced phallus" and of the deity as a "eunuch"), the authors demanded that the book be immediately withdrawn from circulation and that the author and publisher offer an apology to Hindus. The petition received over 4,000 signatures in the first few days and generated considerable anger in the worldwide Hindu community. The book was quickly withdrawn by the Indian publishers, Motilal Banarsidas. Courtright even received death threats on the Internet site, at which point the petition was withdrawn by its originators. Hindu groups in Atlanta subsequently met with Emory University administrators to demand that the university stop defending Courtright and take action to address the misrepresentations in his book and, more broadly, to oversee the way academics portray other cultures and religions.[60] The Courtright issue was discussed in an article in the *Washington Post*, and the book also came under severe attack on e-zines like Sulekha.com.[61]

The issue of the academic portrayal of religion was taken up in a roundtable at the American Academy of Religion in November 2003, titled "Creating Bridges: Dharma Traditions and the Academy." The roundtable was organized by the Dharma Association of North America, an organization that was formed in 2002 with the goals of undertaking "the recovery, reclamation, and reconstitution of Hindu Dharma for the contemporary global era" and of "providing bridges between, and networks among, the practicing Hindu Dharma scholars and the Diaspora Hindu community in North America."[62]

According to one published report, the roundtable provoked a heated discussion, with RISA scholars agreeing that a "fair, respectful and thorough representation of their culture is 'non-negotiable' to Hindus in North America." However, they also insisted that "respect for tenure and free exchange of ideas for the professors was just as 'non-negotiable.'" According to the report, this was "strongly countered" by Balagangadhara of Ghent University, Belgium (the newly elected co-chair of the Hinduism unit of the AAR), who apparently argued that "misrepresentation of the Hindu culture to the point of destroying age-old spiritual experience is an act of violence" and demanded that such misrepresentation was "unprofessional, non-negotiable and must stop."[63]

The last critique revolves around another long-standing emotional issue within the Indian American community—whether Indians should be classified as South Asians, as in the South Asian studies programs around the country. Those who argue for a South Asian identity make the case that forming coalitions to address common issues is advantageous to Indian Americans, who are minorities in the United States. Advocates argue that there are many cultural similarities between individuals of South Asian background and that in this country they also face common concerns and similar treatment as "brown-skinned" individuals. They also point out that policymakers do not see differences between South Asian groups. While agreeing that there are many fundamental issues on which individuals belonging to different South Asian countries do not see eye to eye, they argue that it is still possible to forge alliances by understanding and respecting these differences.[64]

Hindu and Indic activists, however, have long been unhappy with this classification. Members of such groups describe themselves as proud Hindus and patriotic Indians who are trying to build community solidarity and inculcate individual and collective pride on the basis of an identity and culture that is thousands of years old. They maintain that it is disadvantageous for India to be lumped together with the other countries in South Asia, since "India's geographical size, economy and progress are far ahead of these countries." They further argue that the cultural and political gulf between members of these countries is too vast to bridge. Thus, these groups contend that instead of trying to ignore these cleavages, Indian Americans ought to educate their children and the wider American society about the fundamental differences between the countries in South Asia. They characterize members of South Asian organizations as anti-Hindu and anti-Indian, reflecting a "deracinated group" with very little knowledge about Indian history and culture that has bought into the "artificial" U.S. State Department construct of a homogenous subcontinent.[65]

In a series of articles on Rediff.com in December 2003 and January 2004, Rajiv Malhotra elaborated on this latter viewpoint.[66] He argues that U.S. universities play an important role in "India's brand positioning" by influencing the perspectives of the media, government, business, education, and Indian Americans and that, compared with other major countries, a positive stance on India is underrepresented in American academia. According to him, this is because South Asian studies programs are manned by Westerners who are hostile to Indian interests, by "Indian-American Sepoys," and by Indian Americans wanting to be white.[67] Describing the last two groups of Indian Americans as "career opportunists" and "Uncle Toms," he argues that "to become members of the Western Grand Narrative—even in marginal roles—these Indians often sneer at Indian culture in the same manner as colonialists once did."[68] Thus, according to Malhotra, South Asian studies was undermining India by promoting "a perspective on India using worldviews which are hostile to India's interests," and Indian American donors were being "hoodwinked" into thinking that they were supporting India through their monetary contributions to such programs.[69]

Specifically, Malhotra refers to the "identities of victimhood with other Indians depicted as culprits" that he argues South Asianists promote.[70] He claims that such scholarship undermines India "by encouraging paradigms that oppose its unity and integrity" and that South Asian scholars also play "critical roles, often under the garb of 'human rights' in channeling foreign intellectual and material support to exacerbate India's internal cleavages," such as the insurgencies in various parts of the country and the lower-caste movements.[71] Pointing out that September 11 was completely unanticipated by South Asian scholars who were focused on Hindutva but not on the Taliban, Malhotra argues that there is a real chance that under a series of crises, separatist movements could tear India apart "with Indian-American sepoys abetting the process," which in turn could lead to the Talibanization of India and to the subsequent Talibanization of the Association of Southeast Asian Nations (ASEAN). In addition to being devastating for the South Asian region, such a Talibanization, Malhotra stresses, will also have harmful consequences for the United States, and consequently, the "divisive scholarship" of South Asian studies was also "detrimental to US strategic interests."[72] Malhotra indicates that his goal in getting involved in the U.S. academy is to "reposition India's brand" by "challenging the India-bashing club" and emphasizing India's positive contributions.[73] He concludes by calling for a "re-imagining [of] India" as a major partner of the United States and for changing the depictions of India by "retraining" South Asian scholars in the new paradigm.[74]

While it may be too early to say what type of long-term effect Rajiv Malhotra and the other Hindu American leaders will have on the academy, as I have tried to show in this essay, they have made significant headway in having their concerns heard, particularly by scholars specializing in Hinduism and India studies. Several of the issues raised are certainly important—intellectually, culturally, and socially. There are undeniable Eurocentric biases in the academy that need to be corrected. Again, there have been many remarkable Indian achievements of the past and present that ought to be more widely acknowledged. Hindus and Indians should be able to take justifiable pride in their heritage, and Hindus should have the same right to a more positive portrayal of Hinduism as the practitioners of other religious traditions. At the same time, the effectiveness of the critiques launched by Hindu leaders are often diminished by their lack of understanding of the goals of the humanities and the social sciences, by the tendency of many of these leaders to indulge in sweeping generalizations and unsubstantiated allegations, and finally, by their narrow view of Hinduism and their Hinducentric perspective of India. Vitriolic personal attacks against scholars are probably not the most effective way to encourage dialogue!

More serious is the adoption of many elements of the Hindutva discourse by this group, such as the denigration of Abrahamic traditions, the aggrandization of Hinduism, and the diatribes against secularism and secular scholars. There has been a direct relationship between Hindutva supporters and Indic studies in some instances. For instance, several of the invited speakers at the July 2002 international conference on "India's Contributions and Influence in the World", organized by the Center for Indic Studies at University of Massachusetts, Dartmouth, were prominent Hindutva leaders and supporters.[75] The fetishization of the doctrine of indigenousness and the reverse triumphalism of the Hindu American leaders (both of which can also be found in the Hindutva ideology) only undermine their demands for their rights as new citizens of the United States and for pluralism. It is indeed an irony that these groups, which argue for a multiculturalist conception of American identity based on its changing history and the new groups that form the nation, should be simultaneously promoting a chauvinistic Indic-centrism based on a civilization that flourished in a section of northwestern India thousands of years ago. This conception of India ignores how its identity and culture have been irrevocably shaped by the variety of groups and cultures that have been part of the country for millennia, as well as the experiences of the past 5,000 years.

Hindu American strategies for recognition after September 11 are a good case study of how the public activism of immigrant religious groups is powerfully shaped by the religio-cultural context of the country and its official policies. The events of September 11 triggered a process of Hindu American mobilization for a variety of reasons: the need of Hindu practitioners to distance themselves from Islam lest they be mistaken for Muslims and attacked, fears about the marginalization of Hindus if Muslims were also included under the American sacred canopy, resentment and worry about the sudden American rapprochement with Pakistan, and finally, an attempt to exploit the rise of anti-Islamic sentiments in the United States to obtain the recognition and support that Hindus craved.

As the numbers of immigrants increase in the United States and as the children of such immigrants grow to adulthood, there will undoubtedly be more challenges to American academia like that presented by Hindu Americans, particularly to humanities and social science scholarship dealing with non-Western traditions. How these challenges will be met and addressed will be crucial in determining the future contours of American society and culture. Reactionary Eurocentric responses will probably only exacerbate feelings of marginality, leading to a heightened feeling of victimhood and a possible turn toward extremism. At the same time, a multiculturalism that does not address the deeper issues of racism and unequal structures is likely to merely legitimize the development of modular cultural nationalisms among ethnic and racial groups.[76] What is crucial, therefore, seems to be the development of a reconstructed multiculturalism that addresses these issues and thus brings about a genuine change in the conception and treatment of nonwhite and non-Western ethnic communities in the United States.

NOTES

1. Samuel P. Huntington, *Who Are We?: The Challenges to America's National Identity* (New York: Simon and Schuster, 2004).

2. Prema A. Kurien, "Mr. President, Why Do You Exclude Us from Your Prayers? Hindus Challenge American Pluralism," in *A Nation of Religions: The Politics of Pluralism in Multireligious America*, ed. Stephen Prothero (Chapel Hill: University of North Carolina Press, 2006), 119–38.

3. Huntington, *Who Are We.*

4. Jeffrey G. Reitz, "Host Societies and the Reception of Immigrants: Research Themes, Emerging Theories and Methodological Issues," *International Migration Review* 36 (Winter 2002): 1005–19.

5. Anthony M. Orum, "Circles of Influence and Chains of Command: A Structural Perspective on How Ethnic Communities Influence Host Societies," unpublished manuscript, 2002.

6. Ibid., 6.

7. According to the 2005 American Community Survey (table B02006) of the U.S. Census Bureau (www.census.gov), the Indian American population in the United States was 2,319,222. The community registered a growth rate of 105.87 between 1990 and 2000 and 38 percent between 2000 and 2005.

8. According to the 1990 census, the median family income of Indians in the United States was $49,309, well above that for non-Hispanic whites, which was $37,630; 43.6 percent were employed either as professionals (mostly doctors and engineers) or managers; and 58.4 percent had at least a bachelor's degree. In 2000 the median household income of foreign-born Indians was $68,500, compared with $53,400 for native-born whites. Mary C. Waters and Karl Eschbach, "Immigration and Ethnic and Racial Inequality in the United States," in *Majority and Minority: The Dynamics of Race and Ethnicity in American Life*, ed. Norman R. Yetman (6th ed.; Boston: Allyn and Bacon, 1999), 315; Larry Hajime Shinagawa, "The Impact of Immigration on the Demography of Asian Pacific Americans," in *The State of Asian Pacific America: Reframing the Immigration Debate: A Public Policy Report*, ed. Bill Ong Hing and Ronald Lee (Los Angeles: LEAP Asian Pacific American Public Policy Institute and UCLA Asian American Studies Center, 1996), 113, 119.

9. This figure is based on Indian census reports that count Dalit groups (former "untouchable" groups) and tribals as Hindu. However, many members of these groups object to their being included within Hinduism.

10. S. K. Hofrenning and B. R. Chiswick, "A Method of Proxying a Respondent's Religious Background: An Application to School Choice Decisions," *Journal of Human Resources* 34, no. 1 (1999): 193–207. See also *Britannica Book of the Year* and *World Almanac* estimates, found at <http://www.pluralism.org/resources/statistics/tradition.php#Hinduism> (July 9, 2004).

11. While most *Hindutva-vadis* share this common worldview, it is important to emphasize that not all those who support some of these positions can be labeled as a Hindutva supporter.

12. Georg Feuerstein, Subhash Kak, and David Frawley, *In Search of the Cradle of Civilization* (Wheaton, Ill: Quest Books, 1995); Navaratna S. Rajaram and David Frawley, *Vedic "Aryans" and the Origins of Civilization* (St-Hyacinthe, Quebec: World Heritage Press, 1995).

13. Prema Kurien, "Multiculturalism, Immigrant Religion, and Diasporic Nationalism: The Development of an American Hinduism," *Social Problems* 51 (August 2004): 362–85; Vinay Lal, "The Politics of History on the Internet: Cyber-Diasporic Hinduism and the North American Hindu Diaspora," *Diaspora* 8, no. 2 (1999): 137–72; Biju Mathew and Vijay Prashad, "The Protean Forms of Yankee Hindutva," *Ethnic and Racial Studies* 23, no. 3 (2000): 516–34.

14. This essay draws on an eight-year study of the new forms, practices, and interpretations of Hinduism in the United States. Besides participating in the activities and programs of twelve Hindu organizations, I conducted detailed interviews with leaders and many of the members (over 120 first- and second-generation Hindu Americans in all). I have also been following the activities of the Hindu Indian community around the country by reading several Indian American newspapers and the international magazine *Hinduism Today*, published in Hawaii. However, this particular essay is based primarily on an analysis of discussions on Internet groups, websites, and Internet magazines devoted to Indian- or Hindu-related topics. Since the year 2000, when the Internet became a major site of Hindu American activity, I have been monitoring four Internet discussion groups devoted to Indian- or Hindu-related topics, the popular Internet magazines for the Indian diaspora (<http://www.Sulekha.com> and <http://www.Rediff.com>), and several Internet websites devoted to Hinduism.

15. Trisha Pasricha, cited in Rajiv Malhotra, "RISA Lila 2: Limp Scholarship and Demonology," November 17, 2003, <http://rajivmalhotra.sulekha.com/blog/post/2003/11/risa-lila-2-limp-scholarship-and-demonology.htm> (March 6, 2007).

16. Rajiv Malhotra, "The Case for Indic Traditions in the Academy," paper presented at the "Completing the Global Renaissance: The Indic Contributions" conference, New York, July 2002, 8.

17. See the description on the website of the Dharam Hinduja Institute of Indic Research at the University of Cambridge, <http://www.divinity.cam.ac.uk/CARTS/dhiir/default.html> (January 22, 2007).

18. Biju Mathew, "Byte-Sized Nationalism: Mapping the Hindu Right in the United States," *Rethinking Marxism* 12, no. 1 (2000): 108–28; Kamala Visweswaran and Ali Mir, "On the Politics of Community in South Asian–American Studies," *Amerasia Journal* 25, no. 3 (1999/2000): 97–108.

19. As Indic studies became the main activity of the foundation, the ECIT was disbanded.

20. <http://www.infinityfoundation.com/people.shtml> (January 22, 2007).

21. <http://www.infinityfoundation.com/ECITmissionframeset.htm> (December 16, 2000).

22. Rajiv Malhotra, "A Business Model of Religion—1," December 31, 2001, <http://

rajivmalhotra.sulekha.com/blog/post/2001/12/a-business-model-of-religion-1.htm>
(March 13, 2007).

23. Ibid; Rajiv Malhotra, "A Business Model of Religion—2," April 24, 2002, <http://
rajivmalhotra.sulekha.com/blog/post/2002/04/a-business-model-of-religion-2.htm>
(March 13, 2007).

24. <http://www.infinityfoundation.com>.

25. Rajiv Malhotra and David Gray, "Global Renaissance and the Roots of Western Wisdom," *IONS Review* 56 (June 2001): <http://www.noetic.org/publications/review/issue56/
main.cfm> (March 13, 2007). This argument replicates those made by Swami Vivekananda
(see, for example, "India's Gift to the World," lecture delivered in Brooklyn, New York, in
1895, *Brooklyn Standard Union*, February 27, 1895, reprinted in "Reports in American
Newspapers," in vol. 2 of *Complete Works of Swami Vivekananda*, <http://www.ramakrish
navivekananda.info/vivekananda/complete_works.htm> (August 11, 2005).

26. Rajiv Malhotra and Robert Thurman, "Completing the Global Renaissance: The
Indic Contributions: Overview of Mission" <http://www.infinityfoundation.com/indic
_colloq/colloq_mission_long.htm> (July 5, 2002).

27. This concept of a second renaissance originating from Hindu thought was first
propounded by the German philosopher Schopenhauer, and was alluded to by Swami
Vivekananda in a lecture delivered in Colombo, Sri Lanka, in 1897 ("First Public Lecture
in the East," in "Lectures from Colombo to Almora," in vol. 3 of *The Complete Works of
Swami Vivekananda*, <http://www.ramakrishnavivekananda.info/vivekananda/compl
ete_works.htm> (August 8, 2005).

28. <http://s-n-balagangadhara.sulekha.com/blog/post/2002/12/on-colonial-exper
ience-and-the-indian-renaissance/comment/274788.htm> (March 13, 2007).

29. Malhotra, "Case for Indic Traditions in the Academy", 9.

30. Ibid., 8.

31. Ibid., 10.

32. Ibid., 26.

33. Ibid., 30.

34. For a detailed discussion of the work of these scholars, see Edwin Bryant, *The
Quest for the Origins of Vedic Culture: The Indo-Aryan Migration Debate* (Oxford, U.K.:
Oxford University Press, 2001); and Michael Witzel, "Autochthonous Aryans? The Evidence from Old Indian and Iranian Texts," *Electronic Journal of Vedic Studies* 7, no. 3
(2001): <http://www.people.fas.harvard.edu/witzel/EJVS-7-3.pdf> (March 6, 2007).

35. Bryant, *Quest for the Origins of Vedic Culture*; Witzel, "Autochthonous Aryans?"

36. Bryant, *Quest for the Origins of Vedic Culture*; Witzel, "Autochthonous Aryans?"

37. Subhash Kak, "Light or Coincidence" <http://infinityfoundation.com/mandala/
t_es/t_es_kak-s_light.htm> (July 10, 2002).

38. Raja Ram Mohan Roy, *Vedic Physics: Scientific Origin of Hinduism* (Toronto:
Golden Egg Publishing, 1999).

39. For example, see the website <http://atributetohinduism.com> (July 20, 2003),
hosted by an Indian American.

40. For example, see <http://www.infinityfoundation.com/sourcebook.htm> (April 2, 2004).

41. Wilfred Cantwell Smith, *The Meaning and End of Religion* (New York: Macmillan, 1962).

42. S. N. Balagangadhara, *"The Heathen in His Blindness . . .": Asia, the West, and the Dynamic of Religion* (Leiden: E. J. Brill, 1994), 322.

43. Arvind Sharma, "An Indic Contribution Towards an Understanding of the Word 'Religion' and the Concept of Religious Freedom," paper presented at the "Completing the Global Renaissance: The Indic Contributions" conference, New York, July 2002.

44. Balagangadhara, *"Heathen in His Blindness"*; Sharma, "Indic Contribution."

45. Kurien, "Mr. President, Why Do You Exclude Us from Your Prayers?"

46. "The Mission of the Vedanta," in "Lectures from Colombo to Almora," in vol. 3 of *Complete Works of Swami Vivekananda*, <http://www.ramakrishnavivekananda.info/vivekananda/complete_works.htm> (February 4, 2005); Kanchan Banerjee, "What Is Dharma, What Is Religion," *Brochure of the Dharma Conference*, July 25–27, 2003. This is a characterization of Hinduism that can be traced back to the Hindu renaissance movements that were initiated during the colonial period in India.

47. Banerjee, "What Is Dharma, What Is Religion." For criticisms of other religions, see the speeches of the chief guest, Swami Dayananda Saraswati, and David Frawley.

48. Rajiv Malhotra, "Problematizing God's Interventions in History," March 19, 2003, <http://rajivmalhotra.sulekha.com/blog/post/2003/03/problematizing-god-s-interventions-in-history.htm> (March 6, 2007).

49. "Mission of the Vedanta"; Malhotra, "Problematizing God's Interventions in History," 1.

50. Malhotra, "Problematizing God's Interventions in History."

51. Ibid.

52. Rajiv Malhotra, "A Hindu View of the American Academy of Religion's Convention, 2000," <http://www.infinityfoundation.com/ECITAAR2000frame.htm> (January 21, 2007).

53. Rajiv Malhotra, "Who Speaks for Hinduism? A Critique of the Special Issue of the Journal of the American Academy of Religion," <http://www.infinityfoundation.com/mandala/s_es/s_es_malho_critiq_frameset.htm> (January 21, 2007).

54. "Who Speaks for Hinduism? Commentary by the Editors," *Hinduism Today*, September/October 2001.

55. Swami Tyagananda, "Kali's Child Revisited; or Didn't Anyone Check the Documentation?" <http://www.infinityfoundation.com/mandala/s_rv/s_rv_tyaga_kali1_frameset.htm> (March 13, 2007); <http://www.infinityfoundation.com/mandala/s_rv_misce_feed.htm> (July 15, 2004).

56. From an Internet report on the panel that included the papers that were presented: "Defamation/Anti/Defamation: Hindus in Dialogue with the Western Academy," by John Stratton Hawley, <http://web.barnard.columbia.edu/religion/hindu/malhotra_defamation/html> (January 31, 2002).

57. Rajiv Malhotra, "RISA Lila—1: Wendy's Child Syndrome," September 6, 2002,

<http://rajivmalhotra.sulekha.com/blog/post/2002/09/risa-lila-1-wendy-s-child-syndr
ome.htm> (March 6, 2007); Arvind Sharma, "Hindus and Scholars," *Religion in the
News* 7 (Spring 2004), <http://www.trincoll.edu/depts/csrpl/RINVol7No1/Hindus%20
and%20Scholars.htm> (June 24, 2004).

58. Malhotra, "RISA Lila—1: Wendy's Child Syndrome," 15.

59. Sankrant Sanu, "Are Hindu Studies Prejudiced? A Look at Microsoft Encarta,"
September 24, 2002, <http://sankrant.sulekha.com/blog/post/2002/09/are-hinduism-
studies-prejudiced-a-look-at-microsoft.htm> (March 13, 2007).

60. The controversy and the presentations of the group are archived under the title,
"Animal House: The South Asian Religious Studies Circus" (<http://www.jitnasa.india-
forum.com>).

61. Vedantam, "Wrath over a Hindu God: U.S. Scholar's Writings Draw Threats from
Faithful," *Washington Post*, April 10 2004; Vishal Agarwal and Kalavai Venkat, "When
the Cigar Becomes a Phallus—Part I," December 8, 2003, and Vishal Agarwal and
Kalavai Venkat, "When the Cigar Becomes a Phallus—Part II," December 15, 2003,
<http://vishalagarwal.voiceofdharma.com/articles/devis/cigar.htm> (March 6, 2007);
Sankrant Sanu, "Courtright Twist and Academic Freedom," December 20, 2003, <http://
sankrant.sulekha.com/blog/post/2003/12/courtright-twist-and-academic-
freedom.htm> (March 13, 2007).

62. <http://www.danam-web.org/missionpage.htm> (November 4, 2003).

63. Mona Vijayakar, "Western Scholars vs. Hinduism," *India West*, December 12, 2003,
A6.

64. Prema A. Kurien, "To Be or Not to Be South Asian: Contemporary Indian
American Politics," *Journal of Asian American Studies* 6, no. 3 (October 2003): 261–88.

65. Ramesh Rao, "It Is India, Not South Asia," *The Subcontinental: A Journal of South
Asian American Political Identity* 1, no. 1 (2003): 27–40; Rajeev Srinivasan, "Why I Am
Not South Asian," March 20, 2000, <http://www.rediff.com/news/2000/Mar/19rajeev
.htm> (March 13, 2007).

66. Rajiv Malhotra, "America Must Re-Discover India," January 20, 2004, <http://
www.rediff.com/news/2004/jan/20rajiv.htm> (March 6, 2007); Rajiv Malhotra, "Does
South Asian Studies Undermine India?," December 4, 2003, <http:www.rediff.com/
news/2003.dec/08rajiv.htm> (March 6, 2007); Rajiv Malhotra, "Preventing America's
Nightmare," January 21, 2004, <http://www.rediff.com/news/2004/jan/21rajiv.htm>
(March 6, 2007); Rajiv Malhotra, "Repositioning India's Brand," December 9, 2003,
<http://www.rediff.com/news/2003/dec/09rajiv.htm> (March 6, 2007).

67. Malhotra, "America Must Re-Discover India."

68. Ibid.

69. Malhotra, "Does South Asian Studies Undermine India?," 2, 6. He gives as examples of the worldviews hostile to Indian interests the exotic of anthropology, colonial or
Marxist frameworks in history, U.S. foreign policy interests in South Asian studies, and
non-Indian categories in religious studies.

70. Malhotra, "Does South Asian Studies Undermine India?," 5. For instance, Western
feminists telling Indian women that they were victims of Indian culture, Dalit [lower

caste] activists being sponsored to blame Brahmins, and the Aryan theory used to create a separate Dravidian identity and blame Aryan North Indians as foreign imperialists.

71. Ibid.; Malhotra, "Preventing America's Nightmare," 3.

72. Malhotra, "Preventing America's Nightmare," 3; Malhotra, "America Must Re-Discover India," 1.

73. Malhotra, "Does South Asian Studies Undermine India?," 5.

74. Malhotra, "Preventing America's Nightmare," 5, 6.

75. See description of the conference at <http://www.lokvani.com/lokvani/article .php?article_id=410> (November 2, 2004).

76. Mitch Berbrier, "Making Minorities: Cultural Space, Stigma Transformation Frames, and the Categorical Status Claims of Deaf, Gay, and White Supremacist Activists in Late Twentieth Century America," *Sociological Forum* 17 (December 2002): 553–91; Kurien, "Multiculturalism, Immigrant Religion and Diasporic Nationalism."

Brown Is the New Yellow

The Yellow Peril in an Age of Terror

ROBERT G. LEE

"Civilization's going to pieces," broke out Tom violently. "I've gotten to be a terrible pessimist about things. Have you read 'The Rise of the Colored Empires' by this man Goddard? . . . The idea is if we don't look out the white race will be—will be utterly submerged. It's all scientific stuff; it's been proved. . . ." "We've got to beat them down," *whispered Daisy, winking ferociously toward the fervent sun.*
—F. Scott Fitzgerald, *The Great Gatsby*

Fu Manchu, "tall, lean and feline, high shouldered, with a brow like Shakespeare, and a face like Satan," was the face of terror in the early twentieth century.[1] At the beginning of the twenty-first century, Fu Manchu has returned with the face of Osama bin Laden, the Frankenstein of the American empire.[2] Then and now, the "Yellow Peril" imaginary mobilizes a deeply rooted mythic identity of Western civilization as the bulwark of Christendom against the Mongol and the Muslim, the "clash of civilizations" by which the West defined itself as the "West" and its other as the "East."[3]

At turn of the twentieth century and again at the turn of the twenty-first, the Yellow Peril imaginary enables an anxious discourse of Western civilization beset by ancient enemies and of national suicide brought about by the presence of an inassimilable Other. Yellow Peril serves as a way of articulating inchoate terrors about race, class, and national identity when the borders that give structure and meaning to the world appear to be collapsing. In the first decades of the twentieth century, Yellow Peril spoke to deep anxieties about urbanization, immigration, and "race suicide" in a world in which Western civilization, after Verdun, seemed no longer unassailable and in a nation increasingly peopled by immigrants and by people of color. In the twenty-first century, the Yellow Peril imaginary, rewritten to include Latinos, articulates similar anxieties with regard to the collapse of the international system organized by the Cold War, the rise of global capitalism, and the massive migration flows it has engendered. In both centuries, the Yellow Peril imaginary articulates the dread of an empty world without borders, structure, and order. The Yellow Peril spells out the collapse of political and social space as both global and local crises and welds national security to national identity. It demands the simultaneous construction of new world orders and redefinitions of national identity. It sutures the strategic crisis—what is to be done?—to an existential crisis—who are we? The Yellow Peril lives. The assimilation of even "model" minorities is always in doubt. In the hours and days after the attacks on the World Trade Center and the Pentagon, President George W. Bush promised a crusade to smoke the barbarians out of their caves. In the following few days, at least three more Americans were killed: Adel Karas, an immigrant from Egypt, was gunned down in his import shop in San Gabriel, California; Balbir Singh Sodhi, an immigrant from India, was shot to death outside his gas station in Mesa, Arizona; Waqar Hasan, an immigrant from Pakistan was killed in his grocery store in Dallas, Texas. On the front line of America's urban crisis, these immigrants were for most part faceless, except as a discomforting, permanently alien presence; in America after the World Trade Center, they became visible as the barbarians at the gate, suspects in America's global wars.

Civilization Is Going to Pieces

In 1917, amid the carnage of the First World War and the apparent exhaustion of European civilization, Lothrop Stoddard, Tom Buchanan's "Goddard," warned of a racial apocalypse in the immensely popular book, *The Rising Tide of Color*. The white race, he wrote, "might soon be irretrievably lost, swamped by the triumphant colored races, who will obliterate the white man by elimination or absorption."[4] The Bolshevik Revolution represented the apocalypse. Should the proletarian revolution spread, "the [white] race, summarily drained of its good blood, would sink like lead into the depths of degenerate barbarism." In this nightmare the Red Menace and the Yellow Peril had come together; Lenin had become Fu Manchu. In no less lurid images than those Sax Rohmer used to describe the underworld of Fu Manchu, whose Asiatic minions maneuvered to "pave a path for the Yellow Peril" into the citadel of white civilization, Stoddard warned that Bolshevism sought to enlist the colored races in its grand assault on civilization.[5] "Meanwhile," Stoddard wrote, "Lenine [*sic*], surrounded by his Chinese executioners, sits behind the Kremlin walls, a modern Jenghis Khan plotting the plunder of a world."[6] In every corner of the globe, in Asia, Africa, Latin America, and the United States, Bolshevik agitators whispered in the ears of discontented colored men their schemes of hatred and revenge.[7]

Stoddard's book remapped a world shattered by war and revolution and provided a powerful metaphor of a flood of brown and yellow races that threatened to break through what Stoddard called the "Inner Dikes" and inundate "the racial homelands of the Anglo-Saxons." Surrounding the core of white civilization were the "Outer Dikes," the vast areas of the world that were under white political control but largely inhabited by peoples of color. The Inner Dikes were areas, including Canada, the United States, and Australia, that were "peopled wholly or largely by Whites." In the coming racial struggle for survival, these Inner Dikes, Stoddard insisted, were "part of the race heritage, which should be defended to the last extremity."[8]

Like Josiah Strong a generation before him, Stoddard was an Anglo-Saxon nationalist who believed that colonialism was the inevitable expression of White racial supremacy. Stoddard, however, did not share Strong's optimism about the transformative power of Anglo-Saxon Protestant culture. Instead, Stoddard mapped the world in terms of a titanic eugenic racial struggle. In the past the boundaries of civilization had been coterminous with those of race, but the expansion of white civilization and technology had broken down natural boundaries and made migration possible for millions. For Stoddard, the great threat of Asiatic immigration was exacerbated by a tendency toward race suicide from within the Inner Dikes.

Shortly after the collapse of the Soviet empire and end of the Cold War, Samuel Huntington, one of America's most prominent defense intellectuals, warned in an article in *Foreign Affairs* that future global conflict would be organized around the "clash of civilizations." Huntington's civilizational map of the world was remarkably similar to Stoddard's, dividing the globe into seven or eight civilizations: Western (in two variants, Western European and North American), Confucian, Japanese, Islamic, Hindu, Slavic-Orthodox, Latin American, and "possibly" African.[9]

Huntington, a conservative "realist" who served in a number of liberal Democratic administrations, took to task neoconservatives like Francis Fukuyama, who had argued that the fall of the Soviet system had ushered in the triumph of liberal democracy and the "end of history."[10] Huntington insisted that the world was now threatened by older, more enduring civilizational conflicts between the West and its Others, in which the West was at a historical disadvantage. At stake in this struggle is the very survival of Western civilization. In a passage that echoes Stoddard's alarm at the breaching of Western civilization's innermost dike, Huntington writes, "If the United States is de-Westernized, the West is reduced to Europe and a few lightly populated overseas European settler countries. Without the United States, the West becomes a miniscule and declining part of the world's population on a small and inconsequential peninsula at the extremity of the Eurasian land mass."[11]

Stoddard's *Rising Tide of Color* was a racist jeremiad and a critique of imperialism. Stoddard believed that the anti-imperialists' turn-of-the-century admonitions about the dangers of the "white man's burden" had come home to haunt the republic. Although it was the inevitable expression of white racial supremacy, imperialism had led humanity to a potentially disastrous "dysgenic" pass. Modern urban and industrial life, with its huge demand for immigrant wage labor, he wrote, had been "one sided, abnormal, unhealthy . . . dysgenic." In Stoddard's calculus of the ill effects of immigration and miscegenation, the modern world was moving toward the diminishment of "racial values," which would inevitably end in "racial bankruptcy and the collapse of civilization."[12]

Stoddard held that imperialism, modernity, and technology had combined to shorten the "natural" geographical distance that separated the races. The extension of white civilization throughout the world via colonialism had awakened millions in the colored world to the advantages of Western civilization but simultaneously aroused their resentment against the imposition of white dominion. In the wake of Japanese imperialism, the Chinese revolution, the emergence of anticolonialist movements in India, Indonesia, and Indochina, the Kemalist revolution Turkey, and the Bolshevik Revolution at Europe's doorstep, the immediate threat was the "very imminent danger that the White stocks may be swamped by Asiatic blood."[13]

Echoing Stoddard's alarm that the main threat to Western civilization is from the East, Huntington warns that the West is endangered by a likely alliance between militant and revanchist Islam and the capitalist powerhouses of "Confucian" East Asia. Huntington rehearses the powerful but short-lived "Asian Values" discourse of Westernized Asian leaders such as Lee Kuan-yew of Singapore to suggest that Oriental capitalism is fundamentally different than Western capitalism. Rejecting the claims of former U.S. president Bill Clinton and others that it is not Islam but Islamic extremists who are at war with the United States over matters of foreign policy, Huntington insists that Islam itself has been at war with the West for a thousand years. In both cases, civilization is the bedrock of difference that does not yield to politics and leads inexorably to conflict. Huntington, like Stoddard, is wary of the unintended consequences of imperialism. He cautions against the attempt to think of Western values such as democracy as universal and warns against any attempt to spread such values abroad. "Western intervention in the affairs of other civilizations," Huntington writes, "is probably the single most dangerous source of instability and potential global conflict in a multi-civilizational world."[14] The rest of the contemporary world, he holds, should be left alone while the West restores its strength through a reforging of Western identity.

It's All Scientific Stuff; It's Been Proved

In *The Rising Tide of Color*, Stoddard shared Madison Grant's pessimism about the future of American society and his belief in the new science of eugenics. Even as the colored tide from the East threatened to breach the Inner Dikes, the strength of the white race was already threatened by "mongrelization" from within. The "mongrelization" and "devaluation" of the Nordic bloodline in America had already been brought about both by the migrations of various "Alpine and Mediterranean" European racial stocks and the "amalgamation with those already here." At the heart of Stoddard's argument lay the eugenic thesis that Nordic blood carried "superior" or "more specialized" genetic material and was vulnerable to "dilution" by the blood of "lesser breeds."[15] Over-civilization, overconsumption, and collapse of purpose had led the middle classes to forget their racial mission. "Two things are necessary for the continued existence of a race," Stoddard warned; "it must remain itself and it must breed its best." In the past, the white race could always rely on a reserve army of "White barbarians" to forward the militant mission of the race. But by 1920, modernization had spread civilization to all the tribes of the white race and left the race without its redemptive army of "unspoiled, well-endowed barbarians to step forward and 'carry on.' "[16]

Although Huntington is quick to disavow biologically defined racial categories in his analysis, his definition of "civilization" rests on the same principle of indelible difference; it is race without biology. In Huntington's definition, civilization determines a "basic" identity, impervious to politics or historical change. He defines civilization as "the highest cultural grouping of people and the broadest level of cultural identity people have, short of that which distinguishes humans from other species."[17] In this view, civilizational differences are broad but impermeable, "far more fundamental than differences among political ideologies and political regimes."[18] Huntington asserts that an individual might choose to be a socialist, a Catholic, a worker, but one cannot transcend or escape his or her "essential" Armenianness, Japaneseness, or Indianness: "In the conflicts between civilizations, the question is 'What are you?' That is a given that cannot be changed."[19] For Huntington, it is not biology but civilization that is inescapable.

Breaching the Inner Dikes

In identifying the Yellow Peril as the threat to the American nation, Stoddard was in the mainstream of racial geopolitical thinking. However, unlike Alfred Thayer Mahan or Homer Lea, Stoddard did not believe the Asian threat to be a military one.[20] For Stoddard, it was neither military force nor economic competition that posed the principal colored threat to white civilization. White civilization was, he warned, in imminent danger of being swamped by the rising tide of Asian immigration. It was weakness in the West and American political culture and a "dysgenic" tendency toward egalitarianism that made white civilization vulnerable to the advancing tide of colored immigration. He saw immigration, assimilation, and miscegenation between the yellow or brown and white as the vehicle for the total absorption of white into yellow. Stoddard concluded that the question of "Asiatic" immigration was the "Supreme phase of the colored peril. . . . It threatens not merely our supremacy or prosperity, but our very race-existence, the well-springs of being, the sacred heritage of our children."[21] Even though they laid out their template on a global scale, both Huntington and Stoddard insist that immigration and multiculturalism (in Stoddard's case, pluralism and the melting pot) pose the greater threat to national identity. Both contend that American national identity is based on the essential and inseparable European (in Stoddard's case, Anglo-Saxon) character of liberal democracy. In this vision, America is threatened by the demand of non-European Americans for equity and social recognition, which Huntington characterizes as "special rights (affirmative action and similar measures) for blacks and other groups." Such claims, he asserts, undermine "the principles that have been the basis of American political unity." Simultaneously, "multiculturalism" insists on "rewriting American political, social, and literary history from the viewpoint of non-European groups," thereby encouraging "a clash of civilizations within the United States."[22]

Just as Stoddard saw "Asiatic" immigration as a threat to white civilization, Huntington warns that the West is challenged from within by the "immigrants from other civilizations who reject assimilation and continue to adhere to and propagate the values, customs, and cultures of their home societies."[23] Immigration from the non-Western world (both Asia and Latin America) threatens to turn the United States into a "torn society." Huntington sounds the alarm against the "weakening of the European character of American society and culture through non-European immigration and multiculturalism."[24] The Hispanic and nonwhite populations that he fears will soon comprise a majority in the United States threaten to "de-Westernize" America.[25] The rejection of assimilation, Huntington notes, "is also manifest, in a lesser degree, among Hispanics in the United States who are large minority. If assimilation fails in this case, the United States will become a cleft country."[26] "A multicultural America," he writes, "is impossible because a non-Western America is not American. . . . The preservation of the United States and the West requires the renewal of Western identity."[27] He fears that if "Americans cease to adhere to their liberal democratic and European-rooted political ideology, the United States as we have known it will cease to exist and will follow the other ideologically defined superpower on the ash heap of history."[28]

Reforging America

In *Who Are We? The Challenges to America's National Identity* Huntington describes himself as a patriot writing out of concern for the future of the whole nation in a time of crisis. Samuel Huntington saw the September 11 attacks much as Lothrop Stoddard had seen World War I, as a wake-up call for a slumbering America. For Huntington, the attacks "dramatically symbolized the end of the twentieth century of ideology and ideological conflict, and the beginning of a new era in which people define themselves primarily in terms of culture and religion. The real and potential enemies of the United States are now religiously driven militant Islam and entirely nonideological Chinese nationalism."[29]

Who Are We? is a call for the revitalization of America through a restoration of "the Anglo-Protestant culture, traditions, and values that for three and a half centuries have been embraced by Americans of all races, ethnicities, and religions and that have been the source of their liberty, unity, power, prosperity, and moral leadership as a force for good in the world."[30] No longer are broadly Western European values sufficient to sustain America; Huntington now insists that an Anglo-American culture is the necessary core of the national identity, without which "History shows that no country so constituted can long endure as a coherent society."[31] Huntington identifies the "key elements" of Anglo-America culture to include the English language; Christianity; religious commitment; English concepts of the rule of law, the responsibility of rulers, and the rights of individuals; and dissenting Protestant values of individualism, the work ethic, and the belief that humans have the ability to create a heaven on earth, a "city on a hill."[32]

In this view, Anglo-American culture, which is the indispensable core of American identity, is in crisis, beset from above and below, its Anglo-Protestant bedrock eroded by the tides of yellow and brown immigrants crashing at its shore and undermined from within by multiculturalist academics and politicians and multinationalist corporate elites. "The spread of Spanish as a second language and the Hispanization trends in American society, the assertion of group identities based on race, ethnicity and gender, the impact of diasporas and their homeland governments, and the growing commitment of elites to cosmopolitan and transnational identities" all threaten American national identity.[33]

A decade after *The Rising Tide of Color*, Stoddard wrote *Re-forging America*, which, like Huntington's *Who Are We?*, is a restorationist call to remake America's national identity. The Johnson-Reed Act of 1924 sharply restricted immigration from Eastern and Southern Europe through national origins quotas. The compromise enshrined in the Johnson-Reed Act—that immigration should forever reflect the ethnic balance of 1904—seemed to safeguard the dominance of the Nordic "race brethren" and the preservation of the "Anglo-Saxon stamp . . . so deeply impressed upon this virgin land."[34] Stoddard called for a revitalization of America nationalism through the restoration of "Anglo-Saxon" culture as the indispensable core of American national identity. While the curtailment of immigration had made such a national revitalization possible, the task would require reforging the American people. European immigrants, residents and newcomers, would be gradually assimilated into Anglo-America, African Americans segregated, and Asians excluded.

Much like *Who Are We?*, *Re-forging America* is based on a narrative of American history as the rise and fall and rebirth of the "Nordic brethren." The task before "loyal" Americans was "above all to preserve America . . . a nation, whose foundations were laid over three hundred years ago by Anglo-Saxon Nordics, and whose nationhood is due almost exclusively to people of North European stock."[35] Stoddard attacked pluralistic interpretations of American history, which held colonial America to be "a hodge-podge of races and cultures" and modern American society to be "still in the making," as the "emotional protests of dissatisfied, unassimilated elements."[36]

In particular, Stoddard attacked Horace Kallen's pluralist ideal that separated ethnicity from national identity. He described Kallen as a brilliant but unassimilated Jew whose goal was to undermine a distinctive Anglo-American identity and to replace it with a polyglot of hyphenated Americas. Such an abandonment of the true spirit of America would mean the loss of American identity and ultimately national suicide. "Loyal America," Stoddard asserted, "rejects absolutely the concept of a 'pluralistic America,' Balkanized into a haphazard assortment of diverse racial and cultural groups. And loyal America rejects equally the idea of the 'Melting Pot,' the fusion of all existing elements into a mongrel mass devoid of outstanding, dominant qualities."[37]

Stoddard was not unaware that cultures other than the Anglo-Saxon were at play in colonial America, and it is to the baleful influence of the French Encyclopedists that he assigned blame for the idealism that had led to America's mishandling of its two "gravest problems—the negro and immigration. . . . A good instance of this is the changed popular interpretation of that much-discussed phrase in the Declaration of Independence: 'All men are created equal.' "[38] The "equalitarian and cosmopolitan doctrines" introduced by the

French philosophes ran counter to the basic "pragmatic" nature of Anglo-Saxon Americans; the ideal of universal equality had led America into civil war and close to national suicide.[39]

Assimilability as Race

The identification of the Yellow Peril as a problem of immigration was paralleled by the consolidation of whiteness as an exclusive racial category in citizenship law. This involved a shift from definitions of race as a category of nature to a view of race based on civilizational *difference*.[40]

Even though the Johnson-Reed Act had slowed the pace of immigration, race and immigration remained at the center of Stoddard's concern about the future of a reforged America. Immigration was "a supremely vital problem" signifying a national spirit "determined by the blood of its people."[41] Stoddard pointed to World War I as the siren that had awakened Americans to the disaster of immigration. Immigrants who clung to their ethnic identities and demanded a pluralistic interpretation of American history could never be true Americans, and they sapped America's strength in a time of need. World War I, however, was "the 'great awakening," an "'acid test' which revealed latent 'alienism' and 'hyphenism' which had drifted along for generations."[42] This did not apply to all immigrants, but apart from the assimilated middle class, "there lies a polyglot mass of undigested and indigestible material, refractory to assimilation, which already causes us much trouble and which will continue to be a burden, a weakness and potential menace, probably for generations to come."[43]

His negative attitude toward Eastern and Southern Europeans and proletarians of any national origin notwithstanding, Stoddard embraced the grand compromise of the Johnson-Reed Act, which slowed Southern and Eastern European immigration to allow for the gradual "amalgamation" of those lesser ethnics into the Anglo-American bloodstream. The issue was no longer the hierarchy of European races, he wrote; "when we discuss immigration we had better stop theorizing about superiors and inferiors and get down to the bedrock of *difference*."[44] Alpines and swarthy Mediterraneans were "so basically like us in blood [and] culture" that "eventual assimilation is only a matter of time."[45] While Stoddard now believed that European immigrants, "most of whom belong to some branch of the white racial group," might over time become assimilated into Anglo-Saxon American culture, he asserted "most emphatically" that this did not extend to nonwhite immigrants "like the Chinese, Japanese, or Mexicans; neither does it apply to the large resident negro element which has been a tragic anomaly since our earliest times. Here, ethnic differences are so great that 'assimilation' in the racial sense is impossible."[46]

The question of assimilation and race has been central to the struggle over the immigration and citizenship of Asian Americans. In 1854 the California Supreme Court ruled Chinese ineligible to testify against whites, declaring the Chinese presence "an actual and present danger." Justice Charles Murray wrote that the Chinese were "a distinct people, living in our community, a race of people whom nature has marked as inferior, and who are incapable of progress or intellectual development beyond a certain point, as their history has shown; differing in language, opinions, color, and physical conformation; between whom and ourselves nature has placed an impassable difference."[47]

In the notorious 1889 Chinese Exclusion Case, Justice Stephen Johnson Field reiterated the judgment that the Chinese were excludable as a race because they were inassimilable. Field found evidence of Chinese unassimilability in their frugality and lack of family residing in the United States: "It seemed impossible for them to assimilate with our people or to make any change in their habits or modes of living."[48] By the end of the century, so universal was identification of the Chinese with indelible foreignness that Justice John Marshall Harlan wrote famously in his "color blind" dissent in *Plessy v. Ferguson* that the Chinese were "a race so different from our own that we do not permit those belonging to it to become citizens of the United States."[49] Indeed, it was the unassimilable and excluded Chinese against which the offended rights of the African American citizen might be measured. Stoddard echoes this logic of assimilability as a marker of racial difference when he writes of the Chinese: "The Chinese . . . are hard working, temperate, likable, intelligent, and much more besides. But—the Chinese are different! They are so different from us in blood, culture, ideals and general outlook on life that they cannot be assimilated, and we know that if they came to us in vast numbers they would either destroy us or hopelessly mongrel-ize us."[50]

Assimilation is a two-way street. Belief and behavior on the part of the petitioner is less significant than the consent of the adjudicator. At the center of defining whiteness for purposes of citizenship was the question of assimilation. In 1922 and 1923 Takao Ozawa, a Japanese resident of the United States for twenty-six years and who had been denied citizenship, and Bhagat Thind, an immigrant from India whose naturalized citizenship had been revoked, brought the question of assimilation and whiteness to the Supreme Court.[51]

Both argued that, their Asian origins notwithstanding, they, unlike the excluded Chinese, were assimilated immigrants and deserving of naturalization. Takao Ozawa argued that unlike the proscribed Chinese, he was perfectly assimilated and that (following *Dred Scott*) having no "Negro" blood he was white. Furthermore, Ozawa, it was claimed, had a complexion paler than many Americans of European stock. Ozawa testified that he was a true and loyal

American and had broken all ties to Japan and Japanese culture, that he and his family spoke English exclusively, and worshipped with a white church.[52] The Court ruled unanimously that Ozawa could not become a naturalized American citizen, no matter how assimilated he declared himself to be. Nor, it held, was this a matter of racial superiority or inferiority but one of racial difference. A white person was, as a matter of law, "a person of what is popularly known as the Caucasian race."[53]

The next year in *Thind*, the Court ruled that racial categories were contingent not on scientific standards, ethnology, or linguistics, but on contemporary popular standards of assimilability. The Court acknowledged that successive immigration from Southern and Central Europe had brought "the Slavs and dark-eyed, swarthy people of Alpine and Mediterranean stock" to America and that some of these might be of darker hue than the petitioner, but it held that these immigrants were "unquestionably akin to those already here and readily amalgamated with them."[54] "Hindoos," regardless of their lineage or coloration, were not among those "unquestionably akin" or "readily amalgamated with" the common (white) man. In describing the ethnic assimilation of Americans of European descent and the "instinctive" recognition and rejection of assimilation for the American children of Indian immigrants, the Court made a clear distinction between white ethnicity and race:

> The children of English, French, German, Italian, Scandinavian, and other European parentage, quickly merge into the mass of our population and lose the distinctive hallmarks of their European origin. On the other hand, it cannot be doubted that the children born in this country of Hindu parentage would retain indefinitely the clear evidence of their ancestry. . . . What we suggest is merely racial difference [not superiority or inferiority], and it is of such character and extent that the great body of our people instinctively recognize it and reject the thought of assimilation.[55]

As yellow came to signify indelible otherness, whiteness came to signify assimilability. With citizens of "African nativity and descent" disfranchised and segregated by the *Plessy* decision, the Supreme Court in the *Ozawa* and *Thind* decisions articulated a vision of American nationality based on an exclusive and consolidated white race made up of a colorful but white range of European Americans, from the "Nordic" to the "swarthy Mediterranean."[56]

Exclusion in the Time of Peril

In 1889, deciding that the Chinese were as a "race" excludable, Justice Stephen J. Field wrote, "It seemed impossible for them to assimilate with our people or to make any change in their habits or modes of living. As they grew in numbers each year the people of the coast saw, or believed they saw, in the facility of immigration, and in the crowded millions of China, where population presses upon the means of subsistence, great danger that at no distant day that portion of our country would be overrun by them unless prompt action was taken to restrict their immigration." In a passage that echoes Field's fear of being overrun by nonwhite immigrants, Huntington describes late twentieth-century Mexican immigration as an invasion: "A demographic reconquista of areas Americans took from Mexico by force in the 1830's and 1840's . . . blurring the border between Mexico and America, introducing a very different culture, while also promoting the emergence, in some areas, of a blended society and culture, half-American and half-Mexican."[57]

In support of his vision of the *reconquista*, Huntington cites a prediction that by 2080 the southwestern states of the United States will come together to form a new country, "La República del Norte." Huntington imagines that this extraordinary development will be made possible by "the surge of Mexicans northward and the increasing economic ties between the communities on different sides of the border . . . which is 'melting,' moving (northward that is) and as 'sort of a dotted line.' " Huntington fears that these ties will produce in the southwestern United States, and to a lesser extent in northern Mexico, what has be variously termed "MexAmerica", "Amexica," and "Mexifornia."[58]

It is not simply the numbers of Mexican immigrants entering the United States and their proximity to their homeland but what he perceives as their relative lack of assimilation that alarms Huntington. Even though Huntington is willing to acknowledge the rapid acquisition of English among second-generation Mexican Americans, and the rapid growth of evangelical Protestantism among Latinos, he is concerned that the size and concentration of Mexican American communities and Latino markets mean that there will be decreasing need for English language acquisition. Mexican American society and culture "could eventually change America into a country of two languages, two cultures and two peoples," he concludes.[59]

Huntington's fear of the Brown Peril of Mexican immigration brings to mind Stoddard's fear of Yellow Peril of Chinese immigration. Even as Stoddard conceded that the Chinese possessed admirable qualities, he was convinced that the bedrock of unsurmountable difference made their very presence in the United States a gathering peril. If only the Chinese had been simply coolies and sojourners, Stoddard lamented; "unluckily, the coolie is not quite a machine. In fact he is a man—with ideas, and desires, and aims of his own." It is precisely the opposite, the growing settlement of the indelibly alien Chinese in America the that mattered to Stoddard. Like Huntington's Mexicans, "The Chinese element expands by leaps and bounds. Chinese villages, Chinese city quarters, grow like mushrooms. Ultimately the land is transformed into something like a New China. And the native is, for the most part, no more!"[60]

Like Stoddard's unassimilable Chinese, Huntington views Mexican and other Latino immigrants as outsiders to Anglo-Protestant culture, to be excluded. Unless Mexican immigration can be likewise curtailed, "no such transfer of loyalties, convictions, and identities can be expected with Mexican immigrants, and the great American assimilation success story of the past will not necessarily be duplicated for Mexicans."[61]

Huntington is bluntly dismissive of those who believe that Latino Americans might share an "Americano Dream." "There is no Americano dream. There is only the dream created by an Anglo-Protestant society. Mexican-Americans will share in that dream and in that society only if they dream in English."[62]

Mexican exclusion would, in Huntington's view, be something of a panacea. Virtually all the social ills of the United States, from illegal immigration, to low wages, to education and crime, are made worse by the presence of Mexicans in the land. Huntington argues that were Mexican immigrants to be excluded, "the average education and skills of immigrants would again become highly diverse, which would increase incentives for all immigrants to learn English and absorb American culture. The possibility of a de facto split between a predominantly Spanish-speaking America and an English-speaking America would disappear, and with it a potential threat to the cultural and possibly political integrity of the United States."[63]

The Monotonous Refrain of Nativism

Huntington insists that *Who Are We?* is "an argument for the importance of Anglo-Protestant culture, not for the importance of Anglo-Protestant people." Nevertheless, just as Stoddard had insisted that Northern European immigrants were only presumptively more assimilable, Huntington turns to a nativist patriotic movement, "composed largely but not only of white males, primarily working class and middle class, protesting and attempting to stop or reverse these changes and what they believe, accurately or not, to be the diminution of their social and economic status, their loss of jobs to immigrants and foreign countries, the perversion of their culture, the displacement of their culture, the displacement of their language, and the erosion or even evaporation of the historical identity of their country."[64]

Such a movement would be different than the crudely racist and fascist hate groups and paramilitaries. Young, articulate intellectuals armed with degrees from the "most prestigious" universities would lead the Anglo-American na-

tionalist movement. These groups could "be both racially and culturally inspired and could be both anti-Hispanic, anti-black and anti-immigrant. They
would be the heir to the many comparable exclusivist racial and anti-foreign
groups that helped define American identity in the past."[65]

Seeking to blunt criticism of these groups, Huntington claims that "nativist"
has become a term of opprobrium "among denationalized elites." He finds in
John Higham's *Strangers in the Land* a more "neutral" definition: the "intense
opposition to an internal minority on the ground of its foreign (i.e. 'un-
American') connections." In describing this new nativism, Huntington expands
Higham's definition so as to include, "first, opposition to groups, such as
blacks, that lack 'foreign connections' but are nonetheless seen as not a true
part of American society and, second, to include 'opposition to an internal
minority' that is perceived as becoming a majority." Echoing Stoddard's insistence in *Re-forging America* that the issue was not theories of racial superiority
or inferiority but rather the "bedrock of difference," Huntington insists that the
white nationalists do not advocate white supremacy but rather believe in "racial
self-determination and self-preservation" and that "America is fast becoming a
nation dominated by non-white people."[66]

Huntington's new nativists are the intellectual and political equivalent of
Stoddard's "Nordic barbarians," who periodically come forward to protect the
Anglo-American cultural core of the nation. Rising to the threat to their language, culture, and power that they see coming from the expanding presence of
Latinos in American society, these new nationalists resist "the replacement of
the white culture that made America great by black or brown cultures that are
different and, in their view, intellectually and morally inferior."[67]

In his classic study of American nativism, John Higham chose not to incorporate an account of the powerful movements against Asian immigrants because he saw those movements as sui generis. But in the matter of citizenship
and nationality, it was precisely the excluded Asian Other that defined what
constituted the free white person, and it was precisely within the boundaries of
this definition that European immigrants could find their way past race to
ethnicity and to the promised land of citizenship and assimilation. The anti-
Asian movement and the Yellow Peril imaginary that supported it erased the
categorical boundaries between racism and nativism. Nonetheless, John Higham's observation that "hardly any aspect of American xenophobia over its
course from the eighteenth century to the twentieth century is more striking
than the monotony of its ideological refrain" is as appropriate today as was
when it was written forty years ago.[68]

NOTES

1. Sax Rohmer [Arthur Ward], *The Insidious Dr. Fu Manchu* (New York: Pyramid Books, 1913).

2. The similarities of between the fictional Fu Manchu and the presumptively real Osama bin Laden are such that one is tempted to say that if bin Laden didn't exist, he could only be made up as a Fu Manchu sequel. He shares much of the same physical description: tall and lean, and bearded; a wealthy, cunning mastermind, Western-trained, and bitterly revanchist.

3. The phrase "Yellow Peril" (*Gelfelb Gefar*) was coined at the end of the nineteenth century by Kaiser Wilhelm of Germany to justify Germany's grab for concessions in China. To illustrate his point, in 1895 the Kaiser commissioned a painting of the nations of Europe, dressed as female warriors, defending Christendom from the Yellow Peril. This he had reproduced and sent to various European heads of state and to U.S. president William McKinley. For analysis of the painting and its ideology see Gary Okihiro, "Perils of Mind and Body," in *Margins and Mainstreams* (Seattle: University of Washington Press, 1994), 118–47.

4. Lothrop Stoddard, *The Rising Tide of Color against White World-Supremacy* (New York: Scribner's Sons, 1920), 20.

5. Ibid., 220.

6. Ibid., 219.

7. Ibid., 220.

8. Ibid., 226.

9. Samuel P. Huntington, "The Clash of Civilizations," *Foreign Affairs* 72 (Summer 1993): 22–49.

10. Samuel P. Huntington, *The Clash of Civilizations and the Remaking of World Order* (Cambridge, Mass.: Harvard University Press, 1996), 29; Francis Fukuyama, *The End of History and the Last Man* (New York: Free Press, 1992).

11. Huntington, *Clash of Civilizations*, 307.

12. Stoddard, *Rising Tide of Color*, 240.

13. Ibid., 235.

14. Huntington, *Clash of Civilizations*, 318.

15. Stoddard, *Rising Tide of Color*, 236.

16. Ibid., 240.

17. Huntington, *Clash of Civilizations*, 43.

18. Ibid., 25.

19. Ibid., 27.

20. Stoddard, *Rising Tide of Color*, 240.

21. Ibid., 20.

22. Samuel P. Huntington, "If Not Civilizations, What?: Paradigms of the Post–Cold War World," *Foreign Affairs* 72 (November 1993): 190.

23. Huntington, *Clash of Civilizations*, 305.

24. Ibid., 186–94.

25. Huntington, "If Not Civilizations," 191.

26. Huntington, *Clash of Civilizations*, 304.

27. Ibid., 305.

28. Huntington, "If Not Civilizations," 191.

29. Samuel P. Huntington, *Who Are We?: The Challenges to America's National Identity* (New York: Simon and Schuster, 2004), 340.

30. Ibid., xvii.

31. Ibid., 229.

32. Ibid., xvi.

33. Ibid., xvi.

34. Lothrop Stoddard, *Re-forging America* (New York: Charles Scribner's Sons, 1927), 5, 9.

35. Ibid., 101.

36. Ibid., 5.

37. Ibid., 368.

38. Ibid., 41.

39. Ibid.

40. It was not until the passage of the McCarran-Walters Immigration and Naturalization Act of 1952 that the principle of the right to naturalization regardless of race was legislated.

41. Stoddard, *Re-forging America*, 95.

42. Ibid., 181.

43. Ibid., 165, 166.

44. Ibid., 103 (emphasis in original).

45. Ibid., 256.

46. Ibid., 256–57.

47. *The People, Respondent, v. George W. Hall, Appellant*, Supreme Court of the State of California, 1854.

48. The Chinese Exclusion Case, *Chae Chan Ping v. United States*, 130 U.S. 581 (1889).

49. *Plessy v. Ferguson*, 163 U.S. 537 (1896).

50. Stoddard, *Re-forging America*, 119.

51. Sucheng Chan, ed., *Entry Denied: Exclusion and the Chinese Community in America, 1882–1943* (Philadelphia: Temple University Press, 1991); Jeffrey Lesser, "Always Outsiders: Asians, Naturalization, and the Supreme Court, 1740–1944," *Amerasia Journal* 12, no. 1 (1985–86): 83–100.

52. Cited in Yuji Ichioka, "The Early Japanese Immigrant Quest for Citizenship: The Background of the 1922 Ozawa Case," *Amerasia Journal* 4, no. 2 (1977): 1–22.

53. *Takao Ozawa v. United States* (1922), cited in Hyung-chan Kim, ed., *Asian Americans and the Supreme Court: A Documentary History* (Westport, Conn.: Greenwood Press, 1992), 528.

54. Kim, *Asian Americans and the Supreme Court*, 540.

55. Ibid., 541.

56. See Matthew Frye Jacobson, *Whiteness of a Different Color: European Immigrants*

and the Alchemy of Race (Cambridge, Mass.: Harvard University Press, 1999), for an extended account of this phenomenon.

57. Chinese Exclusion Case, *Chae Chan Ping v. United States*, 130 U.S. 581 (1889); Huntington, *Who Are We?*, 306.

58. Huntington, *Who Are We?*, 246.

59. Ibid.

60. Stoddard, *Re-forging America*, 117.

61. Huntington, *Who Are We?*, 229.

62. Ibid., 256.

63. Ibid., 243.

64. Ibid., 310.

65. Ibid., 312.

66. Ibid., 311–12.

67. Ibid., 316.

68. John Higham, *Strangers in the Land: Patterns of American Nativism, 1860–1925* (1963; reprint, New Brunswick, N.J.: Rutgers University Press, 1988), 131.

Rethinking the "Clash of Civilizations"

American Evangelicals, the Bush Administration,
and the Winding Road to the Iraq War

MELANI MCALISTER

In May 2004 the Institute for Global Engagement, a Christian evangelical non-profit focused on international relations, published an article called "Is Evangelicalism Itching for a Civilizational Fight?"[1] No, the report said; or rather, evangelicalism was deeply divided about how to think about Islam. Shortly after September 11, 2001, several conservative evangelicals had made headlines with rhetoric attacking Islam. Jerry Falwell called the prophet Mohammed "a terrorist," while missionary leader Franklin Graham called Islam "an evil and wicked religion." The comments were widely reported in both the U.S. media and in the Arab and Muslim world, and many Americans, including evangelicals, found them offensive. A group of moderate evangelicals with the National Association of Evangelicals called a meeting to discuss "dialogue" with Muslims, to which Falwell was not invited. These moderate leaders were consciously trying to fashion a more positive engagement with Islam. At the same time, they remained convinced that Christianity is the only truth, and they criticized mainline Protestants, whom they said were "naïve" in minimizing the differences between Muslims and Christians.[2] These leaders, like the vast majority of evangelicals in the United States, were interested in evangelizing Muslims, in the Middle East and elsewhere. As activists and thinkers, they were also deeply concerned about the Israeli-Palestinian conflict and the Iraq war; in both cases, Islamist activism was seen as a major threat to peace.

With visions of a "clash of civilizations" prominent in U.S. political and intellectual life, evangelical views of Islam have become matters of national, as well as global, interest. During the first five years of the Bush White House, evangelicals were increasingly visible as a mainstream political force, both as members of the administration (George W. Bush himself, as well as high-level figures from John Ashcroft to Condoleezza Rice) and as activists and lobbyists who have been aggressive on a variety of issues. Domestically, those issues have included gay marriage, abortion, and the teaching of evolution in the schools. On international issues evangelicals have been equally influential. They have organized against the persecution of Christians in countries where they face hostility, and they have lobbied U.S. policymakers on issues including the Israeli-Palestinian conflict, the Sudan, and HIV/AIDS. When the United States went to war against Iraq in 2003, white evangelical Christians supported the war more enthusiastically than any other subset of the population, with 85 percent describing themselves as in favor.[3]

Twenty-five to 40 percent of Americans identify themselves as evangelical or born again—the exact number depends on how you ask the question. One basic definition of evangelicalism, put forward by Mark Noll and others, is that it centers on (1) the idea the Bible is inerrant truth, the word of God; (2) the necessity of personal salvation, (3) the necessity of evangelizing others; and (4) the centrality of Jesus' crucifixion as the path to God.[4] Defined in this way, evangelicals are predominantly white, but the group also includes most African American Christians, whose churches are generally evangelical in theology, and smaller numbers of Latinos, Asians, and others.[5] Evangelicals are far from a cohesive group: they are theologically and politically divided; the movement encompasses deeply conservative leaders like Falwell and Pat Robertson; neo-evangelicals like those at the Institute for Global Engagement; African American leaders who tend to be conservative on social issues but more liberal on foreign policy and domestic economic issues; and a small group of left-liberals who see their faith as a basis for social justice activism.

In recent years, journalists and activists have paid increasingly close attention to evangelicals' influence on U.S. Middle East policy, particularly on the ever-tightening link with the Israeli right and evangelicals' support for prosecuting and expanding the war on terrorism. It is certainly true that conservative Christians have been a key component in the populist coalition for empire that has backed President Bush's transformation in U.S. foreign policy since September 11. But the administration is also engaged in a complex dance with evangelicals, whose fervent beliefs and public visibility on Middle East issues make them at once a core constituency and a rather problematic set of allies.

Since September 11, evangelicals, like most other Americans, have frequently focused on Islam and on defining the relationship between the Muslim world and the United States, both of which have been frequent topics in evangelical magazines, on radio talk shows, and in popular books with titles like *Secrets of the Koran* and *Married to Muhammed*.[6] Conservative evangelicals in particular have been often inclined toward the formulation of a "clash of civilizations" because it highlights the importance of religious identity and the distinction between Islam and Christianity. However, the need to court allies and convince the world that the United States is not at war against Islam meant that the Bush administration found itself frequently at odds with both the rhetoric of civilizational clash and the anti-Muslim sentiments of the evangelical conservatives who were the president's base.

This essay explores the tensions, contradictions, and yet productive work done by the trope of a "clash of civilizations" as it was mobilized, challenged, and captured by policymakers, pundits, and Christian evangelicals alike. The prominence of that formulation, I argue, was part of an ongoing and still partial transformation in the racial politics of global American power. While the privileges that have linked "whiteness," maleness, citizenship, and power remain in place, new and/or revitalized nationalist markers are remaking the landscape. Religion has returned to the center of the explicit and implicit geographies of Americanness that structure daily life. Evangelicals are part of that project: they are globalizing their visions, becoming more interested in foreign policy and increasingly powerful in their lobbying as activists. They are, however, just one part of a much larger conversation, one in which religion, popular culture, and policymaking are closely intertwined, as questions about the nature of Islam have become inseparable from definitions of American national identity and debates about the direction of U.S. policy in the Middle East.

The Clash and the Bush Administration

In the immediate aftermath of the attacks of September 11, President Bush reached out to American Muslims as "true Americans." Islam, he said, was a "religion of peace." He visited a mosque, and a Muslim cleric participated in the National Day of Prayer on September 14, 2001. As Bush launched the war in Afghanistan, and the larger war on terrorism, the president declared repeatedly that his acts were not a "war against Islam" but a war against the "evildoers," on behalf of all who were civilized.[7] The Bush administration surely wanted to set a tone that would discourage hate crimes in the United States; just as surely, policymakers knew from the beginning that they would need to seek allies in the Arab and Muslim world, and that any rhetoric that placed America in opposition to "Islam" would severely hamper foreign policy options.

Yet at the same time, Bush seemed to give another set of messages about the nature of the conflict at hand. In the early days after September 11, he infamously referred to his administration's plans for fighting terrorism as a "crusade," inflaming anger in the Middle East and elsewhere among those who feared exactly that—that the United States had launched its own holy war to take control of the Middle East. Bush also consistently used religious language that went beyond the vague pieties voiced by most presidents and politicians, suggesting a specifically Christian identity for the United States. The president spoke frequently and generically of the importance of "faith" in resolving the nation's crises after 9/11, but he also peppered his talks with insiderish terms of evangelical Protestantism. For example, in the 2003 State of the Union address, he invoked a well-loved hymn when he spoke of the "power, the wonder-working power" of the goodness and faith of the American people. Bush also spoke of "our calling as a blessed country," a distinctly Protestant conception of the American city on a hill.[8]

The tension between embracing Muslim allies, on the one hand, and positioning the United States as a Christian nation with a mission, on the other, was an ongoing rhetorical and political problem in the Bush administration, one that emerged from conflicts among different constituencies and competing policy goals. Domestically, the idea of a fundamental clash with Islam worked as an enabling precept for garnering support for U.S. policy, among both Christian and secular audiences (although, of course, not universally in either case). Internationally, however, it was an unworkable, fundamentally destabilizing posture. For those in the Bush administration who were determined not only to fight terrorism but to remake the political landscape of the Middle East, it was crucial to argue not for cultural clash but for universal values: if given a chance, all nations could and would embrace American-style democracy.

The phrase "a clash of civilizations"—and the concept it succinctly encapsulated—comes from the title of Samuel Huntington's influential book, *The Clash of Civilizations and the Remaking of World Order*, published in 1996.[9] The book was an expansion of a controversial article published in *Foreign Affairs* three years earlier. Huntington was one of the most respected and influential scholars of international relations in the nation, a founder of *Foreign Policy* magazine, and chair of the Harvard Academy for International Affairs. When Huntington's analysis first appeared, it was hotly debated among international relations scholars, many of whom criticized it for the broad strokes of its argument, simplistic statements, and harshly negative views of Islam. That discussion, however, remained largely within the academic and policy community.[10] Then, in the aftermath of September 11, *Clash of Civilizations* was reissued and became a national best seller. The "clash of civilizations" suddenly became a media shorthand—a presumption or a code, a way of "explaining" the origins of terrorism and the nature of Islam.[11]

While the general outlines of Huntington's arguments are well known, the complexity of his argument, and thus its pernicious flexibility, is often ignored. *The Clash of Civilizations* used a relativist argument to posit a deeply conservative position. Western culture, he suggested, should stop trying to assert its values and beliefs—rationality, individualism, human rights, separation of church and state—as if they were universal, when in fact they had little relevance for other cultures. Huntington posited a link between "the West" and Christianity. Other civilizations were similarly defined by cultural/religious characteristics; thus, "Islam" was a civilization, along with "Hindu," "Orthodox," and "Sinic (Confucian)." With the end of the Cold War, he argued, religion, particularly, was coming to matter a great deal; it was taking over from economics and ideologies as the central glue holding groups of people together. "Civilizations" (a term he resurrected from the early twentieth century, when it had distinctly racialist connotations) would replace the nation-state and the Cold War bloc as the primary organizing sites for identity—and thus as the nexus of conflict.

Huntington believed that the West would face its greatest challenges from Islam, which was the most dangerous threat, and from China, which was gaining in economic strength and power. Muslims, he said, were growing in numbers and strength, and were in general more inclined toward violent conflict than people from other civilizations—"Islam has bloody borders," he famously commented.[12] Against those who argued that the conflicts between Western nations and Muslim ones emerged from clashing political interests, such as the history of U.S. intervention in the region, the situation in Israel/Palestine, or the corruption of Arab governments supported by the United States, Huntington posited something far more elemental:

> The underlying problem for the West is not Islamic fundamentalism. It is Islam, a different civilization whose people are convinced of the superiority of their culture and are obsessed with the inferiority of their power. The problem for Islam is not the CIA [Central Intelligence Agency] or the U.S. Department of Defense. It is the West, a different civilization whose people are convinced of the universality of their culture and believe that their superior, if declining, power imposed on them the obligation to extend that culture throughout the world.[13]

Western leaders may have claimed to act in the interests of the "world community," Huntington argued, but in the face of omnipresent cultural clash, such statements were presumptuous and wrong: "Western belief in the universality of Western culture suffers from three problems: it is false; it is immoral; and it is dangerous. . . . Imperialism is the necessary logical consequence of universalism." Western civilization would have renounce its universal pretensions, but it should aim to protect its own interests, maintain its global position, and prevent its "subordination to other economically and demographically more dynamic civilizations.". An honest particularism in defense of Western values, Huntington posited, would be far better than disingenuous talk of a universal world community.[14]

While Huntington supported aggressive action in the war on terrorism, and had backed the war in Afghanistan, the logic of his argument suggested a more cautious view about the advisability of turning to Iraq as the next target. Although Huntington was perhaps strategically silent in this period, there is indeed evidence that he opposed the war, at least initially.[15] But Huntington's general arguments about culture were mobilized in the media to support a broad discourse about the dangers of "the clash of civilizations," one that did not always maintain his realist policymaking assumptions. That discourse, as it was constructed in journals of elite opinion and in small-town newspapers, on television and on radio talk shows, frequently claimed that the United States was the last defender of the noble values of individualism and human rights, which Islamic civilization did not respect. An editorial writer for the *San Diego Union-Tribune*, for example, described his fact-finding trip to the Middle East by contrasting a mosque and a church standing side by side in Istanbul: "The two nearby monuments symbolize the age-old rivalry between two cultures— the largely democratic and secularized West, built on the Enlightenment ideals of reason and individual liberty spawned in 18th century Europe and America; and the largely authoritarian and theocratic societies of the Muslim world, shaped over the past 14 centuries by the unchanging orthodoxy of the Holy Koran."[16] Huntington had been similarly, if implicitly, scornful of non-Western civilizations, but he had insisted that they should be treated as competitors, not potential converts. *Newsweek*, on the other hand, published a long, sweeping cover story by the conservative political scientist Fareed Zakaria, which argued that while the culture of the Middle East "fuels the fanaticism" at the heart of terrorism, it was possible and necessary for Middle Eastern Muslims to come to terms with Western hegemony as the only way out of their political and economic stagnation. "If the West can help Islam enter modernity in dignity and peace," Zakaria contended, "it will have done more than achieved security. It will have changed the world."[17] In the U.S. media, then, the concept of a "clash" was mobile: it hovered between a despairing vision of the dangerous inevitability of conflict and a determined manifesto for America's mission to the world.

Going to War

The ambiguity about Islam was fully present in the lead-up to the Iraq war. At every turn, the administration argued for invasion on two levels. One level focused on the threat to U.S. interests posed by Saddam Hussein, who was said to harbor weapons of mass destruction and to support terrorism. The second highlighted the necessity of freeing Iraqis from tyranny, an argument that implicitly and sometimes explicitly opposed the notion of entrenched cultural differences that would supposedly prevent Muslims from embracing democracy. Speaking at West Point in 2002, President Bush explicitly positioned the United States as the defender of a freedom that all nations equally desired: "When it comes to the common rights and needs of men and women," he said, "there is no clash of civilizations. The requirements of freedom apply fully to Africa and Latin America and the entire Islamic world."[18] A free Iraq would become a model for the "democratizing" of the rest of the region. This argument was one key to the U.S. justification for launching the war in Iraq. Retrospectively, it became even more important, when no weapons of mass destruction were found and Iraq's links to al Qaeda were shown to be a fiction.[19]

President Bush's promise to use U.S. military power as a force for freedom was a dramatic departure from a more traditional realist framework of pursuing only limited U.S. national interests (even when those interests were framed as being justified by claims of U.S. benevolence or stewardship).[20] This stance, at once universalist and proselytizing, represented the ascendance within the administration of a strongly ideological group of neoconservative defense intellectuals and policymakers. As I have argued elsewhere, the term "neoconservative" emerged originally in the 1970s in reference to a specific group of people who had defined themselves as "newly" conservative after turning against the social liberalism of the 1960s.[21] By the 1990s, however, "neoconservatism" referred to a fairly broad set of foreign policy ideas subscribed to in various degrees by a range of people in and out of the Bush administration. Neoconservatives generally supported a more proactive or offensive U.S. posture, a strong pro-Israel Middle East policy, and the aggressive promotion of free markets. They also argued strongly for developing U.S. goals based as much on ideological or moral precepts as on realist ones, though the actual practice of that moralism often proved to be selective and self-interested.

The neoconservatives' offensive-oriented military approach had been codified as the "Bush Doctrine" of preemption; that is, the assertion of the United States' right to strike against foes who posed a potential but not necessarily imminent threat to U.S. interests. Bush had begun to lay out the basic components of that doctrine in his State of the Union address in January 2002, when he had declared that the United States now confronted an "axis of evil" that included Iraq, North Korea, and Iran.[22] Bush finalized his doctrine in his 2002 speech at West Point, when he declared, "If we wait for threats to fully materialize, we will have waited too long. . . . We must take the battle to the enemy, disrupt his plans and confront the worst threats before they emerge."[23] As Bush stated it, the doctrine had no limits; wherever U.S. policymakers saw a potential threat, they would reserve the right to respond with military action, including the overthrow of governments.

Administration officials generally accompanied articulations of the Bush Doctrine with broad statements of the United States' commitment to promoting liberty, fighting tyranny, and supporting democracy. Indeed, the heart of neoconservatism—what most clearly distinguished it from other contemporary and historical forms of conservatism, including Huntington's—was the claim that U.S. foreign policy should be formulated on the basis of (conservative) morality as well as strategic interests. Many of the most prominent neoconservative intellectuals and activists, including Francis Fukuyama, Paul Wolfowitz, and William Kristol, had been influenced by the political philosopher Leo Strauss, who taught that modern politics was being destroyed by moral relativism. What was needed, Strauss argued, were strong leaders who were willing to stand up for what was right and to do battle against "tyranny."[24] The Bush team's characterization of terrorists as those who "hate freedom," and of certain nation-states as part of an "axis of evil," was fundamentally aligned with this kind of moralistic vision of international politics.

Thus, the ideological backing for remaking the Middle East was framed in the language of idealism. To oppose U.S. policy was to suggest that Arab or Muslim peoples did *not* have the right to democracy; the push toward war was brandished as an antiracist credential.[25] For neoconservative policymakers, however, "democracy" meant quite specific things: The Bush administration's National Security Strategy of September 2002 had explicitly committed the United States to lead other nations toward the "single sustainable model for national success," which meant basic formal democratic institutions, such as voting, certainly, and some basic protections for civil rights (including for women and minorities), but also, just as centrally, individualism and capitalism based on a free market.[26] Democracy also was defined as having good relations with the United States.[27]

Despite the universalizing rhetoric, in practice neoconservatives were also far from immune to the "clash" model proposed by Huntington. The nations of the Middle East were considered specifically resistant to democracy, particularly dangerous to the United States, and uniquely oppressive to women. During the lead-up to the war in Iraq, a thirty-year-old book by Rafael Patai, *The Arab Mind*, was popular reading among members of the Bush administration— one observer called the book "the bible of the neocons on Arab behavior."[28] Patai's was a patently racist text that argued, among other things, that Arabs did not really understand time (because of the structure of the Arabic language) and that they were at once sex-obsessed and sexually repressed, both due to perverse childrearing practices. (The implication could be drawn, then, that Arabs were particularly vulnerable to sexual humiliation, and there is some evidence that these seeming insights were put to use in the specific tortures carried out at Abu Ghraib.)[29] The underlying message of the crudely argued book was that the Arab world was fundamentally different and, in key ways, contemptible. Despite their critiques of realism, then, neoconservatives were in no way starry-eyed democratic idealists. They were fully capable of racist theorizing about Arabs and Islam and also completely committed to promoting U.S. strategic and economic hegemony, in the Middle East and elsewhere. In their view, however, the Islamic world was not home to a "dynamic" civilization that would challenge the West for hegemony; it was a place ripe for transformation and, ultimately, incorporation into the global marketplace. There would be no clash of civilizations because the war of ideas, and the struggle for power, had already been won.

Evangelicals as Missionaries and Activists

The Bush administration's dual messages about Islam were both part of its success—the rhetoric spoke to and reassured diverse constituencies, including Republicans who supported civil rights for Muslims in the United States—and a potential Achilles heel in its relations to its base, particularly conservative white evangelicals. Nowhere was the vision of a civilizational clash with Islam discussed with more intensity than among evangelicals. In magazines like *The World* (a deeply conservative journal focused on international issues), *Charisma* (aimed at Pentecostals), and *Christianity Today* (the moderately conservative voice of "mainstream" evangelicalism), multiple articles discussed the "Islamic worldview and how it differs from Christianity," or asked, "Is Islam a religion of peace?"[30] On talk radio and on Christian television, Islam was everywhere, and Christian publishers quickly produced dozens of popular books that explained Islam from a specifically evangelical perspective.

Of course, the views propounded in these diverse media were hardly of a piece. In *Sojourners* magazine, the organ of the left-liberal wing of evangelicalism, the articles tended to criticize all "fundamentalisms" and called for inter-religious dialogue.[31] *Christianity Today*, speaking for moderate conservatives, acknowledged that a significant number of evangelicals viewed Islam as inherently violent and anti-American, but argued that Islam was in fact in the midst of a struggle to define itself and to decide whether it could "find a way to be part of the human community without violently insisting on its own way." Implicitly condescending, *Christianity Today*'s tolerance was nonetheless a far cry from the views of Robert A. Morey, a popular lecturer and author of *The*

Islamic Invasion, who declared that "the blood lust of Islam is thus rooted in a perverted religious impulse to kill and mutilate in the name of Allah."[32]

Morey's views were extreme but were voiced by other conservative Protestants, including Franklin Graham, who continued to insist, well after his infamous comments in the wake of 9/11, that Islam is inherently violent. Graham, after all, is no fringe leader; he is, according to one poll, the second-most admired evangelical leader, after his father, Billy Graham, and is viewed favorably by 73 percent of evangelicals, according to a recent poll. That same poll showed that there is a broad and profound evangelical mistrust of Islam. In this 2003 poll sponsored by the Ethics and Public Policy Center (a Christian think tank) and Beliefnet, 77 percent of evangelicals said their overall view of Islam was "negative." When asked if Muslims and Christians pray to the same God, 79 percent said no.[33]

Evangelical views of Islam have been shaped by many factors, including, of course, the general anger and anxiety that emerged after September 11. In recent years, however, evangelical Christians have also had their own particular set of interests in Islam, emerging from the cultural impact of missionary work and concerns about persecuted Christians, in addition to the centrality of the Muslim world in end-times theology. Each of these issues has been the site of evangelical activism and has been extensively covered in evangelical media and popular culture. Together, they shape the contours of an engagement with the Muslim world that is sometimes contradictory; it combines elements of a clash model with a simultaneous commitment to maintaining good relationships with Islamic governments, so as to allow a missionary and/or aid presence in Islamic countries.

In the Gospel of Matthew, Jesus tells his followers to "go therefore and make disciples of all nations." This injunction, which Christians call the Great Commission, was the impetus for the first great wave of American evangelical missionary fervor at the end of the nineteenth century. Starting in the 1980s, Protestant evangelicals once again made global missions a priority for their ministries, and as a result, they have helped transform the face of international Christianity. Today in several countries in Latin America, evangelicals are more numerous than practicing Catholics. In sub-Saharan Africa, Christianity is growing faster than anywhere else on earth. Within twenty years, Africa, Asia, the Caribbean, and Latin America, and not Europe or the United States, will be the centers of what Philip Jenkins has described as the "next Christendom."[34]

Evangelical Christians in the United States increasingly understand themselves to be part of a truly global community of believers. Of course, Christianity has been a global religion for centuries, and the idea of an international network of Christians has been important to American believers since at least the nineteenth century, when "evangelizing the world in this generation" was a broadly shared Protestant ambition. But something has transformed the way that many American evangelicals understand themselves, as they increasingly talk in terms of their membership and participation in a global community—as very much part of, and in some ways subject to, this global body.[35] This reality has helped to construct a vision of global Christianity that transcends national boundaries and often challenges traditional views of U.S. "national interests." Missionary work has become a central part of that transformation, but in complex ways. The new Christian communities spawned by missions are at the heart of the extranationalist globalizing consciousness, which puts transnational Christian community before mere national interests. Yet missionaries' encounters with Islam lie at the heart of a certain evangelical version of cultural clash, which has worked to undergird popular support for U.S. expansion in the Middle East.

In the late 1980s, several evangelical streams converged to create the "AD2000 and Beyond" movement, chaired by Argentinean evangelical Luis Bush. AD2000's goal was "a church for every people and a gospel for every person" by the end of the millennium. The movement's more specific target was the "10/40 Window," that is, the rectangular region on the world map between ten degrees and forty degrees north latitude, encompassing North Africa, most of the Middle East, and Southeast Asia. This, according to activists, was an area where Islam, Hinduism, and Buddhism "enslave" a majority of the inhabitants. Of these three religions, Islam was of the greatest concern because it was "reaching out energetically to all parts of the globe; in a similar strategy, we must penetrate (its) heart with the liberating truth of the gospel."[36] In 1997 the Southern Baptist Convention responded to the AD2000 and Beyond movement by restructuring its large and well-funded missions program to focus more excitedly on the "Final Frontier"—unreached peoples in the Middle East and South Asia. Since the 1980s, the number of missionaries in Islamic countries has quadrupled.[37]

Franklin Graham, who heads the missionary organization Samaritan's Purse, is well known for his determination to evangelize the Muslim world, even in the face of powerful opposition. Graham delights in telling the story of how he angered General Norman Schwarzkopf during the first Gulf War, by arranging for a shipment of thousands of Arabic-language New Testaments to the troops and encouraging the soldiers to give them out to Saudis. Proselytizing was explicitly forbidden by the U.S. basing agreement, and Schwarzkopf was furious. For Graham, that anger was a badge of pride; it proved that he was willing to take risks and displease the powerful to evangelize those places most in need. Graham later sent a group of missionaries into war-torn Afghanistan in the immediate aftermath of the U.S. war against the Taliban (just a few weeks after

Graham had publicly called Islam "a very evil and wicked religion"), and he also opened up one of the first aid organizations/missions programs in Iraq after the U.S. invasion.[38] Some evangelical thinkers have criticized the practice of sending religious workers into countries on the heels of the U.S. military, while others see these recent incursions as an opportunity to reach countries that have long been off-limits.[39]

But missionary work is carried out by evangelicals of many stripes, and some of these are committed to an "aid first" approach that eschews overt proselytizing in countries where it is not welcome. World Vision, a Christian aid organization that is now the largest privately funded charity in the world, has working relationships with many governments that do not allow explicit missionary work. In those places, they focus only on providing aid—hospitals, clean water projects, microfinancing—in the hope that the Christian message will be carried through the fact that they are there, helping people, rather than by any explicit proselytizing. Some more theologically liberal evangelicals argue that such service is a Christian imperative, even if it never leads to any conversions (a position also taken by left-liberal Catholics).[40]

Even for more proselytizing evangelicals, the situation was complex. During the run-up to the Iraq war, the National Association of Evangelicals was deadlocked and was unable to issue a statement about the war, despite a great deal of pro-war sentiment in its constituency and among its leaders, in large part because of concerns that pro-war statements would endanger the lives of missionaries throughout the Muslim world.[41] So missionary work can be the source of silence on the issue of a "clash of civilizations," and sometimes provides direct opposition to that Manichean vision. In fact, in January 2003 a group of Southern Baptist missionaries sent an open letter to Baptist leaders in the United States decrying the negative comments about Islam, saying that evangelicals should concentrate on speaking the message of the gospel to Muslims, "instead of speaking in a degrading manner about their religion and prophet." Not too subtly, they suggested that their stateside colleagues should engage Islam "in love and in a fashion that is consistent with the life of our Lord Jesus Christ."[42]

Missionary work can also be the source of a great deal of anger and even hatred toward Islam, however, as Luis Bush and Franklin Graham have made clear. This carries over into popular culture: dramatic missionary life stories are often Christian best sellers, particularly those that tell of Western missionaries or newly converted Christians who suffer or die for their beliefs (*If God Should Choose*; *In the Presence of My Enemies*; *Bruchko*; *Vanya: A True Story*) or recount uplifting conversion stories (*Peace Child*; *I Dared to Call Him Father: The Miraculous Story of a Muslim Woman's Encounter with God*).[43] The threats to

Christians living or evangelizing in the Muslim world are highlighted in a great many of these accounts, and Islam emerges as a particular threat to Christians who are simply carrying out the requirements of their faith. The physical dangers of doing missionary work in Muslim nations are in fact enormous, especially in countries like Saudi Arabia, Egypt, or Libya, where proselytizing is forbidden. Missionary reports do often include sympathetic portrayals of the people being evangelized; they are, after all, children of God who will soon be welcomed into the Christian community. But that threat of Islam is also a central part of the appeal of the missionary genre today: stories of stalwart faith in face of persecution are the saint stories of modern evangelicalism.

For many evangelicals, as well as for many mainline Protestants, the persecution of Christians by Muslims is one of the key political issues of our times. Evangelicals were central to the passage in 1998 of the act that produced the U.S. Commission on International Religious Freedom, a government monitoring body that many observers believe was specifically targeted at Muslim nations. The act required the State Department to issue an annual report about the state of religious freedom around the world. The commission stated that one of its first priorities would be religious freedom in the Sudan—a priority that became a problem for the Bush administration when, after September 11, the United States tried to enlist Sudan as a partner in the war on terrorism. That move cost the administration the conservatives who had been involved in religious freedom issues. Upon the release of the State Department's 2001 report, for example, the *National Review* commented, "President Bush's repeated assertions about the peaceful nature of Islam were briefly interrupted . . . [as] our Muslim-world partners in the coalition against terrorism were prominently featured among the most violent, most intolerant regimes in the world."[44]

In the work being done on behalf of persecuted Christians, Islam and Christianity are often posited as "clashing," but, contra Huntington, this evangelical vision does not divide the world up geographically, into the West versus the Rest. Instead, it posits a great multiracial coalition of Christians around the world who support both missionaries and the persecuted Christians who confront Islam in their own nations. Nations do not mark the fault lines of this clash; the real issues are at once subnational, in that they happen within national borders, and genuinely global, in that they are carried out by communities of believers across the globe who see their alliances with each other as more central than national identities or even "Western civilization." In addition, the Christian coalition envisioned in this missions work is *not* a code for white power; it is, instead, one of the signs of the coming transformation in evangelical Christianity, as it becomes increasingly centered outside of Europe and the United States.

Evangelicals and Prophecy

The encounter with Islam is also a key element for more recent incarnations of the prophetic "end times" theology that animates a significant strand of evangelical thought. Prophecy interpreters look to the books of Ezekiel, Daniel, and Revelation for information about the rise of the Antichrist, the battle of Armageddon, and ultimately, the Second Coming of Jesus. Drawing on the interpretations developed by John Darby in the nineteenth century and popularized in the 1909 Scofield Reference Bible, generations of prophecy watchers have held that the Bible's accuracy can be tested and confirmed by political developments, especially those concerning Israel and the Middle East.[45] Within this formulation, it becomes obvious that Christians must pay attention to foreign policy, because the Middle East, particularly the nation of Israel (and its allies and enemies), will be central to the greatest religious test of all time. Political events become important because of how they fit into a biblical scheme, and interpreting that scheme is a complex and politically saturated process.

End-times speculation has been a major component of the rich tapestry of evangelical fiction and nonfiction literature and film over the past twenty-five years. Since 1970, when Hal Lindsey published the hipster-styled book of prophecy interpretation, *The Late, Great Planet Earth*, which went on to become the best-selling nonfiction book of the decade, evangelical prophecy scholars have published one popularizing book after another, many of which were Christian bookstore best sellers. By the 1980s, several authors, including Pat Robertson, started turning pious tracts into rollicking adventure; Frank Paretti's *This Present Darkness* sold several million copies, and the 1999 film *Omega Code* was the year's most successful independent release. In the late 1990s prophecy talk also moved to the Internet, with sites like Raptureready.com, prophecynewswatch.com, and endtimesinsight.com. The latest example of the enthusiasm for prophetic theology is the *Left Behind* series of novels, written by evangelist Tim LaHaye and coauthor Jerry Jenkins. From 1995 to 2004, the series of twelve books sold more than 60 million copies, making it second only to the Harry Potter series as the best-selling fiction of all time.

Both mainline Protestant leaders and many evangelicals have strong theological disagreements with an approach that focuses heavily on apocalyptic longings for Armageddon and the Second Coming.[46] Even conservative evangelicals are quite often not particularly interested in the topic—or, if they are, it is because they are appalled that prophecy watching is considered a representative evangelical activity. And it certainly has far less traction in African American churches, for example, or among liberal evangelicals. Randall Balmer, for example, is a leading evangelical intellectual who has written a series of influential studies of the movement; he says that the focus on prophecy emerges out of a "theology of despair" based on a "slavishly literalistic" reading of Revelation. But the fascination remains. However lacking in intellectual respectability, prophecy watching is an important popular culture pastime for a significant subset of evangelical Christians.[47]

Prophecy interpretation as practiced by evangelicals today requires a constant negotiation between, on the one hand, a belief in the Bible as literally true in its predictions and, on the other hand, a willingness to engage in the most complex hermeneutics, bringing together highly metaphorical passages that are spread across several "prophetic" books of the Old and New Testaments. Even the most rigid prophecy analysts will agree that their interpretations cannot be precise about exactly how political events will unfold, and that is exactly what gives the activity its energy and, ultimately, its profoundly interactive character. Believers pursue their speculations about the role of Iraq, Israel, and/or Islam on dozens if not hundreds of websites, chat rooms, and Christian forums. *Left Behind*, now the dominant name brand of prophecy interpretation, offers its fans the chance to become members of the web-based "Prophecy Club," an impressive site that includes message boards and weekly newsletters. There, Iraq and Babylon were a frequent topic of discussion in the run-up to the Iraq war, always under the presumption that the U.S. invasion of Iraq was necessary to "set the stage" for the rise of Babylon as a world capital during the end times. In this view, "militant Islam" is also a major factor in the increasing turbulence and instability that are predictors of the rise of the Antichrist. Islam, one Prophecy Club newsletter argued, "is contributing to worldwide instability and pushing the world toward globalism even faster than its already accelerating pace. . . . The meteoric rise of militant Islam is also setting the stage for the massive end times invasion of Israel predicted by the Old Testament prophet Ezekiel over 2,500 years ago."[48]

After September 11, several members of the community made it clear that they were shocked and angered by Bush's statements that Islam was a religion of peace and that Christians and Muslims worship the same God. The Antichrist would come bringing offers of false peace, they said, and would, under the guise of that peace, defame and attempt to destroy Christianity. Yet even here, in one of the most conservative corners of evangelical thought, there is a great deal of discussion about Islam that makes clear the complexity of the emotions and values that prophecy-oriented evangelicals hold. During the fall of 2002 and early 2003, for example, there were heated debates about the war. The vast majority of posters were in favor of the war, and in these debates, one could see many arguments that drew on the basic arguments from the Bush administration and the secular media: Hussein had weapons of mass destruction; he supported al Qaeda; he was a brutal dictator.

At the same time, there were passionate arguments about whether the war against Iraq was, essentially, a religious war. On a thread called "Un-Christian if Pro-War?" one poster responded to the question by saying that *of course* Christians could and should support the war: "I don't believe that our military is fighting for a political reason—I look at the war as our military (military of a Christian nation) fighting for God! Against a world who chooses not to know Him. I do believe this is a war of good and evil."[49] Other posters joined in to argue that Christians should never support war, or only in cases of self-defense (the two most adamant antiwar posters named themselves as women), but they were far outnumbered by those who saw the war at least partly in religious terms. Almost all of the commentaries interspersed religious ideals and biblical prophecy with up-to-the-minute discussions of U.S. policy or events in Iraq, as well as a "clash of civilizations" rhetoric. "Kudoes to you for seeing the war for what it is . . . a religious war," wrote "Viewcam," who elsewhere identified himself as a veteran. He continued, "The Koran, as I have previously posted, states that anyone that fails to embrace (convert) to Islam is to be killed or maimed. I'm at war! There will be some shocked antiwar Christians at Armageddon when we must fight on the side of the Lord. . . . Wake up fellow Christians, somewhere out there is a Muslim that wants you, your family, and your nation to be annihilated!"[50]

The tension between the Bush administration's official positions on Islam and the views of conservative evangelicals became starkly apparent in the fall of 2003, when the news media reported anti-Islamic comments made by Lieutenant General William "Jerry" Boykin, the deputy secretary of defense for intelligence. Over the previous year, Boykin had spoken at nearly two dozen churches, telling audiences that he believed that terrorists hated America because "we are a Christian nation," and that they would only be defeated "if we come at them in the name of Jesus." In one speech, he recalled an encounter with a Muslim fighter in Somalia who said he had the protection of Allah against U.S. troops. Boykin told the group: "I knew that my God was bigger than his. I knew that my God was a real God, and his was an idol." When Boykin's comments were reported in the press, he was roundly criticized for promoting a blanket view of Islam as inherently evil; the *New York Times* and the *Los Angeles Times* both called for his retirement or resignation. But the Bush administration refused to consider such a move, in large part because Boykin was a strong favorite among evangelical Christians, who quickly rallied around him. The general's opinions cost U.S. government dearly in negative press, both at home and abroad, but the Bush team knew it could not afford to further alienate evangelicals. As the 2004 election approached, Bush's campaign advisor Karl Rove made clear that he was very concerned about low voter turnout among evangelicals, and he made several tours through the South and Midwest to drum up support.[51]

Conclusion

Writing in the *New York Review of Books* in November 2003, Joan Didion offered a tour de force analysis of the Bush administration's relationship with the Christian right. The essay was erudite, funny, and frightening, as it laid out the president's multiple debts to evangelical conservatives and the ways in which he mobilized his own narrative of being saved to shore up a subtle and not-so-subtle vision of himself as chosen by divine Providence to lead the country during and after the trauma of September 11.[52] Like many liberal or left commentators in recent years, however, Didion was so busy tracing the intersections of interests and ideologies that brought conservative Christianity into the White House that she failed to see the fissures, debates, and tensions that are every bit as much a part of that alliance.

Similarly, many critics of the implicitly and explicitly racist theorizing that has gone on under the rubric of "clash of civilizations" have assumed that the Bush administration's drive for hegemony in the Middle East is fueled by a Huntingtonian vision of "the West versus the Rest." Since the Bush administration has so obviously lied about so many aspects of the war on terrorism and the invasion of Iraq, the argument goes, surely its disavowals about being at war with Islam were equally disingenuous.

While skepticism about the president's arguments for war are surely warranted, and fears about the impact of a conservative evangelicalism on U.S. Middle East policy are well placed, any attempt to fully understand the hegemony of anti-Islamic and pro-war sentiment in the United States after September 11 will need to fully account for the complexities of ideology and interest in the conservative coalition. The "clash of civilizations" emerged as a shorthand for what many Americans (and many people in the Middle East) thought they were facing after 9/11, but the term occluded as much as it revealed. On the one hand, it pointed to a real transformation in global politics; religious identifications were becoming central to the logic of American power (as opposed to being just the atavistic values of a few "fundamentalists"). Moreover, Christian evangelicals were moving increasingly to the center of U.S. political life—powerful in Congress, courted by the White House, and claimed by the president. But Bush's foreign policy was in key ways premised on a very different vision, one that insisted that there was no "clash" of cultures, because such a claim would belie the universalism of American values, the moral stature of the U.S. assertion that it was working to free the world from tyranny. If Islamic culture did not value individualism or human rights, as Huntington claimed, then the administration's insistence that it was speaking on behalf of suppressed longings for freedom might be suspect.

At the same time, Christian conservatives, so strongly supportive of the U.S. war in Iraq, were also torn by competing visions. On the one hand, many resented the Bush administration's argument that Islamic militants and extremists were the problem, not Islam in general. The warm words for Islam affronted the many evangelicals who were angry about Muslim persecution of Christians. The administration perspective was also diametrically opposed to the end-times theology that animated a powerful segment of the community. At the same time, the clash of civilizations rubric did not and could not fully express the moral geographies of even the most conservative of American evangelicals, who increasingly saw themselves as part of a global Christian community. A great many missionary-minded evangelicals did see Islam as a threat and a source of persecution. But others saw their missionary work as part of, and requiring, good relations with Muslims. They insisted that they would work with Muslim governments, and feed the Muslim poor, and even restrict their own proselytizing, because it was service in the name of Jesus, not the promulgation of Jesus' name, that exemplified their mission.

In the end, of course, the elections of 2004 proved that these tensions would not stand in the way of evangelicals' willingness to reelect the president: 77 percent of people who defined themselves as "white evangelicals" voted for Bush; the vast majority of those said they believed that the war in Iraq was "going well."[53] As the first President Bush said, it's a New World Order, one that is transforming the terms of identity, politics, and power. Religious identification and internationalist Christian activism are as much a part of the modern American empire as race and nationalism. The rhetoric of clash of civilizations is, at its core, performative speech, and those who wish to challenge it must understand both the contours of the changing global stage and the complex interconnections of the multiple audiences it speaks to. Put another way, one might simply say that it will be impossible to either comprehend or to influence the direction of U.S. foreign policy in the next decade unless one understands the terms through which neoconservatives have posited their universalism and American Christian evangelicals have constructed their internationalism. Both have played a key role in the making of the world that the rest of us will inhabit for many years to come.

1. Denis Hoover, "Is Evangelicalism Itching for a Civilizational Fight? A Media Study," *Brandywine Review of Faith and International Affairs* 2 (Spring 2004): 11–16.

2. Alan Cooperman, "Ministers Asked to Curb Remarks About Islam," *Washington Post*, May 8, 2003, A3; Laurie Goodstein, "Top Evangelicals Critical of Colleagues over Islam," *New York Times*, May 7, 2003, A22.

3. Pew Center for the People and the Press, "U.S. Needs More International Backing," February 20, 2003, <http://people-press.org/reports/pdf/173.pdf> (February 20, 2007).

4. Mark A. Noll, *The Scandal of the Evangelical Mind* (Grand Rapids, Mich.: W. B. Eerdmans, 1995).

5. Anna Greenberg and Jennifer Berktold, "Evangelicals in America," Survey Results from Greenberg Quinlan Rosner Research, Inc., for PBS, April 5, 2004, <http://www.pbs.org/wnet/religionandethics/week733/results.pdf> (March 13, 2007).

6. Don Richardson, *Secrets of the Koran: Revealing Insights into Islam's Holy Book* (New York: Regal Books, 2003); W. L. Cati, *Married to Muhammed* (Lake Mary, Fla.: Creation House Press, 2001).

7. Dana Milbank and Emily Wax, "Bush Visits Mosque to Forestall Hate Crimes; President Condemns an Increase in Violence Aimed at Arab Americans," *Washington Post*, September 18, 2001.

8. President George W. Bush, State of the Union speech, January 28, 2003, <http://www.whitehouse.gov/news/releases/2003/01/20030128-19.html> (January 22, 2007); John Donnelly, "Fighting Terror/Theologians: Some Voice Concern over President's Religious Rhetoric," *Boston Globe*, February 13, 2003, A20.

9. Samuel P. Huntington, *The Clash of Civilizations and the Remaking of World Order* (New York: Simon and Schuster, 1996); also Huntington, "Clash of Civilizations? *Foreign Affairs* 72 (Summer 1993): 22–49. This analysis of Huntington is adapted from my *Epic Encounters: Culture, Media, and U.S. Interests in the Middle East, 1945–2001* (new ed.; Berkeley and Los Angeles: University of California Press, 2005).

10. See, for example, Fouad Ajami, "The Summoning," *Foreign Affairs* 72, no. 4 (1993): 2–9, which is a discussion of the article version; and Roy Mottahedeh, "The Clash of Civilizations: An Islamicist's Critique," *Harvard Middle Eastern and Islamic Review* 2 (1996): 1–26.

11. "Q&A: A Head-On Collision of Alien Cultures?," *New York Times*, October 20, 2001; Samuel Huntington, "The Age of Muslim Wars," *Newsweek*, December 17, 2001, 14ff; Robert D. Kaplan, "Looking the World in the Eye," *Atlantic Monthly* 288 (December 2001): 68ff. See also Stanley Kurtz, "The Future of 'History,'" *Policy Review* 113 (June/July 2002): 43–58; and Ervand Abrahamian, "The US Media, Huntington, and September 11," *Third World Quarterly* 24 (June 2003): 529–44.

12. Huntington, *Clash of Civilizations*, 254.

13. Ibid., 217–18.

14. Ibid., 310, 303.

15. "Huntington Opposes Invasion," *Dawn* (Pakistani newspaper), August 9, 2002, <http://www.dawn.com/2002/08/09/int8.htm> (January 22, 2007).

16. Robert A. Kittle, "Islam vs. the West; Perilous Rift; Islamic Awakening Pursues an Anti-Western Future," *San Diego Union-Tribune*, July 28, 2002, G1.

17. Fareed Zakaria, "The Politics of Rage: Why Do They Hate Us?" *Newsweek*, October 15, 2001, also available at <http://www.fareedzakaria.com/articles/newsweek/101501_why.html> (October 17, 2001).

18. "President Bush Delivers Graduation Speech at West Point," White House Office of the Press Secretary, June 1, 2001, <http://www.whitehouse.gov/news/releases/2002/06/20020601-3.html> (January 22, 2007).

19. "President Bush Discusses Freedom in Iraq and Middle East," White House Office of the Press Secretary, November 6, 2003, <http://www.whitehouse.gov/news/releases/2003/11/20031106-2.html> (January 22, 2007). For an excellent critique of the overall theory of spreading democracy by fiat, see Thomas Carothers, Marina S. Ottaway, Amy Hawthorne, and Daniel Brumberg, "Democratic Mirage in the Middle East," Carnegie Endowment for International Peace Policy Brief, no. 20, October 2002, <http://www.ceip.org/files/pdf/Policybrief20.pdf> (January 22, 2007).

20. Carl Conetta, "What Colin Powell Showed Us: The End of Arms Control and the Normalization of War," Project on Defense Alternatives briefing report no. 14, May 5, 2003, <http://www.comw.org/pda/0305br14.html> (March 13, 2007).

21. See McAlister, *Epic Encounters*, chap. 4. The analysis that follows is adopted from the conclusion to the new edition of *Epic Encounters*, 266–308.

22. President George W. Bush, State of the Union address, January 29, 2002, <http://www.whitehouse.gov/news/releases/2002/01/20020129-11.html> (January 22, 2007).

23. "President Bush Delivers Graduation Speech at West Point."

24. James Mann, *The Rise of the Vulcans: The History of Bush's War Cabinet* (New York: Viking, 2004), 26–31; Elizabeth Drew, "The Neocons in Power," *New York Review of Books*, June 12, 2003, <http://www.nybooks.com/articles/16378> (January 22, 2007).

25. "President Bush Discusses Freedom in Iraq and Middle East," November 6, 2003. See also George Packer, "Dreaming of Democracy," *New York Times Magazine*, March 2, 2003, <http://query.nytimes.com/search/restricted/article?res=FB071EFF34590C718CDDAA0894DB404482> (January 22, 2007). In addition to other discussions of neoconservative ideology already cited, see Jack Beatty, "History's Fools," *The Atlantic*, May 19, 2004, <http://www.theatlantic.com/doc/prem/200405u/pp2004-05-19> (January 22, 2007).

26. "The National Security Strategy of the United States of America," September 2002, <http://www.comw.org/qdr/fulltext/nss2002.pdf> (January 22, 2007).

27. Francis Fukuyama, *The End of History and the Last Man* (New York: Free Press, 1992).

28. Seymour Hersh, "The Gray Zone," *New Yorker*, May 24, 2004, <http://www.newyorker.com/fact/content/?040524fa_fact> (March 13, 2007); Raphael Patai, *The Arab Mind* (1973; rev. ed., New York: Hatherleigh Press, 2002); Ann Marlowe, "Sex, Violence,

and "The Arab Mind," Salon.com, June 8, 2004, <http://dir.salon.com/story/books/feature/2004/06/08/arab_mind/index.html> (March 13, 2007).

29. Hersh, "Gray Zone"; Mark Danner, "The Logic of Torture," *New York Review of Books*, June 24, 2004, 72; Kate Zernike and David Rohde, "Forced Nudity of Iraqi Prisoners Is Seen as Pervasive Pattern, Not Isolated Incidents," *New York Times*, June 8, 2004.

30. Marvin Olasky, "Islamic Worldview and How It Differs from Christianity," *World Magazine*, October 27, 2001, <http://www.worldmag.com/displayarticle.cfm?id=5476> (January 22, 2007); James Beverley, "Is Islam a Religion of Peace?" *Christianity Today*, January 7, 2002, 32–42.

31. "Fundamentalism in the Modern World: A Dialogue with Karen Armstrong, Susannah Heschel, Jim Wallis, and Feisal Abdul Rauf," *Sojourners*, March–April 2002; Charles Kimball, "Osama and Me: What Osama bin Laden and Jerry Falwell Have in Common," *Sojourners*, January–February 2003, both archived at <http://www.sojo.net> (March 13, 2007).

32. James Beverley, "Is Islam a Religion of Peace?" *Christianity Today*, January 7, 2002, <http://www.ctlibrary.com/ct/2002/january7/1.32.html> (March 13, 2007); Robert A. Morey, "Will Islam Cause WWIII?" *Lion of Judah*, 7 (October 2001), <http://www.thelionofjudah.org/newsletter/oct_2001.htm> (January 22, 2007); Robert A. Morey, *The Islamic Invasion: Confronting the World's Fastest Growing Religion* (Eugene, Ore.: Harvest House, 1992).

33. "Evangelical Views of Islam," Poll for Ethics and Public Policy Center and Beliefnet, released April 7, 2003, <http://www.beliefnet.com/story/124/story_12447.html> (January 22, 2007). However, 52 percent said they believed it was important to "welcome Muslims into the American community."

34. Philip Jenkins, *The Next Christendom: The Rise of Global Christianity* (New York: Oxford University Press, 2002).

35. Among the dozens of commentaries on the transformations in global Christianity, see Lamin Sanneh and Joel A. Carpenter, eds., *The Changing Face of Christianity: Africa, the West, and the World* (New York: Oxford University Press, 2005).

36. <http://www.ad2000.org> (March 13, 2007).

37. "The Southern Baptists Restructure to Reach the Unreached Peoples: An Interview with Jerry Rankin, IMB President, and Avery Willis, Senior Vice President for Overseas Operations," *Missions Frontiers: The Bulletin of the U.S. Center for World Missions*, July–October 1997, <http://www.missionfrontiers.org/1997/0710/jo976.htm> (January 22, 2007); Deborah Caldwell, " 'Poised and Ready': The Evangelist Who Called Islam 'Wicked' Is Ready to Bring Humanitarian Aid to Muslims in Iraq," Beliefnet.com, <http://www.beliefnet.com/story/123/story_12365.html> (January 22, 2007).

38. Graham describes this incident in *Rebel with a Cause* (Nashville, Tenn.: Nelson, 1997); see also Michelle Cottle, "Bible Brigade: Will Franklin Graham Destabilize Postwar Iraq?" *New Republic*, April 21, 2003, <http://www.tnr.com/doc.mhtml?i=20030421&s=cottle042103> (January 22, 2007).

39. Dawn Herzog and Deann Alford, "No Strings Attached: Christians Seek to Balance Relief Work and Evangelism in Iraq," *Christianity Today*, June 1, 2003, <http://www.christianitytoday.com/ct/2003/006/5.44.html> (January 22, 2007).

40. Kevin D. Miller, "De-Seiple-ing World Vision," *Christianity Today*, June 15, 1998, <http://www.ctlibrary.com/ct/1998/june15/8t7049.html> (January 22, 2007).

41. Bill Broadway, "Evangelicals' Voices Speak Softly about Iraq," *Washington Post*, January 25, 2003.

42. Todd Hertz, "Comments on Islam Endanger[s] Missionaries, Letter Says," *Christianity Today*, January 1, 2003, <http://www.ctlibrary.com/ct/2003/januaryweb-only/1-13-53.0.html> (March 13, 2007).

43. Karen Stagg, *If God Should Choose: The Authorized Story of Jim and Roni Bowers* (New York: Moody, 2002); Gracia Burnham and Dean Merrill, *In the Presence of My Enemies* (New York: Tydale House, 2003); Bruce Olson, *Bruchko* ([Carol Stream, Ill.]: Creation House, 1993); Don Richardson, *Peace Child* ([Glendale, Calif.]: G. L. Regal Books, 1974); Bilquis Sheik, *I Dared to Call Him Father: The Miraculous Story of a Muslim Woman's Encounter with God* (Philadelphia: Chosen Books, 2003).

44. Kate O'Beirne, "Martyred: Muslim Murder and Mayhem against Christians," *National Review*, December 3, 2001, 38.

45. For a good discussion of the basics of this theology, see Paul Boyer, *When Time Shall Be No More: Prophecy Belief in Modern American Culture* (Cambridge, Mass.: Harvard University Press, 1992).

46. Karen Long, "*Left Behind* and the Rapture over the Rapture," *Washington Post*, May 5, 2001, B9. The many criticisms published by conservative evangelical groups include the Lutheran Church Missouri Synod's document, "A Lutheran Response to the *Left Behind* Series," April 1, 2004, <http://www.lcms.org/graphics/assets/media/CTCR/LeftBehind.pdf> (March 13, 2007).

47. Randall Balmer, writing in dialogue with Michael Maudlin, "The *Left Behind* Books," Slate.com, June 20, 2000, <http://www.slate.com/id/2000179/entry/1005543> (April 23, 2003).

48. "War on Militant Islam," *Interpreting the Signs* newsletter, April 19, 2004, <http://secure.agoramedia.com/leftbehind/rs-article.asp?ArticleID=542> (December 12, 2005). The *Interpreting the Signs* newsletter is linked to LeftBehind.com, but it is available only by joining the "Prophecy Club" (now $29.95 a year).

49. Posted by Chubear19 (Caroline), March 6, 2003, as part of the thread, "Un-Christian if Pro-War?" (message 76.1), <http://forums.prospero.com/n/mb/message.asp?webtag=lb-prophecyclub&msg=76.1> (January 22, 2007).

50. Posted by Viewcam, March 15, 2003, as part of the thread "Un-Christian if Pro-War?" (message 76.53), <http://forums.prospero.com/n/mb/message.asp?webtag=lb-prophecyclub&msg=76.53>.

51. "US Is 'Battling Satan' Says General," BBC News, October 17, 2003, <http://news.bbc.co.uk/2/hi/americas/3199212.stm> (January 22, 2007); "Holding the Pentagon Accountable: For Religious Bigotry," *New York Times*, August 26, 2004; Ted Olsen, "Web-

log: Should Christians Be Banned from the Military?" *Christianity Today*, October 17, 2003, <http://www.christianitytoday.com/ct/2003/141/55.0.html> (January 22, 2007).

52. Joan Didion, "Mr. Bush and the Divine," *New York Review of Books*, November 6, 2003, <http://www.nybooks.com/articles/16749>.

53. David Finkel, "Ohio Evangelicals Support Bush," *Washington Post*, November 4, 2002, A1.

Contributors

James T. Campbell is a professor of American civilization, Africana studies, and history at Brown University. His research focuses on African American history and on the wider history of the black Atlantic. He is the author of *Songs of Zion: The African Methodist Episcopal Church in the United States and South Africa* (1995), which was awarded the Organization of American Historians' Frederick Jackson Turner Prize and the Carl Sandburg Literary Award for Non-Fiction, and *Middle Passages: African American Journeys to Africa, 1787–2005* (2006), which was awarded the Mark Lynton History Prize and was a finalist for the 2007 Pulitzer Prize in History. He was the chair of Brown University's Steering Committee on Slavery and Justice.

Ruth Feldstein teaches in the history department and the graduate program in American studies at Rutgers University–Newark. She is the author of *Motherhood in Black and White: Race and Sex in American Liberalism, 1930–1965* (2000). Her forthcoming book is tentatively titled *Do What You Gotta Do: Black Women Entertainers and the Civil Rights Movement*.

Kevin K. Gaines is the director of the Center for Afroamerican and African Studies and professor of history at the University of Michigan. He is the author of *Uplifting the Race: Black Leadership, Politics, and Culture in the Twentieth Century* (1996) and *American Africans in Ghana: Black Expatriates in the Civil Rights Era* (2006).

Matt Garcia is an associate professor of American civilization, ethnic studies, and history at Brown University. His book, *A World of Its Own: Race, Labor, and Citrus in the Making of Greater Los Angeles, 1900–1970* (2001), was named co-winner for the best book in oral history by the Oral History Association in 2003. His current book project, *The Rise and Fall of the Farmworkers Movement: Race, Labor, and Justice on the California-Mexican Border, 1940–1980*, explores the farmworkers movement from its formation to the purges and defections of key organizers and members of the United Farmworkers Union.

Matthew Pratt Guterl is an associate professor of African American and African diaspora studies and director of American studies at Indiana University, Bloomington. He is the author of *The Color of Race in America, 1900–1940* (2001) and *American Mediterranean: Southern Slaveholders in the Age of Emancipation* (forthcoming). He is at work on a book on Josephine Baker's adopted family.

George Hutchinson is the chair of the Department of English and the Booth Tarkington Professor of Literary Studies at Indiana University, Bloomington. He is the author of

The Ecstatic Whitman: Literary Shamanism and the Crisis of the Union (1986), *The Harlem Renaissance in Black and White* (1995), and *In Search of Nella Larsen: A Biography of the Color Line* (2006). He is also the editor of *The Cambridge Companion to the Harlem Renaissance* (2007).

Matthew Frye Jacobson is a professor of American studies, history, and African American studies at Yale University. He is the author of *What Have They Built You to Do?: The Manchurian Candidate and Cold War America* (with Gaspar González, 2006), *Roots Too: White Ethnic Revival in Post–Civil Rights America* (2006), *Barbarian Virtues: The United States Encounters Foreign Peoples at Home and Abroad, 1876–1917* (2000), *Whiteness of a Different Color: European Immigrants and the Alchemy of Race* (1998), and *Special Sorrows: The Diasporic Imagination of Irish, Polish, and Jewish Immigrants in the United States* (1995). He is currently editing a reissue of Curt Flood's autobiography, *The Way It Is*, and chipping away at a volume on race and culture in the postwar years, *Odetta's Voice and Other Weapons: The Civil Rights Era as Cultural History*.

Prema Kurien is an associate professor of sociology at Syracuse University. Her research focuses on the relationship between religion, ethnicity, and international migration. She is the author of two books, *Kaleidoscopic Ethnicity: International Migration and the Reconstruction of Community Identities in India* (2002) and *A Place at the Multicultural Table: The Development of an American Hinduism* (2007). Her current work focuses on transnationalism and the generational transmission of religion among a group of Indian American Christians, and on Indian American civic and political activism. In addition to the two books, she has published over twenty articles in journals and edited books.

Robert G. Lee is an associate professor of American civilization at Brown University. He is the author of *Orientals: Asian Americans in Popular Culture* (1999), which was named best book by the New England Popular Culture/American Studies Association and best book on the social construction of race by the American Political Science Association, and was given an honorable mention for the John Hope Franklin Prize for best book in American studies by the American Studies Association. He is also the editor, with Wanni Anderson, of *Displacements and Diasporas: Asians in the Americas* (2005).

Eric Love is an associate professor of history at the University of Colorado at Boulder, where he teaches early national and Jacksonian America, Civil War, Gilded Age and Progressive Era, African American history, and American slavery. He has received fellowships from the Ford Foundation, American Historical Association, the Massachusetts Historical Society, and the Woodrow Wilson Foundation. He is the author of *Race over Empire: Racism and U.S. Imperialism, 1865–1900* (2003) and is presently at work on a second book, *Barbarian Hearts: Power, Culture, and the Opening of Japan, 1853–1854*, a study focusing on blackness and blackface minstrelsy in American world affairs in the antebellum period.

Melani McAlister is an associate professor of American studies and international affairs at George Washington University. She is the author of *Epic Encounters: Culture, Media,* *and U.S. Interests in the Middle East, 1945–2000* (2001). She is currently working on a study of American evangelical Christians, popular culture, and global politics, tentatively titled *Our God in the World: The Global Visions of American Evangelicals.*

Joanne Pope Melish is an associate professor of history and the director of American studies at the University of Kentucky. She is the author of *Disowning Slavery: Gradual Emancipation and "Race" in New England, 1780–1860* (2000) and several articles on race and slavery in the early republic. Currently she is working on a study of the articulation of language, landscape, and raced social identities in the early republic.

Louise M. Newman is an associate professor of U.S. women/gender history at the University of Florida and the author of *White Women's Rights: The Racial Origins of Feminism in the United States* (1999). She is currently working on a project dealing with historical memory of the 1960s, whiteness, and film.

Vernon J. Williams Jr. is a professor of African American and African diaspora studies and also professor of American studies at Indiana University, Bloomington. He is the author of *From a Caste to a Minority* (1989), *Rethinking Race* (1996), and *The Social Sciences and Theories of Race* (2006). He is also the general editor of the Association of Black Anthropologists board.

Natasha Zaretsky is an assistant professor of history at Southern Illinois University, Carbondale. She is the author of *No Direction Home: The American Family and the Fear of National Decline, 1968–1980* (2007).

Index